ALSO BY LOUISE RICHARDSON

When Allies Differ: Anglo-American Relations
in the Suez and Falklands Crises

Democracy and Counterterrorism: Lessons from the Past
(edited with Robert J. Art)

The Roots of Terrorism
(editor)

WHAT TERRORISTS WANT

UNDERSTANDING THE ENEMY

WHAT TERRORISTS WANT

CONTAINING THE THREAT

Louise Richardson

RANDOM HOUSE / NEW YORK

Published in the United States by Random House,
an imprint of The Random House Publishing Group,
a division of Random House, Inc., New York.

RANDOM HOUSE and colophon are registered trademarks
of Random House, Inc.

Grateful acknowledgment is made to the following for permission
to reprint previously published material:

Nasra Hassan: Excerpt from "An Arsenal of Believers" by Nasra Hassan. Originally
published in *The New Yorker,* November 19, 2001. Reprinted by permission of the author.

Taylor & Francis Group, LLC: Excerpt from "The Terrorists in Their Own Words:
Interviews with 35 Incarcerated Middle Eastern Terrorists" from
Terrorism and Political Violence, 15(1). Copyright 2003. Reprinted by permission
of Taylor & Francis Group, LLC, http://www.taylorandfrancis.com.

LIBRARY OF CONGRESS CATALOGING-IN-PUBLICATION DATA
Richardson, Louise.
What terrorists want : understanding the enemy, containing the threat / Louise
Richardson.
p.   cm.
Includes bibliographical references and index.
ISBN 1-4000-6481-3
1. Terrorism. 2. Terrorists. 3. War on Terrorism, 2001–4.
4. September 11 Terrorist Attacks, 2001—Influence. I. Title.
HV6431.R53 2006
363.325—dc22   2006043884

Printed in the United States of America on acid-free paper

www.atrandom.com

468975

Book design by Casey Hampton

To Ciara, Fiona, and Rory

CONTENTS

Introduction   xi

PART ONE: THE TERRORISTS

1. What Is Terrorism?   3
2. Where Have Terrorists Come From?   21
3. What Causes Terrorism?   38
4. The Three Rs: Revenge, Renown, Reaction   71
5. Why Do Terrorists Kill Themselves?   104

PART TWO: THE COUNTERTERRORISTS

6. What Changed and What Did Not on September 11, 2001   139
7. Why the War on Terror Can Never Be Won   169
8. What Is to Be Done?   200

Acknowledgments   241
Glossary   243
Notes   255
Bibliography   285
Index   297

INTRODUCTION

While nothing is easier than to denounce the evildoer,
nothing is more difficult than to understand him.[1]

—Dostoevsky

I N SEPTEMBER 2001, THE OBSCURE ACADEMIC FIELD I HAD
quietly toiled in for many years, terrorist movements, was thrown
into the limelight. I had been thinking about the subject for as long
as I can remember and teaching courses on terrorist movements to
Harvard undergraduates since the mid-1990s. Suddenly invitations to
speak flooded in from all over the country and beyond, and since that
time I have addressed countless audiences. At the end of every talk I
am always asked, "What is the one book I should read to get a handle
on terrorism?" The disappointment of the questioner is palpable when
I respond with a lengthy list of books that address different aspects of
terrorism. I always assumed that authors more entrepreneurial than I
would have rushed to write the one book that addresses the question
of terrorism in all its complexity but with a coherent, comprehensive,
and analytical approach. A book that would present terrorism in a
nonpartisan way as an age-old political phenomenon that can be understood in rational terms. That would help readers to understand

what causes people to resort to terrorism and what terrorists are trying to achieve. I have written *What Terrorists Want* to try to fill this void. Drawing on years of research on the evolution of terrorist movements and counterterrorist strategies throughout the world, it explores the nature of the terrorist threat we face today. It examines the context and the causes behind the terrorists and what drives them to fight us. It explores the experiences of other democracies in countering terrorism and suggests lessons that can be derived from their successes and their failures to enable us to formulate a more effective counterterrorism policy.

———

I have a different perspective from that of most terrorism experts. I come from a background that has produced many terrorists, and I have spent most of my professional life trying to understand them. When I consider a terrorist atrocity, I do not think of the perpetrators as evil monsters; rather, I think about the terrorists I have met and the people I have known who have joined terrorist groups, and I rehearse in my mind their own justifications. I grapple with how a young idealist can believe that in murdering innocent people he or she is battling injustice and fighting for a fairer world. I think, as the Protestant martyr John Bradford said five hundred years ago, "There but for the grace of God, go I."[1] I do not find their justifications convincing. Far from it. In my moral code, nobody has the right to take the life of noncombatants. Nevertheless, I am struck by how futile counterterrorist policies are likely to be when they are based on a view of terrorists as one-dimensional evildoers and psychopaths.

I grew up in a small seaside town in rural Ireland in the 1960s and 1970s. With my classmates I assembled at school every morning to pray beneath a statue of a crucified Christ and a large framed copy of the Proclamation of Independence. The text of the proclamation was surrounded by photographs of the seven men who were executed for their part in the 1916 Easter Rising, which tried and failed to establish a republic of Ireland by force of arms. Their photographs were as familiar to me as the images of America's Founding Fathers are to my children. My classmates and I admired these seven men in much the same way that my children admire Benjamin Franklin, Thomas Jefferson, George Washington, and Abraham Lincoln. The real difference, of course, is that Jefferson and Franklin and the other signatories of the American Declaration of Independence won their war of independence, and the signatories of the Irish Proclamation of Independence lost. They did not hang together, but rather, as Franklin feared, they were executed together.[2] The unstated message of both the crucifix and the proclamation was the same: that the good are often vilified and forced to suffer, that fighting against today's majority and being punished for it does not mean you are on the wrong side, that in time the truth triumphs. My view of the world, in other words, is very different from that of my American children, who have learned to assume that the majority is right and that, as demonstrated by the War of Independence, the Civil War, and the world wars, the good guys win the wars.

Years later, studying Irish history under the tutelage of English historians, I learned that the glorious 1916 Rising, in which we had been taught that the nation rose together to overthrow the British yoke, was in fact an altogether more modest occasion. A motley crew of amateur armed insurrectionists terrorized Dublin city center for a week by taking over the General Post Office and a few other buildings and firing at the British garrison and local police force. In all, 254 civilians, 132 members of the security forces, and 64 rebels were killed in the course of a week of fighting in the densely populated city.[3] It was the reaction, or rather overreaction, of the British government that transformed the affair. The leaders were executed and thereby turned into martyrs, while the foot soldiers and sympathizers were shipped off to internment camps in Britain, there to become radicalized and to return better organized, more embittered, and motivated to launch a war of independence. The resonance to today is inescapable.

The myth of 1916, however, lived on in the popular mind. My childhood was filled with stories from my mother's side of aunts secretly slipping messages into the occupied post office, of guns courageously hidden beneath food in bicycle baskets and brought to "the lads." On my father's side, the story was that my father had gotten his name from his uncle, who died, shortly before my father's birth, at the brutal hands of the Black and Tans. These were ill-trained auxiliaries dispatched to maintain order in Ireland by Britain whose security forces were strained by the demands of the Great War. (They were known as Black and Tans because their uniforms were made up of surplus army and police uniforms.) The story was that my uncle witnessed some thuggish Black and Tans harassing a Dublin girl, and when he went to her defense, they simply shot him in cold blood. It was only later, with the skepticism of the history student trained in research, that I discovered that most of these stories must have been apocryphal. Once while helping my grandmother clean out some drawers, I came across a photo of my father's namesake, the uncle alleged to have died at the hands of the hated Black and Tans, dressed in the uniform of a British soldier. His occupation had never been mentioned in the family. I kept the secret. Less important than the facts of this history was the way it was remembered and passed down. It is this remembered history, invariably oversimplified, with heroes and villains overdrawn, that mobilizes and motivates the next generation. The facts don't seem to matter so much.

Like many around me, I grew up with a passionate hatred of England, which was not shared by my apolitical parents but was certainly never censored at home or at school. At school we learned Irish history as a long series of heroic efforts to throw off the evil yoke of the British. Britain was to blame for all our ills, political, cultural, linguistic, social, and of course religious. I occasionally met English holiday makers visiting our town, which shook my certitude, so I decided that I hated the English government rather than individual English people. As the streets of Northern Ireland exploded in the late 1960s with the civil rights movement and the overreaction of the security forces, it all seemed to be a continuation of the same brutal repression of Irish Catholics. I kept scrapbooks of atrocities against Catholics and wrote diaries filled with invective against the latest example of Britain carrying out her historical role of exploiting and brutalizing Ireland. After the Bloody Sunday massacre in 1972, my anger reached new heights. I was fourteen, and if the IRA would have had me I'd have joined in a heartbeat.[4] My bemused mother had to lock me in my room and forbid me to leave the house to prevent me carrying out my desire to travel to the North to join the civil rights march in Newry the Sunday following Bloody Sunday.

My views were entirely in keeping with the surrounding culture. We all felt differently when we heard a Catholic was killed, as opposed to a Protestant or a British soldier. A Catholic death was a loss to our side, a soldier's death a victory. The extremism I imbibed came from school, books, popular history, and songs. It came from the air around me. I was horrified to discover years later in a peaceful Boston suburb, as I desperately tried to stay awake in the early hours of the morning while rocking one of my infant children to sleep, that I knew only one or two lullabies. But I knew an endless repertoire of Irish songs remembered from my childhood. I found myself sweetly singing one blood-curdling, warmongering song after another to my restless child. They told simple tales of good and evil and the justice of the fight for change.

I arrived at Trinity College Dublin at the age of seventeen, a Catholic country girl very much out of my depth socially on the upper-crust Protestant campus. During freshman week, clubs tried to get the newcomers to join. My closest friend, another Catholic socially out of her element, and I were recruited by the student branch of the IRA. By then I had concluded that killing people was not the right way to advance the cause of reuniting Ireland. I attended meetings and discussions but said I would not join as I could not endorse the use of violence. My friend decided to join. I remained in the background arguing about methods, making sandwiches in the kitchen, until more appealing causes such as antiapartheid in South Africa garnered my attention. Those who did join were like me in almost every respect. They were young idealists wanting to do their part for their country as their forebears had (or as they thought their forebears had). They were motivated by a desire to right wrongs and to do their best for a noble cause. They knew that they were likely to suffer personally from their decisions. They justified the use of force on the grounds that it was the only way to make progress toward the legitimate goals they sought.

At Trinity College I learned the British version of Irish history. When I tried to present evidence to my family challenging the accepted wisdoms of Irish republicanism, it was dismissed as "Trinity talk." I was fascinated, and remain so, by how two entirely different versions of the same event could be believed by well-meaning people living side by side. Years later, while studying for a Ph.D. at Harvard, I read the literature on terrorism. I was profoundly struck by how ill understood the subject was. Terrorists were portrayed as psychopaths, terrorist movements as criminal gangs motivated by desires for personal gain, the term "terrorism" itself a loose and pejorative label attributed to one's enemies. This was not my perspective. It did not describe my fellow students who had joined the IRA, or the parents of my friends, or my teachers in the Gaeltacht (the Gaelic-speaking part of Ireland) who had joined.

———

This sense of the inadequacies of the field led me into a study of terrorism to try to establish why an otherwise responsible parent, student, or teacher would choose to join a terrorist movement and remain in one, and why a group of people would collectively choose to kill innocent people they do not know in order to advance some goal unlikely to be achieved in their lifetime. My research drew me to the source, to the writings of terrorists themselves. There is a great deal of primary source evidence available on terrorists' motivations, aspirations, and justifications. They appear in interviews with imprisoned terrorists and in the publications and Web sites of terrorist groups. I also spoke to any terrorist I could. In the days before September 11, 2001, this was a lot easier than it has been since.

On one occasion a few years ago, some colleagues and I convened a group of what we politely termed "activists," representatives from a number of ethnonationalist terrorist groups, for a secret conference in a private location. We met for several days, during which we conducted ourselves much like an academic conference. I gave a paper on factors driving terrorists' decisions to escalate, and a senior member of a well-known terrorist group served as commentator on my paper. He politely pointed out where he thought I was right and where he disagreed, where my generalizations applied to his movement and where they did not. We all socialized together for several days. It was soon difficult to tell to which camp an individual belonged.

Part of the goal of the gathering was to try to figure out what factors drive a group to escalate to a different level of violence, so we composed some scenarios to try to get at this question. We also engaged in some war games—again in an effort to establish the factors that trigger the decision to escalate. Mixed teams of academics and "activists" participated in each role. I participated in a group that was a Chechen cell based in Moscow. The scenario called for us to be placed under increasing pressure by the authorities, as we were trying to establish what kinds of pressures would force a decision to escalate. The similarities in response between the academics and the insurgents were very striking. While the operational efficiency of those with experience was breathtaking (in a completely matter-of-fact way correcting us academics on how many individuals and what weapons would be required to carry out a particular operation), on the more important question of when one should escalate, the insurgents were not more prone to escalation than the academics. (Indeed, the insurgents were quite taken aback by the belligerence of the academics in the mixed groups.) The only real difference was on an issue of how to respond to an incident that could be seen as an insult to our honor. I argued rationally that we were weak; we had to husband our resources and should not act. An insurgent was adamant that we had to defend our honor no matter what the cost. As to when we should target children and families, it was the academics who were prepared to take this action first. I mention this not to make light of a serious issue, only to make the point that terrorists are human beings who think like we do. They have goals they are trying to achieve, and in a different set of circumstances they, and perhaps we, would lead very different lives.

With colleagues, I helped to organize a second similar gathering, this time with representation from religious terrorist groups. We were scheduled to meet from September 11 to 14, 2001. Six weeks before the planned meeting, worried that one of the groups might make the meeting public and when one of the insurgent groups insisted that there could be no Jews among the academics, we decided to cancel. I have often imagined what it would have been like to have been in that company on that day.

———

As a professor of government at Harvard, I taught courses on international relations and American foreign policy. Coming to my office and seeing my bookshelves laden with books about terrorists, my students asked why I didn't teach about terrorism, to which I responded this was my hobby, not what I taught. But they talked me into it. I agreed to teach a junior honors seminar. These courses are limited in size to 15 and usually have half that number of students. The first time I offered the course, 130 students signed up. As always happens when teaching smart students, you learn as much as they do.

Thinking of my own undergraduate days, I expected that those who wanted to take the course would be the politically disaffected, those with Che Guevara posters in their dorm rooms. But when I went around the class the first day and asked why they were there, the responses invariably were that they wanted to be secretary of state or director of the CIA or the FBI. They were there because they wanted to lock up the terrorists, not because they sympathized with them. I required each student to choose a terrorist movement at the beginning of term and to track that movement, consult its Web site, read the literature, research the leaders and the actions of the group, and then present the group to the class at the end of term. A funny thing happened. Almost without exception, the student would start his presentation (and they were predominantly males) by saying something like "Well, all those other groups are terrorist groups, but if you really look at the ETA [or IRA or Shining Path, or whichever movement he had chosen] you discover that they are not really terrorists. Do you know what happened to them, or do you know what they do for the poor? Or do you know about their cultural programs?"

The depth of students' interest in the subject in the 1990s never ceased to amaze me. My small seminars could not contain the demand, so I offered an undergraduate lecture course. The students poured in. Their desire to grapple with and to understand the phenomenon and to question every assertion was exhilarating.

In the 1990s, terrorism studies was a marginalized field. Terrorism was studied in a range of different disciplines but was central to none. No major universities had positions in terrorism, and very few even offered a course in the subject. There were a small number of dedicated academics around the country, however, who had devoted their lives to studying some aspect of this phenomenon. We were called the terrorism studies community. We were not so interested in counterterrorism—not because we didn't want to counter the terrorists, only because we were more interested in other questions: Why do people do this? How do they recruit? When do they escalate? What are the underlying causes?

Very occasionally, a government official would come by to keep abreast of academic research. In early August 2001, one official came to visit me to ask why I thought no terrorist group had ever used an airplane as a bomb and whether I thought they would. My answer was far from helpful. I said that the tactic was very much under consideration and I suspected that some terrorist groups would use it sooner rather than later. But I wrongly predicted that they would make some coordinated attack on a number of American embassies around the world.

On another occasion a member of the State Department's Office of Counterterrorism visited Harvard to find out what terrorism research was being conducted there. He complained bitterly about how we were not being helpful, going off doing research wherever we liked instead of focusing on the government's policy concerns. I argued back just as vehemently that it was not in our interest, and I didn't think it was even in his, to turn universities into the research arm of the government. Later at an academic conference, in a talk entitled "Long Live the Gap," I argued for preserving the distance between government policy and academic research.

Experience since September 11, 2001, has taught me to moderate this view. Had the American government's policy in the past few years been informed by the views of the terrorism studies community, it would have been a very different policy indeed. Lives have been lost because of our government's failure to understand the nature of the enemy we face and its unwillingness to learn from the experiences of others in countering terrorism. I have emerged from my academic shell, therefore, to argue in this book that we cannot defeat terrorism by smashing every terrorist movement. An effort to do so will only generate more terrorists, as has happened repeatedly in the past. We should never have declared a global war on terrorism, knowing that such a war can never be won. We should never have believed that Osama bin Laden and Saddam Hussein were working together against us. Our objective should not be the completely unattainable goal of obliterating terrorism; rather, we should pursue the more modest and attainable goal of containing terrorist recruitment and constraining resort to the tactic of terrorism.

After September 11 an entirely new breed of terrorism expert emerged. The priority of these experts was counterterrorism policy and American power. They were very knowledgeable about the workings of the American government and about military and security policy. Many had worked on international security issues such as nuclear proliferation or the conduct of the Cold War; others had practical experience fighting, either overtly or covertly, against terrorists; but very few had ever actually tried to understand terrorism. They found the terrorism studies community incurably soft on terrorism, ignorant of policy, and blind to the threat of al-Qaeda. Members of the terrorism studies community tended to console themselves by remarking how little the newly minted experts knew about their subject. It is clearly in everyone's interest for this gap to be eliminated.

———

There is a widespread view that to endeavor to understand or to explain terrorism is to sympathize with it. I reject this view. Indeed, it is a central tenet of this book that the best way to contain terrorism is to understand its appeal and to use this understanding to forge effective counterterrorist policies. The Peruvian government's campaign against the Shining Path is one example of how an effort to understand a terrorist movement can be much more effective at ending terrorism than an effort to smash it. The Shining Path was a Maoist movement with close to ten thousand members at its height in the 1980s that terrorized a large section of the Ayacucho region.[5] It was led by a ruthless academic, Abimael Guzmán, who followed the Maoist prescription for revolution: mobilize the peasantry first and then move into the urban areas. An estimated 69,000 people were killed in the course of the twenty-year terrorist campaign.[6] It is anyone's guess how many of these people were killed by the Shining Path and how many were killed by the military battalions that were sent to the countryside to destroy them. I expect it was a matter of little consequence to those close to the victims.

Successive Peruvian governments dispatched the military to destroy the terrorists, which led to an increase in casualties but no diminution of terrorism. It was only when the government established DIRCOTE, a seventy-man intelligence unit within the police force, to follow the movement that it had results. Those studying the movement soon realized that the real Achilles' heel of the group was its centralized dependence on the charismatic leadership of Guzmán. They decided that if they could eliminate Guzmán they could destroy the movement. They studied everything they could about Guzmán and discovered that he had a particular skin condition. Through old-fashioned police work and good electronic intelligence, they were able to track down Guzmán through his medical prescription. He was captured along with several of his top lieutenants. The movement never recovered.[7] This seventy-man police unit was thereby able to achieve what wave after wave of military deployment could not.

The lesson of the Peruvian case is not that every terrorist movement will disintegrate if its leader is captured. This is not the case. Terrorism is a complex phenomenon, a tactic employed by many different groups, in pursuit of many different objectives, in many parts of the world. The key is to understand the nature of the group you confront. When a group is organized around a single leader, like the Shining Path of Peru, Aum Shinrikyo in Japan, or the PKK in Turkey, it makes sense to try to decapitate the movement.

It does not follow, however, that the capture of Osama bin Laden would deal a body blow to al-Qaeda. There is no evidence to suggest that the movement is organized around him. He has clearly gone to some lengths to ensure that the movement can survive without him. Different terrorist movements are organized differently, and it is essential to know the difference.

Our adversaries fully understand the importance of knowing one's enemy in order to undermine him. Radical Islamic groups have been so effective against us in part because they have used hallmarks of our democracy against us. An al-Qaeda spokesman put it this way:

> Al-Qa'ida can take over the enemy's means and use them against him, while the enemy cannot do the same. The *mujahedeen* can do this because they have come to understand the enemy's mentality and how his society functions; yet the enemy has no way of deterring the believer or influencing his mentality.[8]

We must prove them wrong.

———

In the first half of this book I pay little attention to the policies of our government and look instead to the terrorists themselves. I spell out the meaning of the term "terrorism" and how terrorists themselves feel about that label. I look to the past, to demonstrate the long lineage of the terrorist tactic and to rebut the myth that terrorism, even religious terrorism, is either new or the primary preserve of Islam. I point to the political use of the term, to terrorists who have become statesmen, and to ways in which those quite opposed to terrorism have been labeled terrorists. I argue that terrorists are neither crazy nor amoral but rather are rationally seeking to achieve a set of objectives within self-imposed limits.

I suggest that the causes of terrorism are not to be found in objective conditions of poverty or privation or in a ruthless quest for domination but rather in a lethal cocktail that combines a disaffected individual, an enabling community, and a legitimizing ideology. I believe that terrorists' behavior can be understood in terms of both long-term political motivations, which differ across groups, as well as more immediate motives, which very different kinds of terrorists share. Their record of success in attaining these secondary motives is much better than in achieving fundamental political change. When terrorists act, they are seeking three immediate objectives: they want to exact revenge, to acquire glory, and to force their adversary into a reaction. These are the three Rs of revenge, renown, and reaction.

In the second part of the book I examine the situation in the United States after September 11, 2001. I suggest what changed and what did not that day. The biggest change, and the one with most serious long-term implications, is our government's reaction to terrorism. The declaration of a global war on terrorism has been a terrible mistake and is doomed to failure. I suggest a different approach to containing terrorism, one that relies instead on an appreciation of the factors driving terrorists and is dedicated to depriving them of what they seek. We can learn from the experience of other countries in countering terrorism. We should emulate their success and avoid repeating their mistakes.

Terrorism is a tactic that will continue to be employed as long as it is deemed to be effective. Technological developments will make it easier for ever smaller groups to employ weapons of ever greater lethality against us. Political, social, and economic developments will continue to produce disaffected individuals. We will never be able to prevent every attack. But we can control our reactions to those attacks. If we keep terrorist attacks in perspective and recognize that the strongest weapons in our arsenal against terrorism are precisely the hallmarks of democracy that we value, then we can indeed contain the terrorist threat.

PART ONE

THE TERRORISTS

The difference between the revolutionary and the terrorist lies in the reason for which each fights. For whoever stands by a just cause and fights for the freedom and liberation of his land from the invaders, the settlers and the colonialists cannot possibly be called terrorist, otherwise the American people in their struggle for liberation from the British colonialists would have been terrorists; the European resistance against the Nazis would be terrorism, the struggle of the Asian, African and Latin American peoples would also be terrorism, and many of you who are in this Assembly hall were considered terrorists. . . . As to those who fight against the just causes, those who wage war to occupy, colonize and oppress other people, those are the terrorists. Those are the people whose actions should be condemned, who should be called war criminals: for the justice of the cause determines the right to struggle.

—YASSER ARAFAT, NOVEMBER 1974[1]

WHAT IS TERRORISM?

Terror is nothing else than justice, prompt, secure and inflexible.[1]
—Robespierre, 1794

Today our nation saw evil, the very worst of human nature.
—George W. Bush, September 11, 2001

The best that one can say of these people is that they are morally depraved. They champion falsehood, support the butcher against the victim, the oppressor against the innocent child.
—Osama bin Laden, October 7, 2001

L IKE PORNOGRAPHY, WE KNOW TERRORISM WHEN WE SEE it. Or do we? We know we don't like it. In fact, the only universally accepted attribute of the term "terrorism" is that it is pejorative. Terrorism is something the bad guys do. The term itself has been bandied about so much that it has practically lost all meaning. A casual glance at newspapers reveals currency speculation being labeled "economic terrorism," domestic violence as "domestic terrorism"; crank telephone calls have even been labeled "telephone terrorism." If you can pin the label "terrorist" on your opponent, you have gone a long way toward winning the public relations aspect of any conflict.

Even terrorists don't like the label. An al-Qaeda statement put it this way: "When the victim tries to seek justice, he is described as a terrorist."[2] Many prefer to redefine the term first. In Osama bin Laden's words, "If killing those who kill our sons is terrorism, then let history be witness that we are terrorists."[3] On another occasion, when asked to respond to media claims that he was a terrorist, he replied, "There is an Arabic proverb that says, she accused me of having her malady and then snuck away."[4] Other terrorist leaders have taken a similar perspective. Abimael Guzmán, the Peruvian academic turned leader of the Maoist Shining Path, declared, "They claim we're terrorists. I would like to give the following answer so that everyone can think about it: has it or has it not been Yankee imperialism and particularly Reagan who has branded all revolutionary movements as terrorists, yes or no? This is how they attempt to discredit and isolate us in order to crush us."[5] Shamil Basayev, the Chechen leader responsible for the Beslan school siege, among other exploits, declared, "Okay. So, I'm a terrorist. But what would you call them? If they are keepers of constitutional order, if they are anti-terrorists, then I spit on all these agreements and nice words."[6]

Terrorism simply means deliberately and violently targeting civilians for political purposes. It has seven crucial characteristics. First, a terrorist act is politically inspired. If not, then it is simply a crime. After the May 13, 2003, Riyadh bombings, Secretary of State Colin Powell declared, "We should not try to cloak their . . . criminal activity, their murderous activity, in any trappings of political purpose. They are terrorists."[7] In point of fact, it is precisely because they did have a political purpose that they were, indeed, terrorists.

Second, if an act does not involve violence or the threat of violence, it is not terrorism. The term "cyberterrorism" is not a useful one. The English lexicon is broad enough to provide a term for the sabotage of our IT facilities without reverting to such language.

Third, the point of terrorism is not to defeat the enemy but to send a message. Writing of the September 11 attacks, an al-Qaeda spokesman declared, "It rang the bells of restoring Arab and Islamic glory."[8]

Fourth, the act and the victim usually have symbolic significance.

Bin Laden referred to the Twin Towers as "icons" of America's "military and economic power."[9] The shock value of the act is enormously enhanced by the symbolism of the target. The whole point is for the psychological impact to be greater than the actual physical act. Terrorism is indeed a weapon of the weak. Terrorist movements are invariably both outmanned and outgunned by their opponents, so they employ such tactics in an effort to gain more attention than any objective assessment of their capabilities would suggest that they warrant.

Fifth—and this is a controversial point—terrorism is the act of substate groups, not states. This is not to argue that states do not use terrorism as an instrument of foreign policy. We know they do. Many states, such as Iran, Iraq, Syria, and Libya, have sponsored terrorism abroad because they did not want to incur the risk of overtly attacking more powerful countries. Great powers have supported terrorist groups abroad as a way of engaging in proxy warfare or covertly bringing about internal change in difficult countries without openly displaying their strength. Nor do I wish to argue that states refrain from action that is the moral equivalent of terrorism. We know they don't. The Allied bombing campaign in World War II, culminating in the bombing of Hiroshima and Nagasaki, was a deliberate effort to target civilian populations in order to force the hand of their government. The policy of collective punishment visited on communities that produce terrorists is another example of targeting civilians to achieve a political purpose. Nevertheless, if we want to have any analytical clarity in understanding the behavior of terrorist groups, we must understand them as substate actors rather than states.

A sixth characteristic of terrorism is that the victim of the violence and the audience the terrorists are trying to reach are not the same. Victims are used as a means of altering the behavior of a larger audience, usually a government. Victims are chosen either at random or as representative of some larger group. Individual victims are interchangeable. The identities of the people traveling on a bus in Tel Aviv or a train in Madrid, dancing in Bali or bond trading in New York, were of no consequence to those who killed them. They were being used to influence others. This is different from most other forms of political violence, in which security forces or state representatives are targeted in an effort to reduce the strength of an opponent.

The final and most important defining characteristic of terrorism is the deliberate targeting of civilians. This is what sets terrorism apart from other forms of political violence, even the most proximate form, guerrilla warfare. Terrorists have elevated practices that are normally seen as the excesses of warfare to routine practice, striking noncombatants not as an unintended side effect but as deliberate strategy. They insist that those who pay taxes to a government are responsible for their actions whether they are Russians or Americans. Basayev declared all Russians fair game because "They pay taxes. They give approval in word and in deed. They are all responsible."[10] Bin Laden similarly said of Americans, "He is the enemy of ours whether he fights us directly or merely pays his taxes."[11]

TERRORISTS, GUERRILLAS, AND FREEDOM FIGHTERS

It goes without saying that in the very messy worlds of violence and politics actions don't always fit neatly into categories. Guerrillas occasionally target civilians, and terrorists occasionally target security forces. But if the primary tactic of an organization is deliberately to target civilians, it deserves to be called a terrorist group, irrespective of the political context in which it operates or the legitimacy of the goals it seeks to achieve. There are, of course, other differences between guerillas and terrorists. Guerrillas are an irregular army fighting the regular forces of the state. They conduct themselves along military lines and generally have large numbers of adherents, which permit them to launch quasi-military operations. Their goal is the military defeat of the enemy. Terrorists, by contrast, rarely have illusions about their ability to inflict military defeat on the enemy. Rather, they seek either to cause the enemy to overreact and thereby permit them to recruit large numbers of followers so that they can launch a guerrilla campaign, or to have such a psychological or economic impact on the enemy that it will withdraw of its own accord. Bin Laden called this the "bleed-until-bankruptcy plan."[12]

It is the means employed and not the ends pursued, nor the political context in which a group operates, that determines whether or not a group is a terrorist group.

In his famous 1974 speech to the United Nations renouncing

terrorism, Yasser Arafat, chairman of the Palestinian Liberation Organization and founder of its militant wing, al-Fatah, declared, "The difference between the revolutionary and the terrorist lies in the reason for which each fights. For whoever stands by a just cause and fights for the freedom and liberation of his land . . . cannot possibly be called terrorist."[13] A great many people, including several U.S. presidents, have shared this view. Indeed, the main reason international cooperation against terrorism has been so anemic over the past thirty-odd years is precisely because the pejorative power of the term is such that nobody has wanted to pin the label on a group fighting for what are considered legitimate goals. President Ronald Reagan shared the goal of the Nicaraguan Contras to overthrow the Marxist Sandinista government, so he called them "the moral equivalent of our Founding Fathers."[14] Our European allies saw the Contras as a violent and unrepresentative group attempting to subvert a popular government and considered them terrorists. In fact, the legitimacy of the goals being sought is irrelevant. Many terrorist groups, and especially those that have lasted the longest, the ethnonationalist groups, have been fighting for goals that many share and that may even be just. But if they deliberately kill civilians to achieve that goal, they are terrorists.

Bin Laden has only a slightly different perspective. He thinks that there is good terrorism and bad terrorism:

> Terrorism can be commendable and it can be reprehensible. Terrifying an innocent person and terrorizing them is objectionable and unjust, also unjustly terrorizing people is not right. Whereas terrorizing oppressors and criminals and thieves and robbers is necessary for the safety of people and for the protection of their property. . . . The terrorism we practice is of the commendable kind for it is directed at the tyrants and the aggressors and the enemies of Allah, the tyrants, the traitors who commit acts of treason against their own countries and their own faith and their own prophet and their own nation. Terrorizing those and punishing them are necessary measures to straighten things and to make them right.[15]

Bin Laden evidently believes that terrorism is justified if it is used against those who are unjust, whereas it is unjustified if used against the innocent. His concept of innocent as seen above, however, is an idiosyncratic one. This is a variant on the widely held position that the ends being sought determine whether or not an act is a terrorist act.

Another popular perspective is that an action is terrorist only if it takes place in a democratic state that permits peaceful forms of opposition. Liberal intellectuals made this distinction in reaction to the African National Congress (ANC) in South Africa. Conor Cruise O'Brien and others wanted to argue that members of the Irish Republican Army (IRA) in Northern Ireland were terrorists when they planted bombs in trash cans in Belfast in the 1970s, as they had a democratic alternative to voice their opposition to the state. But the ANC, when it planted bombs in trash cans in Johannesburg in the 1980s, was not a terrorist group because it had no means of political opposition available. This perspective implies that members of the Basque nationalist group Euskadi ta Askatasuna (ETA) were not terrorists when they planted bombs and murdered tourists under the Franco regime but became terrorists when they planted bombs and murdered tourists under the democratic government of Spain. This argument is hardly compelling. The political context in which an act takes place can affect our normative evaluation of the act—the degree to which we might think it morally justified or morally reprehensible—but it does not alter the fact that it is a terrorist act.

Perhaps the most difficult case to make is that of the ANC in South Africa. If ever a group could legitimately claim to have resorted to force only as a last resort, it is the ANC. Founded in 1912, for the first fifty years the movement treated nonviolence as a core principle. In 1961, however, with all forms of political organization closed to it, Nelson Mandela was authorized to create a separate military organization, Umkhonto we Sizwe (MK). In his autobiography Mandela describes the strategy session as the movement examined the options available to them:

> We considered four types of violent activities: sabotage, guerrilla warfare, terrorism and open revolution. For a small and fledgling army, open revolution was inconceivable. Terrorism inevitably reflected poorly on those who used it, undermining any public support it might otherwise garner. Guerrilla warfare was a possibility, but since the ANC had been reluctant to embrace violence at all, it

made sense to start with the form of violence that inflicted the least harm against individuals: sabotage.[16]

These fine distinctions were lost on the court in Rivonia that convicted Mandela and most of the ANC leadership in 1964 and sentenced them to life imprisonment. For the next twenty years an increasingly repressive white minority state denied the most basic political rights to the majority black population.

An uprising in Soweto was defeated, as was an MK guerrilla campaign launched from surrounding states. In 1985, the government declared a state of emergency, which was followed within three weeks by thirteen terrorist bombings in major downtown areas. Reasonable people can differ on whether or not the terrorism of the ANC was justified, given the legitimacy of the goals it sought and the reprehensible nature of the government it faced. The violent campaign of the ANC in the early and mid-1980s, however, was indisputably a terrorist campaign. Unless and until we are willing to label a group whose ends we believe to be just a terrorist group, if it deliberately targets civilians in order to achieve those ends, we are never going to be able to forge effective international cooperation against terrorism.

This same confusion between ends and means is what has given the rather silly adage that "one man's freedom fighter is another man's terrorist" such a long life. Most terrorists consider themselves freedom fighters. Bin Laden told the American people, "We fight because we are free men who don't sleep under oppression. We want to restore freedom to our nation."[17] Shamil Basayev said something quite similar: "For me, it's first and foremost a struggle for freedom. If I'm not a free man, I can't live in my faith. I need to be a free man. Freedom is primary."[18] The freedom for which they fight, however, is often an abstract concept. It means political freedom rather than conceding to others the right of freedom from fear, or freedom from random violence, as terrorists exploit civilians' fear to further their ends. Whether they are fighting for freedom from repression or freedom to impose a repressive theocracy, to suggest that a freedom fighter cannot be a terrorist is to confuse ends and means. The fact that terrorists may claim to be freedom fighters does not mean that we should concede the point to them, just as we should not concede the point that all citizens of a democracy are legitimate targets because they have the option of changing their government and have not done so and are therefore responsible for their government's actions.

———

It is often claimed, and not without reason, that history is written by the winners, so that a victorious terrorist becomes a statesman and a failed terrorist remains a terrorist. Terrorists with whom I have spoken invariably invoke Nelson Mandela and Menachem Begin as evidence that someone considered a terrorist today can be considered a statesman tomorrow. (In the past they also used to invoke Robert Mugabe, but less so now.) Nelson Mandela was for a long time described as a terrorist not only by the South African government but also by our own, as well as by many academics. In fact, Mandela led a campaign of sabotage, not terrorism. Menachem Begin, however, is a different story. Begin led the Irgun from 1943 until its dissolution in 1948. The Irgun was an illegal Jewish right-wing movement made up of revisionist Zionists. They attacked both Arabs and British in an effort to establish a Jewish state on both sides of the River Jordan. In 1938, the Irgun exploded land mines in an Arab fruit market in Haifa, killing 74 people. More famously, in 1946, it blew up the King David Hotel in Jerusalem, killing 91 people. In 1948, the Irgun and its offshoot the Stern Gang attacked the Arab village of Deir Yassin and killed 254 of the inhabitants. Both the Irgun and the Stern Gang were soon absorbed into the fledgling Israeli Army on the expiration of the British mandate in 1948. Notwithstanding this past, Menachem Begin served as prime minister of Israel from 1977 to 1983 and shared the Nobel Peace Prize with Anwar Sadat in 1978. In truth, Begin was a terrorist in the 1940s and a statesman in the 1970s.

So a terrorist is neither a freedom fighter nor a guerrilla. A terrorist is a terrorist, no matter whether or not you like the goal s/he is trying to achieve, no matter whether or not you like the government s/he is trying to change.

TYPES OF TERRORISM

Today the term "terrorist" connotes the image of a radical Islamic fundamentalist from the Middle East. Thirty years ago, the term conjured up images of atheistic young European Communists. At that time terrorists from Sri Lanka to Northern Ireland were also fighting for tradi-tional goals, such as territorial control over a homeland. Aside from their willingness to visit violence on civilians to achieve their objec-tives, all these groups shared one characteristic: they were the weaker party in an asymmetrical conflict. Terrorism is the weapon of those who want to effect change, and to do so quickly, but lack the numbers either to prevail in a democratic system or to launch a viable military campaign.

Terrorism has been practiced by the Right as well as by the Left, by atheists, agnostics, and religious millenarians, by Christians, Jews, Muslims, Hindus, and members of most other religions. It has taken place in rich countries and poor, under authoritarian regimes and demo-cratic governments. Terrorists' objectives range from Maoist revolution in Peru and Nepal to bringing about the apocalypse in Japan; from the destruction of capitalism in Europe to the destruction of the state of Is-rael; from the expulsion of U.S. influence from the Middle East to the return of the caliphate; from the expulsion of Russia from Chechnya and Britain from Northern Ireland to creating homelands for Kurds, Tamils, Sikhs, and Basques. Any attempt to reduce all of them to one simplified notion of terrorism will only cloud our understanding.

Social revolutionary movements, such as the Italian Red Brigades, the German Red Army Faction, the Japanese Red Army, and the French Action Directe, and millenarian movements, such as the Japan-ese Aum Shinrikyo, have arisen primarily in advanced industrialized countries. Maoist movements (such as the Peruvian Shining Path, the Nepalese Communist Party, and the New People's Army in the Philip-pines) have emerged in the developing world. Radical religious move-ments have so far emerged primarily in the Middle East and East Asia (such as Hezbollah in Lebanon and the Abu Sayyaf Group in the Philippines), while ethnonationalist movements have occurred all over the world from India to Ireland.

In spite of the dizzying array of terrorist movements, the two key variables for understanding all terrorist groups are the nature of the goals they seek and their relationship to the community they claim to represent (see Figure 1). This simple matrix enables us to organize the ever-growing and quite disparate set of terrorist movements, but it will also prove essential later in understanding how terrorist groups termi-nate their campaigns and how they can most effectively be countered.

FIGURE 1.1: GOALS OF TERRORIST GROUPS

NATURE OF GOALS[19]

TEMPORAL	TRANSFORMATIONAL

ISOLATED / **RELATIONSHIP TO COMMUNITY**

TEMPORAL (ISOLATED):

Abu Nidal Organization (ANO)
Al-Badhr Mujajedin
Al-Ittihad al-Islami (AIAI)
Cambodian Freedom Fighters (CFF)
Continuity IRA (CIRA)
Ejército de Liberación Nacional (National Liberation Army) (ELN)
Grupo de Resistencia Anti-Fascista Primero de Octubre (First of October Anti-Fascist Resistance Group) (GRAPO)
Irish National Liberation Army (INLA)
Jamiat ul-Mujahedin (JUM)
Lord's Resistance Army (LRA)
Loyalist Volunteer Force (LVF)
Mujahedin-e Khalq (MEK)
Palestinian Liberation Front (PLF)
People Against Gangsterism and Drugs (PAGAD)
People's War Group (PWG)
Popular Front for the Liberation of Palestine (PLFP)
Popular Front for the Liberation of Palestine—General Command (PLFP-GC)
Real IRA (RIRA)
Red Hand Defenders (RHD)
Revolutionary Nuclei (RN)
Revolutionary Organization 17 November (17 November)
Special Purpose Islamic Regiment (SPIR)
Ulster Defense Association, Ulster Freedom Fighters (UDA, UDF)
Ulster Volunteer Force (UVF)

TRANSFORMATIONAL (ISOLATED):

Abu Sayyaf Group (ASG)
Action Directe
Alex Boncayao Brigade (ABB)
Al-Gama'a al-Islamiyya (Islamic Group) (IG)
Al-Jihad
Ansar al-Islam (AI)
'Asbat al-Ansar
Aum Shinrikyo (Aum Supreme Truth)
Battalion of Chechen Martyrs (RSRSBCM)
Brigate Rosse (Red Brigades) (BR)
Cellules Communistes Combattantes (Communist Fighting Cells) (CCC)
Devrimci Sol (Dev Sol)
Eastern Turkistan Islamic Movement (ETIM)
Groupe Islamique Armé (Armed Islamic Group) (GIA)
Groupe Islamique Combattant Marocain (Moroccan Islamic Combatant Group) (GICM)
Islami Büyüledogu Akincilar Cephesi (Great East Islamic Raiders Front) (IBDA-C)
Harakat ul-Jihad-I-Islam (HUJI)
Harakat ul-Jihad-I-Islami/Bangladesh (HUJI-B)
Harakat ul-Mujahidin (HUM)
Hizb-I Islami Gulbuddin (HIG)
Hizb-ul-Mujedhideen (HM)
Islamic Army of Aden (IAA)
Islamic International Peacekeeping Brigade (IIPB)
Islamic Movement of Uzbekistan (IMU)
Jaish-e-Mohammed (Army of Mohammed) (JEM)
Japanese Red Army (JRA)
Jemaah Islamiyan (JI)
Kach (Kahane Chai)
Kumpula Mujadedin Malaysia (KMM)
Lashkar-e-Tayyiba (LT)
Lashkar-i-Jhangvi (LJ)
Libyan Islamic Fighting Group (LIFG)
Movimiento Revolucionario Túpac Amaru (Túpac Amaru Revolutionary Movement) (MRTA)
Nuclei Territoriali Antiimperialisti (Anti-Imperialist Territorial Nuclei) (NTA)
Nucleo d'Iniziativa Proletaria Revoluzionaria (Revolutionary Proletarian Initiative Nuclei) (NIPR)
Palestinian Islamic Jihad (PIJ)
Riyadus-Salikhin Reconnaissance and Sabotage
Rote Armee Fraktion (Red Army Faction) (RAF)
Salafist Group for Call and Combat (GSPC)
Sipah-I-Sahaba/Pakistan (SSP)
Tunisian Combat Group (TCG)

1 | 2
4 | 3

al-Qaeda

Hamas (Islamic Resistance Movement)
Hezbollah (Party of God)

CLOSE

TEMPORAL (CLOSE):

Al-Aqsa Martyrs Brigades
Army for the Liberation of Rwanda (ALIR)
Autodefensas Unidas de Colombia (United Self-Defense Forces of Colombia) (AUC)
Communist Party of Nepal
Euskadi ta Askatasuna (Basque Fatherland and Liberty) (ETA)
Fuerzas Armadas Revolucionarios de Colombia (Revolutionary Armed Forces of Colombia) (FARC)
Irish Republican Army (IRA)
Liberation Tigers of Tamil Eelam (Tamil Tigers) (LTTE)
Maoist Communist Center of India (MCCI)
New People's Army (Communist Party of the Philippines) (NPA)
Partiya Karkeren Kurdistan (Kurdistan Workers' Party) (PKK)
Sendero Luminoso (Shining Path)
Turkish Hezbollah

GOALS OF TERRORIST GROUPS

The goals of all terrorist groups fall into one of two categories: temporal and transformational. By temporal I mean political goals that can be met without overthrowing the political system. An independent homeland for Sikhs, Tamils, Chechens, and Basques qualifies, as do the secession of Kashmir from India and of Northern Ireland from the United Kingdom. This is not to trivialize these aspirations nor to underestimate the difficulty of conceding them. The United States fought a bitter and bloody civil war at a cost of 600,000 lives on the issue of secession. Nevertheless, these goals could be won or lost without overthrowing the fundamental balance of power. They are also issues on which compromise could be negotiated, substituting local autonomy for complete independence, for example.

On the other hand, a transformational goal, by its nature, is not subject to negotiation, and its satisfaction would require the complete destruction of the regional state system. The social revolutionary movements in Europe in the 1970s sought the destruction of capitalism. The desire to replace the states of the contemporary Middle East with the caliphate, the era of Islam's ascendancy from the death of Muhammad until the thirteenth century, is similar in scale. Of course, the declared policy of these movements, much like the stated policy of many governments, should not always be taken at face value. It is essential to understand their degree of commitment to declared goals and whether or not they might actually be motivated by more traditional political aspirations.

The second variable is the relationship of a movement to the community it claims to represent. Some movements are quite isolated from their communities. Those that are have been easiest to defeat. Lacking financial support, they have often been forced to engage in criminal activity to fund their operations, and this in turn exposes them to capture. They have been most vulnerable to defections and internal splits and have proven easiest to counter with traditional security measures. Groups in this category, such as the left-wing extremists 17 November in Greece and GRAPO in Spain, have been able to inflict only limited damage on their enemies.

Far more dangerous are the groups that have close ties in the community they claim to represent. This is the sea in which Mao's fish swim. In a great many instances the broader communities share the as-pirations of the terrorist groups even if they don't always approve of their means of achieving these objectives. A terrorist group can survive and thrive in this kind of complicit society. Though the broader popula-tion will not themselves engage in terrorism or even openly approve of it, they will not turn the terrorists in. They will look the other way and provide crucial, albeit often passive, support. When the authorities come looking, these terrorists are simply absorbed into the community. When the authorities respond harshly to terrorist acts, willing new recruits emerge. These kinds of groups can last indefinitely, but, handled prop-erly, the community can serve as a source of restraint. Terrorist groups with community support can also turn into broad-based insurrectionist movements or, given the right conditions, into political movements.

THE RATIONALITY OF TERRORISM

We often think of terrorists as crazies. How can killing tourists at a shrine in Luxor or airline passengers in the United States possibly help the cause of Islamic fundamentalism? How can killing children in Beslan, shoppers in London, or tourists in Spain advance the cause of Chechen, Irish, or Basque nationalism? Terrorists must be deranged psychopaths. Their actions seem to make no sense.

But terrorists, by and large, are not insane at all. Their primary shared characteristic is their normalcy, insofar as we understand the term. Psychological studies of terrorists are virtually unanimous on this point.[20] The British journalist Peter Taylor remembers asking a young prisoner from Derry, who was serving a life sentence for murder, what an IRA man was doing reading Tolstoy and Hardy. The prisoner replied, "Because an IRA man's normal like everyone else." When Tay-lor pointed out that normal people did not go around killing people, the prisoner replied that normal people elsewhere did not live in Northern Ireland.[21] There are, of course, psychopaths to be found in many terrorist groups, as in many organizations in which violence is sanctioned. But there are not nearly as many psychopaths in terrorist groups as one might imagine. Most organizations consider them a lia-bility and quite deliberately try to select them out.[22] This holds true across different types of groups, from ethnonationalists to religious fundamentalists.

Historically, terrorists have been very conservative in their choice of tactics. The most common terrorist act is a bombing, and it is not hard to see why. It is cheap. It is easy to get away from the scene of the attack. Moreover, it is dramatic and often indiscriminate. The notion that terrorists are mad has been advanced by the increasing use of suicide terrorism. But from an organizational point of view, suicide attacks are very rational, indeed economical. In the words of Dr. Ayman al-Zawahiri, bin Laden's second in command, "The method of martyrdom operation is the most successful way of inflicting damage against the opponent and least costly to the mujahedin in terms of casualties."[23] It is also, of course, more effective.[24]

Even if suicide terrorism makes sense from an organizational point of view, it seems insane from an individual point of view. But the organizations that employ the tactic have more volunteers than they need. They deliberately do not accept volunteers they consider depressed or suicidal. In the words of the Palestinian Fayez Jaber, an al-Aqsa commander who trained suicide bombers, "There are certain criteria that we observe. People with mental or psychological problems or personal family problems—I cannot allow myself to send such people. . . . A person has to be a fully mature person, an adult, a sane person, and of course, not less than 18 years of age and fully aware of what he is about to carry out."[25] Those who become martyrs appear to do so out of a combination of motives: anger, humiliation, a desire for revenge, commitment to their comrades and their cause, and a desire to attain glory—in other words, for reasons no more irrational than those of anyone prepared to give his life for a cause.[26]

Terrorists' behavior has long seemed senseless to onlookers. The actions of the famous medieval sect the Assassins seemed so incomprehensible to others that for centuries it was believed that they were high on hashish when they undertook their suicide operations. It now appears that they were intoxicated only by their own ideology.[27]

THE MORALITY OF TERRORISM

Another almost universally accepted attribute of terrorists is their amorality—in the words of President Bush, "abandoning every value except the will to power."[28] Yet I have never met a terrorist who considered him/herself either immoral or amoral. Quite the contrary. When not acting as terrorists, they practice as much or as little morality in their daily lives as most of the rest of us. Most terrorists, moreover, go to considerable lengths to justify their actions on moral grounds, both in their public pronouncements and in their internal writings.

Albert Camus, in his play *Les Justes,* beautifully captures the sense of morality of the nineteenth-century anarchists, the precursors of many contemporary terrorists. He describes how Kaliayev, seeing two children seated in the carriage next to his intended target, the grand duke, could not bring himself to hurl the bomb. He subsequently does kill the grand duke and is executed, but he could not justify to himself killing children.[29]

Many contemporary terrorists, of course, have no trouble justifying the killing of children. There are generally a number of defenses offered for the resort to terrorism. First, that it is entered into only as a last resort. Bin Laden made this claim in his 1996 fatwa, or declaration of war, against America: "Why is it then the regime closed all peaceful routes and pushed the people toward armed actions?!! Which is the only choice left for them to implement righteousness and justice."[30] This is an empirical claim. As such, it can quickly be refuted with reference to the facts. Many terrorist groups do first try political action, but they have hardly exhausted the options available to them when they resort to terrorism.

The second common claim is that no other strategy is available. Vellupillai Prabakharan, the charismatic leader of the Tamil Tigers, put it succinctly: "We have no other option but to fight back."[31] One member of al-Qassam, the military wing of Hamas, told the Pakistani writer and relief worker Nasra Hassan, "We do not have tanks or rockets, but we have something superior—our exploding human bombs."[32] A young Italian *brigadista* spoke in similar terms: "I'm not a killer, I'm not a terrorist, I'm someone with a series of values, who wants to be active in politics, and today the only way . . . to be politically active is this."[33] If you are the twenty-five members of the Baader-Meinhof Gang in Germany and desire to overthrow the German capitalist state immediately, there are not too many options available. Ulrike Meinhof, in one of the first communiqués of the Baader-Meinhof Gang, declared that urban guerrilla warfare was "the only revolutionary method of intervention available to what are on the whole weak revolutionary forces."[34] The problem with this argument is that there are always other options available. If those who seek change decided to take a longer time frame and embark on a protracted political strategy of propaganda and civil disobedience, they might undermine the state. But they want immediate results. So their weakness is in relationship to both the state and the broader population who do not share their views. If they had broader support, they wouldn't need to resort to terrorism. So terrorism may well be the only option available, but only if one lacks support, wants immediate results, and is prepared to murder innocents.

Third, those who commit terrorist acts often argue that terrorism works. Certainly the actions of Black September Palestinians, famous for hijacking airplanes and, most notoriously, for murdering members of the Israeli Olympic team in Munich in 1972, brought international attention to the plight of the Palestinians, just as IRA violence in Northern Ireland brought attention to the denial of civil rights to Northern Irish Catholics. But to prove that terrorism works, one would have to show that terrorism achieved what the terrorists wanted and what other means could not, and this has never been done. Maybe the IRA campaign and the ensuing loss of 3,500 lives in Northern Ireland has resulted in the power-sharing executive today in Northern Ireland, but this executive (currently suspended) is a far cry from the Irish unity the IRA has always demanded. Moreover, it is surely reasonable to expect that the same result could have been achieved through concerted peaceful political action over the past thirty years and without any significant loss of life.

The two most common arguments to justify the actions of contemporary Islamic fundamentalists are those of collective guilt and of moral equivalence. Palestinian radicals have long insisted that Israeli civilians, all of whom are obliged to serve in the country's security services, are not civilians and hence constitute legitimate targets: "They are not innocent if they are part of the total population, which is part of the army. . . . From 18 on, they are soldiers, even if they have civilian clothes."[35] Similarly, bin Laden has argued explicitly that Americans and Western citizens have the option of changing their governments and when they do not are responsible for their actions. He declared, "The American people are the ones who pay the taxes which fund the planes that bomb us in Afghanistan, the tanks that strike and destroy our homes in Pakistan, the armies which occupy our lands in the Arabian Gulf, and the fleets which ensure the blockade of Iraq."[36]

The final argument is the familiar teenage response: "Everybody does it." Our terrorism is justified because everyone else practices terrorism too. An angry Palestinian told Nasra Hassan, "The Israelis kill our children and our women. This is war, and innocent people get hurt."[37] Eddie Kinner, a young Protestant paramilitary in Northern Ireland, used similar language: "As far as I was concerned, I had joined an army and we were engaged in a war. The enemy had attacked my community and I was prepared to respond in kind."[38] In all his statements bin Laden goes into detail about the iniquities of the United States, the bombing of Hiroshima and Nagasaki, the killing of Iraqi children with U.S. sanctions and Afghan villagers with U.S. bombs. He and his followers believe that the United States lives by force and so they must respond with force. Bin Laden declared long before 9/11, "Through history America has not been known to differentiate between the military and the civilians, between men and women, or adults and children. Those who hurled atomic bombs and used the weapons of mass destruction against Nagasaki and Hiroshima were the Americans. Can the bombs differentiate between military and women and infants and children?"[39]

Even when arguing that it is legitimate to kill civilians and that they are doing to their enemies only what their enemies are doing to them, they continue to impose limits on the degree to which they can inflict harm on their enemies. Ramzi bin al-Shibh, one of the masterminds of the 9/11 attacks, who was arrested in Karachi, Pakistan, on September 11, 2002, composed an ideological justification of the September 11, 2001, attacks intended for internal consumption. He wrote:

> Because of Saddam and the Baath Party, America punished a whole population. Thus its bombs and its embargo killed millions of Iraqi Muslims. And because of Osama bin Laden, America surrounded Afghans and bombed them, causing the death of tens of thousands of Muslims. . . . God said to assault whoever assaults you, in a like manner. . . . In killing Americans who are ordinarily off limits, Muslims should not exceed four million non-combatants, or render

more than ten million of them homeless. We should avoid this, to make sure the penalty is no more than reciprocal.[40]

The fact that a senior al-Qaeda operative feels justified in killing four million Americans and making ten million homeless is hardly grounds for optimism, but it does demonstrate that al-Qaeda does have a code that imposes restraints on its actions. As bin Laden has said, "Reciprocal treatment is fair."[41] The constant declarations of war by fatwa are another attempt to appeal to a higher authority to justify their actions.

Finally, the popularity of suicide attacks, or "martyrdom operations," as those who volunteer prefer to call them, is in itself a moral claim. Our fascination with suicide attack is due to a number of factors: our fear of its destructiveness, our sense that it is crazy and therefore incomprehensible, and, finally, our discomfiture that it doesn't quite sit well with our sense of terrorists as depraved. Part of the popularity of the act among terrorists is, indeed, its destructiveness, but volunteers are also attracted precisely because it is an assertion of a claim to moral superiority over the enemy.

This is most obviously the case for hunger strikers. The tradition of inflicting harm on oneself in an effort to shame one's enemy has a long history in many cultures, and particularly the Gaelic one. When ten imprisoned republican prisoners slowly starved themselves to death in 1981, they were denying the depiction of them as depraved criminals. They were in fact claiming the moral high ground. It was also an enormously effective tactic. Even if they did not thereby gain the immediate goal, political prisoner status, they won worldwide attention and more new recruits than the movement could manage. The popular sympathy was such that one of the hunger strikers was elected to Parliament in a landslide.[42]

It is, of course, easier to justify killing oneself for a cause than killing oneself as a means of killing others, especially when those others are civilians going about their daily lives. Nevertheless, the scores of young men, and increasingly young women and older men, who volunteer for suicide operations do so believing that they are acting morally, selflessly giving their lives for a cause.[43] In one video, made on the eve of a suicide attack on an Israeli bus, a member of Hamas says, "We want to make it clear to the world that the true killer is Israel because our demands are legitimate."[44]

———

Terrorists are substate actors who violently target noncombatants to communicate a political message to a third party. Terrorists are neither crazy nor amoral. They come from all parts of the world. They come from many walks of life. They fight for a range of different causes. Some have support from the communities from which they come; some do not. They range in size from a handful of Corsican nationalists to thousands of armed Tamils. Some are fighting for the same goals that have motivated wars for centuries, such as control over national territory. Some are trying to overthrow the state system itself. They come from all religious traditions and from none. One thing they do have in common: they are weaker than those they oppose.

TWO

WHERE HAVE TERRORISTS COME FROM?

I as chairman of the Palestinian Liberation Organization, hereby once more declare that I condemn terrorism in all its forms, and at the same time salute those sitting before me in this hall who, in the days when they fought to free their countries from the yoke of colonialism, were accused of terrorism by their oppressors, and who today are the faithful leaders of their peoples, stalwart champions of justice and freedom.[1]
—Yasser Arafat, United Nations General Assembly, December 1988

THE THREE TERRORISTS HID 548 POUNDS OF EXPLOSIVES in a thirty-six-gallon beer cask, covered it with tarpaulin, and placed it in a wheelbarrow.[2] They had earlier bought the explosives in small quantities to avoid suspicion. They wheeled the barrow to the prison walls and rested it there. Following a prearranged plan, they tossed a white ball over the prison wall as a signal to the prisoners exercising inside. Then they lit the fuse and withdrew to a safe distance. The fuse spluttered and went out. One of the team came forward, lit the fuse again, and retreated. Again it went out. A third time he came forward, lit the now dangerously short fuse, and retreated. Yet again the fuse went out. The team decided to wheel their explosives away.

The next day the same three men, thought to have been James Murphy, Michael Barrett, and Jeremiah O'Sullivan, again wheeled the barrow to the prison wall. This time they lifted the cask from the barrow, set it against the prison wall, lit the fuse, and withdrew only after establishing that the fuse was well and truly alight. The barrel exploded. The resulting hole in the prison wall was twenty feet wide at the base and sixty feet wide at the top. The prison authorities, having been tipped off about the planned rescue attempt, had removed the prisoners to cells on the opposite side of the prison. The blast was heard forty miles away.

The real impact of the blast was felt in the surrounding neighborhood. Thousands of terrified Londoners spilled onto the streets from their ruined houses. Fires spread through the overcrowded slums. Six people were killed by the explosion, including seven-year-old Minnie Abbot and sixty-seven-year-old Martha Evans. More than a hundred people were injured, including five members of Minnie Abbot's family. More than four hundred houses were damaged; many were destroyed. All army and police leave was canceled, and a nationwide call was made for volunteers to act as special constables in the emergency; 166,000 were enrolled. In the House of Lords a member declared that terror had seized society.[3] *The Times* declared the explosion to be "one of the most heinous, most reckless, and most foolish outrages that are to be found in the records of crime."[4]

This explosion at Clerkenwell Prison in London occurred on December 13, 1867. Except for the type of explosive used—gunpowder rather than fertilizer or semtex—it could have happened this week. Terrorism has been with us for some time. In September 2001, the human race did not suddenly produce a new breed of evildoers. The forces driving terrorists today are similar to the forces that have driven revolutionaries in other countries and in other times.

In the aftermath of the 9/11 attacks, international public opinion rallied around the United States to an unprecedented degree. The warmth of that reaction has modulated with time. Even among our closest allies there has been a degree of exasperation with the American sense that terrorism was invented on September 11. Terrorism has bedeviled many European countries since the late 1960s. But terrorism has a much longer genesis than the last thirty to forty years.

If we want to understand what changed on September 11, we must first understand what happened before. Terrorism is not new, and it is not a modern phenomenon; examples go back at least as far as the first century after Christ. Terrorism is not now, and never has been, the sole preserve of Islam; the examples that follow are drawn from four religions and none, Judaism, Islam, Hinduism, Christianity, and atheism. The mixture of religious and political motives that has marked so much of contemporary terrorism since the Iranian revolution in 1979 is not new either. Rather, terrorism as it exists today has deep roots in several political and religious traditions. Its recent manifestations reflect broader developments in the evolution of ideas about the legitimate use of force to effect political change. The ancient groups reveal striking similarities to many contemporary terrorists. The French Revolution marked the modern incarnation of terrorism, Marx and Bakunin provided the setting in Western political thought, while the Irish nationalists and Russian anarchists were the nineteenth-century forerunners of today's terrorists.[5]

THE ANCIENT TRILOGY

The three most important and most commonly cited historical precursors to contemporary movements were all religiously inspired, drawing into question the conventional belief that the combination of terrorism and religion is a recent phenomenon. These three cases are the Sicarii or Zealots from classical times, the Assassins from the medieval period, and the Thugs, who lasted from medieval to modern times. Their importance stems, in the case of the Thugi, from their brutality and their longevity; in the case of the Assassins from their culture of martyrdom; and in the case of the Sicarii from their ability to mobilize mass insurrections and the devastating political consequences of their failed revolt. Their names have entered our everyday vocabulary. It is no coincidence; terrorist groups do tend to make an impression.

Their preferred weapon, the dagger, gained for the first group the name Sicarii, while their zeal won them the other name, Zealots.[6] Their goal was largely a political one, to eliminate Roman rule in Palestine, but there was a powerful messianic element in their doctrine. They sought to inspire a mass uprising against the Romans and believed that the spiral of violence that would ensue would herald the arrival of the Messiah. Although they survived for only twenty-five years the Sicarii/Zealots were unique among terrorists in successfully generating a mass uprising. While the revolt proved disastrous and led to mass suicide at Masada, the group also inspired two popular uprisings in successive generations, with even more calamitous long-term consequences for the Jewish population of the region.

The fanaticism of the Zealots was unbridled. They deliberately sought to destroy all efforts at conciliation and to provoke increasing repression in the hope that conditions would be so appalling that the public would be forced to revolt. Every concession from the Romans was greeted with another atrocity. While known for their use of the dagger, they used a range of tactics from hostage taking to direct confrontation with the military. In every instance they made a point of defying all normal restraints by slaughtering prisoners, violating truces, and murdering moderates.

Their targets extended far beyond Romans and included any local Jews willing to work with the Imperial Romans, who today would be called collaborators. They terrorized Jewish landowners in an effort to initiate a redistribution of land according to biblical traditions.[7] So while from their perspective the targets were not random, their lists of enemies were so extensive that the killings appeared to onlookers to be indiscriminate and hence instilled widespread fear. As today's terrorists have learned, random violence has a much bigger impact than discriminate violence, because if nobody is selected then nobody is safe. The Sicariis' preferred tactic was to mingle in the crowds at a festival or other large gathering, locate their opponent, pull a concealed dagger from beneath their clothes, stab their victim, and then disappear back into the crowd. By acting in a crowd, they ensured that word of their action would spread. Writers of the period spoke of the widespread terror inflicted: "The panic created was more alarming than the calamity itself; everyone, as on the battlefield, hourly expected death."[8]

There are a number of interesting parallels to be drawn between the Zealots and contemporary terrorist movements, and not just their name. The word Hamas, incidentally, means "zeal." Most modern terrorists argue that they are acting on behalf of "the people" and hope to inspire the people to rise up against the oppressor. The people, by and large, have proven extremely reluctant to do so. The Zealots were unusually successful in this regard. A great many later terrorist movements, from the nineteenth-century Russian anarchists to the twentieth-century European urban social revolutionaries to the Latin American rural movements, have tried and generally failed to inspire the people to rise up behind them.

The extraordinary brutality of the Sicarii/Zealots can be attributed in part to their religious conviction but also to the fact that there were several different groups of Zealots and Sicarii operating simultaneously in pursuit of the same ends. These groups competed with one another to demonstrate the superiority of their commitment and to claim leadership of the movement. This same dynamic of intraterrorist competition has continued to fuel terrorist violence and is particularly evident today among Palestinian groups. The Zealots also understood the importance of publicity, what Prime Minister Margaret Thatcher called the "oxygen" of terrorism.[9] They remained acutely conscious of the impact of their violence on the population at large. Their political goal and international character were also similar to those of many modern movements. Their deliberate attempt to provoke a spiral of violence, of reprisal and counterreprisal, and their lack of concern for the innocents caught in the middle is another hallmark of modern terrorism.

The Assassins operated from the eleventh to the thirteenth centuries. Medieval times are often thought to have been marked by such sheer brutality that terrorism is difficult to distinguish from all the other forms of violence that proliferated, but this is not entirely the case. In the latter part of the Middle Ages, rules of warfare began to develop, partly under the influence of the Church and partly due to the crippling expense of maintaining an army. While human rights were unknown and torture was standard practice, armies were generally relatively small. A medieval army, for example, rarely comprised more than 100,000 soldiers, compared to 350,000 in Roman times or France's 300,000 in 1710. There were also distinct differences in the treatment of peasants and aristocrats. In the battle of Lincoln, England, in 1217 the value of ransoming captives was such that only one knight died on the winning side and two on the losing side while about four hundred were taken prisoner. The number of peasant deaths in the ensuing massacre of civilians was not recorded.

The Assassins were a fanatical and murderous Shia Muslim sect active in the Middle East for about two hundred years.[10] They were inspired by the goal of purifying Islam, which had both political and religious ramifications. Through jihad, or holy war, they sought to reconstitute Islam as a single religious entity. As with the Zealots, their preferred weapon was a knife and the preferred method was stabbing. Their strategy was a policy of assassination, and their victims were orthodox religious leaders who refused to heed their warnings. Like the Zealots, they compensated for the absence of a mass media by choosing prominent victims whom they murdered on holy days, preferably while there were many witnesses around.

Unlike other terrorist groups, they created their own state, a set of scattered impregnable mountain fortresses where they welcomed refugees. There they trained recruits, developed their organization, and dispatched their members to carry out assassinations. They also had an international character and orchestrated a complex network of sympathetic cells in several urban centers across state lines. The fact that they had a dedicated territorial base proved both a strength and a weakness. They were free to train and to plan with impunity even when their support in the urban centers evaporated. When the Mongol and Arab armies sacked the fortresses in 1275, however, the movement was destroyed.

The Assassins too sought to address a wider audience and to generate sympathy for their cause. They demonstrated the patience and long-term planning that has marked recent radical Muslim groups. In an early version of a sleeper cell, they would send a young recruit into the house of an intended victim to develop a relationship with the victim before stabbing him in front of others. The assassination itself was often a public spectacle.

The Assassins, much like some contemporary terrorists, had a culture of the martyr, or *shaheed*. It was considered shameful to escape. Having stabbed his victim, an Assassin would not disappear into the crowd as had the Zealots; rather, he would wait to be beaten to death by the crowd or arrested and executed. By dedicating his life, the assassin added to the spectacle, demonstrated his commitment, and ensured a place in Paradise. This bizarre behavior both appalled and fascinated their contemporaries, so much so that it was widely believed that they were on hashish when committing their attacks. (The term "assassin" is actually derived from the term for hashish eaters, *hashashin*. In fact, there is no evidence that they were on hallucinogens.)

The third member of the ancient terrorist trilogy is the Indian Thugi.[11] They were a large Hindu group who operated in India for about six hundred years before finally being annihilated by the British in the nineteenth century. Their motives were religious rather than political, and for this reason they do not qualify as terrorists by my definition, but I mention them here as they are widely considered terrorists and do have an interesting contemporary resonance. The Thugi were both the longest lasting and most destructive terrorist group in history, being credited by the political scientist David Rapoport with up to half a million deaths. (More colorful and less reliable accounts credit them with a million murders.[12])

As described by Rapoport, the ideology of the Thugi was based on an idiosyncratic interpretation of one of the central Hindu myths. In ancient times the goddess Kali killed an enormous monster that devoured humans as soon as they were created. Kali killed the monster with her sword, but from every drop of blood another monster emerged. The conventional view was that Kali defeated the monsters by licking the blood from their wounds. The Thugi, however, believed that Kali created two men from her sweat and gave them part of her clothes to use to strangle the monsters. Once they had strangled the monsters without shedding their blood, Kali told the men to keep the clothes for their descendants. The descendants became the Thugi, which, unlike other terrorist groups, had hereditary membership. As Kali represented the energy of the universe, the Thugi believed that they were obliged to supply her with the blood necessary to keep the universe in equilibrium.

They operated under very specific constraints and had rules about every aspect of their behavior. Victims were not chosen randomly. Instead they had very elaborate rules as to who could and could not be killed: they killed only travelers and no Europeans and only those with whom they had developed a friendship, whom they then offered as a gift to their God. Their method of killing was strangulation with a silk tie and without shedding blood, and in the most painful way possible. They believed that Kali was more pleased the more terror she witnessed. To compound the atrocity and enhance the psychological impact, they dismembered the corpses in order to prevent cremation or proper burial. Unlike other groups, they shunned publicity. The injunction against killing Europeans proved quite debilitating to the movement when the British finally decided to challenge them. Some contemporaries mistakenly thought they operated out of self-interest in order to steal the belongings of their victims, but in fact this was not the case at all. They were forbidden to take property without killing and burying the owner first, and they were disdainful of ordinary robbers.[13] They used the booty they did acquire to pay off their sponsors, not for their own enrichment.

They resonate with contemporary terrorists in a number of ways. First, they were the first precursors of state-sponsored terrorism, which in part explains their longevity. While they did not have their own political ambitions, they served the political agendas of their sponsors. They took as loot the belongings of their victims and used it to pay princes who provided their expeditions with sanctuaries. Dissatisfied with the lack of cooperation from surrounding states, the British eventually employed the international law on piracy to seize and punish Thugi wherever they found them. Britain's successful campaign against them was criticized for violating the sovereignty of independent states.

Second, they demonstrate how knowledge of a group's philosophy can be used against them. The British knew that the Thugi believed that Kali would destroy the order when its members no longer served her. Aware that some members of the brotherhood were developing an unseemly interest in booty, the British appealed to the more traditional members of the group and helped persuade them that their responsibility now was to assist Kali by becoming informers.

Finally, the authorities were stunned by the depth of commitment of the members of the group, the cheerfulness with which they met their deaths, and their supreme confidence that they were en route to Paradise.[14] During one interrogation session the infamous Thug Buhram proudly claimed to have murdered 931 victims during his forty-year career. When the judge expressed incredulous horror, Buhram is reported to have benevolently replied, "Sahib, there were many more, but I was so intrigued in luring them to destruction that I ceased counting when certain of my thousand victims."[15]

TERROR FROM ABOVE: THE FRENCH REVOLUTION

We acquired names for nasty characters like thugs and assassins from early terrorist groups. We acquired the term "terror" itself from the French Revolution, but in those days it referred to terror from above, terror imposed by the state, rather than from below, from insurgents. The regime of terror in France in 1793 to 1794 incorporated many of the themes that were to become familiar to succeeding generations. Fundamentally, the Terror was simply the logical application of a particular philosophy: the people had to be reborn in a new way, and if some of them got in the way they were enemies of the revolution and had to be removed. In the words of Saint Just, one of the architects, "We want to establish an order of things such that a universal tendency toward the good is established and the factions find themselves suddenly hurled on the scaffold."[16] The problem, of course, is with the concept of "we." Initially "we" was the people, broadly defined, but the concept was progressively narrowed to become only a subgroup of the Committee of Public Safety. The narrowing of the category of those entitled to act on behalf of the people was matched by a continued widening of the range of the victims. Initially, the Terror was aimed only at aristocrats. In the end, only about 37 percent of those guillotined during the reign of terror were actually aristocrats. Eventually the machine turned in on itself and its chief architect, Robespierre, was himself guillotined. His death heralded a reaction against state terror.

A key legacy of the French Revolution to contemporary terrorism has been this notion of the killers as the self-appointed guardians of the will of the people—though it must be said that when one has the apparatus of the state at one's disposal, as Robespierre and some more recent autocrats have, one can do a lot more damage than any latter-day terrorist movement has ever managed.

The second essential legacy is the introduction of political ideology as a substitute for religion as a motivating force for terrorism. Prior to the French Revolution, all terrorist groups had religious motivations, though in most instances these religious motivations had political ramifications.

After the French Revolution, and until the Iranian revolution in 1979, terrorist movements were motivated by political aspirations and political ideologies. These quite different ideologies were based on a number of assumptions that had been launched in the course of the French Revolution. The first was the belief that radical change was possible—society could be remade. The second was the idea attributed to Rousseau that man is naturally good, that evil comes not from inside man but from the external structures of society. Destroy these structures, and you have destroyed evil. This lent itself to a crusading aspect to politics as well as to the identification of an out-group. For Robespierre it was the aristocrats, for Marx the capitalists, for Hitler the Jews, for Fanon the imperialist powers, for bin Laden the Israelis and Americans, and so on. This new style of politics as crusade lent itself to interpretations that make the use of terrorism for ideological ends appear to be a natural outgrowth of the idealistic belief in man's natural goodness.

Finally, there was the doctrine of popular sovereignty as a basis for political legitimacy. Again, it is easy to see how this doctrine, which was intended to liberate the masses and inaugurate an era of harmony, might instead produce the opposite. As we have seen, the concept of "the people" can be defined in any way at all. Popular sovereignty can be invoked by anyone wishing to defy a government by claiming to be a truer representative of the popular will than the established authority. This idea has been particularly useful to all kinds of contemporary terrorists, who are invariably outnumbered by their adversaries and who claim to act in the name of the people. Most actually believe that they are doing so.

After the French Revolution and the defeat of Napoleon, the forces of conservatism and reaction dominated European politics, but on the ground nationalism, liberalism, and republicanism were gaining adherents. Secret societies and conspiratorial student groups proliferated in European coffeehouses, culminating in the year of revolutions of 1848. These revolutions, which occurred in capital cities all over Europe, were an ignominious failure.

MARX AND BAKUNIN

The destruction in 1848 of revolutionary aspirations for a spontaneous uprising of the people led to a hardening of the nature of the opposition to the status quo and the gradual transformation from gentleman guerrilla to hardened terrorist. Nineteenth-century thinkers then sought to explain the absence of revolutionary ardor on the part of the people. Auguste Blanqui concluded that revolution could be achieved only through a coup d'état and decided that the public had to be organized along military lines to take over the state. Karl Heinzen, in a tract called, simply, *Murder*, argued that 1848 demonstrated that the authorities were too ruthless and too powerful for a popular uprising ever to stand a chance of success. He concluded that murder is the chief instrument of historical progress and argued that as the authorities maintained themselves by murder it was legitimate for the revolutionary to do so too. Added to his faith in murder was his faith in science, which he believed would enable the few to murder the many and thereby compensate for the paucity of recruits to the cause. This core philosophy of the terrorist has since been adapted by groups in pursuit of a range of different objectives.

The two nineteenth-century thinkers most often linked to terrorism (one more legitimately than the other) are Karl Marx and Mikhail Bakunin. Marx was denounced as a terrorist because of his support for the Paris Commune in 1871, but he did not consider himself a supporter of terrorism at all. He dismissed Bakunin's idea of a peasant revolution as "schoolboy's asininity." Marx saw the Commune as the first stage of a workers' state, a radically democratic government, and an authentic representation of the French proletariat. He worried that terrorism might pose a premature threat to the state before the workers were ready to take it over. Marx objected to the efforts to destroy the state, arguing instead that the goal of the organized urban proletariat should be to master the apparatus of the state.

Marx's two daughters, Jenny and Laura, were ardent supporters of the Fenians, who had carried out the Clerkenwell explosion, but Marx himself was not. While he shared the Fenian view of the injustice of British rule in Ireland, he had his eyes firmly fixed on the goal of proletarian revolution. He wrote to his close collaborator Friedrich Engels the day after the explosion, "The last exploit of the Fenians in Clerkenwell was a very stupid thing. The London masses who have shown great sympathy for Ireland will be made wild by it and driven into the arms of the government party. One cannot expect the London proletarians to allow themselves to be blown up in honor of Fenian emissaries."[17] Engels replied on December 19, "The stupid affair in

Clerkenwell was obviously the work of a few specialized fanatics. . . . In particular, there has been a lot of bluster in America about this blowing up and arson business, and then a few asses come and instigate such nonsense. Moreover these cannibals are generally the greatest cowards . . . and then the idea of liberating Ireland by setting a London tailor's shop on fire."[18]

Engels's family, like Marx's, was more sympathetic. Engels's common-law wife, Lizzy Burns, was a staunch supporter of the Fenians. Their home in England was a hotbed of Fenian activity and provided shelter to members on the run. It was even decorated in the Fenian colors of green and black. Later Engels was outraged by the Fenian campaign of the 1880s in which bystanders were again killed. He argued that even revolutionaries must behave like soldiers and kill only those actually fighting against them.

Marx's nemesis Mikhail Bakunin was in many ways the prototype of the modern social revolutionary terrorist and was the most influential of the nineteenth-century thinkers on terrorism. An aristocrat bored with debate, he wanted immediate action. His goal was to seize power quickly with a small group of elite coconspirators and unleash a mass revolt against property and authority. He traveled indefatigably around Europe to any place experiencing civil disturbance and tried to mobilize a revolution. His critics said of him that his revolutionary fervor never flagged, his plotting never ceased, and his rebellions never succeeded. He believed that violence could generate immediate justice by sweeping away the oppressive institutions of the state. So you had in Bakunin the completion of the transition from the old-style insurrectionist, whose emphasis was on mass violence, to the advocate of violent terrorism by small groups claiming to represent the masses.[19]

IRISH NATIONALISTS

Two late-nineteenth-century terrorist groups are worth mentioning as precursors of contemporary terrorism: the Irish nationalists and the Russian anarchists. The Irish Republican Brotherhood (IRB), the forerunner of the contemporary IRA, was a secret society dedicated to achieving an independent Ireland by force. There was a significant degree of support for this aspiration in Ireland, though most of the politically aware population favored the peaceful policies of the Irish Home

Rule Party, which sought to achieve these ends through parliamentary action. The IRB, like the Jacobins before them, claimed an exclusive right to decide what was best for the Irish people, though this did not actually make them terrorists. They were so convinced that the people would follow their lead that they actually preferred the old-fashioned tactic of open insurrection. In fact, their one effort at open insurrection, in the Fenian Rising of 1867, was an unmitigated disaster, not least because almost nobody rose up to join them. The event was hardly noticed in Britain.

Among those who had fought with the Fenians in 1867 were Irish Americans who were recruited at the end of the American Civil War to deploy their military training on behalf of Ireland. Some who did not return to Ireland launched a number of quixotic attempts to invade Canada from the United States. Their plan was to seize Canada's transportation network and force Britain to exchange Ireland's freedom for possession of its province of Canada.

In Britain the group was widely denounced as terrorists, though they were often given credit for the actions of several more radical off-shoots that launched a bombing campaign in England in the 1880s. One such group was the Clan na Gael (Irish Family), which was actually funded by Irish immigrants living in the United States. This is the first known instance of a pattern that was to become quite common a century later: members of diaspora communities, feeling out of place in their new homes, develop a powerful affinity for their homeland and finance movements for radical change back home. Simplicity of interpretation tends to increase with distance from the conflict. The Fenian campaign was unsuccessful, not least due to a reluctance to cause civilian casualties, and without deaths they couldn't garner attention.

One act of violence did gain a lot of attention. In a case known as the Phoenix Park murders, an offshoot of the IRB murdered two leading representatives of British rule in Ireland. In 1882 a new chief secretary, Lord Frederick Cavendish, arrived in Dublin. On the evening of his arrival in May, while walking with his undersecretary T. H. Burke, they were attacked and stabbed to death by a group calling themselves "The Invincibles." This action really belongs in the tradition of the Sicarii and the Assassins, a precise action against carefully chosen targets. The reputation of the Irish separatists for terrorism, then, is somewhat misplaced, though it is easy to see where it came from. While the actual actions of these groups were fairly minor, their rhetoric was extremely bloodthirsty. On paper they loudly called for all kinds of acts of aggression, but on the ground they never quite managed to pull them off. Jeremiah O'Donovan Rossa, one of the great Fenian heroes and a prominent figure in republican mythology to this day, actually once produced a scheme for spraying the House of Commons with a lethal gas, probably the first known terrorist plan to deploy chemical weapons. In actuality the man was completely squeamish and never managed to get even a minor bombing campaign off the ground.

RUSSIAN ANARCHISTS

The other groups best known as the precursors of contemporary terrorism are the Russian Anarchists of the late nineteenth century. The best-known group was the Narodnaya Volya (People's Will), which operated in Russia from 1878 to 1881. The group's philosophy was a kind of idealistic anarchism that required the destruction of the existing order as a prelude to a new and better society. Like other terrorist groups and other revolutionaries from Marx on, the Narodnaya Volya tended to be vague about the details of this new world. The group spent far more of its energy attacking the iniquities of the present system than in describing the virtues of the one with which it would have liked to replace it. This trait can also be found in most terrorist groups today.

Like Bakunin, the group believed in immediate action, arguing that a single act of destruction could achieve more than could ever be achieved by debates and publications. It believed that the assassination of a few government officials would ignite revolution across the land. Its actions were therefore precise and concentrated on killing a few key government players, most notably the tsar. It did succeed, in fact, in killing Tsar Alexander II in 1881. Far from the act's igniting a revolution, the peasantry did not react at all, urban public opinion was horrified, and the radical cause lost support.

Credited with creating the notion of propaganda by deed, the Russian anarchists in fact created more propaganda than deeds. This was true even of more extreme groups such as the Russian Socialist Revolutionary Party, which carefully sought to avoid the death of innocents and constrained itself within clearly defined limits. Its members believed, for example, that terrorism was justified only when the perpetrator was prepared to sacrifice his own life to atone for his actions. The government's response was much less restrained and dealt effectively with these groups through brutal repression. The fact that these groups were fighting for many rights we take for granted today does not make them early democrats. Their fatal weakness—one shared with their twentieth-century successors—was their tendency to arrogate to themselves the right to decide what was good for the people. Their failure was in part due to the fact that the elitist self-confidence that came from this viewpoint blinded them to both the degree of their isolation from the people and the strength of their opponents. Nevertheless, their methods revealed a strong sense of moral responsibility that was not always reciprocated by the governments they opposed.

Curiously enough, Vladimir Lenin, who was to prove such an inspiration for the social revolutionary terrorist movements of the late twentieth century, was critical of the Russian anarchists, whom he considered misguided zealots. (When Lenin was seventeen, his older brother, Alexander, was convicted of attempting to assassinate the tsar and was hanged in Saint Petersburg.) He believed that he had a more efficacious way of overthrowing the system. Rather than throwing bombs at ministers, Lenin advocated the creation of a revolutionary elite dedicated to one simple goal, the seizure of power. Far from being isolated from those around them, Lenin's cadre of revolutionaries exploited popular grievances as a means of consolidating their support. It did not matter to Lenin that the complaints might be from nationalists, aspiring landowners, or others unsympathetic to his cause. What did matter to the ultimate pragmatist was that animosity toward the authorities made them potentially sympathetic to subversives, whose political powerlessness left them free to make empty promises. Lenin's key contribution to terrorist strategy, therefore, was the importance of exploiting every fragment of local alienation for its own ends. It is very clear from reading bin Laden's public statements that he has taken this lesson to heart. He criticizes the United States for everything from support for Israel to the deployment of troops in Saudi Arabia to its refusal to sign on to the international criminal court to profiteering by the Halliburton Company.[20]

There were a number of other anarchist groups operating in Europe and the United States at the same time. Among them they managed some significant assassinations, including the prime minister of Spain in 1892, the Empress Elizabeth of Austria in 1898, King Umberto I of Italy in 1900, and U.S. President William McKinley in 1901.[21] These actions provided an early spur to international cooperation against terrorism. Then, as now, initiatives on the counterterrorism front were usually driven by an atrocity. When international cooperation to combat crime was formalized in extradition treaties in the early nineteenth century, the principle of nonintervention was enshrined through the inclusion in the treaties of a clause excluding political offenders from extradition. But an attempt on the life of Napoleon III in 1855 led to a modification of the political exception clause so as to make the murder of a head of state or his family an extraditable offense. Then, in the 1890s, Britain decided to extradite a French anarchist wanted for the bombing of a French café in which two civilians had died. The court ruled that, as anarchists did not believe in government, they could not avail themselves of the political exclusion clause in extradition treaties.

Compared to the levels of violence practiced by twentieth-century terrorists, these nineteenth-century precursors seem anemic indeed. The two world wars of the twentieth century did a great deal to eliminate the distinction between combatant and noncombatant by legitimating the deliberate massacre of civilians, even by the "good guys." Disregard of this distinction is, as I pointed out earlier, a defining characteristic of terrorism. In the twentieth century, nation-states mobilized their power to kill people from other countries for political reasons. Examples from the Second World War would include the London blitz, the siege of Leningrad, and the bombing of Dresden, not to mention the bombing of Hiroshima and Nagasaki. In each case the motives of the killers were political, the victims were random civilians, and the message was aimed at a wider audience, whether it was the general public, the armed forces, the government, or the emperor of the country concerned. Indeed, in the first half of the twentieth century some leaders mobilized the resources of their governments to murder their own people, not just foreigners, the most egregious cases being Stalin and Hitler. The point here is that the greater brutality of terrorists reflects a greater brutality in political life generally. The nineteenth-century terrorists were more restrained and more discriminating than their twentieth-century successors. Their abandonment of the combatant/noncombatant distinction, however, occurred after the distinction had been profoundly challenged by the conduct of states during the world wars.

The deliberate targeting of civilians, even if it has a great many precedents, remains difficult to understand. The act of deliberately blowing up a school or a government or corporate office building, not to mention killing fellow passengers on a bus or subway, is a more personalized act than dropping a bomb from an aircraft at 30,000 feet in time of war. We find the latter much easier to understand. We see it as a matter of discipline, training, and commitment to a righteous cause articulated by a representative government. An act of terrorism is much harder to fathom. There is no doubt that the Fenians betrayed an extraordinary disregard for human life when they set alight almost 550 pounds of gunpowder a few yards from a densely populated area. (I believe it fair to assume that had they known that their explosion would kill six women and children and destroy hundreds of homes, they would have devised a different rescue effort.) Had many modern terrorists anticipated that their plan would cause only six fatalities, they would have also devised a different plan, one designed to inflict *more* harm. What causes people to be so immune to the suffering their actions cause, and what do they hope to achieve by inflicting it? These are the questions to which we will now turn.

THREE

WHAT CAUSES TERRORISM?

Thinking people, when disaster strikes, make it their priority to look for its causes, in order to prevent it happening again.[1]

—Osama bin Laden, October 2004

I still remember those distressing scenes: blood, torn limbs, women and children massacred. All over the place, houses were being destroyed and tower blocks were collapsing, crushing their residents, while bombs rained down mercilessly on our homes.[2]

—Osama bin Laden, October 2004

AHMED OMAR SAEED SHEIKH, BETTER KNOWN AS OMAR Sheikh, seems an unlikely terrorist. Born in London, he enjoyed a comfortable upbringing. His father, a Pakistani businessman, sent him to the expensive private Forest School, where he was a contemporary of the English cricket captain, Nasser Hussain. His economics tutor at Forest School said of him, "The chap we knew was a good all round, solid and very supportive pupil . . . he was in the premier league of students. . . . He was a nice bloke and very respectful."[3] Another of his superiors said of him, "He was a very nice guy, well mannered and educated."[4] Sheikh passed four A levels with good grades and was ad-mitted to the prestigious London School of Economics to read applied mathematics, statistical theory, economics, and social psychology.

Aside from his evident intellect and charm, Sheikh was a compassionate young man. In 1992, a man waiting for a train at Leytonstone tube station in east London lost his balance and fell onto the tracks. Sheikh, who was then eighteen, witnessed the incident. Ignoring the danger from a train pulling into the station, he jumped down onto the tracks and saved the man. He later received a commendation from the London Underground for this selfless act of bravery.[5]

When Sheikh matured from charming schoolboy to committed terrorist, he did not lose this compassionate side. An Indian newspaper acquired a copy of the diary Sheikh wrote while in prison. While he was on a mission to trap and kidnap foreign visitors in India, one of his colleagues moved out of their shared apartment. Sheikh wrote, "He left. I had the room to myself. Now, since I had been in India, the sight of emaciated beggars everywhere particularly around the Markaz had posed a serious dilemma for me. I had never seen so much poverty first hand in my life before. But I soon realized that superficial help was only perpetuating the problem—most of the money they received was spent on cigarettes or charas. But they were genuinely needy people. Anyway, that night I decided that since I had the room to myself, I would offer to share it with an old one-legged man who sat outside the Markaz. I went and brought the old man to the room. We had dinner."[6] In the same diary Sheikh details how he befriended traveling Westerners and then kidnapped them, chaining them to furniture at gunpoint and holding them hostage.

In July 2002, Omar Sheikh was convicted of kidnapping and murdering *Wall Street Journal* reporter Daniel Pearl. Sheikh pleaded not guilty to the Pearl charges but in one of his court appearances shouted to reporters that he was responsible for other celebrated terrorist atrocities, including the bombing of the Kashmir Parliament in October 2001, the attack on the Indian Parliament two months later, and the attack on the American Cultural Center in Calcutta in January 2001.

It is simply baffling that someone with a background no different from many others' and a great deal more privileged than most would choose to become a terrorist. In attempting to understand the causes of terrorism, one must look for explanations at the level of the individual, such as Omar Sheikh, but that is not enough. Explanations are found at national and transnational levels too. The emergence of terrorism requires a lethal cocktail with three ingredients: a disaffected individual, an enabling group, and a legitimizing ideology.

———

In the wake of the September 11, 2001, attacks, Americans flocked to bookstores to buy copies of the Koran; books about Islam enjoyed unprecedented popularity. Bin Laden himself noted the phenomenon. He told some friends, "I heard someone on Islamic radio who owns a school in America say: 'We don't have time to keep up with the demands of those who are asking about Islamic books to learn about Islam.' "[7] Americans were trying to understand the causes of what happened. The presidential adviser Karl Rove was quite wrong to criticize this effort to understand. Rove told the New York Conservative Party, "Conservatives saw what happened to us on 9/11 and said: we will defeat our enemies. Liberals saw what happened to us and said: we must understand our enemies."[8] The public's desire to understand—which does not mean to sympathize or empathize with—the causes of the terrible violence wreaked upon us constitutes one of the strongest elements in the American counterterrorist arsenal.

Of course there is no single cause of terrorism, any more than there is a single cause of killing. People kill for many different reasons. A soldier kills because he is trained to do so. An inebriated driver kills because he has diminished control, a psychopath because he is crazy, a battered woman because she is frightened, a teen in a fight because he is angry, and so on.

There are at least two reasons why it is very difficult to come up with a convincing explanation for terrorism. The first is that there are so many terrorists. The second is that there are so few. Terrorism is a tactic employed by many different groups in many different parts of the world in pursuit of many different objectives. It occurs in democracies, autocracies, and, most often, transitional states. On the other hand, there are actually very few terrorists. If Islam causes terrorism, with 1.2 billion Muslims in the world and, at most, a few thousand Islamic terrorists, why are there not more? If the social revolutionary movements in Europe in the seventies were caused by the alienation of disaffected youths, why were there not more terrorists? Alienation was widespread among European and American youths, but there were actually very few members of the RAF, Action Directe, the CCC, and the Red Brigades in Germany, France, Belgium, and Italy, respectively.

We can seek the causes of terrorism at a number of different levels. The level of the individual terrorist, the terrorist organization, and the sponsoring state all suggest causes. At the level of society, socio-economic factors such as poverty and inequality reveal causes, while at the transnational level, causes of terrorism can be found in religion and globalization. Many of these causes are interconnected.

INDIVIDUAL-LEVEL EXPLANATIONS

Why does an individual decide to join a terrorist organization, to stay in one, to lead one, or to leave one? Why does a human being decide to kill others he does not know in furtherance of an objective unlikely to be realized in his lifetime, and in so doing put himself outside the law and dramatically increase the likelihood that he will be killed or imprisoned and his family will be at risk? In the most extreme cases, why does someone kill himself as a means of killing others? The most obvious and common explanation is that he is crazy. But terrorists, as I have said, are, by and large, not crazy at all. Interviews with current and former terrorists as well as imprisoned terrorists confirm that the one shared characteristic of terrorists is their normalcy, insofar as we understand the term. Efforts to produce a terrorist profile have invariably failed. Some are introverted, some extroverted; some loud, some shy; some confident, some nervous.

Simplicity, Identification, and Revenge

From the vast literature on psychology, three points in particular stand out.[9] Terrorists see the world in Manichean, black-and-white terms; they identify with others; and they desire revenge. They have a highly oversimplified view of the world in which good is pitted against evil and in which their adversaries are to blame for all their woes. They tend to act not out of a desire for personal gratification but on behalf of a group with which they identify (though the two motives can of course coexist). Islamic terrorists, for example, regularly invoke the suffering of Palestinians and other Muslims.

The identification with others and the desire for revenge commonly emerge in conversations with rank-and-file terrorists as well as with their leaders. The German militant Michael Baumann, in his book *How It All Began,* writes that it was the unprovoked killing by the German police of a student demonstrator against the shah that turned him into a terrorist. Italian and German activists told similar tales to an Italian sociologist, Donatella Della Porta. Members of the Finucane family described to the British reporter Kevin Toolis how they had been radicalized by the experience of being driven from their home by Protestant mobs, while Protestant paramilitaries told the BBC's Peter Taylor of being radicalized by the sight of neighbors injured by IRA bombs.[10]

Omar Sheikh wrote in his confession that while a student at the London School of Economics in 1992, "Bosnia Week" was observed and a number of documentary movies were shown. He wrote that one film, *The Death of a Nation,* which depicted Bosnian Muslims being murdered by Serbs, "shook my heart" and launched his political awakening and subsequent radicalization. He helped organize a student conference on Bosnia and then began fund-raising for a convoy of relief materials for Bosnia. Soon he was making contact with Islamic militants.[11]

Terrorist group leaders have told similar stories of being radicalized by identifying with the suffering of others. Renato Curcio, the intellectual leader of the Italian left-wing social revolutionary group the Red Brigades, says that he was converted to violence in reaction to an incident in which the police fired on farmworkers, killing two and injuring several children among many others. Vellupillai Prabakharan, the poorly educated leader of the Sri Lankan nationalist group the Tamil Tigers, said, "It is the plight of the Tamil people that compelled me to take up arms. I felt outrage at the inhuman atrocities perpetrated against an innocent people. The ruthless manner in which our people were murdered, massacred, maimed . . ."[12] Abimael Guzmán, the academic leader of Peru's Maoist Shining Path, spoke in a similar vein: "I'd say that what has most influenced me to take up politics has been the struggle of the people. I saw the fighting spirit of the people during the uprising in Arequipa in 1950—how the masses fought with uncontrollable fury in response to the barbarous slaughter of the youth."[13] Each of these men led very different types of terrorist movements pursuing very different political objectives in very different parts of the world, yet all speak in very similar terms about how they were radicalized by their sense of identification with others.

The power of the desire for revenge is discussed more fully in the next chapter. Terrorists invariably cast their actions in terms of revenge. Osama bin Laden's speeches, for example, are suffused with the language of revenge. Just a couple of weeks after September 11, he told al-Jazeera television, "Here is America struck by God Almighty in one of its vital organs, so that its greatest buildings are destroyed. Grace and gratitude to God. America has been filled with horror from north to south and east to west, and thanks be to God that what America is tasting now is only a copy of what we have tasted. Our Islamic nation has been tasting the same for more than 80 years, humiliation and disgrace, its sons killed and their blood spilled, its sanctities desecrated."[14]

The two biggest gaps in how terrorists see themselves and how they are seen by others are precisely on the points of being altruistic versus being self-serving, and being defenders versus aggressors. Terrorists see themselves as working heroically for the benefit of others, not for themselves. In this way they see themselves as morally distinguishable from criminals out for their own selfish gain. Bin Laden once described how the idea of blowing up the twin American towers came to him:

> God knows that the plan of striking the towers had not occurred to us, but the idea came to me when things went just too far with the American-Israeli alliance's oppression and atrocities against our people in Palestine and Lebanon. The events that made a direct impression on me were during and after 1982, when America allowed the Israelis to invade Lebanon with the help of its third [Sixth] fleet. They started bombing, killing and wounding many, while others fled in terror. . . . It was like a crocodile devouring a child, who could do nothing but scream. Does a crocodile understand anything other than weapons? The whole world heard and saw what happened, but did nothing. In those critical moments, many ideas raged inside me, ideas difficult to describe, but they unleashed a powerful urge to reject injustice and a strong determination to punish the oppressors.

> As I looked at those destroyed towers in Lebanon it occurred

to me to punish the oppressor in kind by destroying towers in America, so that it would have a taste of its own medicine and would be prevented from killing our women and children.[15]

Addressing a joint session of Congress on September 20, 2001, President Bush gave a rather different version of the forces driving al-Qaeda: "They stand against us because we stand in their way. We're not deceived by their pretenses to piety. We have seen their kind before. They're the heirs of all the murderous ideologies of the twentieth century. By sacrificing human life to serve their radical visions, by abandoning every value except the will to power, they follow in the path of fascism, Nazism and totalitarianism."[16]

We see them as violating all moral codes in pursuit of power and domination. They see themselves as defending the weak against the strong and punishing the strong for their violation of all moral codes. From a counterterrorism point of view, the distinction is important. If one is trying to affect the incentive structure that causes people to join or to leave a movement, knowing why they join in the first place is essential. Bin Laden, for example, scoffed at American efforts to put a price on his head. He told al-Jazeera that his followers "left the world and came to these mountains and land, leaving their families, fathers and mothers. They left their universities and came here under shelling, American missiles and attacks. Some were killed. . . . These men left the world and came for the jihad. America, however, which worships money believes that people here are of this [same] caliber. I swear that we have not had the need to change a single man from his position even after these reports [that the United States was offering a $5 million reward for information leading to his arrest]."[17] If terrorists are engaged in self-gratifying behavior, it is more likely to be a desire for significance, for glory, than for material gain.

Defenders Versus Aggressors

The sociologist Mark Juergensmeyer asked Dr. Abdul Aziz Rantisi, one of the founders of Hamas (assassinated by Israel in April 2004), in what way he thought Hamas was misunderstood. He said, "You think we are the aggressors. That is the number one misunderstanding. We are not: we are the victims."[18] Bin Laden, characteristically, phrased it more dramatically: "The truth is the whole Muslim world is the victim of international terrorism, engineered by America and the United Nations."[19] A member of the IRA explained to Kevin Toolis why he had joined the terrorist movement: "I knew that the IRA were our defenders, looking after our interests, fighting for our rights. There was a great sense of anger."[20] On another occasion bin Laden used a homely analogy to explain his followers' behavior: "Let us look at a chicken, for example. If an armed person was to enter the chicken's home with the aim of inflicting harm on it, the chicken would automatically fight back."[21] Seeing oneself as a victim who is fighting defensively, of course, makes it altogether easier to justify one's actions.

LEADERS AND FOLLOWERS

An individual seeking revenge and identifying with others does not become a terrorist in a vacuum. For someone who rankles at injustice, identifies with the disadvantaged, and wants to help them, becoming a social worker is a more typical career path. It requires a charismatic leader or a functioning organization to mix these feelings with the desire for revenge and turn them into action.

In terrorist organizations, as in most others, the leaders tend to be different from the followers. They often, for example, come from higher educational and socioeconomic backgrounds. In attempting to understand terrorist organizations, it is therefore important to recognize that the motives driving the leaders of organizations are often distinguishable from those of the followers. The role of the leader is crucial in turning the eager volunteers into an organized force. The leader not only arranges training but provides an ideology, identifies the enemy, and articulates a strategy. In some cases the leader becomes the personification of the group or ideology. Some leaders have almost godlike status among their followers, such as Osama bin Laden of al-Qaeda, Vellupillai Prabakharan of the Sri Lankan Tamil Tigers, and Shoko Asahara of Aum Shinrikyo. Some organizations create a cult of personality around their leaders, such as Abimael Guzmán of the Shining Path and Abdullah Öcalan of the PKK.

This can be a real vulnerability for the movement, as the removal of the leader can do irreparable damage to the organization. Cool organizational thinker that he is, Osama bin Laden is well aware of this vulnerability and has gone to pains to point out that his demise will not weaken his movement. He claims that the United States and Saudi Arabia have been trying to assassinate him since 1990 but have failed because only Allah can decide when he should die, so he has no fear of death. "Being killed for Allah's cause is a great honor achieved by only those who are the elite of the nation. We love this kind of death for Allah's cause as much as you like to live. We have nothing to fear for it is something to wish for."[22] Other terrorist groups have a collective leadership, such as the Army Council of the IRA, or otherwise play down the importance of individual leaders. The motivations of these individuals are often different from those of the rank and file of the movements. Some Palestinian families, for example, have pointed out that it is not the sons of the leaders who are volunteering for suicide missions.

The leaders of terrorist movements tend to be older and more highly educated than their followers, no matter what part of the world they come from. Latin American terrorist leaders have consistently been older than their followers. The doyen of the group, Pedro Antonio Marín, better known as Manuel Marulanda Vélez, the leader of Colombia's FARC, was born in 1928. Brazil's Carlos Marighella, author of *Minimanual of the Urban Guerrilla,* the most prominent terrorist manual before al-Qaeda's own, was fifty-eight at the time of his violent death. Abimael Guzmán, the leader of the Shining Path, was also aged fifty-eight at the time of his arrest in 1992. Raúl Sendic Antonaccio, leader of the Uruguayan Tupamaros, was forty-two when he launched his movement. Mario Roberto Santucho, leader of the Argentine ERP (People's Revolutionary Army), was forty at the time of his violent death. Guzmán, an academic, Sendic, a lawyer, and Santucho, an economist, also had considerably more education than did most of their followers.

The leaders of the European movements were younger than the Latin American leaders but still older than their followers and consistently middle and upper middle class. Most of the leaders of Italy's Red Brigades were college professors in their thirties. Among the leadership of the German Baader-Meinhof Gang, Baader was the son of a historian, while Meinhof was a journalist and the daughter of an art historian; Horst Mahler was a lawyer and the son of a dentist. Susanne Albrecht was the daughter of a wealthy lawyer, and Holger Meins was the son of a business executive. Most were university dropouts. The pattern of middle-aged leaders and younger followers is found in different types of terrorist movements throughout the world. In Japan, Shoko Asahara, the leader of Aum Shinrikyo, was born in 1955. Vellupillai Prabakharan, the leader of the Tamil Tigers in Sri Lanka, was born in 1954. Abdullah Öcalan, the founder and leader of the Kurdish Workers Party, the PKK, in Turkey, was born in 1949.

This pattern is less true of Islamist groups, which appear to recruit successfully from all sections of society. Osama bin Laden has the most famous and most unusual profile. A multimillionaire who studied economics in Jeddah, he was born in 1957. His second in command, Ayman al-Zawahiri, is a doctor who was born in 1951. Mohamed Atta, the leader of the 9/11 team, was the son of an Egyptian lawyer and had earned a Ph.D. in urban planning. George Habash, the leader of the Popular Front for the Liberation of Palestine, the PLFP, was also a medical doctor, born in 1926. Abdul Aziz Rantisi, one of the founders of Hamas and another doctor, was fifty-six when he was killed by the Israelis. Sheikh Ahmed Yassin, the spiritual leader of Hamas, trained as a teacher. He was sixty-eight when he was killed by the Israelis. The PLO's Yasser Arafat was a graduate engineer and died at the age of seventy-five. Unlike these leaders, Hassan Nasrallah, the leader of Hezbollah, was born into a modest home in 1960. He was the eldest of nine children, and his father was a grocer.

Marc Sageman studied the biographies of 172 members of al-Qaeda and found that two thirds were middle or upper class and that 60 percent had gone to college; several had doctorates.[23] Their average age was twenty-six. Similarly, Gilles Keppel studied 300 Islamic militants in Egypt and found that they too were more highly educated and of a higher socioeconomic status than most terrorists.[24] Peter Bergen's examination of the backgrounds of 75 terrorists responsible for some of the most damaging attacks found that 53 percent had attended college, while 2 had doctorates from Western universities and 2 others were working on Ph.Ds.[25] While every terrorist army has need of foot soldiers and cannon fodder, Islamist groups have successfully recruited a cadre of more educated followers. Men such as Omar Sheikh and Mohamed Atta are required for the kind of international operations that necessitate international travel and functioning in different societies. Moreover, increased reliance on the Internet, essential for secure transnational communication, requires operatives with some technological facility.

TERRORIST ORGANIZATIONS

The two key differences that divide terrorist groups mentioned in the last chapter—the nature of the goals sought and the relationship to the broader community—have significant psychological implications too. Jerrold Post has made the point that there are real psychological differences between those who are carrying on the work of their parents, that is, the ethnonationalist groups such as the ETA, the IRA, the LTTE, and the PKK, and those who are trying to destroy the world of their parents, the social revolutionary groups such as the RAF and Red Brigades.[26] Nationalist groups see themselves as occupying a place in their group's historical struggle. Social revolutionary groups completely reject the past. In her seminal book *Hitler's Children,* Jillian Becker describes the members of the Baader-Meinhof Gang, the precursor to the RAF, as "children without fathers."[27]

In looking back at their life as terrorists, many activists speak of the intense feeling of camaraderie within the group. Jerrold Post, after interviewing thirty-five imprisoned Middle East terrorists, describes the process by which "an overarching sense of the collective consumes the individual."[28] Italian and German militants describe a similar process by which the ties to the small collective become stronger as ties to all others become weaker. Former members all attest to the powerful emotional draw to their comrades in arms.[29] One Italian activist put it this way: "We shared the idea that the armed struggle, besides its historical necessity, was also an occasion to build human relations which had to be, I don't know how to say, absolute, based on the readiness to die, the opposite of everyday life, of the individualization of a capitalist society."[30]

It should come as no surprise that ethnonationalist terrorist groups are those that have tended to last the longest, not least because they have close ties to their communities. Psychologically, this means that membership in the group does not cut you off from a broader population that can serve as a counterweight to the mores of the movement. Conversely, groups that are isolated from the community, like most social revolutionary groups and millenarian cults, tend to have no external source of information or security, nor any perspective with which to question the dictates of the movement. Members of these isolated groups create a subjective reality that they inhabit and that their isolation prevents being subject to rational tests. Contemporary Islamist groups seem to be able to combine the transformational aspirations of the social revolutionaries with the community ties of the ethnonationalist groups. It is a very powerful combination.

Most psychologists agree that group, organizational, and social psychology are more helpful than individual psychology in explaining terrorist behavior. Anne Marie Oliver and Paul Steinberg, in describing the streets of the West Bank and Gaza, and Kevin Toolis, in his depiction of the streets of Belfast, provide riveting accounts of the cultures that make joining a terrorist movement the most natural thing in the world for a young man to do.[31] They describe whole societies collectively engaged in protest and providing encouragement and support for those who take up arms. They describe young men getting together with their friends and deciding to fight for the cause. This social setting can motivate even the most introverted and independent individuals. Eamon Collins was an unusually ruthless and cold-blooded killer who plotted the assassination of men with whom he worked. Even he describes being caught up in the popular demonstrations in favor of the H Block prisoners that finally led him into the arms of the IRA.[32]

Aspects of what I call a "complicit surround" that are conducive to terrorism are cultures in which violence is condoned and even glorified. This is more often the case in societies in which there is a history of violence in the region. Another essential ingredient is a religion or ideology that makes sense of violence and legitimates its use, whether it be the Maoism of the Shining Path and the Nepalese Communist Party; the nationalism of the Basques, the Kurds, or the Chechens; the Marxism-Leninism of the RAF and the Red Brigades; or the Islamic Fundamentalism of al-Qaeda, Algeria's GIA, or Egypt's al-Gama'a al-Islamiyya. Practical possibilities can be provided by an available enemy against whom to organize; whether it be American soldiers in Baghdad, British soldiers in Belfast, or Jewish settlers in the Gaza Strip, they are available as targets. A sense of injustice can provide a personal incentive to act. An individual is more likely to do so if he sees empirical evidence of injustice as well as evidence that the identified enemy is to blame.

STATE-LEVEL EXPLANATIONS

States are accustomed to dealing with other states, so it is attractive for a state to see terrorism as a threat from another state. There are fairly clear-cut policy implications to this perspective. If one sees terrorism as being caused by the behavior of an adversarial state, the traditional methods for conducting relations with adversaries will be invoked. Since time immemorial, the armed forces have been the means of conducting interstate behavior. But an examination of known terrorist cases suggests quite powerfully that neither the nature of the state nor the sponsorship by a state is a cause of terrorism.

The idea that democracy is the best antidote to terrorism has enjoyed widespread acceptance recently. This is too simplistic. Terrorism has occurred in democracies the world over. Terrorism is employed by minorities. (If they were not in a minority, they would not need to resort to terrorism.) To be a permanent minority within a democracy can be a frustrating position, and unless democracies can demonstrate that they provide not only a nonviolent means of expressing dissent but also a nonviolent means of redressing the grievances of minorities, they are unlikely to be an acceptable substitute. The leader of the Tamil Tigers could have been speaking for many ethnic minorities when he put it this way: "The Tamil people have been expressing their grievances in Parliament for more than three decades. Their voices went unheard like cries in the wilderness. In Sri Lanka there is no parliamentary democracy where our people could effectively represent their aspirations. What passes as Parliament in Sri Lanka is an authoritarian rule founded on the tyranny of the majority."[33]

Terrorist movements have often emerged in democracies when those trying to change the current system realize that they do not have the numbers required to prevail in a democracy. What's more, many of the hallmarks of democracies, such as freedom of movement and freedom of association as well as protections of privacy and personal rights, have made them convenient operating grounds for terrorism.

STATE SPONSORSHIP

I have argued that, by definition, terrorism is the behavior of substate groups. This view is not universally shared. The idea that terrorism is fundamentally a question of state behavior has long dominated American discourse on the subject. In the 1980s, when terrorism was high on the list of the public's priorities, it was seen as another front in the Cold War. The prototypical terrorist was a Communist controlled by Moscow, while Colonel Qaddafi was the bête noire of the Middle East. In April 1986, ten days after the bombing of a Berlin discotheque in which two American servicemen were killed, the United States bombed Tripoli in retaliation, killing at least a hundred people. In a familiar pattern, most of our allies were outraged; some refused even to allow use of their airspace by American bombers; but Britain, under Prime Minister Margaret Thatcher, permitted American planes to take off from military bases in the United Kingdom.

Cast in terms of state sponsorship of terrorism, it is hard to see how any self-respecting state could engage in the crime. Perceived, however, as the use of terrorism as an instrument of foreign policy, the same actions can be seen to have many advantages for many states, not just international pariahs. If a self-interested government is opposed by a much stronger state, it will be creative and avoid a head-on clash it would inevitably lose. State sponsorship of terrorism has had relatively low risk because it is so difficult to prove and may serve to achieve a state's foreign policy objectives. If it does not, it is easily deniable. Moreover, the primacy placed on human life by Western democracies leaves them very vulnerable to attack through their individual citizens because there are so many of them in so many places. So state sponsorship is often low cost, easy to deny, and difficult to prove, and has a potential for a high payoff. It should come as no surprise that relatively weak states resort to the support of terrorists to strike against their more powerful enemies.

It is often, in fact, a political judgment as to who is or is not a state sponsor of terrorism and who does and does not use terrorism as an instrument of foreign policy. In the 1970s, the USSR and Cuba topped the American public's list of state sponsors of terrorism. In the 1980s, it was Iran and Libya. In the 1990s, Iraq and Syria. Yet if you were to ask people in other countries, even in allied countries, you would find the United States high on most lists, and if you were to ask people in countries hostile to us you would find the United States at the top of their list. The examples invoked in support of the contention that the United States has sponsored terrorism would include the Contras in

Nicaragua, the American support for the mujahedin in Afghanistan, and support for local groups trying to overthrow Castro in Cuba and Allende in Chile. An examination of these cases reveals that the United States had very good reasons to object to the governments of Chile, Cuba, and Nicaragua. Their ideological orientation was inimical to its own, so it supported local groups that used whatever means were available to them to try to bring them down. To have engaged in open warfare against these governments, which were allied with its enemy, the Soviet Union, would have provoked an international uproar.

These are very much the same type of justifications state sponsors of terrorism in the Middle East would use. They perceive the existence of the state of Israel as inimical to their interest, they cannot directly and openly fight Israel, so they do so surreptitiously. The only real difference between their position and ours is that if we had chosen to fight openly we could be confident of winning, but we were not prepared to pay the price. These countries believe that they cannot defeat Israel militarily (they have tried and failed many times), so they fight Israel in other ways. Moreover, given the nature of our economic and political power, we have many more options at our disposal in terms of isolating inimical governments than most state sponsors of terrorism have had. So in some ways they have a better case than we did for using terrorism as an instrument of their foreign policy. It's not only the bad guys who use terrorism as an instrument of foreign policy. Sometimes the good guys do too. But in every instance, the sponsoring state is capitalizing on the availability of preexisting terrorist movements, not creating them.

States have sponsored terrorism not only as a means of conducting foreign policy; they have done so for domestic reasons too. The two most persistent and generous state sponsors of terrorism have been Iran and South Africa (though the latter never made it onto the U.S. State Department's list of state sponsors). Iran sponsored terrorism as a means of exporting revolution, while South Africa sponsored terrorism as a means of preventing the importation of revolution from abroad.

Iran has been the most consistent and most active state sponsor of terrorism. This has been driven by a desire to export its revolution, to undermine unfriendly regimes, and to remove what Supreme Leader Khomeini referred to as the "cancerous tumor" that is Israel. As soon as the Ayatollah Khomeini came to power in 1979, he set about trying to export his brand of fundamentalist Islamic revolution by backing radical groups throughout the Middle East, especially in Kuwait, Saudi Arabia, and Bahrain, as well as Shiite groups in Iraq and terrorist groups in Egypt. At one point, after the death of 260 Iranians in Mecca in the course of a riot during the hajj, Iran publicly called for the overthrow of the Saudi ruling family. Iran continues the policy of supporting Hezbollah in Lebanon and Palestinian rejectionist groups such as Hamas, Palestinian Islamic Jihad, and the Popular Front for the Liberation of Palestine—General Command by providing funding, safe haven, training, and weapons. The U.S. government has also accused Iran of encouraging Lebanese and Palestinian groups to coordinate its anti-Israel activities.[34] Suspicions abound that Iran has tolerated an al-Qaeda presence in, or at a minimum transit through, Iran and has helped to facilitate the operations of some sections of the anti-American insurgency in Iraq.

South Africa is never counted among the ranks of state sponsors of terrorism, yet it was quite a successful one for a time and had a deliberate and sophisticated policy. Finding itself surrounded by unfriendly frontline states in the wake of the wave of independence in Southern Africa in the 1960s and 1970s, the Pretoria government undertook a policy of supporting terrorist movements in neighboring frontline states. These movements were hostile to the new postindependence governments. Pretoria supported them as a means of perpetuating the dependence of the frontline states on the more powerful South African economy, of destabilizing unfriendly regimes, but, most important, to discourage and prevent support for the ANC. The policy was clearly dictated by domestic needs. South African support for Renamo, a brutal terrorist organization in Mozambique, is a case of a government supporting one terrorist organization outside the country as a way of undermining what it perceived to be a terrorist organization, the ANC, within its own country. It was a creative strategy, and eventually Prime Minister Samora Machel approached the South African government offering a deal: You stop supporting Renamo, and we'll stop supporting the ANC. They signed a nonaggression pact, the Nkomati Accord, in 1984. (Ironically, Prime Minister Machel's widow later became Nelson Mandela's wife.)

South Africa followed a similar strategy in another former Portuguese colony, Angola. South Africa supported UNITA against the government of Jonas Savimbi. Ultimately, as a part of the American-sponsored Namibian peace settlement, South Africa ceased its support of UNITA in return for Angola closing down ANC training camps and expelling its members.

Supporting terrorist movements was just one piece of the South African strategy. The government also used more conventional military attacks against ANC targets in the frontline states—Angola, Zambia, Zimbabwe, Mozambique, and Tanzania—and actually invaded Angola at one point. Attacks were launched as far north as the ANC head-quarters in Lusaka, Zambia. For all South Africa's military predomi-nance, and for all the government's willingness to use it against the ANC, and neighboring states that supported it, the government even-tually realized that the threat was political, not military, and could not be won with military force. The white minority regime ultimately ceded power to the "terrorist" ANC.

There can be no doubt that having a state sponsor strengthens ter-rorist movements. It is hard to see how Hezbollah could ever have de-veloped into the powerful and sophisticated terrorist movement it became without Iran's generous support. The existence of safe training grounds in the Bekaa Valley of Lebanon, protected by Syria, greatly augmented the military skills of a range of terrorist movements and helped them to develop relationships with one another. Osama bin Laden understood the value of having space within which to train and organize, first in the Sudan and later, when exiled from the Sudan under U.S. pressure, in Afghanistan. As the subsequent history of Afghani-stan has demonstrated, however, having a state sponsor is not enough. Having a generous sponsor can make terrorist movements more lethal by facilitating training and providing weapons, but ultimately a large part of terrorism's appeal is the fact that it is so cheap. Terrorists can survive without state sponsorship. Our attack on Afghanistan de-stroyed al-Qaeda's base of operations but it has not destroyed al-Qaeda. Generous state sponsors strengthen preexisting terrorist movements; they are not a cause of terrorism.

President Bush made his position on this point very clear in the aftermath of September 11. He declared, "Every nation in every region now has a decision to make. Either you are with us or you are with the terrorists. From this day forward, any nation that continues to harbor or support terrorism will be regarded by the United States as a hostile regime."[35] As it has turned out over the past few years, however, many countries, including our allies, have unwittingly harbored terrorists. Moreover, the history of state-sponsored terrorism suggests that relationships between terrorist movements and their state sponsors are far from uniform. In some instances states provide direction; in some they provide support; in some states simply turn a blind eye to the activities of resident groups; and in some states are unaware of the activities of terrorists in their midst.[36]

If a government assumes that state sponsorship is a basic cause of terrorism, that government is likely to be drawn into wars against other states, as the United States has been in Afghanistan and Iraq. The history of terrorism suggests that waging war against states will not eliminate terrorism.

SOCIETAL-LEVEL EXPLANATIONS

While terrorism can and does occur in both rich and poor countries, it is more likely to occur in developing countries, especially in countries experiencing rapid modernization. Changing economic conditions are conducive to instability, and traditional means of making sense of the world, such as religion or local power structures, are challenged by the scale of the change. In the face of sweeping socioeconomic changes, the promulgation of a particularist ideology that explains what is happening, provides something constant to hold on to, and values the identity being challenged is likely to be well received. On a more practical level, two of the most commonly shared characteristics of terrorists, their gender and their youth, are very often in ample supply in transitional societies or societies feeling the effects of rapid modernization. Modernizing societies experience a disproportionate growth in the youth population due to improvements in the health care system. If the structures are not in place to absorb these young men into the workforce, they are likely to have time to contemplate the disadvantages of their position and to be available to be mobilized behind a cause that promises to change it.

The relationship between poverty and terrorism has long been debated, with one side pointing to the impoverished refugee camps of the Middle East as spawning grounds for terrorists and the other side pointing to the relative affluence of many individual terrorists, such as Mohamed Atta, leader of the 9/11 attacks, and especially to the personal wealth of Osama bin Laden. Both are right, and neither tells the whole story.[37] If there were a direct link among poverty, inequality, and terrorism, the areas with the highest rates of poverty and inequality would have the highest rates of terrorism, but they do not. If there were a direct link between poverty and terrorism, then Africa, the poorest continent on the planet, would be awash in terrorism. It is not. If terrorism were caused by inequality, the countries in Africa and Latin America with the highest rates of inequality would have the highest rates of terrorism, but they do not.[38] Conservative opponents of this liberal view point to the wealth of individual terrorists as proof positive that there is no relationship among poverty, inequality, and terrorism. Indeed, many nationalist terrorist movements have broken out among ethnic groups that are relatively well off, such as the Tamils in Sri Lanka, the Sikhs in India, the Basques in Spain, and the Catholics in Ireland. The relationship, once again, is more complicated than either of these positions suggest.

What appears to drive some people to violence is not their absolute levels of poverty but rather their position relative to others.[39] (The essence of the concept "relative deprivation" is well known to every parent who tries to ensure tranquillity at home by treating and being seen to treat all children equally.[40]) Northern Irish Catholics did not compare themselves to southern Irish Catholics, who enjoyed a much less generous social welfare system at the time the civil rights movement emerged; rather, they compared themselves to Northern Irish Protestants. Impoverished Palestinians are not comparing themselves to other impoverished Arabs in Egypt, Jordan, or elsewhere, but to the much wealthier Israeli settlers. With global mass communications and American TV shows broadcasting American affluence around the world, it is not difficult to mobilize a sense of resentment of American wealth. Previously one compared oneself to others nearby, but the contrast between American wealth and Arab poverty is now being broadcast daily into people's tiny homes. The world's very poorest people, preoccupied with survival, do not even realize the extent of their relative deprivation.

RISK FACTORS

Rather than causing terrorism, poverty and inequality are risk factors that increase the likelihood of terrorism. Moreover, once terrorism has broken out, poverty and inequality increase the likelihood that it will acquire adherents. Individuals may not be driven to terrorism by poverty and inequality, but the alienation that these conditions breed may lead others to support them. With the impact of globalization and especially global media and communications, the relative economic inequalities of the world are increasingly known. They become known both to those who experience them and to those recruited to empathize with them. A young British cricket player may not therefore have to endure poverty himself to feel outraged at the poverty of Palestinians in refugee camps. The occupant of the camps can be persuaded to blame the satellite TV–owning Israeli settlers a few miles away for his relative poverty. But poverty and relative deprivation are far more widespread than terrorism, so this does not tell the whole story.

Part of the success of many Islamist groups, especially well-established groups such as Hamas and Hezbollah, is due to their understanding of the recruitment potential of social services. These groups painstakingly built up their support by attending to the social needs of their potential recruits far more effectively than governments did. They established hospitals, schools, and orphanages. The Islamic Group (al-Gama'a al-Islamiyya) in Egypt adopted a similar strategy with similar success. High unemployment rates, ranging from 11 percent in Egypt to 18 percent in Lebanon to 50 percent in Gaza and the West Bank, ensure continued economic privation.[41] These rates also raise another risk factor for terrorism, the existence of large numbers of unemployed young men. The demographics of many modernizing societies result in a population shift, leading to a disproportionate increase in the number of young people and the inability of the economy to integrate them. The percentage of the population under fifteen years of age is 46 percent in the Palestinian Territory, 42 percent in Iraq, 37 percent in Saudi Arabia and Jordan, and 36 percent in Egypt, as compared to 21 percent in the United States and 18 percent in the UK.[42] These developments are not unique to the Middle East. The ranks of the Shining Path in Peru, for example, were swelled by young men from the indigenous population. They were the first in their families to go to college. They received an education and the heightened expectations that accompany education but were unable to find employment. In this way well-meaning reforms on the part of the government backfired, producing unintended consequences. The Peruvian government created universities in the remote countryside, such as in Ayacucho, in order to bring education to the local populations. It was through the university that Abimael Guzmán recruited followers to his Maoist interpretation of the reason for their problems. This case speaks to the importance of thinking through the implications of social reform policies. It is not enough to provide education if you do not provide the means to employ those you have educated. The same risk factor is very much in evidence in the Middle East and North Africa. In countries such as Egypt and Algeria, only about half of the university graduates are able to find jobs and even fewer are able to find jobs commensurate with their expectations. Similarly, in the period leading up to the first Intifada, the number of men with twelve or more years of education doubled while their real wages dropped by 30 percent and their unemployment rates soared.[43]

Different terrorist groups have tended to attract people from different socioeconomic backgrounds. Between 50 percent and 70 percent of the members of the Latin American urban terrorist groups were students. Japanese and European social revolutionary movements in the 1970s were populated predominantly by middle-class dropouts. By contrast, large-scale ethnonationalist movements, such as the IRA, the FARC, the LTTE, and the PKK, have generally been more working class. In the Middle East, in the past at any rate, the foot soldiers have tended to be poor while the leadership, as in most political organizations, tends to come from the middle class. More recently ideology appears to trump class as recruits are drawn from around the world. Many of these recruits, whether homegrown, as in the case of the British suicide bombers, or members of the diaspora, as in the case of the Spanish bombers, are by no means destitute; on the contrary, they are often quite highly educated though underemployed.

Asked to explain the apparent incongruity of a man of his wealth and background fighting on the front lines, bin Laden responded:

We believe that livelihoods are preordained. So no matter how much pressure America puts on the regime in Riyadh to freeze our assets and to forbid people from contributing to this great cause, we shall still have Allah to take care of us; livelihood is sent by Allah; we shall not want.

He also dismissed the notion that there were any economic explanations for the surge of Islamic radicalism:

They claim that this blessed awakening and the people reverting to Islam are due to economic factors. This is not so. It is rather a grace from Allah, a desire to embrace the religion of Allah. And this is not surprising. When the holy war called thousands of young men from the Arab Peninsula and other countries answered the call and they came from wealthy backgrounds.[44]

The trial transcripts of those accused in the bombing of the U.S. embassies in Nairobi and Dar es Salaam reveal that not all the members of al-Qaeda were as otherworldly as their leader. Jamal Ahmad al-Fadl went into intricate detail in his testimony about the salaries paid to various members and the resentment bred by the apparent inequities in salaries.[45] Another defendant, L'Houssaine Kherchtou, described how he began to resent al-Qaeda when the organization refused to pay $500 for his wife's medical expenses. He found this particularly unfair as the organization was prepared to send a group of Egyptians to Yemen for a month with all expenses paid in order to renew their passports.[46]

Examining economic causes of terrorism leads one back to the same conclusion: it's complicated. Terrorism has occurred in both rich and poor countries but most often in developing countries and in societies characterized by rapid modernization. Rapid socioeconomic changes are conducive to instability and tend to erode traditional forms of social control. These situations are then open to exploitation by militants offering to make sense of these changes, to blame others for the dislocations and humiliations involved, and to offer a means of redress. Only a tiny percentage of the population needs to be persuaded. Whether this small group remains small and isolated or grows into a broadly based movement will depend on a range of factors, from the response of the authorities to the extent of the social dislocation being experienced, as well as the success of the militant leadership in integrating their message with historical, cultural, or religious traditions.

TRANSNATIONAL-LEVEL EXPLANATIONS

Globalization

Globalization is alternatively offered as both a cure for and a cause of terrorism. Again, it is neither and both. Countries that have benefited most from globalization and those that have benefited least have not produced significant terrorist movements.[47] It is often argued that the most open or the most globalized countries are most vulnerable to terrorism in that their permeable borders and advanced technologies are so easy for terrorists to exploit. Yet the countries that have topped the globalization index in recent years, the Republic of Ireland, Singapore, and Switzerland, have not experienced terrorism. On the other hand, India, Indonesia, and Egypt, which along with Iran occupy the bottom of the globalization index, have indeed experienced terrorism.[48] For many of the weak globalizers, the advantages have not been shared and the result has often been an increase in structural inequalities along with a sense of humiliation as traditional cultures are seen being diluted by foreign influences. Abu Shanab, a leader of Hamas, was expressing a widely held view when he told interviewer Jessica Stern:

> Globalization is just a new colonial system. It is America's attempt to dominate the rest of the world economically rather than militarily. It will worsen the gap between rich and poor. America is trying to spread its consumer culture. These values are not good for human beings. . . . It leads to disaster for communities.[49]

The ideology of militant Islamist movements is, of course, radically antiglobalization. They want to remove external influence and return to the traditional rule of Islamic law, called Sharia. These are the very groups, however, that have most creatively exploited globalization to their own advantage. While articulating a vision of a premodern future, they seek to achieve it by ultramodern means. They rely on the Internet, for example, to communicate, to recruit, to mobilize, and to organize and even to fund-raise. They seem quite untroubled by the inconsistency.

RELIGION

In recent years religions, and particularly Islam, have been widely seen as the cause of terrorism. As with all single explanations, this is an over-simplification. Most religious traditions have produced terrorist groups, and many terrorists have been atheists, so the notion that Islam and terrorism are inextricably linked is simply wrong. Islam is a large and disparate religion. Muslims constitute about a fifth of the world's population, form a majority in forty-five countries ranging from Africa to Southeast Asia, and exist in significant and growing numbers in the United States, Europe, and the former Soviet Union.

Nevertheless, there has been an extraordinary growth in the number of terrorist groups with religious motives over the past thirty years. In 1968, of the eleven known terrorist groups, none had any kind of religious affiliation. By the mid-1990s, of the fifty known groups, about a dozen had religious motivations.[30] In 2004, of seventy-seven terrorist groups designated or listed by the U.S. Department of State, forty appeared to have some mixture of religious and political motives. Of these thirty-seven are Islamist groups.[51] Historically, terrorist groups with a mixture of religious and political motives have shared two characteristics: they have been more transnational than groups with purely secular motives, and they have exercised less restraint. Religious boundaries have never conformed to political borders, so religious groups have always managed to operate across borders. This has made them more difficult to contain.

Even more damaging is their relative lack of restraint. A great many terrorist groups have controlled their behavior and the extent of the casualties they have been prepared to inflict out of a desire not to alienate their core constituency. The IRA, for example, planted a bomb outside Harrods and killed six people in December 1983. It could just have easily planted that bomb in the Harrods food court on the first day of the after-Christmas sale and thereby killed many hundreds of people. It feared alienating its core constituency, the Catholic population of Northern Ireland. Indeed, an analysis of the pattern of IRA violence reveals a chronic concern on its part to tailor its targeting strategies in this sort of way. Religious groups are different. If one's audience is God, then one does not need to worry about alienating him.

These groups have therefore tended toward inflicting mass casualties, as the only constraint is their own capabilities.

Religious terrorists are not all the same; far from it. Religion can play different roles in different terrorist groups. For many groups religion is just a badge of ethnic identity. It serves to solidify alliances and divisions, to identify enemies and friends. In this way religion has made several conflicts more intractable, but the underlying conflict has little to do with religion. In the Northern Irish conflict, for example, mavericks such as the Reverend Ian Paisley have sought to cast the conflict in doctrinal terms on the loyalist side, and on the republican side local Catholic curates have often reflected the republican instincts of the communities that produced them. The leadership of both churches, however, have invariably counseled nonviolence, and there is no doctrinal dispute involved. The goals of both sides are entirely political; religion just sharpens the differences.

In other cases religion appears to provide the objective for the terrorist group, but it is usually very difficult to separate religious from political motives and both are usually operating inextricably together. Yigal Amir, the man who assassinated Israeli Prime Minister Yitzhak Rabin in November 1995, offered this explanation: "I have no regrets. I acted alone and on orders from God."[52] On the face of it he would appear to have been motivated exclusively by religion. But his act was calculated to achieve a political objective, the destruction of the Arab-Israeli peace process, even if it was also motivated by a desire to fulfill what he perceived to be a divine command. Jewish groups use the Torah to justify not giving up Judea and Samaria. Islamic groups use the Koran to stake their claim to the same territory. But it is not clear that the political can be separated from the religious in these instances.

Even the case of the Aum Shinrikyo group, the Japanese cult that released sarin gas on the Tokyo subway in March 1995, ostensibly in an effort to bring about the apocalypse, is not a clear-cut case of religiously driven terrorism. It too had political aspirations and turned to terrorism only once its political aspirations were thwarted. The organization put up twenty-four members in the 1989 parliamentary elections, but none was elected. Moreover, its actual attack was precipitated not by any religious doctrine but rather by the paranoid fear that the police were closing in on it.[53]

To this day we do not know quite how much relative weight Osama bin Laden attributes to his religious and his political goals. The manner in which he has altered the listing of his various aspirations in his various statements suggests that the political is primary and religion a tool. But we do not know that for sure, and he would certainly deny it. Bin Laden has long listed the American presence in Saudi Arabia as the primary offense. When asked by Peter Arnett whether an end to the American presence in Saudi Arabia would lead to an end to his call for jihad against the United States, bin Laden replied, "The cause of the reaction must be sought and the act that has triggered this reaction must be eliminated. The act came as a result of the US aggressive policy toward the entire Muslim world and not just towards the Arabian peninsula. So if the cause that has called for this act comes to an end, this act in turn will come to an end. So the defensive jihad against the US does not stop with its withdrawal from the Arabian peninsula but rather it must desist from aggressive intervention against Muslims in the whole world."[54]

Evidently he has no interest in attempting to convert Americans or others; he wants the West to remove itself from the Muslim world, broadly defined, so that it can return to the days of the caliphate and the law of Sharia. We may never know whether bin Laden would be satisfied with assuming control of one country, most likely Saudi Arabia, and trying to impose an Islamist state there. Interestingly enough, when this hypothesis was put to him and he was asked what would happen to the price of oil if an Islamic state were to be established in Saudi Arabia, he replied like the student of economics he once was: "As for oil, it is a commodity that will be subject to the price of the market according to supply and demand. We believe that the current prices are not realistic due to the Saudi regime playing the role of a US agent and the pressures exercised by the US on the Saudi regime to increase production and flooding the market that caused a sharp decrease in oil prices."[55]

For many groups religion plays a role not unlike that of a political ideology, like Maoism for the Shining Path or Marxism-Leninism for the social revolutionary movements. It provides a unifying, all-encompassing philosophy or belief system that legitimates and elevates their actions. The number of Maoist and Marxist-Leninist groups, however, has declined in the course of the past thirty to forty years, while the number of religiously motivated groups has increased dramatically.

The evolution of a philosophical justification for radical Islamism began with the founding of the Muslim Brotherhood in 1920. The most influential of the thinkers were the Egyptian Sayyid Qutb and the Pakistani Sayyid Abul A'la Mawdudi. Three political events were enormously influential in making these fundamentalist views popular beyond an isolated number of marginalized intellectual extremists. The three events were the Iranian Revolution and the wars in Lebanon and Afghanistan.

The revolution in Iran in 1978–1979 overthrew the shah, who was much despised and very closely identified with the West, and established a Muslim Shiite state under a radical cleric, the Ayatollah Khomeini. The success of the revolution proved inspirational to other groups and provoked a wave of Shiite militancy throughout the Middle East. The new Iranian leaders were only too delighted to export their revolution and provide material as well as moral encouragement to those in other countries seeking to emulate their success. Moreover, the revolution gained widespread admiration throughout the Muslim world for the manner in which the new regime humiliated the United States by seizing the U.S. Embassy, holding the staff hostage for more than a year, and forcing the United States to negotiate a settlement.

Second was the war in Lebanon, where Iranian-inspired Shiite terrorists, especially from Hezbollah, again enjoyed considerable success against American and Israeli forces. Hezbollah was, of course, enormously assisted by the $60 million to $80 million a year provided by Iran. Hezbollah became famous for three terrorist tactics in the 1980s. First was hijacking, with the most celebrated case being the protracted media extravaganza surrounding the hijacking of TWA flight 847. In this case a U.S. serviceman was brutally killed and the United States was perceived as conceding to the terrorists by pressuring Israel to release hundreds of prisoners in return for the release of the hostages. The second tactic was the kidnapping of high-profile Western targets, with significant repercussions for domestic U.S. policy once it was learned that U.S. officials had negotiated an arms-for-hostages deal with Iran. The third tactic, and the one with the longest shelf life, was suicide bombings. The most successful example of this tactic occurred on October 23, 1983. A suicide car bomb exploded outside the U.S. Marine barracks near the Beirut airport and killed 241 American soldiers serving as peacekeepers in Lebanon. That same evening, another bomber drove to the French headquarters and killed 58 French soldiers. The American and French forces promptly withdrew from the country.

The Iranian Revolution had occurred on President Carter's watch, and he was widely perceived as being weak and soft on terrorism. Ronald Reagan, by contrast, was elected, in large part, because he articulated a vision of a strong and powerful America. Yet he too withdrew in the face of attack. This exploded the myth for many in the Middle East that there was any essential difference between Democrats and Republicans in the United States. Both were paper tigers. To this day, Osama bin Laden repeatedly invokes the American withdrawal from Lebanon after the attack on the Marines as evidence of American cowardice and unwillingness to fight. In his 1996 Declaration of War, bin Laden made note of a statement from the "crusading" American defense secretary, William Perry—that, in bin Laden's words, "the explosion at Riyadh and al-Khobar had taught [Perry] one lesson: that is not to withdraw when attacked by cowardly terrorists"—and responded by saying: "We say to the defense secretary that his talk can induce a grieving mother to laughter. . . . Where was this false courage of yours when the explosion in Beirut took place in 1983? . . . And where was this courage of yours when two explosions made you leave Aden in less than twenty-four hours?"[56] The withdrawal from Lebanon provided example number two of how a superpower can be humiliated by a determined and much weaker adversary prepared to use violence against it.

The third, and most important, political event leading to the escalation of Islamic fundamentalist terrorism was the war against the Soviet Union in Afghanistan. This war demonstrated to Islamists not only that a superpower could be forced to withdraw peacekeepers, as in Lebanon, but that it could actually be defeated by motivated, armed mujahedin. The Soviet Union invaded Afghanistan in 1979, fearing that a surge in Islamic fundamentalism there inspired by the Iranian Revolution would spread to the neighboring Soviet republics of Uzbekistan, Tajikistan, and Turkmenistan. Ten years later, after the deaths of 1 million to 1.5 million Afghans and 15,000 Soviet troops and the creation of 5 million Afghan refugees, the Soviets withdrew. Afghanistan proved to be a training ground for Islamic militants who were recruited from across the Middle East to come to Afghanistan, to train, and to fight. In the course of the decade fighting the Soviets, they acquired ideological unity, international connections, and experience in warfare and in the use of sophisticated weaponry (often provided by the United States in an effort to help defeat the Soviet Union). At the end of the war the mujahedin, hardened and radicalized by the experience, returned to their home countries, joined preexisting terrorist groups, and radicalized them. The Afghan experience demonstrated to them that they could bring down a superpower. The sole remaining superpower was the United States. Returning to their home countries, they encountered American influence everywhere and often faced harsh repression from secular Muslim governments anxious to preserve stability. They blamed the United States for propping up many of these governments and despised the governments for selling out the cause of Islam, as they saw it.

The two main branches of Islam, Sunni and Shia, both experienced fundamentalist revivals among intellectuals in the twentieth century. These three political events ensured that the writings of these intellectuals and extremist thinkers, such as the Sunni Sayyid Qutb, in his treatise *Milestones,* and the Shia participants in the al-Dawa movement, did not remain marginalized but rather received widespread circulation when embraced by militant leaders. This combination of a philosophical justification for terrorism with empirical evidence of its success proved lethal.

The interplay of religion and politics is an essential part of Islam, which does not recognize the compartmentalization of society into public and private realms. There has never been an Islamic equivalent of the Reformation leading to the legal or constitutional separation between religion and state. Rather, Muslims are called upon to bring the behavior of the wider world into conformity with the religious teaching and moral precepts of the Koran (God's written revelations through Muhammad) and *hadith* (the divinely inspired traditions of Muhammad's sayings and practices).

Fundamentalists have a fairly simple and powerful message: The problems Muslims face are due to the pervasiveness of foreign ideologics, be they capitalist or Communist, which have displaced the much nobler cultural values and philosophy of Islam. Muslims will be able to develop their own modern civilization and address the social, economic, political, and moral problems they face only if they reject these alien influences and embrace Sharia. The fundamentalist appeal, therefore, is to blame the social and economic problems of the region on corrupt secular leaders and the nefarious external forces that support them. The political symbol of the failure of their leadership is the existence of the state of Israel in their midst; the social symbol of failure is the spread of Western culture unaccompanied by a Western standard of living. Fundamentalist leaders have therefore successfully linked economic privation with religious decline.

Islamic fundamentalists differ from Muslim traditionalists in their emphasis on the state as the means for religious reform. Their immediate goal, therefore, is to capture the state. By invoking Islam's gloried past, they both dramatize the humiliation of the present situation and hold out a vision for a proud future. Moreover, the teachings of the fundamentalists such as Qutb promise that ultimate victory is assured.

We in the West have long recognized that democracy can facilitate terrorism. We do not, however, consider democracy a cause of terrorism. Religion too facilitates terrorism. It not only facilitates terrorism among those who live together in the slums and refugee camps of the Middle East but, more dangerously, it facilitates the functioning of terrorism across borders. Earlier I mentioned the capacity to identify with others, a capacity many terrorists share. It has long been recognized that a capacity to identify and empathize is a human trait but one that is held in differing degrees toward different groups. We identify most closely with our families, then our neighbors and our professional colleagues, our town, state, country, in ever-widening and -weakening circles. Does anyone doubt that the West's dilatory response to the Rwandan atrocity was in large part due to the failure to identify with the victims? Had they been closer, whiter, more like us, would we have delayed so long? I doubt it. Or why did the IRA's terrorist campaign, which claimed 3,500 lives in thirty years, get such coverage in the United States, when the terrorist campaigns of the Shining Path, which claimed 69,000 lives in twenty-three years, and of the PKK, which claimed 35,000 over twenty years, got so much less attention? I expect it was because Americans could identify with the white, English-speaking residents of Northern Ireland more than with Peruvians, Kurds, and Turks.

Fundamentalist Islam can cause a young educated Briton to identify not with his neighbors, teammates, or school friends but with Palestinians in a country he's never seen. That is part of its power. In a video made by the two British jihadists Omar Khan Sharif and Assaf Mohammed Hanif on the eve of their martyrdom operation in Gaza, they argued, "But Muslims are being killed every day." Similarly, it appears to have been religiously fostered identification that caused the twenty-two-year-old, college-educated, cricket-playing, Mercedes-driving, young Briton Shehzad Tanweer from the suburbs of Leeds to plant a bomb in a London subway. Religion can serve as a link between the personal and the political. Interviews with terrorists often reveal their sense of frustration, bred of failure. Religion provides them with a means of dealing with these personal issues in a way that addresses their personal inadequacies by making them part of a more powerful movement and promising ultimate victory.

Religion cannot, therefore, be said to have caused terrorism, but Islamic fundamentalism has provided a justification for the use of terrorism in the interests of achieving a greater good. The economic and social failures of many Muslim countries have produced adherents willing to embrace the method as a means of redressing humiliations, improving economic and social conditions, and effecting change. In this way, religion interacts with social, economic, and political factors and contributes to the creation of a culture of violence. It makes recruitment, mobilization, and retention easier for the leaders of these groups. Religious groups can have more staying power because they have an ideology that legitimates their actions and gives each individual a role.

Religion is never the sole cause of terrorism; rather, religious motivations are interwoven with economic and political factors. Yet religion cannot be reduced to social and economic factors. It is a powerful force in itself. Religion serves to incite, to mobilize, and to legitimize terrorist actions. Moreover, religions' preoccupation with fundamental notions of good and evil tends to ensure that movements with religious motives are much less prone to compromise. Islamic fundamentalists tend to see the world in terms of an enduring and cosmic struggle between good and evil. Religiously motivated terrorist groups, therefore, tend to be more fanatical, more willing to inflict mass casualties, and better able to enact unassailable commitment from their adherents. As such, they are much less susceptible to conventional responses such as deterrence or negotiation. So while religion is a cause of terrorism only in combination with other social and political factors, religion does make terrorist groups more absolutist, more transnational, and more dangerous.

———

The two most common explanations of terrorism are that it is the work of either crazy individuals or of warmongering states, but the best explanations are not at these levels at all but at the level of the societies that produce them. Terrorism needs a sense of alienation from the status quo and a desire to change it. Terrorism needs conditions in which people feel unfairly treated and leaders to make sense of these conditions, to organize a group and make it effective. Terrorism needs an all-encompassing philosophy—a religion or secular ideology—to legitimize violence action, to win recruits to the cause, and to mobilize them for action. Terrorism, to survive and thrive, needs a complicit society, a societal surround sympathetic to its aspirations.

In light of these requirements one can see why diaspora communities have become such fertile recruiting grounds for Islamic fundamentalists. Removed from the sureties of their own culture, disaffected because marginalized and undervalued in their new one, immigrants are vulnerable to the appeals of radical clerics attacking the inequities of the society from which they are disaffected and offering an alternative community. But recruits are found not just among the physically displaced. Militant leaders and the organizations they lead are more likely to find followers in situations in which economic developments and rapid change are increasing inequalities and disrupting traditional structures, when expectations are being raised and not met, where feelings of frustration and humiliation are widespread among underemployed youth. These leaders are more likely to be successful in winning recruits if they can construct an ideology that is rooted in religious or historical traditions and thereby legitimizes and even glorifies their actions and offers a path to a different future.

Social, economic, and cultural factors are the underlying risk factors that make a society more or less susceptible to the appeal of terrorist groups. But they are not the cause. The cause lies in the interplay between these broad factors and the actions, beliefs, and political aspirations of a small group of people: the founders, leaders, and members of terrorist groups and the complicity of the community from which they come. Terrorism is caused by the lethal triple cocktail of personal disaffection, an enabling society, and a legitimizing ideology. But what are terrorists fighting for? What motivates them? What do they want?

FOUR

THE THREE Rs: REVENGE, RENOWN, REACTION

If we are mark'd to die, we are enow
To do our country loss; . . .
I am not covetous for gold,
Nor care I who doth feed upon my cost;
It ernes me not if men my garments wear;
Such outward things dwell not in my desires.
But if it be a sin to covet honour,
I am the most offending soul alive . . .
We would not die in that man's company
That fears his fellowship to die with us. . . .
Then shall our names,
Familiar in his mouth as household words—
Harry the King, Bedford and Exeter,
Warwick and Talbot, Salisbury and Gloucester—
Be in their flowing cups freshly remembered.
This story shall the good man teach his son;
And Crispin Crispian shall ne'er go by,
From this day to the ending of the world,
But we in it shall be remembered—

We few, we happy few, we band of brothers;
For he today that sheds his blood with me
Shall be my brother.

        —William Shakespeare, *Henry V*

NINE-YEAR-OLD DERMOT FINUCANE SAT ON THE STAIRS with his brothers, who were eleven and twelve. He remembers the fear etched on his parents' faces and audible in their muffled voices as they looked out their bedroom window. "You would be sitting there terrified, not making a sound; you were like a mouse, just listening." The children carried hammers, hatchets, and the poker from the fireplace to defend themselves when the mob outside broke down the door to their house to burn them out. They were a Catholic family living in a fine big five-bedroom house on a mixed street. Their Protestant neighbors wanted them out. Two older brothers, John and Pat, who were sixteen and eighteen at the time, were not able to get back to the house to help them. The policemen outside watching the mob burn and loot the "Catholic" houses were not about to help them. Dermot remembers, "The thing I most clearly remember is that the adults were terrified and as a child you picked that up. I can remember thinking we were going to be killed soon, our area would be overrun by hostile Indians." They were not killed, but they lost their house and their dad and oldest brother lost their jobs, having been threatened with death if they showed up for work. The family's fortunes plummeted. The parents and eight children squatted in a two-bedroom flat in the Catholic part of town.

Dermot was ten when his brother John joined the IRA. His younger brother Seamus explained, "We were all proud of John. There was a sense of adventure about people taking up the gun and the bomb at that time. Yes, it was exciting at times. You got satisfaction out of it." Immediately the rest of the family became suspect. Their house was regularly raided by soldiers. Dermot estimated that their house was raided more than a hundred times. His father would make tea for the raiding soldiers to try to show that they were a respectable family and in the vain hope that they would not then beat his children. The children reacted differently. Martin, two years older than Dermot, remembers the raids: "I remember them telling my father what to do. It was my father's house, it was my mother's house. But they were telling them what to do and going about our house as if they owned it, searching it, looking at personal things and private things. I began to hate them." Martin never joined the IRA. Instead, unable to handle the constant harassment on account of his brother, he fled the country. His sister Rosie fled too. It wasn't long before their brother Seamus was caught up in the excitement. At the age of fifteen he was picked up by the British Army and interned without trial for more than a year. In the internment camp it was the regular army visits with dogs that scared him the most. "It was frightening, they had the dogs in and big batons and if you moved when you were not supposed to they just clipped you with them." When he emerged he was more committed than ever to the IRA.

Dermot was eleven when his brother John died. What Dermot remembered most was the funeral: "the crowds were massive. . . . My older brothers told me that it was the biggest funeral up until that time to leave Andersonstown. I remember being very proud that John was getting a military funeral." The brothers describe the way the entire community was united against the enemy. In Dermot's words, "The whole area was against them so I was against them, it was a community thing." Martin agreed: "You just got involved because you were caught up in it."

When Dermot was seventeen, the army raided the house again. He assumed that they had come for his older brother and turned to Martin, saying, "They are here again for you." But this time they had come for Dermot. "I got a bit of a beating . . . and after that I just collapsed. I would have told them anything, signed anything. But luckily I didn't know anything." The day after he was released, his father died of a heart attack. The family blamed his premature death on the strain of The Troubles. Dermot decided it was time to join the IRA. He had trouble doing so at first, as he didn't know whom to talk to or how to join. Having been accepted into the IRA, he had to undergo training. He made an excuse to his mother to explain his four-day absence, but when he returned he was proud as punch. "We got a big buzz out of the arms training. I came back with my chest sticking out—Big Man. I should have had a sticker printed on my forehead 'Top Man Now.' It gave you a lift and a sense of achievement." Once a member of the movement, he thought, "In three years' time I will be dead so I am going to do my damnedest to hurt those who have hurt my family, my community."

When Dermot was twenty, he was charged with murder but in the absence of any evidence against him he was released. When he was twenty-one, he was convicted of terrorist offenses and sentenced to eighteen years in prison. At the age of twenty-three he escaped. He fled to the Republic of Ireland, where he lived on the run for four years before being caught. He successfully fought extradition proceedings brought against him and was freed in Dublin in 1991. By then his oldest brother, Pat, a prominent solicitor, had been assassinated in his home in front of his wife and three children in an apparent act of collusion between Protestant paramilitaries and the security services that is being investigated to this day.

The story of the radicalization of Dermot Finucane contains many of the themes found in the stories of other terrorists in other parts of the world. In particular, the sense of being part of a larger community and the desire for revenge are ever present when terrorists explain their motivations. For Dermot the glory of a big funeral was matched by the glory of being listed on a wanted poster. When looking at a poster of three of the most wanted men in Ulster, he remembers thinking, "That's what you want, you want to inflict so much damage on the enemy they want you badly. There is no point doing it Mickey Mouse style; I was always putting myself on the front line. . . . I wanted the honor of doing it." The honor and glory of the battle is another constant theme in the conversations of terrorists everywhere from Andersonstown to Afghanistan.

Another constant theme among terrorists is confidence in victory, the belief that as a result of their violence the enemy will react. Dermot Finucane, looking at Northern Ireland during the mid-1990s, insisted, "Britain is finished in Ireland. It's over. It's all a question of when, when do they decide to pull out." Looking back on his career as a terrorist, Dermot says, "Militarily and politically, I have inflicted damage and I am glad. I am glad I have been a thorn in their side. I did set out to fight them and I fought them." When asked to specify how much damage he had inflicted, he was vague. "Let's just say it is in double figures."[1]

There has been a vigorous debate on the question of whether or not terrorism works. I must confess to finding this entire argument quite pointless. You cannot know whether or not it works until you know what it is terrorists are trying to achieve. Those who argue, for example, that the establishment of the power-sharing executive in Northern Ireland has rewarded the terrorism of the IRA are quite wrong.[2] The IRA did not wage a terrorist campaign to share power with Protestants in Northern Ireland. Quite the contrary; the IRA and the republican community from which it comes have always refused to participate in the running of the province, as to do so would be to concede the legitimacy of its existence. The IRA campaign was fought to bring about a united Ireland, which they have not succeeded in achieving.

Alan Dershowitz's provocative argument in his book *Why Terrorism Works* is based almost entirely on his interpretation of the Palestinian case.[3] He argues that the Palestinians' terrorist tactics have brought more attention and sympathy for their cause than those with better national claims who have not resorted to terrorism, such as the Tibetans and Armenians. If the goal of terrorism is attention and sympathy, Dershowitz might be right in the Palestinian case, though hardly in many others. If the goal is a national territory commensurate with their nationalist aspirations, the Palestinians, like the Tibetans and the Armenians, have a long way to go.

All terrorist movements have two kinds of goals: short-term organizational objectives and long-term political objectives requiring significant political change. This distinction is crucial to understanding their actions and places the current debate on whether or not terrorism works in a very different light.

Hannah Arendt once wrote, "Violence being instrumental by nature is rational to the extent that it is effective in reaching the end that must justify it."[4] If one keeps in mind the terrorists' ultimate objective, the violence may indeed appear to be irrational, but it is important to bear in mind that there are often secondary or more immediate objectives to be pursued. The record of terrorists in obtaining these second-tier objectives is much better than their record in achieving the fundamental political change they generally seek.

Long-term objectives differ. Ethnonationalist groups are looking for traditional territorial gains, such as independence and secession.

(Examples include the PLO in Palestine, the PKK in Turkey, the LTTE in Sri Lanka, and the IRA and ETA in Europe.) Social revolutionary groups are seeking to overthrow capitalism. (Examples include the Red Brigades in Italy, the RAF in Germany, Action Directe in France, and the CCC in Belgium.) Maoist groups—such as the Shining Path in Peru and the Communist Party of Nepal—seek to remake society. Some religious sects, such as Aum Shinrikyo in Japan, seek to bring about the millennium; fundamentalist groups seek to replace secular law with religious law. Some movements, such as Hamas and Hezbollah, appear to be hybrids, and some groups evolve from one kind to another like the transformation of the isolated "old" IRA to the pragmatic and broader-based Provisional IRA. In every instance, they are driven by an ideal.

SECONDARY MOTIVES

Those who argue that terrorism works are often confusing the primary and secondary motives. Unlike the primary objectives, the more immediate or secondary motives for specific acts are often shared across all kinds of terrorist movements. These secondary motives include:

Exacting Revenge

The desire of individual terrorists for revenge serves as a powerful motive. A captive on hijacked TWA flight 847, for example, could not understand why a hijacker kept running up and down the aisle with a grenade and shouting the name of her home state: "New Jersey, New Jersey." He remembered, though she certainly did not, that it was the USS *New Jersey* that had fired on Shiite sites in Lebanon. The desire for revenge explains why so many attacks take place on the anniversary of earlier actions. The Oklahoma City bombing, for example, occurred on the anniversary of the storming of the Branch Davidian compound in Waco, Texas. Colonel Qaddafi, the Libyan head of state, used to mark the anniversary of the 1986 U.S. bombing of Tripoli by providing funding to terrorist groups.

Generating Publicity

Since the days of the Zealots, terrorists have understood the value of publicity, and those operating in democracies have been singularly successful in achieving this objective. Even before the most recent terrorist spectaculars, an estimated 500 million people watched the abduction and murder of the Israeli Olympic team in Munich in 1972. More recently, the Túpac Amaru, a small group unknown outside Peru, where they were overshadowed by the much larger Shining Path movement, became virtually a household name throughout much of the industrialized world after it took over the Japanese Embassy in Lima and held members of the political, military, and diplomatic elite hostage. No spectacular, however, quite compares with the image of airplanes crashing into the Twin Towers and the subsequent collapse of those bastions of American capitalism. Celebrating this case of propaganda by deed, bin Laden said to a colleague:

> Those young men [inaudible] said in deeds, in New York and Washington, speeches that overshadowed all other speeches made everywhere else in the world. The speeches are understood by both Arabs and non-Arabs, even by Chinese. It completely dominated the media.[5]

Achieving Specific Concessions

Sometimes a terrorist act is conducted in an effort to procure specific concessions. Most often the concession sought is the release of comrades imprisoned either by the country in which the incident occurs or by an ally of that country. In one of the most dramatic instances, Lebanese hijackers agreed to release 145 passengers on board TWA flight 847 in return for Israel's agreement, under intense pressure from the United States, to release 766 detained Lebanese. In another case, in December 1999, the Indian authorities agreed to negotiate with the al-Qaeda-affiliated group Harakat ul-Mujahidin (HUM) in return for the release of 154 passengers on board an Indian Airlines Airbus, flight IC-814. India released three imprisoned Islamic fundamentalists, including the British-educated Omar Sheikh. In another case, in 1974, the Japanese Red Army seized the French Embassy in The Hague and held nine hostages, including the French ambassador, until they were exchanged for one of the group's imprisoned leaders, Yoshiaki Yamada.

This strategy does not always work. The U.S. government's refusal to negotiate with Black September terrorists led to the assassination of Ambassador Cleo Noel, Deputy Chief of Mission George Curtis Moore, and a Belgian diplomat named Guy Eid in Khartoum in 1973.[6] Similarly, Pakistan's refusal to negotiate with the HUM in an earlier effort to secure the release of Omar Sheikh and Maulana Masood Azhar led to the deaths of five kidnapped Western tourists. While the U.S. government and many other governments have an official policy of no concessions to terrorists, terrorists have often, in fact, achieved their limited objectives in these circumstances.

More recently hostages have been taken in an effort to secure a commitment from the victim's government to withdraw troops from Iraq. Japanese, Romanian, and Bulgarian hostages have been taken in an effort to force their governments to withdraw. In the case of the Philippines, fifty-one medics, engineers, and soldiers were withdrawn in July 2004 in response to the kidnapping of a truck driver.

Causing Disorder

Very often terrorists act with the intention of undermining the legitimacy of the state by demonstrating that it cannot protect its citizenship. Generally, they try to make themselves more trouble than they are worth in the hope that this will encourage capitulation to their broader objectives. The IRA in Northern Ireland frequently said that its immediate goal was to make Northern Ireland ungovernable. Terence, better known as "Cheeky," Clarke, who was subsequently to become Gerry Adams's chief of security and who spent twenty-one years in prison for terrorist offenses, told the journalist Peter Taylor, "The more you hurt them, I thought, the more fed up they'll get and want to get out. At that time there were British politicians saying, 'Why are we there? Why are our boys dying?' "[7] This same dynamic is repeating itself in Iraq today.

Provoking Repression

Very often the goal of a particular action is to provoke the government to retaliate forcefully. The hope is that in so doing it will alienate the public and thereby force recruits into the arms of the movement. The Sicarii/Zealots practiced this to devastating effect. The most articulate spokesman of this tactic was the nineteenth-century Russian populist Sergey Nechayev, who advocated violent attacks to force the government into repression, deny it legitimacy, and radicalize the masses, in his famous handbook, "Cathechism of the Revolutionist." The Spanish group ETA discussed the theory behind this tactic in its Fourth Assembly, held in 1965, and formally adopted it in its Fifth Assembly. In the 1980s a prominent leader of the ETA who went by the *nom de guerre* "Antxon" complained that the Spanish authorities were becoming too professional and discriminating in their responses to ETA action.[8] This tactic, of course, lends itself to a vicious cycle of violence that has rarely brought the ultimate objective any closer.

REINFORCING ORGANIZATIONAL DYNAMICS

Occasionally a terrorist action has little to do with external actors and everything to do with the internal dynamics of the group that carries it out. A particular action may be decided upon as a test of loyalty, to enforce obedience to a code, to initiate newcomers, or to demonstrate the prowess of a particular leader or faction. On some occasions the intensity of the internal dynamics is such that the actions undermine the group. One of the more extreme examples took place in the mountains of central Japan in 1972, when fourteen members of the United Red Army were brutally killed by their peers as part of a reeducation process.

Making a Show of Strength

Often, after the capture of a leader or a particularly damaging government action, a group will commit another terrorist attack in an effort to demonstrate to the public at large, to the government, and, most important, to its own supporters, that it is still a force to be reckoned with.

After the arrest of her husband, Renato Curcio, a founder of the Red Brigades, the young Mara Cagol came into her own. A talented musician and practicing Catholic, she grew up in a conservative, supportive, and solidly middle-class family. Cagol enjoyed many activities like tennis and skiing when she wasn't performing in concerts and competing in national competitions with her favorite instrument, the classical guitar. She was also a deeply caring young woman and at the age of twenty spent long hours comforting the sick and volunteering in hospices in nearby towns. She was enormously popular among the elderly patients, who called her "La Margherita." Cagol went to college and obtained a Ph.D. in sociology.

When Curcio and several of the other leaders of the Red Brigades were captured in 1974, Cagol took over, determined to demonstrate that the organization had not been decapitated. She not only organized and sustained the movement through its first crisis but also managed to rescue her husband from prison in February 1975. She died that June in a gun battle with the carabinieri.

REVENGE, RENOWN, REACTION

All of these secondary or more immediate motives can be subsumed under three motivations: Revenge, Renown, Reaction. If we ask ourselves whether Sidique Khan, Shehzad Tanweer, Hasib Hussain, or Germaine Lindsay, the four young men who blew themselves and fifty-two others up in London on July 7, 2005, honestly thought that by placing bombs on the London Underground they were really going to hasten the return of the caliphate, the answer must be no. But if we wonder whether they expected to get revenge, renown, and reaction, then they probably did. If so, they were correct. By inflicting suffering, they presumably thought, they were simply causing the British public to reap what they had sown in the Muslim world. They got renown; the bombing managed even to sideline the much-anticipated G8 summit. The names and photos of the four suspects are familiar all over the world. The reaction they got may have disappointed them. Rather than eliciting the language and actions of warfare, even of a crusade, the British prime minister spoke instead of police work, crime scenes, and criminal investigation. There were no official attempts to denounce Muslims, though there appears to have been an increase in hate crimes and petty discrimination against British Muslims. As a result of the bombings, there has also been increasing pressure on the United Kingdom to withdraw from the wildly unpopular Iraq war, but this has been countered with a reluctance to do so for fear of being seen as giving in to terrorism.

Terrorist movements pursue these two sets of long- and short-term motivations simultaneously. Moreover, philosophical or political aspirations are of greater interest to the leadership of the movements, while followers are more attracted by the nearer-term appeal of revenge, renown, and reaction. Terrorist groups have been singularly unsuccessful in delivering the political change they seek, but they have enjoyed considerable success in achieving their near-term motives. It is this success that appeals to disaffected youths seeking a means of rapid redress.

This distinction in the interests of leaders and followers is evident across all kinds of terrorist groups. In 1971, the IRA's political cover, Sinn Féin, held a party conference (Ard Fheis) and approved political plans for a New Ireland (Eire Nua). Once they achieved Irish unification, they envisioned there would be four regional Parliaments. To the men in the street, however, this did not resonate. According to "Cheeky" Clarke: "I was politically naïve. I thought I was doing the right thing because it was for my people. . . . I hadn't a political thought in my head other than that I knew what we were doing was right because it was to get the Brits out of Ireland."[9] Another member of the IRA, Raymond Gilmore, who was subsequently to become a notorious informant, was sworn in nine years later, in 1980. He describes how he was required by the IRA's education officer to study the IRA's "Green Book" in a school building in the evenings before being allowed to join.[10]

A member of al-Qaeda told a very similar story. In his trial for terrorist conspiracy in the Federal District Court in Manhattan, Ali Muhammad told the judge that "The objective [was] . . . just to attack any Western target in the Middle East, to force the government of the Western countries just to pull out from the Middle East."[11] Young European social revolutionaries often felt the same way. One German militant explained, "Most of the comrades of my group called themselves 'anarcho–trade unionists' and so did I, although I did not really understand what it meant."[12]

PRIMARY MOTIVATIONS

Generally, ethnonationalist terrorist movements, those with political aspirations that could be realized without overthrowing the current order, have been much more clear-cut in spelling out their objectives, though generally vague on the details of a postconflict society. They suggest that in the new order present inequities will be redressed, but few offer details on how this might be accomplished. Some adopt the language of socialism or Marxism, but all are driven primarily by nationalist aspirations. Euskadi ta Askatasuna, or Basque Fatherland and Liberty (ETA), was founded in 1959 with the aim of establishing an independent Basque homeland in the northern Spanish provinces of Vizcaya, Guipúzcoa, Álava, and Navarra and the southwestern French provinces of Labourd, Basse-Navarre, and Soule.

The Kurdistan Workers' Party (PKK), founded in 1974, is composed primarily of Turkish Kurds with the goal of establishing an independent democratic Kurdish state. The Irish Republican Army (IRA) wants a united, thirty-two-county island of Ireland. The Liberation Tigers of Tamil Eelam (LTTE), better known as the Tamil Tigers, was founded in 1976 with the goal of establishing an independent Tamil state.

Maoist groups such as the Shining Path in Peru, the Communist Party of Nepal, and the Communist Party of the Philippines, better known as the New People's Army, seek to overthrow the state and replace it with a proletarian dictatorship. Each of these groups was based initially in the countryside, in keeping with Maoist dogma. In Colombia, in the words of a terrorist spokesman, "The FARC's goal is to be the government. The FARC wants to become a new government to offer the Colombian people the possibility of a worthy life. The FARC wants to begin to build socialism in Colombia."[13] The FARC appears to combine a rural insurgency with a social revolutionary leadership.

There are also a large number of smaller, more urban Marxist-Leninist groups, such as the MRTA in Peru, GRAPO in Spain, 17 November in Greece, and Dev Sol in Turkey. These contemporary groups are of a similar ilk to the social revolutionary movements that proliferated in the 1970s, such as the Japanese Red Army, the RAF in Germany, the Red Brigades in Italy, and so on. They seek to overthrow the institutions of the state and replace them with an ill-defined but perfect classless society.

Terrorist groups do not remain static. They often split in response to peace overtures as the more extreme elements reject the compromises of the leaders. Examples include the Continuity IRA and Real IRA, which split from the Provisional IRA in response to the peace process in Northern Ireland. The Palestinian movement over the years has split and split again on issues of personality, tactics, and strategy, leading to a whole array of movements with compatible but not identical aspirations.

In Chechnya, what started out as a number of nationalist groups seeking independence from Russia have become infiltrated by Islamists, who are turning what was a more narrowly focused nationalist terrorist campaign into a front in the broader-based conflict between Islamists and the West. There are three main Chechen groups today. The Riyadus-Salikhin Reconnaissance and Sabotage Battalion of Chechen Martyrs (RSRSBCM) is led by Shamil Basayev. The Special Purpose Islamic Regiment (SPIR) was led by Movzar Barayev until he was killed in the seizure of the Dubrovka Theater in Moscow in October 2002. The Islamic International Peacekeeping Brigade (IIPB) is jointly led by the Chechen Basayev and an Arab mujahedin leader, currently Abu al-Walid.

The Harakat ul-Mujahidin (HUM) in Pakistan is another case of a group with primarily a territorial objective—liberating Kashmir from India—joining forces with radical Islamist groups. The HUM signed bin Laden's 1998 fatwa against the West, and its members are now an essential part of the al-Qaeda front.

Few terrorist movements have been as consistent and coherent in spelling out their objectives as has Hezbollah. Its program stipulates:

Let us put it truthfully: the sons of Hezbollah know who are their major enemies in the Middle East—the Phalanges, Israel, France, and the United States. The sons of our *umma* [community of Muslims] are now in a state of growing confrontation with them and will remain so until the realization of the following three objectives:

a) to expel the Americans, the French, and their allies definitely from Lebanon, putting an end to any colonialist entity on our land;

    b) to submit the Phalanges to a just power and bring them all to
        justice for the crimes they have perpetuated against Muslims
        and Christians;

    c) to permit all the sons of our people to determine their future
        and to choose in all liberty the form of government they de-
        sire. We call upon all of them to pick the option of Islamic
        government, which alone is capable of guaranteeing justice
        and liberty for all. Only an Islamic regime can stop any fur-
        ther tentative attempts at imperialistic infiltration.

These are Lebanon's objectives; those are its enemies. As for our
friends, they are all the world's oppressed peoples.

This document goes on to reveal that the moderation implied by the
objectives does not run very deep. Of Israel, Hezbollah's program
states:

We see in Israel the vanguard of the United States in our Islamic
world . . . our primary assumption in our fight against Israel states
that the Zionist entity has been aggressive from its inception, and
built on lands wrested from their owners, at the expense of the
rights of the Muslim people. Therefore our struggle will end only
when this entity is obliterated. We recognized no treaty with it, no
cease-fire and no peace agreements, whether separate or consolidated.[14]

Osama bin Laden has been less consistently coherent in his articu-
lation of the objectives he is trying to achieve. In his 1998 fatwa against
Jews and Crusaders, bin Laden listed three "facts"—American occupation of Saudi Arabia, American sanctions against Iraq, and American support for Israel—as a clear declaration of war against Allah.
When asked, however, whether he would call off his jihad against the
United States if the United States were to withdraw from Arabia, bin
Laden replied that he would not stop until the United States stopped
all aggressive actions against Muslims everywhere.[15] Later in the same
interview, he referred to bringing an end not just to occupation but to
"Western and American influence on our countries." On other occasions, bin Laden has articulated an even more ambitious agenda, the

restoration of the caliphate. This would require the elimination of current political boundaries throughout the Middle East and beyond and a return, in essence, to the Middle Ages. Bin Laden, for all his carefully choreographed statements and all the colorful descriptions of the iniquities of the West, has completely failed to articulate a positive political alternative. Like other revolutionaries before him, therefore, he appears to be more enamored of the revolution itself than of the new world it would herald.

A striking and quite surprising aspect of most terrorist movements is how little of their attention is devoted to describing the new world they intend to create. They are happy to provide the outlines of their future world, such as rule by Sharia law or national independence, but they are very short on detail. They are not unique in this. Readers of Marx have invariably been disappointed by the absence of a coherent picture of the new world. In all his voluminous writing Marx devotes only a paragraph in *The German Ideology* to a description of the future, a world in which workers would have time to explore their hobbies: "While in communist society, where nobody has an exclusive sphere of activity but each can become accomplished in any branch he wishes, society regulates the general production and thus makes it possible for me to do one thing today and another tomorrow, to hunt in the morning, fish in the afternoon, rear cattle in the evening, criticize after dinner, just as I have a mind, without ever becoming hunter, fisherman, herdsman or critic."[16] Terrorist leaders today also appear altogether more interested in the process by which the present system will be destroyed than in the functioning of the new system. By contrast, Martin Luther King eloquently described his vision of the new America he sought to bring about. Possessing a vision of the future may well serve to constrain one's behavior in the present. Certainly, igniting a race war would, for King, have been unlikely to bring about a peaceful, equitable multiracial democracy. But if one does not have a coherent vision of the future, then one's means are more likely to be determined not by the needs of the society one is trying to create but rather by the iniquities of the society one is trying to destroy.

This inattention to the details of the future world they are trying to create holds true across the leaderships of very different terrorist movements. When asked by Peter Arnett of CNN in March 1997 what kind of society would be created if the Islamic movement were to take over Arabia, Osama bin Laden was extremely vague. He replied, "We are confident, with the permission of God, Praise and Glory be to him, that Muslims will be victorious in the Arabian peninsula and that God's religion, praise and glory be to him, will prevail in this peninsula. It is a great pride and a big hope that the revelation unto Mohammed, peace be upon him, will be resorted to for ruling. When we used to follow Mohammed's revelation, peace be unto him, we were in great happiness and great dignity, to God belong credit and praise."[17]

Abimael Guzmán, leader of the Maoist Shining Path, was equally vague in describing what his perfect society would be like. He responded to a sympathetic question about life after the triumph of the revolution:

> We have not studied this question sufficiently, because it involves problems that will pose themselves in the future. We have general guidelines, but we agree with what Lenin said: You want to know what war is like? Wage it. And let us have inexhaustible confidence in the international proletariat, in the oppressed nations, in the people of the worlds; and most particularly in the communists, in the parties and organizations, whatever their level of development. Holding fast to our ideology, Marxism-Leninism-Maoism, we will advance, even if we begin by feeling our way in the dark, finding temporary solutions for certain situations for brief periods of time, until we find the definitive one. As Lenin taught us, no revolution can be planned out completely ahead of time.[18]

Paul Reyes, a member of the Secretariat of Colombia's FARC and a spokesman for the organization, was also remarkably vague when asked by a sympathetic Cuban reporter what the ruling program of the FARC would be. He said:

> I must admit that we have yet to define this aspect. However, we have thought about it to some extent. We start out based on the idea that the type of government that should be installed in Colombia must be in accordance with the country's situation and in accordance with the world's technical and scientific development. We are

aware that Colombia is an immensely wealthy country, a country which can feed itself and finance itself and a country which cannot be blocked completely. We are also aware that imperialism and foreign financial capital will exert pressure, they will always exert pressure and we know this. Likewise, we believe that the socialist model we should implement in Colombia is a socialism for Colombians.[19]

The charismatic leader of the Tamil Tigers, Vellupillai Prabakharan, was only a little more specific in answer to a question posed by an Indian reporter. She asked, "If and when Eelam is achieved, what sort of a nation do you conceive it to be?" He responded:

Tamil Eelam will be a socialist state. By socialism I mean an egalitarian society where human freedom and individual liberties will be guaranteed, where all forms of oppression and exploitation will be abolished. It will be a free society where our people will have maximum opportunity to develop their economy and promote their culture. Tamil Eelam will be a neutral state, committed to nonalignment and friendly to India, respecting her regional policies, particularly the policy of making the Indian Ocean a zone of peace.[20]

The Chechen leader Shamil Basayev was asked a similar question by a Russian journalist who wanted to know who would rule Chechnya when the Russians left. He replied, "First thing that comes to mind are the words 'power to the people.' I have never sought power and I have never fought for power. I have always fought for justice and justice has been my only goal."[21]

Here we see the leaders of five of the bloodiest terrorist movements in the world whose campaigns have cost tens of thousands of lives over many years and several continents in pursuit of religious, secular, Maoist, and nationalist objectives, and none of them is able to describe the society they are trying to create.

These very vague notions of the future world are hardly enough to motivate followers to lay down their lives for the cause. By contrast, all of their statements and interviews are full of invective about the evils of their enemies. It is not so much a vision of a new world, therefore, that drives even the leaders of these groups but rather their outrage at the injustices of the present one. What appears to drive most terrorists, therefore, is not the desire or expectation of achieving the primary political objective articulated by their leaders but rather the desire for, and reasonable expectation of achieving, revenge, renown, and reaction.

THE THREE Rs: REVENGE, RENOWN, REACTION

Revenge

The most powerful theme in any conversation with terrorists past or present, leader or follower, religious or secular, left wing or right wing, male or female, young or old, is revenge. It is not the objective severity of the grievance any more than it is the objective severity of poverty that drives terrorists, but a desire for revenge is ubiquitous among them.

Suhail al-Hindi, older brother of the suicide bomber Abu-Surur, captured the power of revenge in his entry in the martyr book compiled after his brother's death:

> That day he was born for revenge . . . revenge for me and my country and my people and the honor of the umma. Revenge for Majdal from which my parents were forced to flee, despite their passionate love of their soil, despite their sweat and blood, despite their huge love of its soil. Yes, he will take revenge, he will take revenge, he will take revenge, Allah permitting. And at the moment of this cry, the soldiers of Zion were breaking into houses, searching for cells of fedayeen belonging to the Liberation army or other groups as was their wont during that long period during the history of Palestine. At the moment they entered, upon hearing the voice of Mohammad of al-Qassam, they looked into the face of the newborn and asked his mother, What is his name? And she replied in the voice of revenge, "Mohammad."[22]

Before his own death on a suicide mission, Abu-Surur approached the mother of a friend who had blown himself up and assured her, "I will kill everybody who killed your son."[23] A video he made on the eve of his death makes clear that he and his co–suicide bombers saw themselves as avenging the deaths of those who had gone before them.

The thirst for revenge pervades the posters, songs, and popular culture of the Intifada as well as the official communiqués. Posters of martyrs declare, "The right of revenge is ours." Popular songs ask, "The scoundrels have taken Palestine—who will bring revenge?" Popular poetry and ubiquitous graffiti call for vengeance. In a communiqué issued on June 4, 1994, the Qassam Battalion announced the group's responsibility for a revenge attack shortly after the Hebron massacre: "To the leadership of Israel: You turned Eid al-Fitr into a black day so we swore to turn your independence holiday into Hell. This is our first reply to the Hebron slaughter."[24]

The ideologically driven social revolutionary movements were also driven in large part by a desire for revenge. The people they chose to murder were usually held up as symbols of the corrupt capitalist system they wished to replace, but the lengthy and often turgid communiqués they delivered to the media after most of their atrocities usually spelled out more banal explanations for the selection of particular targets. After the attempted assassination in July 1990 of Hans Neusel, a senior official in the German Interior Ministry, the RAF issued a communiqué saying that it was punishing him for his crimes, that is, his work coordinating European counterterrorist efforts.[25] Similarly GRAPO, the Spanish group, issued a communiqué a day after it murdered Dr. José Ramón Muñoz in 1990. He was murdered to avenge his role in force-feeding prisoners. The communiqué declared: "The socio fascist government swine have not shrunk from applying any means to undermine the prisoners' will to resist, including force feeding to make them abandon the struggle for their just demand."[26]

The powerful appeal of revenge is equally strong among ethnonationalist movements such as the IRA. The ranks of the IRA swelled after events like "Bloody Sunday" in January 1972, in which British paratroopers shot dead thirteen Catholic civil rights marchers. Far from taking all comers, the IRA sought to ensure that recruits were not volunteering on a whim. Raymond McCartney, who later spent fifty-three days on a hunger strike while serving a life sentence for murder, remembers the devastation in his family when one of his cousins was killed on Bloody Sunday. His older brother, however, advised him not to act precipitously, but to think it over: "I should take time to make up my mind so that no one could ever accuse me of letting emotions cloud my judgment, so no one could say 'you're joining the IRA just because of Bloody Sunday.'" He waited a few months and then approached a senior IRA member to tell him that he was thinking of joining. Again he was sent away, given some books to read, and told to think through his decision. Only then was he permitted to begin the process of joining.[27]

The desire for revenge does not end with the decision to join a terrorist movement. On the contrary, once a person becomes involved in violence the grievances to be avenged multiply and the opportunities for and means of vengeance expand dramatically. In Northern Ireland, IRA members sought vengeance against the British Army for events such as Bloody Sunday and the introduction of internment. They avenged the ill treatment of prisoners by murdering prison officers and wreaked vengeance on the Protestant community for burning them from their homes.

The attacks on the Protestant community had the effect of spawning more terrorist organizations designed to wreak vengeance on them. A month after the introduction of internment without trial, the IRA expanded its attacks beyond "economic" targets. They bombed a pub in the Protestant Shankill Road, killing two. The Protestant terrorist group the UVF retaliated by bombing a "Catholic" pub. Fifteen people were killed, including the owner's wife and child, who lived upstairs. One week later the IRA took revenge by bombing a "Protestant" furniture shop. Two adults and two toddlers were killed. Several of those who arrived on the scene soon joined loyalist terrorist groups. One, Eddie Kinner, explained:

> If somebody had handed me a bomb to plant anywhere you want in the Falls (a Catholic area) I would have done it. . . . I was angry and wanted to do just as much damage to the community responsible for those actions. My mentality then would have been, whenever they blow up a location in the Shankill, killing one or two people, I would want to blow up somewhere in the Falls killing double. Doing twice the amount of damage that they were doing in my community.

When it was pointed out to him that it was not the Catholic community but the IRA who planted the bomb, he replied: "I think you're right about that, but that's not how I saw it then. I would have linked it into other events that were taking place and would have seen it as not necessarily the Catholic community carrying it out but it being done on their behalf. So they were part of it.[28]

Individual sectarian killings were one of the most gruesome aspects of the Northern Irish conflict as each side tried to avenge the other. These tit-for-tat murders were anathema to the political ideology of the organizations that carried them out. Similarly, just as large-scale events like Bloody Sunday swelled the ranks of the IRA, large-scale IRA atrocities such as Bloody Friday, when the IRA planted twenty-two bombs in the center of Belfast, swelled the ranks of Protestant paramilitary organizations.

In Italy too the dynamics of violence were driven not just by conflict between the Left and the state but by violence between left- and right-wing militant groups. Just as Catholics and Protestants became abstract, depersonalized enemies to each other in Northern Ireland, Left and Right became abstract, depersonalized enemies to each other in Italy. One militant right-wing radical explained his involvement in political violence as part of a spiral of revenge: "There had been violence against my brother, and I felt a sense of injustice that pushed me to get involved, as he was, in politics. My first attitude was one of retaliation: my mother's car had been burned, and I burned other cars. I returned to others the blows my brother had received. It grew year after year. Violence produced violence."[29] The story on the Left was quite similar. "If you see black [the fascist color] shoot at once, that was the slogan . . . there was a manhunt, without any pity, it was a hunt against the fascists that then had repercussions for us, because there was a spiral of revenge."[30]

In the narrow confines of Northern Ireland the defended community is small; the names of the victims and sometimes the victims themselves are known to their murderers. In Italy the stage was larger and the arguments different, but the dynamic was very similar. Vengeance, however, can be sought with equal fervor on behalf of a much larger group such as the world's Muslims. Nowhere is the power of revenge more vividly portrayed than in the writings of Osama bin Laden, which are suffused with the language of revenge. In appealing to the American people over the heads of their leaders in October 2004, bin Laden declared, "Just as you lay waste to our nation so shall we lay waste to yours."[31] In some cases the act for which he seeks vengeance is quite specific, such as Israel's assassination of the Hamas leader, Ahmed Yassin: "The act that horrified the world; that is the killing of the old, handicapped sheikh Ahmed Yassin, may God have mercy on him. . . . We pledge to God that we will punish America for him, God willing."[32] More often it is revenge for a long train of abuses by the United States and its allies:

> The youths hold you responsible for all of the killings and evictions of the Muslims and the violation of the Holy Places, carried out by your Zionist brothers in Lebanon; you openly supplied them with arms and finance. More than 600,000 Iraqi children have died due to lack of food and medicine and as a result of the unjustifiable aggression [sanctions] imposed on Iraq and its nation. The children of Iraq are our children. . . . Our youths knew that the humiliation suffered by Muslims as a result of the occupation of their Holy Places [Mecca and Medina in Saudi Arabia] cannot be kicked and removed except by explosions and jihad.[33]

In the infamous "Dinner Party Tape," in which bin Laden is shown discussing the September 11 attacks with a coterie of supporters, one described learning of the attacks. "I was sitting with the Shaykh [bin Laden] in a room, then I left to go to another room where there was a TV set. The TV broadcasted the big event. The screen was showing an Egyptian family in their living room, they exploded with joy. Do you know when there is a soccer game and your team wins, it was the same expression of joy. There was a subtitle that read: In revenge for the children of Al Aqsa Usama bin Laden executes an operation against America."[34]

Once the United States invaded Afghanistan, there were, of course, a great many more actions to be avenged. In November 2001, bin Laden railed against the injustice of the attack on Afghanistan:

> The entire West, with the exception of a few countries, supports this unfair, barbaric campaign, although there is no evidence of the involvement of the people of Afghanistan in what happened in America. The people of Afghanistan had nothing to do with this matter. The campaign, however, continues to unjustly annihilate the villagers and civilians, children, women and innocent people.[35]

The next month, in an interview on al-Jazeera, he spoke even more vehemently:

America bears an unspeakable crusader grudge against Islam. Those who lived these months under continuous bombardment by the various kinds of US aircraft are well aware of this. Many villages were wiped out without any guilt. Millions of people were made homeless during this very cold weather. Those oppressed men, women, and children now live in tents in Pakistan. They committed no [crime].[36]

The Iraq war has provided a great many more grievances to be avenged. Hesmat Abdul Rahman, a Jordanian mother, described how her twenty-five-year-old son, Zaid Horani, became angrier and angrier as he watched television images of the American invasion of Iraq. He and his friends became so angry that they decided "Let's go do jihad" and went off to the local mosque. Horani is now on trial, accused of establishing a recruitment network for Jordanian jihadists.[37]

The ongoing conflict between Israel and the Palestinians provides an endlessly renewable stream of recruits mobilized by a desire for revenge for endless new Israeli atrocities. In the minds of those avenging them, these new atrocities are all mixed in with received wisdom about earlier Israeli actions. One incarcerated Islamist declared:

You Israelis are Nazis in your souls and in your conduct. In your occupation you never distinguish between men and women, or between old people and children. You adopted methods of collective punishment, you uprooted people from their homeland and from their homes and chased them into exile. You fired live ammunition at women and children. You smashed the skulls of defenseless civilians. You set up detention camps for thousands of people in sub-human conditions. You destroyed homes and turned children into orphans. You prevented people from making a living, you stole their property, you trampled on their honor. Given that kind of conduct, there is no choice but to strike at you without mercy in every possible way.[38]

In Europe, too, members of social revolutionary groups describe themselves as being radicalized by encounters with an "unfair" state.

One young militant looking back remembered it this way: "We reacted with stones against those who had guns . . . and clubs. This difference was for me a justification: it legitimized the defensive use of violence."[39] In both Italy and Germany the death of activists at the hands of either the police or their enemies on the Right had a dramatic radicalizing effect. A former Italian activist remembered, "The deaths . . . were the moment when rage and the desire to rebel came to possess all of us. . . . Those deaths gave us a strange feeling, almost as if it were not possible to go back anymore."[40] A desire for revenge, therefore, can get people to join a terrorist movement in the first place, but once they are involved it keeps them there, as the conflict provides so many other grievances to be avenged and so many opportunities to seek vengeance.

From a counterterrorist point of view there is a limit to what can be done to deny terrorists the revenge they desire. There is little correlation between the nature of a grievance and the vehemence of the power for revenge. Once engaged in a campaign against terrorism, however, a state can take care not to provide excuses for those wishing to use violence. Unlike revenge, however, which terrorists take for themselves, renown has to be given by others, by a complicit community, or by the adversary.

Renown

Publicity has always been a central objective of terrorism. It brings attention to the cause and spreads the fear terrorism instills. Renown, however, implies more than simple publicity. It also implies glory. Terrorists seek both individual glory and glory for the cause in an effort to redress the humiliation they perceive themselves as having suffered. For the leaders this glory comes on the national or, increasingly, global stage. For the followers, glory in their own community is enough.

The fact that terrorists have been extremely successful in gaining publicity has led some observers to conclude, rather simplistically, that terrorism works. If the goal of terrorism were simply publicity, one could conclude that it does work, but one could also devise a ready means of defeating it: deny it publicity. The sensitivity of al-Qaeda to publicity was spelled out in an article on the movement's online magazine, al-Ansar, by Abu Ubeid al-Qurashi, a leading member of the group. He wrote that the 1972 "Munich Massacre" was the greatest media victory, and the first true proclamation to the entire world of the first of the Palestinian resistance movements . . .

In truth, the Munich operation was a great propaganda strike. Four thousand journalists and radio personnel and two thousand commentators and television technicians were there to cover the Olympic Games; suddenly, they were broadcasting the suffering of the Palestinian people. Thus, 900 million people in 100 countries were witness to the operation by means of television screens. This meant that at least a quarter of the world knew what was going on at Munich; after this, they could no longer ignore the Palestinian tragedy.

The September 11 [operation] was an even greater propaganda coup. It may be said that it broke a record in propaganda dissemination.[41]

He was of course right; the depiction of the collapsing towers made Osama bin Laden and al-Qaeda into household names all over the world.

There have been any number of lesser examples of terrorists gaining attention, though rarely sympathy, for their cause through terrorist atrocities. IRA bomb attacks in both Britain and Northern Ireland have won widespread recognition of the organization's aspirations. The kidnap and subsequent murder of the former prime minister and elder statesman Aldo Moro by the Italian Red Brigades received extensive coverage. The release of sarin gas on the Tokyo subway by the Japanese Aum Shinrikyo cult brought international notoriety to a group largely unknown even inside Japan. The siege of a school in Beslan by Chechen rebels brought the issue of Chechnya to the world's televisions. The larger the number of casualties, the more innovative the tactic, the greater the symbolic significance of the target, the more heinous the crime, the more publicity accrues to the perpetrators.

The timing of bin Laden's October 2004 "Message to America" was clearly designed to gain maximum publicity, timed as it was to appear right before the American election. This video also reveals the desire for more than publicity. Gone were the Kalashnikov and the rugged mountainous terrain; instead, bin Laden was seated behind a desk, playing the part of a statesman, addressing the American people over the heads of their leaders.

Abimael Guzmán was known to his followers in the Shining Path as Chairman Gonzalo. He placed himself among the pantheon of Communist revolutionaries with his program known as "Gonzalo Thought." He described it as follows:

> It is the application of Marxism-Leninism-Maoism to the Peruvian revolution that has produced Gonzalo Thought. Gonzalo Thought has been forged in the class struggle of our people, mainly the proletariat, in the incessant struggles of the peasantry, and in the larger framework of the world revolution, in the midst of these earthshaking battles, applying as faithfully as possible the universal truths to the concrete conditions of our country.[42]

Guzmán evidently saw himself and sought to be seen as a world-historical figure through his leadership of the Peruvian peasantry of the Ayacucho region.

Other terrorists too have delighted in the attention their global exploits have brought them. When he was captured in Pakistan, Ramzi Yousef, subsequently convicted for his role in the 1993 attack on the World Trade Center, had a large collection of newspaper clippings about his exploits. Similarly, the infamous Carlos "The Jackal," among whose more famous exploits was his kidnapping of the OPEC oil ministers in Vienna in 1973, also carefully clipped newspaper articles about himself. He once declared to a colleague, "The more I'm talked about the more dangerous I appear. That's all the better for me."[43]

Mere membership in a terrorist group also brings a degree of glory to the rank and file. This is true across different kinds of terrorist groups. A nationalist member of Fatah reported, "After recruitment, my social status was greatly enhanced. I got a lot of respect from my acquaintances, and from the young people in the village."[44] An IRA member, Shane Paul O'Doherty, who was sentenced to thirty life sentences for his bombing campaign in England, later described how he felt when waging his war against Britain: "I was no longer an insignificant teenager. I became heroic overnight. I felt almost drunk with power."[45]

Organizations understand this and treat their "patriot dead," as the IRA calls them, or their "martyrs," as Islamic fundamentalists call them, with great respect. The likenesses and names of those who have died for the cause are to be found in the streets of Gaza, the West Bank, Derry, and Belfast. Moreover, the status of the families of those who have died for the cause, whether in Gaza, Belfast, or Sri Lanka, is increased. One Islamist prisoner explained:

> Families of terrorists who are wounded, killed or captured enjoyed a great deal of economic aid and attention. And that strengthened popular support for the attacks. Perpetrators of armed attacks were seen as heroes, their families got a great deal of material assistance, including the construction of new homes to replace those destroyed by the Israeli authorities as punishment for terrorist acts.[46]

Shane O'Doherty describes how he threw nail bombs at British soldiers at the age of sixteen and almost hoped that he would be shot dead, "fantasizing that his sacrifice would inspire a mural, or better yet, a song," ensuring his immortality.[47]

Many terrorist groups engage in complex rituals to convey a sense of glory to their followers. Members eagerly participate. Frankie Ryan would die in 1991 while planting an IRA bomb in St. Albans, England. The bomb was to have exploded while members of a military band were playing to a civilian audience in the town's civic center. Before going on the operation, Frankie bought the tricolor that was to wrap his coffin. The funerals of fallen soldiers are another way in which significance and glory are conveyed to members of terrorist groups by the organization. Military escorts, flag-draped coffins, rifle volleys, and patriotic speeches over the grave are ways of investing glory on people who might easily be perceived as ignominious murderers. In bin Laden's words, "Being killed for Allah's cause is a great honor achieved by only those who are the elite of the nation. We love this kind of death for Allah's cause as much as you like to live."[48]

Many terrorist leaders delight in their status of being most wanted. This too invests them with glory. When an Indian journalist asked

Prabakharan what it felt like to be the most wanted man in Sri Lanka, he answered by invoking a terrorist leader from the other side of the world: "An Irish leader once remarked that when the British indict a person as a terrorist it implied that he was a true Irish patriot. Similarly when the Sri Lanka government refers to me as the most wanted man it means that I am a true Tamil patriot. Hence I feel proud to be indicted as a wanted man."[49] A Russian journalist prefaced a question to Shamil Basayev by referring to him as "the second most wanted terrorist in the world." Basayev replied, "First of all I'm not the second. And secondly, I'm not wanted. I myself am trying to find these terrorists. I'm looking for them in all of Russia And I'll keep on looking and I'll keep on finding them. And I'll keep on punishing them. So, don't tell me they're trying to find me. I'm trying to find them."[50] Abimael Guzmán was also asked a similar question: How does it feel to be the man most wanted by the repressive forces of the government? He replied in terms similar to those of his counterparts in other countries: "It feels like you're doing your job and working hard at it."[51] For his part, bin Laden delighted in the popularity of the September 11 attacks. In a statement two months after the attacks, he invoked public opinion polls, saying, "Polls show that the vast majority of the sons of the Islamic world were happy about these strikes."[52] In one of his stranger comments, bin Laden seemed almost peeved when he complained at American hypocrisy in calling militant Muslims terrorists while receiving the Irish republican leader, Gerry Adams, in the White House.[53]

Reaction

Terrorists, no matter what their ultimate objectives, invariably are action-oriented people operating in an action-oriented in-group. It is through action that they communicate to the world. This phenomenon has been called "propaganda by deed." Action demonstrates their existence and their strength. In taking action, therefore, they want to elicit a reaction.

Terrorists often have wildly optimistic expectations of the reactions their action will elicit: American and Israeli withdrawal from the Middle East, British withdrawal from Northern Ireland, the collapse of capitalism. There are several revealing accounts of the first meeting between British politicians and leaders of the IRA in July 1972, including

Martin McGuinness and a very young Gerry Adams, who was released from Long Kesh internment camp for the occasion.[54] The British officials were stunned by the expectations of their interlocutors, whom they considered, at best, young hooligans. The IRA representatives insisted upon an immediate declaration from Britain of its intent to withdraw from Northern Ireland and for the withdrawal to be completed by January 1, 1975.[55] In the 1970s, former members of European social revolutionary movements similarly remember drinking and celebrating the imminent collapse of the capitalist states in which they lived.[56] For radical Islamists their faith that Allah is on their side best explains their optimism. In the words of the Taliban leader, Mullah Muhammad Omar, "America is very strong. Even if it were twice as strong or twice that, it could not be strong enough to defeat us. We are confident that no one can harm us if God is with us."[57] This optimism is reinforced by the group members, who create their own reality. The more isolated from their society they become, the more their optimistic fantasies go unchallenged.

It appears as though terrorists rarely have a very coherent idea of what kind of reaction they will get. They often expect complete capitulation. Bin Laden and other terrorist leaders constantly invoke the U.S. departure from Lebanon and Somalia after the death of American servicemen as evidence of American cowardice and corruption. They seem to extrapolate that after they have killed some Americans again, the United States will simply withdraw. On other occasions terrorists clearly hope to provoke a forcible response from their adversaries. By provoking democratic governments into draconian repression, they can demonstrate to the world that the governments really are the fascists they believe them to be. Moreover, the experience of state repression will bring new recruits to the fold. This approach has been advocated by theorists from Nechayev to Marighella and self-consciously practiced by groups as different as the nationalist ETA and the social revolutionary Red Brigades.

It is often thought that bin Laden was deliberately trying to provoke a war between Islam and the West by the 9/11 attacks. He hoped that the United States would respond militarily and that the Islamic world would then unite against it. It is also perfectly possible that bin Laden was simply trying to provoke any reaction and that either withdrawal or repression, capitulation or crusade would serve his purpose. In a famous essay, bin Laden's second in command, Ayman al-Zawahiri, explained why he thought it necessary to attack the United States:

> The masters in Washington and Tel Aviv are using the regimes [like Saudi Arabia, Egypt and Jordan] to protect their interests and to fight the battle against the Muslims on their behalf. If the shrapnel from the battle reaches their homes and bodies, they will trade accusations with their agents about who is responsible for this. In that case, they will face one of two bitter choices: Either personally wage battle against the Muslims, which means the battle will turn into clear cut jihad against infidels, or they reconsider their plans after acknowledging the failure of the brutal and violent confrontation against Muslims. Therefore we must move the battle to the enemy's grounds to burn the hands of those who ignite fire in our countries.[58]

So long as there is a reaction, therefore, the terrorist purpose is served.

———

Not reacting is hardly an option for a democratic country with a free press. The actions of the terrorists and the spectacular nature of their attacks are designed to make good television coverage. The media then become tools for terrorists to spread fear. Though it should be said that the media rarely spread sympathy for or understanding of terrorists, they do publicize their actions and thereby serve their purpose. The public are frightened and insist on action to ensure their security. It is part of the power of terrorism that the fear it spreads, due to the random nature of the victims, tends to be out of all proportion to the actual threat posed. In an effort to try to ensure the safety of their citizens and to demonstrate their competence, governments invariably react strongly, and often forcibly. Moreover, if governments do not act, not only do they jeopardize their own political survival, but they run the risk that terrorists will feel compelled to commit ever-larger atrocities in order to elicit a reaction.

Al-Qaeda's al-Qurashi declared triumphantly: "The Western propaganda machine's size did not keep it from being defeated by Sheikh Osama with what resembled a judo move. The aggressive Westerners became accustomed to observing the tragedies of others—but on September 11 the opposite happened."[59] Al-Qaeda insists upon a confrontation with the West and refuses to allow itself to be ignored. Its release of audio- and videotapes threatening the security of its adversaries, and the bombings in various parts of the world, all serve to magnify the threat it poses. As the first purpose of any government is to defend its citizens, governments are compelled to react. The competitive nature of Western democracies and the short-term thinking that is encouraged by the electoral cycle combine to ensure that governments react forcefully and quickly. Speed and force are both critical elements in a successful military campaign; it is far less clear that they are necessary ingredients of a successful counterterrorism policy.

Terrorists rarely have territory under their control. They have no structures to which they can point. Their clandestine existence means that the only way that they can demonstrate their existence is to act. In so doing they communicate not only with their adversaries but also with their supporters and their followers throughout the world. By reacting, governments communicate for them too. By bombing their training camps or labeling them public enemy number one, governments also demonstrate the existence and strength of their terrorist adversaries. Any government that refused to react, however, would soon be dismissed as weak. President Jimmy Carter failed to win reelection in 1980 in large part because he was perceived as weak in the face of terrorist aggression. He sought to address underlying conditions that he thought spawned terrorism, and he failed in the effort to rescue the Americans held hostage in Tehran. In South America civilian governments were replaced by the military when they were perceived as weak in the face of terrorism. In Uruguay the terrorism of the Tupamaros was used to justify a military coup against a democratic government in 1973. In Brazil the terrorism of Action for National Liberation (ALN) was used to justify the transformation of a moderate military regime into a repressive military dictatorship. In both Brazil and Uruguay, the brutal behavior of the military state did succeed in destroying the terrorist movements, but the costs were far higher than any democracy could pay. Part of the genius of terrorism, therefore, is that it elicits a reaction that furthers the interests of the terrorists more often than their victims.

HUMILIATION

The powerful appeal of renown and the desire for a reaction are clearly related to the fact that terrorists are attempting to redress a perceived sense of humiliation. Sometimes this is a personal experience. Eamon Collins, who would become a cold-blooded member of the IRA before he betrayed it and was assassinated, wrote of one of the turning points in his decision to join the IRA. He was visiting a hunger striker, Raymond McCreesh, a neighborhood friend, in prison when he gave another prisoner some cigarettes. "A screw [prison officer] yelled at me that if I was caught doing that again I'd never be allowed back in. I had to swallow his dressing down, feeling humiliated in front of Raymond. At that moment I thought that if I had a gun I would shoot the bastard, and I left the prison an angry man."[60] There is no doubt that several people can experience the same situation and not all would consider it humiliating. Nevertheless, the experience of humiliation is a constant refrain among members of terrorist organizations.

The experience of humiliation occurs at several levels. In many cases individuals feel personally humiliated. Communities also feel collective humiliation, as Palestinians passing through checkpoints in and out of Israel commonly do. In Northern Ireland the marches by Protestant members of the Orange Order in full regalia through Catholic areas of Northern Ireland were invariably perceived by the Catholic residents as designed to assert Protestant ascendancy and to remind Catholics that their forefathers had lost historical encounters such as the Battle of the Boyne in 1691. Bernard Lewis has written of the broad-based sense of humiliation among Muslims who have witnessed the relative political, economic, and cultural decline of Islam in the face of Western advancement.[61]

The desire for glory as well as publicity can be understood against this background of a pervasive sense of humiliation. The evident pleasure of so many people after September 11 must be seen in this light. It was not pleasure that individual human beings were massacred but pleasure that the mighty and arrogant United States had been brought down by one of their own, a David-and-Goliath story.

Bin Laden's statements and interviews constantly reassert his desire to redress Muslim humiliation. Declaring to his followers, "Death is better than life in humiliation," bin Laden calls on his Muslim brothers "to expel the enemy, humiliated and defeated, out of the sanctuaries of Islam."[62] Bin Laden's belief in the liberating power of violence is evident throughout. This theme is repeated by his followers. In a pre-attack video made by one of the 9/11 hijackers, Ahmad al-Haznawi al-Ghamidi declared, "The time of humiliation is over. It is time to kill the Americans in their own backyard, among their sons, and near their forces and intelligence."[63]

Bin Laden's insistence on the equivalence of Muslim and Western lives, his insistence on his right to possess nuclear weapons, and his efforts to establish himself as an interlocutor on equal footing with Western leaders by offering a truce or addressing specific leaders are driven by his refusal to take a subordinate position to anyone.[64] The successful defeat of the Soviets in Afghanistan was a point of enormous pride for Islamists but was followed by the humiliation of the deployment of American troops on Saudi soil.[65] By challenging the only remaining superpower, bin Laden is asserting the pride of Islam and refusing "servitude to anyone but Allah."[66]

––––––

Terrorists need rely only on themselves to get revenge. They take it; it is not given to them. Terrorists also want renown, and they cannot get this for themselves. It must be given to them by their community and their adversaries. The desire for renown, over and above simple publicity, speaks to the desire to redress the perceived sense of humiliation at the hands of the enemy and is linked to the conviction most terrorists have that they are acting morally and on behalf of others. Finally, terrorists want to elicit a reaction to their action that will demonstrate their strength and communicate their message. Terrorists appear more interested in the scale of the reaction than the details. They can countenance opposite reactions, from capitulation to widespread repression, and be almost equally pleased. By focusing on these more immediate objectives rather than the underlying political change terrorists seek, we can get a much clearer picture of the situation we face today.

FIVE

WHY DO TERRORISTS KILL THEMSELVES?

Dulce et decorum est pro patria mori.[1]

—Horace (65–8 B.C.)

*Whole regiments melted in a few minutes, but others took their place,
only to perish in the same way. "It is a battle of madmen in the midst of
a volcanic eruption" was the description of a staff captain . . . they
fought in tunnels, screaming with the lust of butchery.*

—The New York Times, 1916[2]

ON JULY 7, 2005, THIRTY-YEAR-OLD MOHAMMAD SIDIQUE
Khan traveled from his home in Leeds to London with three
friends. Mr. Khan was the father of a fourteen-month-old daughter, Maryam, and worked as a mentor for elementary school children
with learning disabilities. He was a well-respected teacher and a committed advocate for the children he taught. One of his pupils said of
him that "He seemed a really kind man, he taught the really bad kids
and everyone seemed to like him."[3] Mr. Khan was born in Leeds to
parents from Pakistan. He was raised in Beeston and attended univer-

sity in Leeds, where he met his Indian wife, Hasina Patel. His mother-in-law was also a dedicated educator and had received an award at a royal ceremony for her work as a teacher specializing in bilingual studies.

Traveling with Mr. Khan was twenty-two-year-old Shehzad Tanweer. The younger man was social and sporty. He loved cricket and martial arts and enjoyed driving his father's Mercedes. He studied sports science at Leeds Metropolitan University, and in his bedroom in his family's house he displayed the trophies he had won at school for athletics. Born in Bradford, he had moved to Leeds at the age of two with his parents and three siblings. His father was a successful small businessman who had been born in Pakistan. The family had no financial worries, and his parents were loving and supportive. A friend described him as "not interested in politics" and added, "He is sound as a pound."[4]

Mr. Khan and Mr. Tanweer traveled by train with two friends to London the day after the city had been selected by the International Olympic Committee to host the 2012 Olympics. The attention of the news media, however, had moved to Scotland, where the G8 summit was taking place. The four friends arrived together at Kings Cross station and then separated to go on four different Tube lines. Mr. Khan entered the third carriage of a train bound for Liverpool Street. Mr. Tanweer took the second carriage on a Circle Line train. At 8:50 they blew up themselves and everything around them. Together with their two colleagues they killed fifty-six people, including themselves, and injured seven hundred in the first suicide attack in Europe. A group calling itself al-Qaeda Europe claimed responsibility for the attack.

SUICIDE TERRORISM

Few terrorist tactics have elicited as powerful a sense of horror as suicide bombing. It is all the more troubling because it is so effective. The tactic is not only growing in popularity, it is also growing in geographic reach. From 1981 to 1999, suicide attacks took place in seven countries. Since 2000, they have taken place in about twenty. The year 2005 witnessed escalation in a number of other dimensions too, including the appearance in London of British-born suicide terrorists, the emergence in Iraq of a Belgian-born female suicide bomber, and in

Jordan of a husband-and-wife team acting in the name of al-Qaeda in Iraq.

Suicide terrorism is deeply unsettling as it suggests a degree of fanatical commitment to a cause with which we feel quite unfamiliar. It is further unsettling because there are so few obvious countermeasures. No threats of punishment are likely to influence someone who is willing to kill himself or herself. The American public has grown familiar with the concept of deterrence. This is the edifice upon which our national security has rested since 1945. By threatening massive retaliation against our enemies, we deterred hostile action against us. This policy defended us against the armed might of the Soviet Union, yet is toothless in the face of small groups of fanatics willing to kill themselves. Suicide terrorism is unsettling to us because it does not quite fit the popular image of terrorists as self-serving evildoers. In willingly taking their own lives, terrorists are staking a claim to moral superiority that is quite incompatible with our notion of their moral depravity.

If one accepts the perspective on terrorism that I have been presenting, however, one sees that there is nothing fundamentally different about suicide terrorism. Suicide terrorism today is simply the tactic of choice among many terrorist groups, much as hijacking was in the 1970s. I have argued that terrorists are motivated by both long-term political objectives and short-term immediate objectives and that the most powerful of these are the three Rs of Revenge, Renown, and Reaction. Suicide terrorism has been growing in popularity precisely because it has proven to be an effective means of exacting revenge, attaining renown, and eliciting a reaction. As with terrorists generally, the necessary components for suicide operations are a disaffected individual, a supportive and enabling community, and a legitimizing ideology.

In killing themselves in order to kill others, suicide terrorists are behaving in a way that is entirely consistent with the behavior of soldiers throughout the ages. Military historians long ago convinced us that what drove young men over the trenches and out of the foxholes was fierce loyalty to their small band of brothers. This may appear surprising, as we tend to think of suicide attacks as individual actions, but in fact there has been no recorded case of a terrorist simply deciding to become a martyr, finding the explosives, and making a plan. Instead, in every known martyrdom operation, a group plays an essential role in planning the terrorist attack and in training, sustaining, and supervising the volunteer. The average martyrdom operation requires a supporting cast of about ten others. Societies the world over reserve their highest honors for those who have given their lives for their country. Public squares everywhere are filled with monuments to those who have been victorious in battle. Suicide terrorists seek honors like these, and their handlers make sure that they get them.

HISTORICAL PRECEDENTS

The most frequently cited precursors to contemporary suicide terrorists are the Jewish Sicarii in the first century and the Islamic Assassins in medieval times. Both showed complete disregard for their own lives, and the Assassins in particular had a culture of martyrdom reminiscent of the culture one finds today in the Gaza Strip. The difference between them and those we know today is that for these earlier groups, who murdered by stabbing their victims, it was not necessary to kill themselves in order to kill their victim. Psychologists such as Ariel Merari argue that this difference is essential. He argues that a commitment to undertake an operation with a very small chance of success is psychologically quite different from undertaking an operation that requires one's own mortality, for which there is no possibility of escape.[5] By this thinking the ancient groups would have more in common with contemporary terrorist operations such as the Lod Airport attack in 1972 by the Japanese terrorist group the JRA, or indeed the willingness to climb out over the trenches at the Somme, in which there was very little chance, but still the theoretical possibility, of survival. Psychologists are no doubt correct in making this distinction, but for our purposes it is not relevant, as the motivating factors were, I believe, the same. (In the case of the attack on the Lod Airport in Tel Aviv, in which three terrorists massacred twenty-five people and injured seventy-six in a gun-and-grenade attack, the terrorists did not expect to survive. Two were killed, but one, Kozo Okamoto, survived and was sentenced to life in prison.)

Less well known are the historical cases in which anticolonial campaigns by Muslims in India, Indonesia, and the Philippines deployed the tactic against militarily superior European and American colonial powers.[6] There were significant similarities between these campaigns in Malabar, Atjeh, and the Philippines. In each case the *shaheed* (martyr) or *juramentado* (one who took the oath), as the Spanish called him, would prepare by engaging in certain religious rites and prayers, then dress in white uncut cloth, the uniform of *hajj* or pilgrimage, and the burial shroud before flinging himself on the enemy. In each case a heroic literature emerged with songs and poems glorifying martyrdom. Individual sacrifices were vividly memorialized and the divine rewards for martyrdom widely promulgated. Volunteers were generally very young, though occasionally very old, and all were impoverished. At the time both Dutch psychiatrists and British administrators independently concluded that suicide terrorists were not suffering from any particular psychological disorder. It is taking years for contemporary observers to relearn the lesson. The cases are also instructive in that neither the British, French, nor Spanish authorities succeeded in defeating the tactic by either improved police work or military reprisal. These campaigns ended only when the broader political climate changed.

While religion provided the legitimizing ideology for these earlier groups, this has not always been the case. For the Turkish PKK, Marxism-Leninism was the ideology, and for the Tamil Tigers and several Palestinian groups, it was nationalism. The PKK carried out fifteen suicide attacks in a three-year period, from 1996 to 1999. Most were directed against police and military targets and were carried out by women. The tactic was adopted in a deliberate attempt to escalate pressure on the government in the wake of the capture of the movement's leader, Abdullah Öcalan. Öcalan asked his followers to use suicide operations to secure his release from prison. When the tactic failed, Öcalan called it off. In this instance there was no broad-based effort to support the martyrs, nor did a culture of heroism emerge around them. Rather, a few long-serving members of the organization resorted briefly to the tactic in the face of the disastrous capture of their leader. While the tactic did not achieve its object in securing Öcalan's release, which was a fairly fanciful aspiration to begin with, it was also not very effective. Each attack resulted in the death of fewer than two victims, which by the standards of suicide terrorism is very anemic indeed.

The Tamil Tigers have been altogether more serious and effective in their use of suicide terrorism. Alone of terrorist groups, the LTTE has assassinated two heads of state, Prime Minister Rajiv Gandhi of India in 1991 and Sri Lankan President Ranasinghe Premadasa in 1993.

The current president of Sri Lanka, Chandrika Kumaratunga, was severely injured in another LTTE terrorist attack and has survived at least four attempted assassinations by the LTTE, which has murdered government ministers, local politicians, and moderate Tamil leaders. It has attacked naval ships, oil tankers, the airport in the country's capital, Colombo, and Sri Lanka's most sacred Buddhist relic, the Temple of the Tooth. It has also attacked Colombo's World Trade Center and the Central Bank as well as the Joint Operations Command, the nerve center of the Sri Lankan security forces. Unlike other suicide terrorists, its members do not deliberately target civilians, but they kill large numbers of them regardless. In the attack on the Central Bank in 1996, for example, ninety people were killed.

Until the escalation in the use of suicide terrorism among the insurgents in Iraq, the LTTE had carried out more suicide attacks than any other terrorist group. Different academics count incidents differently, so while there may not be agreement on the precise figures, there is agreement on the scale. By one such account, Robert Pape calculates that between 1987 and 2001, 143 Tamil Tigers carried out 76 suicide attacks, killing 901 people.[7] Most other reliable accounts put the figure much higher. *Jane's Intelligence Review* says there were 168 LTTE suicide attacks in this period, while Luca Ricolfi says 191.[8] The LTTE itself claims to have carried out 147 suicide operations between 1987 and 1999, but it claims responsibility publicly only for military attacks, not attacks on civilians, politicians, or economic targets.[9] More important than the precise number of attacks is the fact that until recently the most consistent and deadly deployer of suicide attacks was not a religious group but a nationalist one.[10] Its ideology is the entirely secular one of national liberation. Its commitment is fueled by hatred of the enemy and desire to avenge its attacks, not by God.

The Tamil Tigers have a special elite unit called the Black Tigers that specializes in suicide missions. The Birds of Freedom, a special unit of female terrorists, contributes Black Tigresses. The LTTE deploys the Black Tigers strategically both to compensate for its military weakness relative to government forces and also to carry out difficult operations, such as the assassination of senior politicians, without having to worry about an escape plan. The commitment of members of the movement to the cause of national liberation is evidenced by the fact that each member carries a cyanide capsule that she or he will take in the event of arrest, a demonstration of commitment that has a practical side, as members know that taking the capsule will spare them brutal treatment by the security forces. More than 600 Tamil Tigers are reported to have died in this way.[11] Taking one's life to avoid torture and probable death is a defensive act of prudence, though it speaks to the power of the commitment to the cause. Willingly volunteering for offensive martyrdom operations is something else.

Just as Islamists reject the notion of suicide and prefer martyrdom, so too the Tamils. The Tamil word for suicide is *thatkolai;* the Tamil Tigers prefer *thatkodai,* meaning "to give yourself."[12] As with other terrorist movements, the LTTE has more volunteers for the role of martyrdom than it has need for. A person who wishes to become a Black Tiger or Tigress writes a letter of application to the organization's leader, Vellupillai Prabakharan. He then goes through each application and selects only those he considers most suitable based on his sense of their emotional stability, motivation, experience, and family circumstances. His preference is for young people, usually aged between fourteen and sixteen, and for girls, who form about two thirds of the suicide squads.[13] This preference appears to be more tactical than philosophical. As Palestinian groups have found, women generally find it easier to conceal explosives in their clothes and tend to be searched less rigorously when stopped.

The LTTE, like other groups, has developed a cult of hero worship around those who deliberately die for the cause. Prabakharan apparently has said, "The death of a liberation hero is not a normal event of death. This death is an event of history, a lofty ideal, a miraculous event which bestows life. The truth is that a liberation tiger does not die. . . . Indeed, what is called 'flame of his aim' which has shone for his life will not be extinguished. The aim is like a fire, like a force in history and it takes hold of others. The national soul of the people has been touched and awakened."[14] Those selected for suicide receive special training and are considered the elite corps. Prior to going out on an operation, they are said to have a final meal with Prabakharan himself and to have their picture taken with him.[15]

The Tamil Tigers ensure that their martyrs are accorded renown among the Tamil community. The names of deceased Black Tigers are publicized along with their rank so that they can be honored in Tamil newspapers and Web sites. Their garlanded photos adorn the walls of the Tigers' training camps. When they go on their mission, many carry identity cards to ensure that their identity will be known. Sometimes they film their attacks. CDs with songs of tribute to the martyrs and videos of their attack on the airport can be bought in shops in Tamil-controlled areas. They have their very own "Heroes' Day," July 5, which is the anniversary of the first LTTE suicide attack in 1987. This day of remembrance is separate from the movement's "Heroes' Day" on November 27 each year. This pattern is exactly the same as the practice in Lebanon, where "Martyrs' Day" is celebrated each year on November 11 in commemoration of Hezbollah's first suicide bomber, who exploded himself at an Israeli military post on that date in 1982.

Local Tamil districts construct memorials to Black Tigers who came from their area. These memorials consist of a photograph that is garlanded with flowers on Black Tigers Day and a flame of sacrifice lit in front of each one. Those who have died for the cause are given the title *mahaveera*, meaning "brave one," and their mother is called *veeravati*, or "brave mother." In the Kantharuban Arivuchcholai orphanage in Tamil-controlled territory, there is a shrine. It contains a picture of Kantharuban, who blew himself up in 1991, and a picture of the first and most famous of the Tamil Tigers' suicides, Captain Miller, who drove a truck full of explosives into an army camp and killed forty soldiers. The children in the orphanage learn that at his meal with Prabakharan on the eve of his operation Kantharuban, an orphan himself, requested that a home be built for children like him.[16]

Along with the appeal of attaining renown, the desire for revenge is everywhere. Twenty-two-year-old Mahendran, whose three brothers were killed fighting for the Tigers, explained why he too was thinking of joining: "The harassment that I and my parents have suffered at the hands of the army makes me want to take revenge. It is a question of Tamil pride, especially after so much sacrifice."[17] Another young man destined to be a suicide terrorist explained that he thought the action was necessary to get a reaction, to get a homeland: "This is the most supreme sacrifice I can make. The only way we can get our *eelam* [homeland] is through arms. This is the only way anybody will listen to us."[18]

Those who volunteer to be suicide terrorists in Sri Lanka do so not with visions of virgins in Paradise on their minds, nor with guarantees that Allah will look after those they have left behind. They volunteer to avenge the atrocities committed against their communities, to further the cause of national liberation, and to bring glory to themselves. They do so because they have been personally affected by the conflict in which they live, because their community supports their action, and because their movement's ideology legitimizes it. Religion has nothing to do with it. A man whose three sons died fighting for the Tamil Tigers, one of whom was a Black Tiger who blew himself up, said that on learning of the death of his third son, "It was heartbreaking but I also knew that they had done it for a cause, for the country, for the people. I bore the sadness, with the thought that they were doing a very desirable thing."[19]

Many of the martyrdom operations in the Middle East have also been carried out by secular, rather than religious, groups. The current wave of suicide terrorist attacks began in December 1981, and the first target, ironically in light of how the tactic has since developed, was the Iraqi government of Saddam Hussein. This attack took place in the context of the Iran-Iraq War. This was the war that witnessed the phenomenon known as human-wave attacks, in which thousands of very young Iranians, many completely unarmed, stormed Iraqi positions or deployed their bodies to demine vast tracts of land in massive suicidal assaults.[20] Not much is known about this Iranian wartime tactic, but its influence on the godfathers of modern suicide terrorism, the Lebanese Hezbollah, is unmistakable.

In the first reported attack, a man drove a car laden with explosives into the Iraqi Embassy in Beirut, killing himself as well as sixty-one others and injuring many more. The Iraqi government blamed Iranian and Syrian intelligence officials. In this period there were estimated to be more than a thousand Iranian Revolutionary Guards in Lebanon.[21] They sought to influence the outcome of the ongoing civil war by bankrolling and training the groups that were to emerge as Hezbollah. The systematic use of the tactic of suicide bombing began a little over a year later.

The year 1983 witnessed the full-scale emergence on the modern scene of suicide terrorism. On April 18, 1983, a truck containing a large amount of explosives was driven into the American Embassy in Beirut and killed 80 people. On October 23, both the U.S. Marine barracks and the headquarters of the French paratroopers were hit by car bombs driven by suicide terrorists; 241 people, 220 Marines, and 21 other U.S. servicemen were killed in one blast, and 58 French paratroopers and 2 civilians were killed in the other. A couple of weeks later, on November 4, a driver bent on suicide drove a car full of explosives into the Israeli government building in Tyre, southern Lebanon, killing 88 people, almost exactly a year after a similar attack in the same place that had killed 90 people, including 15 civilians. The following month, December 1983, the American Embassy in Kuwait was hit by yet another suicide attack.

These early attacks were carried out by Islamist militants, but, as with every successful military tactic, its adoption soon spread. By 1986, several secular Lebanese groups, like the Socialist National Party, the Communist Party, the Lebanese Ba'ath Party, and the Syrian Ba'ath Party were all carrying out suicide attacks. These secular groups were backed by the Syrian government, whose agents recruited, trained, and equipped the operatives.[22] Like those of the Tamil Tigers and the PKK, their targets were primarily political and military, but they showed wanton disregard for civilian casualties.

Aiming specifically at civilians, however, is not the preserve of religious groups. Secular Palestinian groups also employed suicide attacks, and they did deliberately target Israeli civilians, on the quite spurious grounds that there are no civilians in Israel. Two secular Palestinian groups have carried out suicide attacks, the al-Aqsa Martyrs Brigades and the Popular Front for the Liberation of Palestine (PFLP), though the two Islamist groups Hamas and Palestinian Islamic Jihad (PIJ) have carried out significantly more.

The idea of suicide terrorism traveled from Iran to Lebanon, but from Lebanon it spread a long way. A number of Tamil insurgents received training in Lebanon in the early and mid-1980s and took the tactic back to Sri Lanka. Moreover, the Israeli decision to deport 415 Palestinian militants to Lebanon in 1992 had disastrous unintended consequences as the Palestinians learned the value of the tactic from Hezbollah. In this way the skill set was transferred from Shiite (Iran and Hezbollah) to Sunni (Hamas and later al-Qaeda) Muslims, as well as to secular Palestinian and Tamil groups. The modern phenomenon of suicide terrorism, therefore, can be traced to the Lebanese Civil War of 1973–1986.[23] A tradition of martyrdom is helpful in securing the commitment of recruits, as was the case for Shiite Muslims in Hezbollah and their Iranian backers, but it is by no means necessary, as demonstrated by the Sunni and secular examples.

VARIATIONS ON SUICIDE TERRORISM

There have been a number of variations on suicide terrorism. The human-wave attacks deployed by the Iranians in the Iran-Iraq war are one example. The kamikaze attacks launched by Japan in the later stages of the Second World War are better known. Peter Hill has demonstrated that these attacks were not as effective as claimed by the Japanese, but they were more effective than conventional attacks. Moreover, their most pronounced effect was on the morale of their potential victims. The fear they inspired was such that American commanders stopped warning their crews when mass attacks were coming.[24]

There was a marked diminution in the enthusiasm of the kamikaze recruits as the war progressed and younger and more educated volunteers were solicited. The crucial motivational factors appear to have been less commitment to an almost mythical emperor and more a commitment to family, country, and colleagues. One wrote, "I didn't see myself throwing my life away for him [the emperor] nor for the government either, nor for the nation. I saw myself dying to defend my parents, my brothers and sisters." He went on to explain his commitment to his colleagues: "I couldn't bear the idea of sacrificing someone else by quitting. I knew that if I did, I'd regret it for the rest of my life, even if I never knew his name. I hated the thought that I'd fail and they'd say 'those reservists are no good.' I couldn't do that to the others."[25]

Recent research on the kamikaze reveals a number of other similarities to contemporary suicide terrorists that have not been widely acknowledged. Pilots were given an escort on their missions, just as Palestinian handlers often accompany contemporary *shaheed*s on their missions into Israel. The escorts helped guide and protect the kamikaze and later would report on the mission, but they were undoubtedly also used as an element of control to make it more difficult for the pilot to change his mind. Moreover, the writings of those who participated suggest that they were not one uniform group of like-minded individuals, even though each volunteered for this highly unusual suicide mission. Rather, as with any group of significant size, they had a variety of motivations.

The other significant similarity between the kamikaze and contemporary suicide terrorists is the degree of glory that came with the role. Like other groups today, they were rewarded with renown, with glory for themselves and their families. Families of kamikaze were given the title *homare no ie*, meaning "household of honor." They received more tangible benefits, too: increased pension rights, better rations, and places of honor at official ceremonies. The pilots were eulogized in the press and public statements and were referred to as god-heroes. In this they were elevated even higher than other soldiers who died in battle, who had already become national gods.[26]

Like contemporary *shaheed*s, the kamikaze were deployed by the weaker side in the conflict. Like their modern counterparts, they inflicted more damage on the enemy than conventional attacks did, and again like contemporary suicide terrorists, the fear they inspired outweighed the damage they inflicted, considerable as it is and was. They appear to have been motivated by a sense of commitment to their community and their colleagues as well as a desire for glory. The two significant differences are that their targets were exclusively military and their action was ordered by the military hierarchy, acting on behalf of the government, during a time of interstate war. These two differences make their actions both easier to understand on a personal level and easier to exculpate on a moral one. They were motivated by desire for renown and reaction but not revenge, and they were sustained by their commitment to their colleagues, the support of their community, and the ideology of Japanese nationalism.

Another variation on the theme of suicide terrorism is the action of the imprisoned members of the IRA who starved themselves to death in an effort to secure political prisoner status.[27] Given the protracted and painful manner of their deaths, it is perhaps even harder to understand their action in personal terms though easier to understand in moral terms. The tradition of punishing oneself to shame one's enemy also has a long tradition in Celtic culture. It was not uncommon under the ancient Gaelic legal system known as Brehon law for a man who was owed something by his neighbor to sit outside his neighbor's house and refuse to eat until the embarrassed neighbor righted the wrong. While this tradition lay in the cultural background, it was probably not foremost in the minds of those who decided to go on hunger strike in the Maze prison in Belfast in 1981. A historical example that was foremost in their minds was that of Terence Mac Sweeney, the lord mayor of Cork, who had died on hunger strike in Brixton prison in 1920 during Ireland's war of independence against Britain.

With his death, Mac Sweeney joined the pantheon of Irish martyrs alongside the fifteen men executed for their role in the 1916 Easter Rising and Thomas Ashe, who died in 1917 after being force-fed while on hunger strike to demand political prisoner status. Mac Sweeney's famous words, spoken during his inauguration as lord mayor, would become the mantra of the movement: "It is not those who inflict the most but those who suffer the most who will conquer," he declared.

The crucial distinction between these terrorists who committed suicide and suicide terrorists is that they did not kill others while killing themselves. Theirs was a powerful claim to moral superiority over their enemy. In the short term the effort failed, in that the government of Prime Minister Margaret Thatcher allowed the first ten hunger strikers to die and the families of the remaining prisoners authorized the authorities to feed them. Over the longer term, however, the hunger strike was an enormous success.

Given the depth of the suffering that the republican prisoners were prepared to endure for the sake of a principle, that they be treated as political prisoners, the government could no longer reasonably claim that they were wanton criminals. Sympathy for the hunger strikers and fury at the intransigence of the government proved to be a recruitment bonanza for the IRA at home, a fund-raising bonanza abroad, and a public relations bonanza everywhere. The hunger strike had been undertaken by the prisoners acting without official sanction from the IRA, but the movement soon capitalized on the event. The leaders took advantage of the popular sympathy for Bobby Sands, the first of the prisoners to go on strike. (The prisoners decided to space out the beginning of their strikes in order to space out their deaths and thereby prolong the pressure on the government.) The IRA's political wing, Sinn Féin, ran Bobby Sands in a by-election for a seat in Westminster, and he won handsomely. When he died a month later, it was as an elected member of the British Parliament. This political success also had the long-term and quite unanticipated consequence of demonstrating to the membership of the IRA the advantages of political over military action and proved a spur to the pragmatists within the movement who sought to develop a political strategy.

The action of the hunger strikers cannot be explained in religious terms. The Catholic Church unequivocally forbids suicide, and the Church hierarchy was fairly unsympathetic, though curates drawn from the local community were more sympathetic to the prisoners and their families. Nor were the hunger strikes trying to exact revenge; on the contrary, their moral claim was based on their willingness to suffer. They did expect to elicit a reaction. The reaction they received in the streets of Northern Ireland was a great consolation to them and helped sustain the later strikers, who were also sustained by loyalty to their friends. Once Sands died, others felt compelled to go all the way too, as to fail to do so would be to let down their colleagues. To this day Bobby Sands and his nine fellow hunger strikers who died after him are heroic republican martyrs. Their portraits are painted on gable ends, songs recount their stories, and their deaths are commemorated annually.

The popular claims that suicide terrorists are desperate or crazy are not consistent with any of the research on the subject. Suicide terrorists do not act alone; they are selected, trained, supervised, and encouraged by a group. Moreover, those who do the selecting from among the many volunteers competing for the honor consistently argue that they do their best to ensure that those who are selected are psychologically sound. Hamas made a strong point of telling the Palestinian community in Gaza that produced more volunteers than the organization was prepared to deploy that it would take only "normal" people. It was not interested in those who might be depressed or suicidal or crazy.[28] A PIJ spokesman made the same point: "We do not take depressed people. If there were a one-in-a-thousand chance that a person was suicidal, we would not allow him to martyr himself. In order to be a martyr bomber you have to want to live."[29] Fayez Jaber, speaking for the al-Aqsa Martyrs Brigades, also insists that his organization accepts only fully mature, psychologically sound volunteers and not those who are trying to escape personal or family problems.[30] The truth is that suicide terrorists are not crazy in any meaningful sense of the word.

The notion that poverty drives people to suicide terrorism is also exposed by the demographics of those who volunteer for the role, from the Egyptian Mohamed Atta, with his Ph.D. in urban planning, to the Briton Shehzad Tanweer, the son of a successful small business man. It is nevertheless the case that successful professionals have not volunteered to be suicide terrorists and a great many of those who have come from economically deprived areas such as the Gaza Strip. The act of martyrdom, however, is not an act of desperation, as can be seen in the evident exuberance of the young people in the Gaza Strip who flock to Hamas headquarters to volunteer.

The growth in popularity of suicide terrorism has exceeded social scientists' capacity to keep up. All the carefully constructed data sets calculating the lethality of attacks or percentage of attacks carried out by different groups have been confounded by the extraordinary escalation in suicide attacks in Iraq since the U.S. invasion of the country. There have been more suicide attacks in Iraq alone in the years since the fall of Saddam Hussein in April 2003 than in the rest of the world since the tactic was first adopted in 1981. In May and June 2005, there were more suicide attacks in Iraq than had been recorded by the Israelis since the tactic was first used in Israel in 1993.[31]

We know very little about those who are carrying out these attacks in Iraq.[32] Many are local Iraqis; others are foreign, especially Saudi, Syrian, and Algerian mujahedin. Many of the attacks have been carried out by al-Qaeda in Iraq, which is led by Abu Mus'ab al-Zarqawi and part of the al-Qaeda consortium. Among other groups that have deployed suicide attackers are Ansar al-Islam and Ansar al-Sunna. Many of these groups are made up of Iraqis, though some consist largely of foreign fighters recruited to join the battle against the United States. There can be little doubt that the objective of these attacks is to expel the United States from Iraq. In volunteering, the young men are seeking to avenge the occupation of Iraq and the American war on terror, which they perceive as a war on Islam. They are also seeking a reaction. They are clearly hoping that they can raise the cost of occupation to the point that the American government will decide to withdraw. It is hard to see how they can expect to get renown. There are simply so many recruits and so many attacks that it is difficult to see how they are being managed.

Some light was shed on the situation by an interview the reporter Aparisim Ghosh managed to arrange with a young martyr-in-waiting, "Marwan." Like his colleagues in Gaza, he described the day he learned that he had finally been put on the list of suicide candidates as "the happiest day in my life." He was hoping that with the rate of attacks he would not have to wait long: "I can't wait. I am ready to die now," he said. Marwan, who came from a successful middle-class family, explained that he had expected the United States to bring down Saddam Hussein and then leave, but the United States had remained as an army of occupation. He described himself as radicalized by an incident in April 2003 in which U.S. soldiers fired at a crowd of demonstrators at a school, killing twelve and wounding many others. He witnessed the incident and decided to join the fight against the United States in earnest.[33]

Marwan claims to be fighting first for Islam, second to become a martyr and win acceptance into heaven, and third for his country. He concedes that he has given little thought to the nature of the Islamic state he would like to see established, declaring, "The first step is to remove the Americans from Iraq. After we have achieved that, we can work out the other details."[34]

As in other places, many of these volunteers make a videotaped testimony prior to their operation and their names are glowingly recorded in jihadist Web sites, both to encourage others and to lionize the volunteers. Unlike in other cases, however, Iraqi insurgents are not guaranteed the same kind of glory that their Palestinian and Tamil counterparts get. This is due largely to the nature of the occupation and insurgency. There are no family celebrations on the death of a martyr, for example, for fear of reprisals against the family. But Marwan claims not to be worried about this. He says, "It doesn't matter whether people know what I did. The only person who matters is Allah—and the only question he will ask me is 'How many infidels did you kill?'"[35]

The godfathers of suicide terrorism in Iraq do manage to ensure group support for the volunteers, providing them with a mentor to support them through the final weeks and providing a ritual set of preparations to be followed prior to the operation. Nevertheless, they appear to have sought to persuade their volunteers to do without the degree of renown that other martyrs are assured, or rather to settle for renown in the afterlife instead of renown on the ground. The appeal of earthly glory, however, is not entirely absent even here. Marwan said that he hoped that he would be chosen for a high-profile attack, the kind that will get headlines everywhere and that al-Zarqawi himself will direct personally.

———

Another variation on the profile of suicide terrorists that has come to light recently is the significant number of women martyrs. The Kurdish and Tamil terrorist groups have been using women as suicide terrorists for many years, but this has gone largely unnoticed in the West. Generally speaking, women are underrepresented in terrorist groups, but they are overrepresented among PKK and LTTE suicide terrorists. In recent years women have also been very much in evidence among Chechen suicide terrorists, and their attacks have been deliberately targeted at civilians, as when two young Chechen women strapped themselves with explosives and blew themselves up at a crowded outdoor rock concert in Moscow in July 2003. It was only when Palestinian groups started to deploy women, however, that people in the West started to really pay attention.

Islamic fundamentalists have a view of women as property to be protected that would appear to be incompatible with their playing the role of soldiers, much less martyrs. Al-Qaeda, for example, has not yet deployed a woman on a suicide mission, although in late 2005 al-Qaeda-affiliated organizations appeared to be willing to do so. The experience of other Islamist groups suggests that expediency can trump dogma on this issue. Therefore, if al-Qaeda finds it to be in its interest to deploy women as suicide terrorists, it is likely to adjust its religious rulings on the subject accordingly. The use of women against Israel appears to be a consequence of the rivalry among religious and secular groups battling for the role of legitimate representative of the Palestinian people. The first women martyrs acted under the rubric of the secular al-Aqsa Martyrs Brigades, the suicide terrorist offshoot of Yasser Arafat's Fatah movement.

On January 27, 2002, Wafa Idris, a twenty-six-year-old Red Crescent volunteer, became the forty-seventh Palestinian suicide bomber and the first woman to act in the name of the Palestinians. Just as in 1985, when Syrian President Hafez al-Assad decided to try to secularize suicide bombing in Lebanon and thereby win away support from the religious extremists, so too Yasser Arafat at the outbreak of the second Intifada in September 2000 decided that he could not leave all the martyrdom operations to the Islamist members of Hamas and PIJ. More than a year later, the ever-manipulative president of the Palestinian Authority decided to try another twist and exploit one of the advantages of the secular groups, their female supporters. In January 2002, Arafat addressed a crowd of more than a thousand Palestinian women. He pronounced them to be the equal of men and declared, "You are my army of roses that will crush Israeli tanks." In this speech he coined the feminine form of the word *shaheed*, chanting "shahida, shahida until Jerusalem."[36]

That afternoon Wafa Idris blew herself up in a Jerusalem shopping mall, killing an eighty-one-year-old Israeli man and injuring more than 130 people. Initially reluctant to claim her publicly as one of their own, once it was clear that the reaction on the street was overwhelmingly positive, Fatah claimed her and instructed her family to rejoice in her death. A few weeks later the al-Aqsa Martyrs Brigades officially opened a woman's unit, the Shawaq al-Aqsa, in Idris's honor.

The secular groups were not the only ones to respond to popular sentiment. Initially Sheik Ahmed Yassin, the spiritual leader of Hamas, declared that any man who recruits a woman to be a martyr is breaking Islamic law: "He is taking the girl or woman without the permission of her father, brother, or husband and therefore the family of the girl confronts an even greater problem since the man has the biggest power over her choosing the day that she will give her life back to Allah."[37] Even Hamas soon changed its tune. Yassin later said that as there were plenty of men "demanding to participate," it didn't need women. He wrote in *al-Sharq al-Awsat*, the London-based newspaper, that women would require male escorts and that it was preferable to use men.[38] Then later again he completely reversed his earlier position, insisting, "The Prophet always emphasized the woman's right to wage Jihad."[39]

Dr. Abdul Aziz al-Rantisi, the Hamas spokesman, before he was assassinated by the Israelis, explained to the writer Barbara Victor that the fatwa had been adjusted and that women are welcome as *shahida*s but they must first produce one son and one daughter. "After she fulfills her demographic role then she can participate in armed struggle."[40] The movement was not long in finding a candidate. On January 14, 2004, Fox News announced, "Homicide bomber–mom kills four at Gaza border." A twenty-two-year-old mother of a three-year-old boy and one-year-old girl had blown herself up at the main border crossing. Hamas and al-Aqsa Martyrs Brigades issued a joint claim of responsibility. Hamas conceded that this was a first for it but explained the move in purely tactical terms, because of Israeli security impediments to its male bombers. Before her death Reem al-Reyashi made the now-familiar videotape. Smiling into the camera, she explained that she had dreamed since she was thirteen of becoming a martyr and dying for her people. She added, inexplicably, "God gave me two children and I loved them so much. Only God knew how much I loved them."[41]

Reem was not the first mother to volunteer to be a suicide bomber. Exactly a year earlier, forty-year-old Suhad Gadallah had been prevented from blowing herself up only by the swift action of a passing young Israeli. She left at home a handicapped husband and four children between the ages of five and fifteen. She explained her action in the familiar language of revenge: "My oldest son Abdullah was twenty when he was shot and killed by the soldiers. My child is dead. I had no reason to live. I only wanted to avenge his death. I knew Allah would care for my other children and my husband."[42]

Much has been made in the West of the motivating power of the promise of seventy-two virgins awaiting the martyr in Paradise. This prospect undoubtedly holds less appeal for women. Several women who have been incarcerated by Israel for attempting to become martyrs told the writer Manuela Dviri that a woman martyr "will be the chief of the 72 virgins, the fairest of the fair."[43] Sheik Yassin, having decided that he would permit female martyrs, interpreted the Koran to say that women martyrs become "even more beautiful than the seventy-two virgins." They are not, however, guaranteed their own seventy-two virgins; rather: "If they are not married they are guaranteed a pure husband in Paradise." While not prepared to grant women equality on that front, he is on another. Like their male counterparts, "they are entitled to bring seventy of their relatives to join them there without suffering the anguish of the grave."[44]

Interviews with the family and friends of the first female Palestinian suicide bombers suggested that the motives of these women might be somewhat different from those of their male counterparts. Behind the

usual rhetoric, these first female trailblazers were also fighting powerful personal demons. Wada Idris had been divorced by her husband because of her failure to produce a child, and she had been forced to
return to her fatherless family who could ill afford to support her. Her
one child was stillborn, bringing shame on herself and her family. A
month later Darine Abu Aisha followed in her footsteps. This twenty-
year-old university student was profoundly depressed and under intense pressure from her family to marry. She had been forced by Israeli
guards to kiss a male cousin in public at a border crossing, which
had deeply shamed her. The cousin had then offered to marry her. She
wanted a professional career, not marriage.

Ayat al-Akhras's action appears to have been a mix of a desire to
avenge the Israeli occupation and to save her family from the disgrace
and the danger of deriving their livelihood from her father's work at an
Israeli construction company. Hiba Daraghmeh had been raped as a
fourteen-year-old. And so the litany continued. Among those who tried
and failed to explode themselves, familiar stories of being raped or
bearing illegitimate children are told.[45] An Israeli prison guard in the
prison that houses jailed would-be female martyrs describes the in-
mates and their motivations:

> There are 30 of them, between 17 and 30 years old, some of them
> are married and others aren't, some of them have children. Their
> stories come out of the Thousand and One Nights. Some of them
> did it to make amends for a relative who was a collaborator, others
> to escape becoming victims of honor killings, and for the psycho-
> logically frail or depressed it was a good way to commit suicide and
> at the same time become heroines.[46]

If this is the case, it suggests that the movements' insistence on taking only psychologically sound volunteers does not extend to women.

With the increase in numbers of female martyrs, however, the profile appears to have been normalized. Since those first few attempts, female suicide bombers have reflected a cross section of Palestinian
society from the lawyer to the housewife. With Andalib Suleiman, the
normalization seems complete. She seems to have been motivated not
by a desire to exorcise any personal demons but rather by a desire to
become a superstar. She was fascinated by the celebrity of martyrs and

replaced the pop star posters on her bedroom walls with those of martyrs. Her trainer explained that she wanted to be a *shahida* to avenge
the killings of women and children by the Israelis, to prove that women
were as brave as men and that her family were resolute fighters, and
"She also wanted the assurance that after she died she would be famous
all over the Arab world."[47] Female suicide terrorists in the Palestinian
territories, therefore, clearly share their male counterparts' desire for
revenge and renown. They appear, however, to stress nationalism more
and religion less than their male counterparts. This difference is probably attributable to the fact that nationalism is more compatible with
gender equality than religion and many of the women bombers do
wish to make a claim for their sex as well as their communities. Even
in death, however, they do not quite attain equality. The families of
male suicide bombers receive a lifetime stipend of $400 per month
from the sponsoring organization, while families of female *shahida*s
receive $200 per month.[48]

ORGANIZATIONS AND INDIVIDUALS

Suicide terrorism is a very effective tactic for the weaker side in a conflict. The Tamil Tigers' Prabakharan explained, "With perseverance
and sacrifice, Tamil Eelam can be achieved in 100 years. But if we conduct Black Tiger operations, we can shorten the suffering of the people
and achieve Tamil Eelam in a shorter period of time."[49] According to
Hamas's Sheik Yassin, "Once we have warplanes and missiles, then we
can think of changing our means of legitimate self-defense."[50] The trick
for the organization is to ensure a steady stream of volunteers. In at
least one case, a terrorist group decided to launch a suicide attack but
was unable to find any volunteers. Inspired by the success of the 9/11
attacks, the leadership of the Fuerzas Armadas Revolucionarias de
Colombia (FARC) tried to recruit a volunteer to fly an airplane into the
Presidential Palace during a ceremony installing the newly appointed
president, Álvaro Uribe Vélez. In spite of offering $2 million in com-
pensation for the family of the pilot, they were unable to find one. The
organization had to be content with setting off several bombs outside
the palace.[51]

When leaders of terrorist groups speak of suicide attacks, they are
hard-nosed and tactical. When volunteers speak of suicide attacks, they

are emotional and excited. Bin Laden's right-hand man, Dr. Ayman al-Zawahiri, speaks in a cost-benefit fashion of the advantages of inflicting the maximum number of casualties with the minimum number of losses among the mujahadeen.[52] Sayyed Nasrallah, the secretary general of Hezbollah, has been even more explicit:

> In Lebanon, in order to carry out an operation with an outcome of 8 or 9 dead soldiers, it would need training, equipping, observations, frontier groups, rockets, explosives. . . . After all these preparations, the outcome would only be 3 or 4 deaths due to the strong fortifications of the enemy. On the other hand, one single [martyr] without any training or experience, driving a bus without any military back-ups, was able to kill 8 or 9, wound 21, and scare the entire "Israeli" entity.[53]

A Palestinian security official explained to Nasra Hassan that, apart from a willing candidate, all that is needed are common items such as nails, gunpowder, a battery, a light switch and a short cable, mercury, acetone, and a belt wide enough to hold the explosives. "The most expensive item is transportation to a distant Israeli town. The total cost of a typical operation is about $150."[54] The most expensive suicide operation in history was the 9/11 attacks, and they cost an estimated $500,000 while inflicting tens of billions of dollars in damage, quite aside from the enormous human cost. But those planning to volunteer do not speak in terms of costs at all but rather of the glory of their deaths for the cause. One would-be Palestinian martyr who survived his operation described the preparations as "The happiest days of my life. . . . We told each other that if the Israelis only knew how joyful we were they would whip us to death."[55]

It has not gone unnoticed among the families of some martyrs that the leaders of the organizations have not offered their own children as *shaheed*s. When this suggestion was made to him, Sheik Yassin responded cleverly but implausibly, "We do not choose martyrs to die. Allah chooses them."[56] This is not to suggest that the leaders of these movements do not believe their own rhetoric; I expect they do. It does suggest, however, that they are altogether more pragmatic about martyrdom operations than are the many young people who volunteer for them. As one Hamas leader explained, "Our biggest problem is the hordes of young men who beat on our doors clamoring to be sent. It is difficult to select only a few. Those whom we turn away return again and again, pestering us pleading to be accepted."[57] A senior al-Qassam leader agreed: "The selection process is complicated by the fact that so many wish to embark on this journey of honor. When one is selected countless others are disappointed."[58]

The organizations that recruit them understand the motivations of their followers. Once they have selected a volunteer, the organization engages in a well-honed training process. During the period of indoctrination, the volunteers, who are already converts to the cause to begin with, are subjected to a constant barrage of information and ideology designed to strengthen their commitment. The organization appeals to the desire for revenge by telling stories and showing movies of atrocities against Muslims or Israeli atrocities against Palestinians. The operation is explained in terms of the group's ideology—religious fundamentalism in the case of Islamist groups or nationalism in the case of secular groups. (Most Palestinian groups include both, with greater or lesser emphasis depending on the nature of the organization.) The action is legitimized and glorified in terms of the movement's ideology and the history of the community from which the volunteer comes. They appeal to the desire for renown by glorifying the actions of earlier martyrs and treating them in heroic terms. It is at this point too that an effort is made to strengthen the commitment of the volunteer still further by outlining the rewards that will come to him and his family.

The trainers also understand the power of group solidarity and play on this to their advantage. In Hamas and PIJ the preparation for suicide attacks is often done in cells, consisting of three to five volunteers. These cells are characterized as "martyrdom cells" to differentiate them from the regular military cells.[59] In their account of the road to Martyrs Square, Oliver and Steinberg provide riveting accounts of tight social networks and intense small group loyalty. At one point they write, "What the rank and file [of Hamas] seemed to live and die for, in the end, was neither hospitals nor politics nor ideology nor religion nor the Apocalypse, but rather an ecstatic camaraderie in the face of death on the path to Allah."[60] The powerful sway of group solidarity is further evidenced by the clustering of the places of origin of so many suicide bombers. Ricolfi has observed that a significant majority of suicide bombers come from a small number of refugee camps around the West Bank towns of Hebron, Nablus, and Jenin. He points out that on May 17–18, 2003, three students from Hebron Polytechnic University each carried out a martyrdom operation. Even more striking is the case of the "Jihad Mosque," a soccer team from Hebron that provided eight volunteers out of its eleven-man team. Six of the eight were next-door neighbors and members of the same extended family.[61]

Some volunteers make group videos on the eve of their operation, and these films clearly convey the depth of the camaraderie among them. Eve-of-operation videos have become part of the ritual of suicide attacks. Young people pose before the camera against a range of backgrounds and explain what they are about to do and why. In many cases these videos are carefully scripted, with the volunteer reading a statement written by their sponsoring terrorist group. In others, however, they are more informal. In a video called "The Giants," three soon-to-be martyrs take turns on center stage before coming together to make a collective vow to complete their operation. They had been told that "In Islam it's a horrible thing to run away" and that there is a verse in the Koran that says that anyone who runs away in the middle of a battle goes straight to Hell.[62] Through these videos the volunteers explicitly—or more often implicitly—pledge publicly that they will go through with their mission. Ariel Merari has argued convincingly that the main purpose of these videos is to ensure that the volunteer goes through with the mission. In the case of Hamas and PIJ, the candidate is formally referred to as "the living martyr"—*al-shahid al-hai*—from that point on.[63] It would be deeply shameful to oneself and one's family to change one's mind, having gone this far. The videos serve other purposes too, as useful propaganda tools and help in the glorification of the martyr that in turn helps to attract new volunteers.

What appears to be a profoundly individual action—blowing oneself up in an effort to kill others—is actually a very social one. Individuals often volunteer with their friends, and even when they do not they are drawn from a community that is supportive of their action, their determination is fueled by a sense of commitment to their group, and they expect to be rewarded with renown in their community. Public opinion polls suggest that support for suicide attacks among the Palestinian population has fluctuated and ranged from a low of around 20 percent in the early 1990s to a high of around 75 percent a decade later. A poll in March 2005 suggested that Palestinians' support for bomb attacks inside Israel had dropped from 77 percent in September 2004 to 29 percent in March 2005, though only 40 percent believe the perpetrators should be punished.[64] Other polls in May 2005 saw the Palestinian population as evenly divided on the subject.[65] The suicide bombing of Maxim's restaurant in Haifa that killed twenty-one Israelis, including four children, and injured sixty others, garnered the support of 75 percent of Palestinians.[66] Among the tight social and family networks that produce volunteers, the percentages are possibly even higher.

In attempting to ascertain what it is that drives an individual to volunteer to be a martyr in the first place, the evidence that, as with terrorism in general, the key motivators are revenge, renown, and reaction is very strong. From Chechens to Tamils to Palestinians to Saudis, from women to men, from young to old, the words of volunteers for suicide are replete with the language of revenge. A senior member of al-Qassam told Nasra Hassan: "After every massacre, every massive violation of our rights and defilement of our holy places, it is easy for us to sweep the streets for boys who want to do a martyrdom operation. Fending off the crowds who demand revenge and retaliation and insist on a human bombing operation—that becomes our biggest problem."[67] During the October 2002 theater hostage crisis in Moscow, al-Jazeera aired a prerecorded tape featuring five of the female Chechen hostage takers, who expressed their willingness to die and explained that they were acting in order to "avenge their losses." There is a special unit of the Chechen terrorists called the "Black Widows," made up of women who become terrorists once their husbands are killed. The final videotapes made by living martyrs speak incessantly of the desire to avenge the atrocities committed against their communities. Posters and commemorative cards to the martyrs declare, "The Right of Revenge Is Ours." In the mid-1990s in Gaza, there emerged a popular music genre known as "revenge songs." Sometimes the desire is to avenge a personal injury, the death or arrest of a relative, and sometimes it is to avenge the ill-treatment of people they do not know but with whom they identify. Often it is to avenge a sense of humiliation. The longer a conflict continues, the more atrocities there are to be avenged.

While the desire for revenge has proven to be a powerful motivator in the human condition generally, in the past it has not sufficed to pro-pel people to commit suicide in large numbers. There are other moti-vations at play too, and these are the social motivations, the desire to be loyal to your peers and to be revered in your community. I cannot help getting the sense in seeing some of the final videos, especially the less carefully scripted ones, that the volunteers' desire to be the center of attention is being briefly indulged by the movement's leaders before they are dispatched to war as cannon fodder.

The PKK leader, Abdullah Öcalan, speaking of the first female Kurd-ish suicide terrorists, said, "These women were fully aware and fully desirous of being free women with an important message to pass on and capable of being examples to all women the world over."[68] The leaders of the organizations understand the power of this appeal and hence have created a culture of hero worship around the *shaheed*s. Songs extol their virtues and their bravery. Their likenesses adorn walls in the streets of their communities and the homes of their would-be emulators. Their stories are told on the Internet for all the world to see. Calendars depict a "martyr of the month." An underemployed youth has no way of realizing a dream to be a superstar like Diego Maradona or Britney Spears (especially if s/he is not good at soccer or singing). But s/he knows just how to become a Wafa Idris or a Captain Miller, and s/he doesn't need any special talents to do so.

In addition to the worldly renown that the volunteers know they will achieve, they are also guaranteed a direct route to Paradise, where everything they have wanted in this life will be provided. Volunteers are also promised places in Paradise for seventy of their nearest and dearest friends and relatives. Many volunteers conclude that it is an offer they cannot refuse. They give up the life they enjoy now and in so doing take a strike at the hated enemy and force the enemy to respond to them; in return they provide for their family in this world and the next while acquiring for themselves an honored place in Heaven. If you believe in the payout, it's not a bad deal, really. But the fact that there are so many volunteers in secular groups that do not offer a place in Paradise indicates that this is no more than an added inducement, not an explanation of the decision to become a martyr.

Once a martyr dies, the family holds a celebration not unlike a wed-ding. Hundreds of friends and neighbors flock to the home, and parents distribute sweets to the neighborhood children. Parents and siblings speak of their pride and are honored in their communities. Interviews after the fact, however, suggest that at least in some cases the families are just playing a part, doing what is expected of them while privately grieving in an altogether understandable way. Mabrook Idris, the mother of the first female Palestinian suicide bomber, initially declared, "I am proud that my daughter died for Palestine, proud that she gave her life for us all. Thank God. Thank God." As word of Wafa's death spread, the leaders of al-Aqsa arrived at her home in Ramallah with sweets and posters emblazoned with photographs of Wafa. The atmosphere was joyous; a neighbor described it as "a wedding with eternity." Not long afterward, however, the mother confessed, "If I had known what she was going to do, I would have stopped her. I grieve for my daughter."[69] The father of Ayat al-Akhras used almost the same words: "Had I known she was planning to do such a thing I would have locked the door and thrown away the key."[70] Another mother told Nasra Hassan that had she known her son's plans, "I would have taken a cleaver, cut open my heart, and stuffed him deep inside. Then I would have sewn it up tight to keep him safe."[71]

While the family expresses public pride and private grief, the euphoria of the martyrs themselves seems genuine. In 1983, a young guard at the Marine barracks in Lebanon caught a glimpse of the man driving the truck full of explosives toward the building. He remembers no physical features, only that the man had an enormous smile on his face.[72] Israeli survivors of suicide attacks on buses similarly describe the bombers as wearing big smiles. This is what is known in the Shia tradition as the *bassamat al-farah,* or "smile of joy," prompted by one's impending martyrdom. More than twenty years after the Lebanese attack, the Iraqi martyr in waiting, Marwan, described how he had been asked to mentor a friend in the final weeks before his suicide attack. "My friend was happier than I had ever seen him. He felt he was close to the end of his journey to heaven."[73] In their final video the three "giants," Abu-Surur, Uthman, and al-Hindi, cannot contain their excitement. Smiling and laughing into the camera, they are savoring every moment of being center stage. They are the very epitome of the "happy death" constantly celebrated in the slogans of the Intifada. Hamas slogans declare, "I will die smiling in order that my religion live" and "O Muslim, say Allahu Akbar with joy." Nationalist groups simply replace religion with the homeland, as in "How sweet is death for the

sake of the homeland" and "Mother I am happy, happy to die for freedom."[74] Far from committing lonely acts of desperation, these martyrs
are going gleefully to their premature graves.

Though individuals choose martyrdom in order to exact revenge
and attain renown, they also want to advance their cause. They want
to elicit a reaction from the enemy because in reacting the enemy ac-
knowledges their importance. Few volunteers believe that their individual action alone can cause Turkish, Russian, Sri Lankan, or American
withdrawal or Israeli destruction, but they certainly do hope that their
action in concert with others will bring about political change in the
long term and in the short term that it will be at least acknowledged by
the enemy. In some cases the suicide action is carefully designed to ensure the maximum number of casualties possible, as was the case on
9/11, but in many instances in which suicide bombing has become almost commonplace, one gets the sense that the volunteers are more enamored of the dying than the killing. On their videotapes they speak
happily and at length about their deaths and far less about those they
are going to kill. Moreover, they very often detonate themselves in situations in which they do not cause nearly as many casualties as they
might. In one fairly extreme example, in August 2001, twenty-eight-
year-old Muhammad Mahmoud Nassr approached a waitress in the
Wall Street Cafe in Haifa. He was carrying enough explosives in his
belt to destroy the restaurant. He lifted his T-shirt to show the belt to
the waitress and asked if she knew what it was. The terrified customers
fled the restaurant in a panic. When he was left alone, he cried "God is
great" and blew himself up, and nobody else.

A large part of the appeal of suicide attacks, especially to the leaders
of terrorist organizations, is that historically they have been effective in
eliciting a reaction, even in getting results. In the case of Lebanon, the
suicide attacks against American and French forces led directly to the
withdrawal of the multilateral force. "We couldn't stay there and run
the risk of another suicide attack on the marines," wrote President
Ronald Reagan in his memoirs, explaining the American decision to
withdraw.[75] Osama bin Laden has often invoked this example as evidence of American cowardice. The withdrawal had portentous ramifications for Lebanon and permitted the unimpeded growth of Syrian
influence in the country. By 1985, these attacks arguably led to Israel's
decision to concede most of the gains it had made during its 1982 in-

vasion of Lebanon and to withdraw to a narrow strip of land in southern Lebanon from which it subsequently withdrew in May 2001. Later suicide attacks by Hamas and PIJ in Israel were designed to derail the peace process launched by the Oslo agreement in 1993. They largely succeeded. Suicide attacks also influenced the outcome of the 1996 Israeli elections. Prior to the elections Shimon Peres, widely perceived as a dove, was twenty points ahead of his hawkish rival, Benjamin Netanyahu. Yet after suicide attacks in Jerusalem and Tel Aviv, the majority of the Israeli electorate decided that the situation required a hawk and the election went the other way. There can be no doubt that the massive and quite unprecedented escalation in suicide attacks against the United States and her allies in Iraq since the beginning of the American occupation is designed to cause the United States to withdraw.

On the face of it, neither Sidique Khan nor Shehzad Tanweer appears to fit into the type of situations just described. They were both British born and lived in suburban England, where the biggest rivalries are over soccer and cricket teams, not national liberation or religious fundamentalism. They appear not to have left behind much that might help explain their action, and those who knew them best appear to be among the most baffled. Less than two months after the attack, however, a brief videotape was aired on al-Jazeera television depicting Sidique Khan wearing a red *keffiyeh* and speaking in a broad northern England accent. Khan described himself as a soldier and said that he was acting to avenge the atrocities against his people (meaning other Muslims). Ayman al-Zawahiri was then shown praising the London bombings and describing them as "a sip from the glass that the Muslims have been drinking from."[76]

The bombers did carry identification with them on their mission, so presumably they wished to be identified. Even their families had no idea what they were up to. Indeed, the first lead in the case was when the family of another of the terrorists, Hasib Hussain, called the police out of concern as he had not returned home.

The statement claiming the action by al-Qaeda Europe declared it to have been designed "to take revenge against the British Zionist Crusader government in retaliation for the massacres Britain is committing in Iraq and Afghanistan." The statement then threatened other governments that "they will be punished in the same way if they do not withdraw their troops from Iraq and Afghanistan."[77] At this point we do not know whether the claim is legitimate, nor do we know whether it reflects the motivations of all of the bombers. It is reasonable to assume, however, that it does.

From what we know of other suicide terrorists, it is reasonable to assume that these four were also motivated by a desire to avenge British and American actions in Iraq and Afghanistan. We do not know whether they desired renown, but, given the motives of others, they probably did. They certainly achieved it. Pulling off the first suicide operation in the heart of Europe and at a time when the world's leaders were in the country was bound to ensure that their names would be circulated the world over. In his message Khan did say, "I'm sure by now the media's painted a suitable picture of me." So he was evidently anticipating being recognized. We do not know whether the example of their Spanish counterparts came to mind. On March 11, 2004, a group of Moroccan immigrants detonated ten explosions on commuter trains in Madrid, killing 191 people. The bombing is widely credited with ensuring the unexpected defeat of the conservative party of Prime Minister Aznar and the surprise election of the Socialist Party, dedicated to withdrawing Spanish forces from Iraq. One could certainly imagine the young men from Leeds thinking that it would be far better to die gloriously than to be hunted down by the police and waste away in prison for the rest of their lives. It is also reasonable to assume that they thought they could expect a reaction, British withdrawal from Iraq. The war is deeply unpopular in Britain, and one could well imagine them thinking that they could bring about a British withdrawal as the Spanish train bombers had done.

While revenge, renown, and reaction were certainly available to them, they also had a legitimizing ideology in radical Islam, and they were, almost by definition, disaffected individuals. The missing piece seems to be the enabling community. These men were born and grew up in suburban Britain, not the Gaza Strip.[78] Everything we know about suicide terrorists suggests that there must have been a collective component to this. The supportive community was evidently not their family, neighbors, and friends; they were probably deeply committed to one another. The most likely explanation for the fact that one of the four bombs exploded an hour after the others and on a bus, not a train, is that the perpetrator, Hasib Hussain, was prevented from taking the intended Underground train and took a bus instead. Knowing that his colleagues had exploded their bombs, he could have defected from the group but instead decided to improvise within the terms of the original plan. His commitment to his colleagues was presumably such that he acted as they had out of loyalty to them and their group project.

The question then becomes, Where did this small group get the social support they needed to sustain them? Khan and Tanweer had traveled to Pakistan together and presumably made contact with radical fundamentalists there. They may have had support from a small number of local extremists affiliated with nearby mosques, but there is no evidence so far to support this. It is also possible that they managed to attain the support of a virtual *umma,* or Muslim community, through the Internet. Thanks to the powers of the Internet, one can gain access to Islamist Web sites, read and watch endless propaganda against the West, or communicate with radical imams in any part of the world, all from one's bedroom in Leeds. The Internet has truly provided the means of globalizing terrorism, and even globalizing the tactic of suicide terrorism.

One of the striking novelties of the London bombing is that it reversed the usual pattern of terrorist violence. Terrorist violence usually starts locally and then goes global. In this instance it started globally and then went local. This is not an auspicious development.

What is so shocking about Khan and Tanweer, aside from the inhuman horror they inflicted on hundreds of people, is that they did not come from a community that overtly supported their action, nor did they suffer discrimination or privation themselves, nor did they know people whose grievances they sought to avenge, nor were they known to be members of a radical group, nor were they even known to be interested in politics. As a friend said of Tanweer, "It's not in his nature to do something like this; he is the type of guy who would condemn things like that."[79] They did not appear to fit any known profile of suicide bombers and they were acting in a country and a region that had not previously experienced a suicide attack. The London attacks, therefore, represent a sinister escalation in the terrorist threat.

Having examined the emergence of terrorism and the causes and motives of terrorists, it is now time to turn our attention to the situation facing Western countries today to see how this knowledge can help us confront the threat we face. It has often been said that the world changed on September 11, 2001. But did it?

PART TWO

THE COUNTERTERRORISTS

Americans are asking, why do they hate us? They hate what we see right here in this chamber—a democratically elected government. Their leaders are self-appointed. They hate our freedoms—our freedom of religion, our freedom of speech, our freedom to vote and assemble and disagree with each other.[1]

—GEORGE W. BUSH, SEPTEMBER 2001

Later [after the attack on the USS *Cole*] the Mujahideen saw that the gang of black hearted criminals in the White House was misrepresenting the event, and that their leader, who is a fool whom all obey, was claiming that we were jealous of their way of life, while the truth—which the Pharaoh of our generation conceals—is that we strike at them because of the way they oppress us in the Muslim world, especially in Palestine and Iraq, and because of their occupation of the Land of the Two Holy Places. When the Mujahideen saw this they decided to act in secret and to move the battle right into his [the U.S. president's] country and his own territory.[2]

—OSAMA BIN LADEN, MARCH 2003

WHAT CHANGED AND WHAT DID NOT ON SEPTEMBER 11, 2001

Night fell on a different world—a world where freedom itself is under attack.[1]

—George W. Bush, September 20, 2001

At the time of the Clerkenwell explosion terror took possession of society.[2]

—Lord Campbell, March 18, 1868

EFORE BOARDING THE PLANE ON THAT BRIGHT, CLEAR September morning the young man telephoned his wife to tell her, three times, that he loved her.[3] She was not able to accompany him as she was studying in dentistry school in Germany. Only the night before, he had written her a love letter. It began, "Hello my dear Aysel. My love, my life. My beloved lady, my heart. You are my life. . . . I love you and will always love you." The letter ended by declaring, "I am your prince and I will pick you up. See you again!! Your man always."[4]

The couple had been separated for fourteen months while each attended school in different countries. He had gone to Germany five times to visit her during that time, and she had gone to visit him in the United States once. Six months earlier, he had traveled home to visit his father, who was having heart surgery. Before returning to school, he had spoken to Aysel, who had found him to have been deeply moved by his father's illness. He had said that he wanted to have children soon so that his father could see them before he died. His father had been generously supporting his studies, sending him $2,000 a month and making sure that his young wife was well supported. The family had been pleased to see the handsome happy-go-lucky playboy get married. In the elite private schools in which he had been educated, he had seemed, or so his family complained, more interested in girls than geometry. While not spectacularly wealthy, his family was very comfortably off. They owned two homes, drove fashionable Mercedes, and enjoyed good whiskey. Their only son and middle child enjoyed spending their money. When visiting his wife, the young couple would take a trip to Paris to eat, drink, and take in the sights, and when she came to visit him they took a trip to the Florida Keys. Rather than staying with those he knew, he was quick to make friends with classmates at his new school and took a fun trip with them to the Bahamas. He often stayed in their apartment, cooking dinner for them in the evening and making everyone an early-morning cup of tea. "He was a friend to all of us," said the head of his school.[5]

Unlike the other passengers who said good-bye to their family members that morning, however, the twenty-six-year-old Lebanese student, Ziad Jarrah, knew that he would not be seeing them again. He boarded United Airlines flight 93 on the morning of September 11 with no intention of ever stepping off the plane.

———

By exploring the degree to which the terrorism we encountered on September, 11, 2001, in the United States differs from the terrorism that preceded it, I want now to challenge the view that we inhabit an entirely new world in which the experience of other countries has no relevance, our national security doctrine is inadequate, and our protections of civil liberties are unaffordable. The terrorists' preference for conventional technology, symbolic targets, spectacular actions, and even suicide bombing was far from new. Religiously motivated violence appeared new but was not, and the prominence of the political motives mixed in with the religious ones was underappreciated. Despite previous attacks on American citizens abroad, with attacks on American soil the sense of U.S. vulnerability was entirely new, and the country's counterterrorist policy changed accordingly. The biggest change that occurred on 9/11, therefore, was not in the forces arrayed against us but in Americans' reaction to those forces. There was a newfound sense of insecurity. With it came a loss of perspective and, ultimately, a willingness to support a response that was destined to make the situation worse.

The scale of the atrocity committed on 9/11 was unprecedented in the lengthy annals of terrorism. With a final casualty figure just under three thousand, almost ten times as many people were murdered that day than in any previous terrorist action. Previously the point of terrorism had been for the psychological impact to be greater than the actual physical act. This is how terrorists have leveraged their relative weakness. But in this instance the physical act itself was unprecedented in its destructiveness outside wartime. Of course, from the terrorists' point of view, they were at war. Bin Laden had declared war on us in 1996. The destruction in New York, Washington, and Pennsylvania made this war a reality. We countered with our own declaration of war.

One of the most striking things that changed on that day, therefore, was that for the first time terrorists had succeeded in killing very large numbers of people, the kind of casualties that had previously occurred only in interstate or civil warfare. Historically, terrorists have not taken the opportunities available to them to murder on a grand scale. They have not needed to. They could further their objectives and inflict widespread terror without inflicting widespread casualties. The most frequently cited aphorism making this point was made by the RAND analyst Brian Jenkins in 1974: "Terrorists want lots of people watching, not lots of people dead."

Most terrorist groups rely for support on members of their ethnic group or adherents of their ideology, and so operatives have been careful to ensure that their actions do not alienate this support base. When the audience is God, however, you do not need to be so constrained. God is unlikely to announce his reaction, so terrorists are free to interpret his reaction as they choose. Like most other terrorist groups with religious motives, however, al-Qaeda also has an audience on the ground. For al-Qaeda this audience is vast and geographically dispersed; it is the entire Muslim world, amounting to 1.2 billion people, as well as the population of the United States, whose policies they seek to change. In order to make an impression on such a vast group, an action has to be quite spectacular, as indeed the 9/11 attack was.

This was not the first time terrorists had tried to kill the maximum possible number of people. The group of New Jersey Islamists who drove a yellow Ford Econoline rental van filled with 1,500 pounds of urea nitrate into the basement of the World Trade Center in February 1993 had clearly intended to kill as many people as possible. They succeeded in killing six and injuring more than a thousand. Philippine authorities had similarly found plans for inflicting mass casualties when in 1995 they found a laptop containing plans devised by Khalid Shaikh Mohammed, the mastermind of the 9/11 attack. The plans involved simultaneously blowing up eleven airplanes over the Pacific. They required that a bomb be left under a seat and that the bomber leave the plane during a stopover. The computer contained a number of other plans too, including flying airplanes into major American buildings such as the World Trade Center. At the same time the interrogation of one of those arrested, Abdul Hakim Murad, revealed plans to fly airplanes into CIA headquarters in Langley, Virginia.[6]

This was the first time, however, that terrorists had succeeded in inflicting such massive casualties. The previous year 19 Americans had died as a result of international terrorism, 405 people worldwide.[7] The year before that, 5 Americans and 233 people of all nationalities had died at the hands of international terrorists.[8] A leap from 200 to 400 to 3,000 is dramatic by any standard. Another way of getting a sense of the scale of the escalation is to look at the United Kingdom. Britain had been fighting a campaign against the IRA, a thoroughly professional and ruthless terrorist organization, in Northern Ireland for several decades. Yet Britain lost 67 of its citizens in the September 11 attacks, more than in any single terrorist attack by the IRA in over thirty years.

So while the scale of the attack was unprecedented, the nature of the violence was also quite different from what had previously been experienced. That nineteen men, a group the size of an average sports team, would willingly blow themselves up in unison in order to kill American office workers seemed completely beyond the bounds of comprehension.

Americans tend to see themselves as being on the side of those who seek to overthrow the yoke of colonialism. They have never seen themselves as colonial oppressors and were spared the political traumas experienced by many of their allies in accommodating themselves to the demand for independence that swept the colonial world after the Second World War. We are not very familiar with the writings of Frantz Fanon, who wrote of violence as liberating, as necessary to the perpetrator as a means of freeing himself from oppression. This is not the instrumental violence of the robber or Mafia member. This is expressive violence to cleanse the soul.⁹ This was the kind of violence that confronted the American public on September 11 and for which they were quite unprepared.

The first thing that changed, therefore, was the scale and the nature of the violence that confronted the United States. The second essential innovation of 9/11 was that this attack hit America at home, exposing its vulnerability. The United States, unlike most of its allies, had been relatively untouched by domestic terrorism. The Days of Rage of the Weathermen, the violent offshoot of the Students for a Democratic Society (SDS) in the 1960s, were a distant memory. Aside from the earlier attack on the World Trade Center, the one notable exception was the bombing of the Alfred P. Murrah Federal Building in Oklahoma City on April 19, 1994, which left 168 people dead, including 19 children. That bombing was carried out by a twenty-six-year-old American survivalist, Timothy McVeigh, who was in police custody ninety minutes after the attack.¹⁰ While deeply shocking, McVeigh's action, for which he was executed on June 11, 2001, appeared to be a one-off attack by a deranged extremist.

Not only has the United States been spared domestic terrorism, but it has also been extraordinarily lucky in managing to conduct its wars largely beyond its own shores. Other than the Japanese attack on the Pacific Fleet in Pearl Harbor on December 7, 1941, which resulted in the deaths of 2,403 American servicemen and 68 civilians, one has to return to the Civil War to find domestic casualties on the scale of 9/11. In this case, however, the victims, with the exception of some of the 125 people killed in the Pentagon, were all civilians.

The ability of al-Qaeda to carry out a sophisticated attack within the United States was deeply shocking. It exposed the fact that for the first time in its history America's oceans and geographic location no longer sufficed to keep her enemies at a distance. In the words of Vice President Dick Cheney, "9/11 changed everything. It changed the way we think about threats to the United States. It changed about our recognition of our vulnerabilities. It changed in terms of the kind of national security strategy we need to pursue, in terms of guaranteeing the safety and security of the American people."[11] The American public was confronted with the reality of globalization. The world was a smaller place, and they no longer felt safe. In a poll conducted by CBS News a month after the attack, 88 percent of the respondents said that they considered it likely that there would be another terrorist attack within the United States within a few months.[12]

The American public was also confronted with the fact that the United States, both its government and its people, were deeply reviled by a group of radical Islamists half a world away of whom they had never heard. Some reacted by asking, How do we get them? Applications to the military and intelligence services soared. (Applications to the CIA rose by 50 percent from 2001 to 2002.) Others reacted by asking, Why do they hate us? These people sought to learn more. (Applications to the Peace Corps rose by 40 percent that year.) For the U.S. public it was an unconscionable, unprovoked attack on innocent civilians. For the perpetrators of the violence, however, it was a glorious blow by the weak against the strong. It was giving the Americans a taste of their own medicine. It was in effect the story of David and Goliath. In bin Laden's own words:

> They carried out the raid by means of enemy planes in a coura-
> geous and splendid operation the like of which mankind had never
> before witnessed. They smashed the American idols and damaged
> its very heart, the Pentagon. They struck the very heart of the Ameri-
> can economy, rubbed America's nose in the dirt and dragged its
> pride though the mud. The towers of New York collapsed and their
> collapse precipitated an even greater debacle: the collapse of the
> myth of America the great power and the collapse of the myth of
> democracy; people began to understand that American values
> could sink no lower. The myth of the land of freedom was de-

stroyed, the myth of American national security was smashed and the myth of the CIA collapsed, all praise and thanks to Allah.[13]

Americans would have been stunned to learn that al-Qaeda believed that it had warned the United States time and time again to change its policies in the Middle East but that the United States had arrogantly ignored all warnings. While the American public focused on the individual tragic stories of fathers, mothers, and children whose lives had been torn apart by the attack, the perpetrators saw the victims as depersonalized agents of their message. Their rancor was toward America, the most powerful country in the world, not the individual people they had murdered. They held individual Americans collectively accountable for the actions of their government. Their hearts had been hardened to the individual tragedies they inflicted, as they believed that their side had experienced many more. For their part, most Americans had never heard of al-Qaeda or Osama bin Laden.

For the United States, the world appeared to have changed on 9/11, but it's not so clear that it did. Certainly the scale and the nature of the violence visited on the United States were unprecedented, but this change was a long time in the making. The exhaustive work of the 9/11 Commission and the work of many academics before 2001 attested to the growth in radical Islamic movements, their antipathy toward the United States, the impact of the successful end of the mujahedin campaign against the Soviet Union, and the activities in terrorist training camps in Afghanistan and elsewhere. Investigations of earlier attacks outside the United States had also revealed to the security services the extent of the transnational networks that were operating and the degree of financial backing they enjoyed. There was no shortage of evidence attesting to the fact that the stability of our most powerful allies in the Middle East was often purchased by repression of domestic opponents, as in Egypt, or exportation of the radical message, as in Saudi Arabia.

None of this, however, had penetrated the popular consciousness in the United States, so that this act was seen as coming completely out of the blue. Americans have long been a relatively insular people, with comparatively low rates of foreign travel, passport ownership, and foreign-language fluency. This tendency to look inward has been reflected in Washington, where the national interest is narrowly defined and foreign policy is conducted with a keen eye to domestic politics and not with an eye to the impact of American policies on other countries.

A case in point is the deployment of American troops in Saudi Arabia at the end of the first Gulf War. Few Americans were aware of the commitment that was made, ostensibly as a deterrent to aggression against the friendly Saudi regime. This deployment was enormously unpopular on the ground and was used as a rallying cry for Islamic extremists, most notably bin Laden. He argued repeatedly that the deployment of American troops was humiliating and evidence of nefarious American designs on Saudi oil reserves and independence.

Before September 11 I heard Michael Sheehan, the Coordinator for Counterterrorism in the State Department between 1998 and 2001, respond to a question posed by a student: "Why do they hate us?" He replied with the government's line that they hate us because we love freedom, because we love democracy. I countered with another question: "What if we learned that, in fact, what they hated was our policies? If we learned that the deployment of our troops in Saudi Arabia was what caused the enmity against us, would this cause you or the administration to reevaluate the wisdom of our policies?" He responded emphatically: "No. We will never let terrorists determine our policies." He won the debating point, but I was stunned then, and remain so now, by how shortsighted a policy this was. There were many alternatives to this deployment that would have provided ample reassurance to Saudi Arabia: an additional American aircraft carrier in the Persian Gulf, for example. But we insisted on our right to implement a policy that was hugely unpopular, and we appeared to be completely oblivious to the way it could be used against us. This was the hubris of great power.

The American government did not see the attacks of September 11 as an attack on American policies. President Bush was speaking for many when he said on the night of September 11, "America was targeted for attack because we're the brightest beacon for freedom and opportunity in the world. And no one will keep that light from shining. Today our nation saw evil, the very worst of human nature."[14] Four years later his position remained unchanged: "Our enemies murder because they despise our freedom and our way of life."[15] The American public, however, appears to have had a more nuanced view. In a Harris poll conducted just over a week after the attacks, Americans were asked: "Which ONE of the following do you think is the main reason why those who attacked us and their supporters hate the United States?" Twenty-six percent answered, "Our democracy and freedom"; 20 percent answered, "Our values and our way of life." Both of these responses were consistent with the administration's interpretation. However, 22 percent responded, "Our support for Israel"; 17 percent thought it was "Our influence on the economy and lives of Middle Eastern countries," and 11 percent answered that they hated us because of "our economic and military power."[16]

While there was some disagreement on the reason for the attack, there was little dispute that "the events are a turning point that will fundamentally change things forever."[17] Terrorism is, above all, a game of psychological warfare. As pointed out earlier, terrorists are invariably weaker than their opponents, so they try to compensate for this weakness with dramatic effect. They were extraordinarily successful in inflicting almost three thousand casualties on the United States in a single day. They were even more successful in eliciting a reaction even more powerful than the harm they inflicted. The discrepancy between the harm they inflicted and the impact they had was considerable. They succeeded in persuading Americans that the world had changed and that they were no longer safe. The United States responded in the strongest way possible, with a declaration of war.

With the conviction that their world had changed came a willingness on the part of Americans to change the way they faced the world. While the nature and the scale of the atrocity were bound to have an enormous impact, there was nothing inevitable about the conclusion that the world had changed. Three thousand casualties was an appalling figure, but in a country that experienced 30,000 suicides, 16,000 homicides, and 15,000 deaths from falls in the same year, a more moderate reaction might have been expected. It is part of the genius of terrorism that it causes us to emphasize the harm it inflicts as compared to other tragedies. Consider the fact that six times as many Americans are killed by drunk drivers every year than were killed by the terrorists on 9/11.[18] The difference in reaction is due partly to the spectacular effect of terrorist atrocities, which is magnified by the media with their compelling stories of heroism, chance, and tragedy. As I will argue later, an essential element of any successful counterterrorism strategy must be the development of public resilience so that we cannot be manipulated by terrorists so easily.

Americans felt much less safe after 9/11, but were they? On the face of it, American citizens were a great deal safer in the fall of 2001 than they were throughout the Cold War, when the armed might of the Soviet Union, including more than ten thousand strategic and close to thirty thousand nonstrategic nuclear warheads, was trained on the United States and its allies. During the Cold War, its enemy was a global superpower in possession of vast arsenals rivaling its own and an army considerably larger than its own. It was ruled by authoritarian leaders espousing a hostile and expansionist ideology utterly at variance with the American belief in democracy. The enemy in 2001 was a stateless band of fanatical fighters sponsored by one of the poorest and most isolated countries in the world.

It is perhaps worth remembering that when the threat from communism was first felt after the Second World War, there was an intense popular reaction as "Reds" were sought under beds, in Hollywood, in academia, and, most of all, in the government. Alliances were struck with unsavory dictators who shared none of our commitment to civil and human rights and democratic principles but who shared our loathing of communism. Then, too, we embarked on costly foreign wars when we mistook nationalism for communism and failed to understand the profound distinction between the two. By 2001, more than a decade after the end of the Cold War, even the threat from communism had become a distant memory. Its place in the American psyche has been more than supplanted by the threat of terrorism.

There were two aspects of al-Qaeda violence in particular that left Americans thinking that indeed the world had changed and that they would have to change in response. First was the sense that the organization was driven by irrational religious fanatics, so their behavior was likely to be both unpredictable and unconstrained. Policies such as mutually assured destruction (MAD) had worked against the Soviet Union, as they assumed the rationality of the adversary, but suicide terrorists could not be deterred. Second was the belief that al-Qaeda wanted to kill as many Americans as it could; if it would destroy the World Trade Center, al-Qaeda would not hesitate to use weapons of mass destruction against the United States.

Unlike many countries in Europe, the United States does not have a large Muslim community. Estimates vary widely, but the most accurate suggest that there were 2.8 million Muslims in the United States in 2001. This represents less than 1 percent of the population and is significantly less than the Muslim populations in allied countries such as Britain, France, Germany, and Spain. Not having much exposure to Islam, many Americans seemed frightened and prepared to confound the extremist perversion of Islam represented by bin Laden and his relatively small group of followers with the vast global religion. Only a religion seemed capable of legitimizing such action. President Bush sought to make clear in his public pronouncements that al-Qaeda did not speak for Islam, declaring instead that Islam's "teachings are good and peaceful and those who commit evil in the name of Allah blaspheme the name of Allah."[19] Nevertheless, the view that there was indeed a clash of civilizations in the making received growing currency. Asked whether they thought the attacks were the start of a major conflict between the people of America and Europe versus the people of Islam or only a conflict with a small radical group, in October 2001, 28 percent of Americans thought we were in conflict with Islam; a year later, that number had grown to 35 percent.[20]

For all the religious rhetoric of bin Laden, however, he has persistently articulated a set of political demands linked to American policy in the Middle East. In the wake of the attack, however, public discourse did not focus on these political demands but rather on the grandiose religious rhetoric. In the president's words, "Al Qaeda is to terror what the mafia is to crime. But its goal is not making money; its goal is remaking the world—and imposing its radical beliefs on people everywhere. . . . These terrorists kill not merely to end lives, but to disrupt and end a way of life."[21] Later he would refer to its ideology as "Islamofascism."[22] There can be no doubt that terrorist groups that have enjoyed a mix of religious and political motives have been both more transnational and less constrained than other terrorist groups. Religion, however, is rarely a cause of terrorism; rather, religion serves to "absolutize" conflicts, in the word of sociologist Mark Juergensmeyer, making compromise more difficult.[23]

Terrorist leaders have found religion enormously useful in legitimizing their actions and in winning recruits for the cause. Religion enables terrorist leaders to cast a conflict in terms of cosmic warfare and their followers to see themselves as soldiers in a divinely inspired army. Religion facilitates recruitment both by providing legitimacy and by providing rewards in the afterlife to people prepared to pay a considerable cost in this one. The organizational networks available through religions have long been a powerful resource for the weak in their efforts to mobilize against the strong. In the case of apartheid South Africa, for example, which banned most forms of political organization among the black majority, churches remained one of the few places in which those seeking change could congregate. Churches, especially among diaspora communities, have also always served to draw in those seeking comfort in an alien culture. So on both a practical and an ideological level, at the level of personal rewards for the followers as well as tools for the leaders, religion and terrorism have often been linked.

In responding to the attacks on 9/11, Americans opted to accept al-Qaeda's language of cosmic warfare at face value and respond accordingly, rather than respond to al-Qaeda based on an objective assessment of its resources and capabilities relative to their own. There is no doubt that the sheer spectacle of the crumbling towers certainly appeared consistent with a view of cosmic warfare. But in point of fact, three thousand casualties, in a country long accustomed to more than five times that many homicides a year, might have elicited a more focused and more moderate reaction. Part of the reason it did not was the sense that if, in the name of their God, they would fly planes into American buildings, what else would they do? The biggest fear is that they might try to use weapons of mass destruction.

WEAPONS OF MASS DESTRUCTION

It is ironic that an attack using primitive box cutters and relying on no technological innovation since the jet engine managed to propel fear of terrorists' use of weapons of mass destruction to the top of the national agenda. But it did. In the words of the president, "In the Cold War, weapons of mass destruction were considered weapons of last resort as they risked the destruction of those who used them. Today, our enemies see weapons of mass destruction as weapons of choice."[24] Public opinion polls in the months after 9/11 attest to the widespread fear of an imminent attack on the United States using weapons of mass destruction.[25] Ever since the Japanese cult Aum Shinrikyo had released sarin gas on the Tokyo subway in 1995, American officials have been deeply troubled at the prospect that terrorists might use weapons of mass destruction against the United States. After 9/11 these fears became endemic, with most officials saying it was simply a matter of time.

The term "weapons of mass destruction," or, more often, "WMD," is used to describe broadly three types of weapons: chemical, biological, and nuclear. Distinctions are not often drawn among the different types of weapons, but it is actually very important to understand that they differ significantly from one another in their lethality, their novelty, in the ease of their deployment, and their usefulness to terrorists. Just as it is imperative to disaggregate the notion of terrorism and differentiate among types of terrorist groups with different motives and different capabilities, so it is crucial to understand that the term "WMD" is a very broad one and incorporates very different types of threat to the United States. In order to understand the extent to which there was a change in the threat posed to the United States, therefore, we must disaggregate this concept of weapons of mass destruction and explore the nature of the different types of weapon that fall under this rubric.

CHEMICAL WEAPONS

There are four major categories under which chemical agents can be classified according to their effects: blister agents, choking agents, blood agents, and nerve agents. Blister agents are designed to cause injury rather than death. So if a murderous group wanted to cause chaos and overload a region's medical facilities without actually killing many people, it might opt for a blister agent such as mustard gas. It is hard to imagine, however, how this approach would appeal to any known terrorist group. Choking agents were widely used in World War I. They are designed to kill their victims, and their biggest attraction from a terrorist point of view is that they are so easy to obtain. Cyanide-based compounds are the main components of blood agents. These work best for individual assassinations rather than mass attacks because of the rapid rate of evaporation. The newest trend in chemical weapons has been nerve agents. These weapons, such as sarin, tabun, and soman, have been the main weapons stockpiled as chemical weapons. These were the types of weapons deployed by Saddam Hussein against the Kurdish city of Halabja in March 1988. In general, they are hundreds of times more lethal than blister, choking, and blood agents. They are particularly attractive to those seeking to do harm because of the small amount needed to do a lot of damage.

The advantages of chemical weapons for terrorists include the fact that they are cheap and easy to obtain, little training is required in their use, and production of the crude agents is fairly straightforward. The most difficult part is dispersing the weapons correctly. Chemical weapons can also be quite dangerous to handle and quite difficult to control, so their appeal to terrorists has been quite limited. Over the years a number of terrorist groups have been linked to chemical weapons, but these episodes remain quite rare. Lacking the dramatic effect of a bombing or hijacking and entailing considerable risk to the handlers, they have not been an attractive option for terrorists.

The one exception occurred on March 20, 1995. On that day, at the height of the morning rush hour, five teams of two members each of Aum Shinrikyo, a Japanese sect led by Shoko Asahara, smuggled small gas dispensers onto several subway trains in Tokyo. The trains were all due to arrive at the Kasumigaseki Station, in the heart of the capital's government district, shortly after 8 A.M. The cult members were smartly dressed in business suits and carried umbrellas, as well as plastic bags of sarin concealed in the morning newspaper. As the trains pulled into the station, they left the bags on parcel racks, punctured them with the tips of their umbrellas, quickly alighted from the trains, and promptly swallowed an antidote. The dispensers released the nerve gas, causing pandemonium. Many thousands of commuters were overcome, 12 people died, and 5,500 were injured. The attack was the first successful use of chemical weapons by a terrorist group, and it appeared to demonstrate just how easy it could be for terrorists to deploy chemical or biological weapons in an open society. The casualties in this instance would have been considerably higher if the chemists had made the concoction stronger. Moreover, it became clear once the group's headquarters were raided that it had the facilities to produce several other nerve agents as well.

Aum Shinrikyo, however, was a highly unusual case, as the testimony presented at the trials of those accused in the Tokyo attack attest. In spite of a series of indications of their illegal activities, their status as a religious organization had protected them from police investigation. The organization had global assets estimated at $1 billion and a membership estimated to be about fifty thousand. It had twenty scientists with graduate degrees among its membership as well as extensive, elaborate, and highly modern technical facilities. Indeed, Masami Tsuchiya, Aum's top scientist, who held a master's degree in organic chemistry from Tsukuba University and who confessed to having created the sarin, explained that he had joined the cult because it had far better laboratory facilities than his university.[26] It recruited the top science graduates from Tokyo's best universities. They practiced for five years and made nine attempts before successfully pulling off the sarin gas attack. Two further failed attempts followed the March attack. In all, they launched twelve attacks, and only the Tokyo attack made an impact, though far less than intended by the group. The experience of Aum suggests that developing these weapons is not as easy as it is often presented and requires scientific expertise, significant funding, and secure laboratories. These means are not readily available to a terrorist group, though they could, of course, be provided to one by a sponsoring state. Aum itself was dismantled after the Tokyo attack and has reemerged as a peaceful group.

There were many reports, prior to 9/11, of al-Qaeda's interest in securing chemical weapons, though these reports rarely made an impact on the public. In one instance they did. On August 20, 1998, charging that al-Qaeda was producing chemical weapons at the al-Shifa Pharmaceutical Factory in Khartoum, Sudan, the United States bombed the factory, killing one worker and injuring twelve others. This action was partly in retaliation for the bombing of the American embassies in Nairobi and Dar es Salaam. Subsequent reports suggested that the information on which the attack was based was inaccurate, and the factory's owner, Salah Idris, filed suit against the U.S. government, claiming compensation. In response the U.S. Treasury unfroze Idris's American bank accounts, thereby implicitly acknowledging that it lacked the evidence to justify its action against him.[27]

There were a variety of other reports in the 1990s of plans by al-Qaeda to develop and deploy chemical weapons, in particular cyanide. There were reports of crude laboratories in Khost, Jalalabad, and Charassiab, Afghanistan.[28] There were also reports that bin Laden had bought chemical and biological weapons from former Soviet states.[29]

More fanciful reports declared that bin Laden had bought no fewer than three CBW factories in the former Yugoslavia and hired a number of Ukrainian biologists and chemists to train his members.[30] Ahmad Rassam, who pleaded guilty to plotting to bomb Los Angeles International Airport, claimed in court that he had witnessed a dog being gassed with cyanide. These claims were consistent with an al-Qaeda video broadcast on CNN showing dogs being killed by toxic chemicals, probably a crude nerve agent or hydrogen cyanide gas.[31] The Italian government claims that by arresting nine Moroccans in February 2000 it foiled a plan to poison the water supply of the U.S. embassy in Rome using a cyanide compound.[32] When U.S. forces toppled the Taliban, however, they found evidence only of very primitive laboratory facilities.

Most of the reports since 9/11 have been about al-Qaeda's interest in these weapons while in Afghanistan. An al-Qaeda computer that fell into the hands of a *Wall Street Journal* reporter, Alan Cullison, in Kabul, for example, contained details of a project, code-named "Curdled Milk," that was under the direction of Ayman al-Zawahiri and included plans to launch a chemical and biological weapons program.[33] With the capture of Khalid Shaikh Mohammed in 2003, more detailed information on the progress of this program appears to have been acquired. According to reports, captured documents indicated that al-Qaeda had the requisite material to manufacture cyanide and two biological toxins and were close to producing anthrax bacteria.[34] Other post-9/11 reports claimed that al-Qaeda members were being trained in secret camps near Baghdad in how to use chemical and biological weapons by instructors from the secret Iraqi military intelligence unit.[35] The United States found no evidence to verify these reports once it occupied Iraq. In all likelihood, these reports were fabricated, or at best exaggerated, in order to satisfy the American conviction that terrorists were developing chemical weapons.

While there can be little doubt that some members of al-Qaeda displayed a keen interest in acquiring chemical weapons, there is no evidence that they succeeded in doing so. The ability of the organization to pursue this interest, moreover, was far greater prior to the fall of the Taliban, when it could operate openly in Afghanistan. It appears, therefore, that the fear of its using chemical weapons increased just as its capacity to do so declined.

DIOLOOIOAL WCArONS

Far from being new, biological weapons have been around as long as warfare itself. The term essentially means the intentional use of biologically derived agents or disease to undermine the adversary's strength. There are two categories of biological warfare agents: microorganisms, which are living organic germs such as anthrax, and toxins, which are the by-products of living organisms or essentially natural poisons such as botulism or ricin. There are also a great many natural and man-made variants. Biological warfare includes such well-honed ancient practices as catapulting carcasses of dead animals into a besieged city to spread disease or placing dead horses in the enemy's water supply (a common practice in the American Civil War).

One of the most famous cases of biological warfare in American history occurred during the French and Indian War (1754–1767). The English believed that the Indians holding Fort Carillon were loyal to the French. In 1763, in an apparently altruistic gesture, they offered blankets to the Indians, but before handing over the blankets they exposed the blankets to the smallpox virus. The Indians got sick, the epidemic spread, and the British attacked and defeated them handily.

There have been a variety of very minor incidents of the use of biological weapons by terrorists. In the 1980s, a number of Red Army Faction (RAF) safe houses in Germany and France were found to have bathtubs full of biological agents. More serious were a number of assassination attempts made with ricin-tipped umbrellas. One of the more famous of these incidents was the murder of Georgi Markov, a BBC World Service journalist and active critic of the Communist Bulgarian regime. He was killed by being poked with a ricin-tipped umbrella while waiting at a bus stop in London in 1978. Though labeled terrorism at the time, these assassination attempts were actually the covert actions of governments trying to eliminate difficult dissidents overseas.

Generally, biological agents are many times deadlier than chemical agents pound for pound. Ten grams of anthrax spores, for example, would kill as many people as a ton of the nerve gas sarin. Indeed if the Aum Shinrikyo group had used anthrax instead of sarin, it would have killed many more people in Tokyo. One of the big advantages of biological weapons from the point of view of the terrorist is how difficult they are to detect while they are being produced or transported. If one

were carrying a biological agent in a briefcase onto an airplane, for example, there are no mechanisms that would identify it. Alternatively,
the agent could easily be concealed in an aerosol can. Readers of Tom
Clancy novels will have come across many other ideas too.

The fact that members of al-Qaeda were willing to kill as many
people as possible led to the fear that they would not hesitate to use
biological weapons. These fears were greatly exacerbated by a series of
anthrax attacks that occurred shortly after the demolition of the World
Trade Center. Exactly a week after 9/11, five letters containing anthrax
were mailed to media outlets in the United States. Three weeks later,
two further letters were mailed, this time to two Democratic senators
and this time containing a more potent and highly refined form of anthrax. In all, seven letters were mailed, five people died, and nobody
has yet been charged with the crime. The consensus among the investigators is that these letters were mailed not by a member of al-Qaeda but
rather by an American with a grudge, probably one who had worked
in one of the country's most sophisticated biolabs, such as the Level 4
Laboratory at Fort Detrick, Maryland. The appearance of anthrax
greatly contributed to the sense of fear and insecurity as local officials
were deluged with calls from a frightened public fearing that every
white powder they encountered might be anthrax.

Al-Qaeda's continued interest in biological weapons, particularly in
ricin, is evidenced by a number of arrests in Europe that have found
traces of the toxin and equipment for its production. These arrests include the December 2002 arrest of Menad Benchellali, known as "the
chemist" because of his chemical weapons training in Chechnya or
Afghanistan and later in Georgia. He had a makeshift laboratory in the
spare bedroom of his parents' home in Lyon, France, where he developed ricin and stored it in Nivea face cream jars before giving them to
a chemist for safekeeping. Two years after his arrest, several members
of his family were charged with involvement too. Authorities believe
that there are interconnected cells of North Africans attempting to develop ricin operating in France, Britain, and Spain, but this has yet to
be proven.[36]

In January 2003, nine Algerians were also arrested in London after
a makeshift ricin lab appeared to have been found in their flat above a
chemist shop. This incident was deeply troubling to the British public
and was invoked by the British prime minister, Tony Blair, as well as

the American secretary of state, Colin Powell, in an effort to gain support for the American-led invasion of Iraq. It subsequently transpired, however, that traces of ricin had not been found in the flat.[37] In April 2005, four of those charged were acquitted and charges against four others were dropped. Only one man was convicted, and that was for murdering a policeman in the course of the raid. While the alleged discovery of ricin received worldwide attention, the revelation that no traces of ricin had been found, just a number of recipes downloaded from the Internet, went largely unnoticed.[38] This case speaks to the way the media can help to exaggerate our reactions. Finding a ricin factory in London was big news, all the more so when the governments involved constantly referred to it; the fact that there was no factory after all did not make such a good story, and so it got lost. Meanwhile, the public perception that underground bioweapons factories are proliferating remains.

One of al-Qaeda's manuals, known as *The Encyclopedia of Jihad,* actually commends ricin as relatively easy to produce and harmless to the developer, and provides instruction on its production from readily available castor beans.[39] While undoubtedly deadly, ricin is more appropriate for assassination than for mass attacks. Given the relative ease with which it can be produced, one can understand its appeal to terrorists, though far more readily available ingredients such as fertilizer can inflict far greater harm. Remember that Timothy McVeigh managed to take down the Murrah Federal Building with a readily available agricultural fertilizer and some motor-racing fuel.

Earlier claims about al-Qaeda's cache of bioweapons also appear to have been exaggerated. A number of defendants on trial in Egypt claimed that al-Qaeda had obtained biological weapons substances, including the Ebola virus and salmonella bacterium, through the mail from countries of the former Soviet Union as well as anthrax-causing bacteria from East Asia and botulinum toxin from the Czech Republic.[40] Shortly after 9/11, there were also reports that Mohamed Atta, the leader of the suicide team, had had a meeting in Prague with an Iraqi intelligence agent who had allegedly given him a vial of anthrax. The Czech government has vehemently challenged the veracity of this claim.[41] There were reports from U.S. forces in Afghanistan in late 2001 that the homes of al-Qaeda leaders in Kabul tested positive for anthrax, but these claims too have been challenged. John Walker

Lindh, the so-called American Taliban, allegedly told his interrogators that battlefield rumors were rife that there was going to be a second wave of attacks by al-Qaeda and that they would be biological attacks.[42] It now appears that most claims about biological weapons were just that—rumors—and many were elicited in response to the evident American interest in the subject.

American forces did appear to find a biological weapons plant under construction in Afghanistan. It was apparently being built to produce anthrax, though no traces of any biological agents were found there.[43] The French prime minister, Dominique de Villepin, asserted in January 2005 that al-Qaeda affiliates had moved to the Pankisi Gorge region of Georgia after the fall of the Taliban in order to continue their efforts to produce anthrax bacteria, ricin, and botulinum toxin.[44] Still other reports have said that two groups closely allied to al-Qaeda, Ansar al-Islam and Jemaah Islamiyah, have both sought to develop biological weapons.[45]

Many of these reports were of questionable reliability. Most appear to have been ignored prior to 9/11 and to have been taken on face value after 9/11. The truth probably lies in between. As with chemical weapons, al-Qaeda has clearly had an interest in developing biological weapons, not least because of their scare value. There is not much evidence to suggest, however, that it has succeeded in acquiring these weapons in any meaningful numbers. As it has lost the sanctuary of Afghanistan, it has become extremely difficult for it to acquire the capacity to produce them in significant quantities.

It is worth remembering the experience of Aum Shinrikyo in this respect. In spite of its excellent facilities, its trained scientists, and its immunity from police oversight, Aum did not succeed in deploying biological weapons. Initially Aum opted for biological weapons over chemical weapons because of their greater lethality. In its first several attempts, Aum actually tried to use biological toxins and failed. It developed an anthrax bomb, which it tried to deploy twice, once from a truck and once from a skyscraper, to no effect. After four failed attempts with biological weapons, it turned to chemical weapons and produced sarin. The first time the group used it, it killed one of the group's own scientists, so it diluted the gas. It was this diluted concoction that was deployed in the fatal attack in Tokyo. This attack was followed by two further failed attempts, one involving cyanide.[46] None of this is to suggest that we should ignore the possibility that terrorists might use chemical or biological weapons. Followers of bin Laden have demonstrated an interest in acquiring them. It is to suggest, however, that the fears of their use that were prompted by 9/11 are probably overblown, that chemical and biological weapons are more difficult to develop and to deploy effectively than is widely believed, and that, thanks to the destruction of its sanctuary in Afghanistan, al-Qaeda is likely to find it more difficult to acquire them now than before 9/11. The constant allegations of weapons finds, however, greatly fed into the fear generated by the 9/11 attacks.

Including biological and chemical weapons under the broader rubric of weapons of mass destruction is itself questionable, though it predates 9/11. In fact, chemical and biological weapons have in the past in-flicted far fewer casualties than more conventional forms of weaponry. Biological weapons, while relatively easy to acquire, are extremely dif-ficult to deploy effectively, while chemical weapons have to be used in vast quantities in order to be effective. It is probably for these reasons that biological and chemical weapons have seen so little use by states in wartime. On the relatively rare occasions when they have been used, they have not been responsible for a significant percentage of the over-all casualties. World War I saw the heaviest use of chemical weapons, which caused 5 percent of the overall casualties. Chemical weapons caused less than 1 percent of the Iranian casualties when used by Iraq in the Iran-Iraq War.[47] Reportage of every purported incident in which a terrorist might have acquired these weapons and thereby feeding the public fear that mass casualties are just around the corner is, of course, exactly the kind of reaction terrorism attempts to elicit.

NUCLEAR WEAPONS

The biggest fear of all, of course, is that terrorists might use nuclear weapons. In the 2004 presidential debate, both President George Bush and his opponent, Senator John Kerry, ranked nuclear proliferation and, in particular, weapons falling into the hands of terrorists as the biggest security threat facing the United States. The risk of "loose nukes" had been a constant concern to American administrations since the end of the Cold War. The fear was that the collapse of the Soviet Union would facilitate trafficking in nuclear weapons. There was considerable concern at the quality of security in Russian nuclear facilities. There were also concerns that underpaid Russian scientists might attempt to sell their knowledge or some of the contents of their labs or that the Russian Mafia might attempt to raise significant amounts of cash by acquiring nuclear materials. Any of these groups, it was thought, could take advantage of the permeability of Russia's southern borders. These concerns were heightened when Aum Shinrikyo broke the taboo on terrorist use of WMD. The imperviousness to any constraints on civilian casualties exhibited on 9/11 led to widespread concerns that al-Qaeda would not hesitate to use nuclear weapons.

Official pronouncements by the government tended not to distinguish between different types of weapons of mass destruction. But evidently the public did. Specifically, the public consistently found that a nuclear attack posed less of an immediate threat than did a chemical or biological attack, by 13 percent to 75 percent.[48] That said, fully 16 percent said they expected terrorists to detonate a nuclear device within the United States within a year, and a further 23 percent said they expected it within the next five years.[49]

Notwithstanding the availability of nuclear materials technologies and expertise, there was nothing to suggest that al-Qaeda had the ability or even the motive to use nuclear weapons against the United States. The consequence of such an action would be so catastrophic, however, that the possibility was widely discussed. Developing nuclear weapons is far from easy. Nevertheless, the task would be rendered a lot easier with a sponsoring state to provide protected facilities in which to work or even the fissile material itself. It was precisely the fear that Saddam Hussein was developing weapons of mass destruction and that he might put them into the hands of terrorists that led the American public to support the invasion of Iraq.

Bin Laden himself did not help matters; on the contrary, he appears to have been happy to exploit American fears. He simply insisted that he had the same right to possess nuclear or any other weapons that the West had. In an interview with al-Jazeera television in 2001, bin Laden was asked how true were the reports that he sought to acquire nuclear, chemical, and biological weapons. He replied:

> We are seeking to drive them [the United States] out of our Islamic nations and prevent them from dominating us. We believe that this

right to defend oneself is the right of all human beings. At a time when Israel stocks hundreds of nuclear warheads and when the western crusaders control a large percentage of this weapon, we do not consider this an accusation but a right.[50]

As with chemical and biological weapons, prior to 9/11 there were a great many reports that bin Laden had acquired nuclear weapons, but these reports did not penetrate the popular consciousness in the United States. In the case the United States brought against bin Laden for the embassy bombings, a prosecution witness, Jamal Ahmad al-Fadl, testified that as early as 1993–1994 he had been charged by al-Qaeda to acquire uranium in Khartoum. In August 1998, a leaked Israel intelligence report stated that bin Laden had paid more than two million British pounds to a middleman in Kazakhstan for a "suitcase" bomb. A few months later, Russian intelligence services informed their American counterparts that bin Laden had given a group of Chechens $30 million in cash and two tons of opium in exchange for twenty nuclear warheads.[51] In September 1998, a full three years before 9/11, an alleged aide of bin Laden, Mamduh Mahmud Salim, was arrested in Germany for trying to obtain highly enriched uranium for al-Qaeda.[52] There were other reports of expensive failed efforts by bin Laden to acquire enriched uranium in Eastern Europe.[53] In December 2000, Arab security sources alleged that a shipment of about twenty nuclear warheads originating from Kazakhstan, Turkmenistan, Russia, and Ukraine had been intercepted en route to bin Laden.[54]

Reports after 9/11 were even more alarming. One report, this time in November 2001, claimed that al-Qaeda had acquired a Russian-made suitcase nuclear bomb from Central Asian sources. The device was reported to weigh eight kilograms and to possess two kilograms of fissionable uranium and plutonium. The report said that the device, with a serial number of 9999, had been manufactured in October 1998 and could be set off by a mobile phone.[55] On February 8, 2004, the Egyptian newspaper al-Hayat reported that al-Qaeda had bought tactical nuclear weapons from Ukraine in 1998 and was holding them in storage. The Ukrainian government denied the claim and insisted that it had transferred all nuclear weapons to Russia by 1996.[56] No evidence was discovered in Afghanistan suggesting that al-Qaeda had nuclear weapons, but evidence of its interest in nuclear weapons was found. A London *Times* reporter discovered a blueprint for a "Nagasaki bomb" in files in an abandoned al-Qaeda house in Kabul. The "super-bomb" manual, as it was called, discusses the advanced physics of nuclear weapons and dirty bombs. There can be little doubt, therefore, that al-Qaeda has contemplated the acquisition of nuclear weapons.[57]

Asked in September 2001 and again two months later whether they thought bin Laden currently had access to nuclear weapons, 63 percent of Americans replied "yes."[58]

It is impossible to know for certain, but there can be little doubt that most of these reports are as reliable as the reports that Saddam Hussein was developing and stockpiling weapons of mass destruction. All the indications are that al-Qaeda has tried and failed to procure nuclear weapons and that it is very far from being in a position to deploy them. Its statements claiming a right to possess nuclear weapons have been misinterpreted as expressing a determination to use them. This in turn has fed the exaggeration of the threat we face.

DIRTY BOMBS

A far more likely scenario than a nuclear attack is the detonation of a "dirty bomb." Often confused with nuclear weapons, a dirty bomb uses conventional explosives to disperse radioactive materials. Even a small amount of radioactive material, if properly milled into fine particles and dispersed by a conventional explosive, could spread radioactive particles over an area of several blocks. The most devastating aspect of a dirty bomb is the panic it would in all likelihood cause. The lethality of a dirty bomb, however, is quite limited when compared to the impact of even a crude nuclear bomb, in which there is a nuclear chain reaction that can kill tens of thousands of people within a three-mile radius of the blast as well as thousands more from radiation poisoning.

Again, there have been many reports of al-Qaeda's interest in procuring a dirty bomb. A month after 9/11, *The Sunday Times* of London reported on meetings at which bin Laden had sought to purchase nuclear and radiological materials.[59] In November 2001, the Italian organized crime office alleged that bin Laden had obtained seven enriched uranium rods from Mafia connections. The rods had apparently been made in the United States.[60] In early 2003, British intelligence sources indicated that they had found documents that suggested that al-Qaeda members had built a dirty bomb in Afghanistan with the assistance of medical isotopes provided by the Taliban.[61] Other reports claim that bin Laden bought radiological materials through contacts in Chechnya.[62] There have also been many reports of intercepted efforts to purchase radioactive materials by al-Qaeda operatives. Again, it is impossible to assess the accuracy of these reports.

The case that generated the most concern in the United States was the case of Jose Padilla, a former gang member and United States citizen who was arrested in Chicago in May 2002 on the grounds that he was planning to organize a dirty-bomb attack on the United States for al-Qaeda. Padilla has been held as an enemy combatant, the only American citizen arrested in this country to be so classified. Two years after his arrest, the Justice Department revealed that in fact he had not been planning to deploy a dirty bomb but instead to blow up some apartment buildings. The plan had apparently been a modest one that involved Padilla and an accomplice renting two apartments. They then planned to turn on the natural gas and set off conventional explosive devices simultaneously in both buildings.[63] As an enemy combatant, Padilla has not yet been brought to trial. In the minds of most Americans, however, he has been incarcerated for planning a dirty bomb attack on this country. In December 2005, the Bush administration decided to change course and sought to have Padilla released from military custody and tried in civilian court. In the case of both Padilla's dirty bomb and the Algerian ricin ring in London, the conviction that al-Qaeda was pursuing WMDs appears to have outweighed the evidence that it has done so. Reports of these cases helped to instill fear and exacerbate the sense of insecurity occasioned by 9/11. From the terrorists' point of view, the mere suggestion that they have or plan to use WMDs serves their purpose by exaggerating their capabilities and frightening their adversary.

Bin Laden has long understood the essential role of terrorism as communication. His regular video and audio appearances, as well as those of his senior associates, have sought to intimidate the enemy and hearten his followers. As a regular follower of the Western media, bin Laden is well aware of the fear weapons of mass destruction evoke in the American public. He has deliberately fueled concerns about his possible use of WMDs by declaring it to be a religious duty to acquire them and a right to use them. He has been very successful and, I expect, deliberately so in exploiting these fears.

On a number of occasions, bin Laden and al-Zawahiri have claimed to have nuclear weapons. In an interview in early 1999 with *Time* magazine, bin Laden asserted, "Acquiring weapons for the defense of Muslims is a religious duty. If I have indeed acquired these weapons, then I thank God for enabling me to do so. And if I seek to acquire these weapons, I am carrying out a duty. It would be a sin for Muslims not to try to possess the weapons that would prevent the infidels from inflicting harm on Muslims."[64] A Pakistani reporter, Hamid Mir, claims to have interviewed bin Laden in November 2001 and says that bin Laden asserted, "We have chemical and nuclear weapons as a deterrent and if America used them against us we reserve the right to use them."[65] Five months later, an al-Qaeda leader, Abu Zubayda, claimed that al-Qaeda had the interest and the know-how to produce radiological weapons and knew how to smuggle them into the United States.[66] On another occasion, Ayman al-Zawahiri went considerably further. He told Hamid Mir that al-Qaeda possessed nuclear weapons purchased in Central Asia. Al-Qaeda's second in command asserted that operatives had been sent to Central Asia to purchase portable nuclear material. He is quoted as having said, "If you have $30 million, go to the black market in central Asia, contact any disgruntled Soviet scientist and a lot of . . . dozens of smart briefcase bombs are available."[67]

In making these claims al-Qaeda is undoubtedly attempting to carry out the essential psychological aspect of its terrorist campaign. Aware of Americans' fears of WMDs, al-Qaeda will further its efforts to acquire them and by announcing that it has them will try to acquire the benefits of possession even if it lacks the reality. One gets the clear impression that bin Laden is skillfully engaged in a game of manipulation, trying to stoke the fears that he has generated. In fact, the risk of WMD was actually greater before 9/11 than afterward due to the sanctuary provided in Afghanistan and access to opium to trade for weapons. Most Americans appreciated the risk only after 9/11, and then it became a preoccupation. The American government became obsessed with the fear that an enemy state might provide terrorists with weapons of mass destruction. This fear led the country into war.

In all the discussions of our vulnerabilities to WMDs, there was almost no public discussion of the nature of the threat, no distinctions drawn among chemical, biological, nuclear, and radiological weapons, nor any public discussion of the limitations of these weapons. Rather, government statements have tended to group all forms of weapons of mass destruction together as an apocalyptic means of destroying the country. In fact, as I have pointed out, there are very real differences between the different types of weapons that are linked under the rubric of WMD. Moreover, the lethality of any biological and chemical weapons or dirty bombs likely to be acquired by terrorist groups pales in comparison to that of natural disasters such as Hurricane Katrina.

The numbers killed by all forms of weapons of mass destruction throughout history come to about 400,000.[68] The bombs dropped on Hiroshima and Nagasaki killed more than 100,000 people. Nuclear technology has undoubtedly come a long way since then, but it is worth remembering that conventional weapons, whether deployed by states or by terrorists, have killed a great many more people. Our preoccupation with WMDs, however, has greatly enhanced their benefits to our adversaries. As they want to intimidate us, they know that they can do so by having, or pretending to have, access to weapons of mass destruction. If some al-Qaeda sympathizers were to get access to some ricin, they could not kill many people, but they could be confident of having a major psychological impact. In this way our emphasis on WMDs runs the risk of creating a self-fulfilling prophecy.

The detonation of a nuclear bomb would undoubtedly be devastating and would indeed constitute a turning point in history. But the conflation of this risk with that posed by a hapless Frenchman concocting ricin in his parents' spare bedroom serves only to undermine our ability to formulate coherent and effective counterterrorist policies. While the probability of any terrorist group obtaining access to nuclear weapons is very low, due to the difficulty of acquiring facilities to develop them and the unwillingness of states to provide them, the consequences would be so enormous that the risk has to be taken very seriously and focused policies developed to address it.

The fear inspired by the 9/11 attack and the government's response to that attack led us to conflate the threats instead of analyzing them, gauging the risks, and responding appropriately. Just as distinctions were not drawn among the types of weapons that could be used against us, distinctions were also not drawn among the enemies we faced. The fear that terrorists might acquire WMDs from an enemy state was such that we did not stop to analyze the relations between the terrorists and those states. We developed a plan to prevent Saddam Hussein from giving weapons to Osama bin Laden without any consideration of the likelihood that he would do so or the relations between the two men. Middle East experts in the State Department and terrorist experts around the country were quick to point out that Saddam Hussein was exactly the kind of secular, corrupt Islamic leader that bin Laden was dedicated to overthrowing. They sought to remind the country that when Hussein had invaded Kuwait in 1990, bin Laden had approached the Saudi authorities and offered to mobilize the mujahedin, who had fought successfully in Afghanistan, to fight Hussein and expel him from Kuwait. Knowing only that both Saddam and bin Laden were our enemies and ignoring the fact that they were each other's enemies too, we conflated the threat and eventually created a self-fulfilling prophecy.

Saddam Hussein, of course, was notorious for having deployed chemical weapons against Iran and against the Iraqi Kurds in the course of the Iran-Iraq War. Of the 600,000 Iranians killed in the Iran-Iraq War about 5,000 were killed by chemical weapons deployed by Iraq.[69] Estimates of the number of Kurds killed by Iraqi chemical weapons in Halabja range from several hundred to 5,000. The fact that Saddam Hussein was prepared to use chemical weapons was considered enough to justify the conviction that he would hand some of these weapons over to terrorists to use against us. The heightened sense of insecurity caused by the 9/11 attacks appears to have prevented public discussion of the logic of this assumption. We felt that we could not afford to take the chance.

Terrorists were no more likely to use WMDs after 9/11 than before. And in fact, given the loss of their sanctuary in Afghanistan, they were even less likely to use them. What changed on 9/11 was that terrorists demonstrated that they could land a powerful blow on us. They did not demonstrate that they had the wherewithal to repeat the act or to wage a military campaign against us; we just assumed that they could. The public attitude toward weapons of mass destruction changed dramatically. One year after the Oklahoma City bombing, 66 percent of Americans said that they were not worried about terrorism in public places in the United States.[70] September 11 changed all that.

Through a combination of failures on our part and a long series of lucky breaks on theirs, al-Qaeda managed to hit us and hit us hard. But it could not follow up. It did threaten the lives of American civilians, but it posed no real threat to the security of the state itself. It would be extraordinarily difficult for it to repeat such an attack on the United States. What changed was that the American public was now prepared to believe that terrorists wanted WMDs and wanted to use them. When this conviction was added to the widespread belief that al-Qaeda was linked to Saddam Hussein and the fear that Hussein would give these weapons to al-Qaeda, the combination became a crucial factor in mobilizing support for the war on Iraq, which was to have such portentous ramifications for the campaign against terrorism.

It is not quite true, therefore, that, in the words of President Bush, "September 11 changed our world." Rather it was our reaction to September 11 that changed the world. Americans suffered a terrorist attack unprecedented in its scale and destructiveness and in so doing lost their sense of security and their sense of perspective. The fear engendered by the attack was out of proportion to the threat we faced. We believed that we now faced a powerful enemy driven by irrational religious fanaticism and determined to use weapons of mass destruction against us. In fact, our enemy was much less powerful than we thought, demonstrated a persistent capacity for rational behavior, and had concrete political as well as religious motivations, and its interest in weapons of mass destruction was driven more by a desire to intimidate us and defend itself against us than by the desire to deploy them in the United States.

At home Americans became convinced that it was unsafe to fly, even though the facts clearly indicated otherwise.[71] (Economists have calculated that among the uncounted casualties of 9/11 are the extra 1,200 fatalities on the road occasioned by the diversion from air to road transport after 9/11.[72]) Abroad, the American government conflated the threats it faced and based its policies on the vulnerabilities it felt, rather than the threats it faced. The heinousness of the attack, moreover, blinded the United States to some of the legitimate objections to its policies overseas. One thing that did not change was Americans' confidence in the rectitude of their actions or the unassailability of their moral position.

Domestically, a weak and unpopular president, recently elected with a highly questionable mandate, was transformed into a war leader by a population seeking the security of a strong leader. Believing that the world had changed, we were prepared to accept changes in our long-standing national security doctrine and infrastructure in response. The enormous scale of the atrocity seemed to merit a powerful response, and the United States responded with the most potent weapon in its armory, a declaration of war. But the war was not declared on those who had committed the crime, but rather on the tactic they had used to hurt us. It was a war we could not win.

SEVEN

WHY THE WAR ON TERROR
CAN NEVER BE WON

The security forces set about their work in a manner which might have been deliberately designed to drive the population into our arms. On the pretext of searching they burst into people's homes by day and night, made them stand for hours with their hands up, abused and insulted them. . . . These attempts to frighten the people away from EOKA always had exactly the opposite effect to that intended: the population were merely bound more closely to the Organization and the young scorned the threat of the gallows.[1]

—George Grivas, leader of EOKA

The story had already started with the Shah's visit of '67, when Ohnesorg was shot—a completely harmless man. After that, things were different.

Two days earlier he had been in the Extrablatt office making an order, and I had happened to be helping out at the sales desk where I saw him briefly. Then three or four days later I was standing by his casket, and that gave me a really crazy flash. It's hard to describe it: something terrible got started in me. I couldn't get over it, that some idiot comes along and guns down an unarmed man.

I had been in a lot of barroom fights, and even though they were often really tough, you always kept some semblance of fairness. . . . But a thing like this was just straight out murder to me.

Benno Ohnesorg. It did a crazy thing to me. When his casket went by, it just went ding, something got started there.[2]

—Bommi Baumann, member of the German June 2nd Movement

WHEN THE HISTORY OF THE IMMEDIATE POST-9/11 YEARS comes to be written, it will be seen as a period marked by two major mistakes and two major missed opportunities. The mistakes were a declaration of war against terrorism and the conflation of the threat from al-Qaeda with the threat from Saddam Hussein. The missed opportunities were the opportunities to educate the American public to the realities of terrorism and to the costs of our sole superpower status and the opportunity to mobilize the international community behind us in a transnational campaign against transnational terrorists.

As soon as the enormity of the atrocity became clear on September 11, the U.S. government reacted with a declaration of war. In an address to the nation on the night of the attack, the president declared, "Immediately following the first attack, I implemented our government's emergency response plans. Our military is powerful, and it's prepared. . . . America and our friends and allies join with all those who want peace and security in the world, and we stand together to win the war against terrorism."[3] Nine days later, when the president addressed a joint session of Congress and the American people on September 20, 2001, the declaration of war on the tactic of terrorism was cast as a declaration of war on the emotion of terror: "Our war on terror begins with al Qaeda, but it does not end there. It will not end until every terrorist group of global reach has been found, stopped and defeated."[4]

The scale of the attack was so enormous that there was little question that war was the right response. On September 18, the U.S. Congress authorized the president to "use all necessary and appropriate force against those nations, organizations, or persons he determines planned, authorized, committed or aided the terrorist attacks that occurred on September 11, 2001, or harbored such organizations or persons, in order to prevent any future acts of international terrorism against the United States by such nations, organizations or persons."[5]

Only hours after the attack on Pearl Harbor, the U.S. Congress voted a declaration of war against Japan, and President Roosevelt signed the declaration the following day, December 8, 1941. In 2001, the memory of Pearl Harbor was often invoked. Also invoked was the 1996 fatwa of Osama bin Laden entitled "Declaration of War against the Americans Occupying the Land of the Two Holy Places [Saudi Arabia]" and his second fatwa two years later: "The ruling to kill the Americans and their allies—civilians and military—is an individual duty for every Muslim who can do it in any country in which it is possible to do it, in order to liberate the al-Aqsa Mosque and the holy mosque from their grip, and in order for their armies to move out of the lands of Islam, defeated and unable to threaten any Muslim."[6] As bin Laden had declared war against us and in bombing our cities had committed an act of war against us there was little doubt that war was the appropriate response. Nor was there much doubt about the outcome of the war: "People have declared war on America and they have made a terrible mistake," declared the president.[7] Polls indicated that more than 90 percent of the American public were confident of victory.[8]

Bin Laden's al-Qaeda was not the first violent group to declare war on America. On July 31, 1970, in Berkeley, California, Bernardine Dohrn, an attractive young woman in her signature outfit of short skirt and high boots, issued communiqué No. 1 from the Weather Underground, a militant offshoot of the SDS. It was entitled "A Declaration of a State of War." The statement read, in part:

> All over the world, people fighting Amerikan imperialism look to Amerikan youth to use our strategic position behind enemy lines to join forces in the destruction of the empire. . . . Tens of thousands have learned that protest and marches don't do it. Revolutionary violence is the only way. . . . We will never live peaceably under this system. . . . Within the next fourteen days we will attack a symbol or institution of American injustice.[9]

The words of the Weather Underground proved to be more violent than its deeds. Although it did bomb more than two dozen buildings, it sought to avoid human casualties. It generally did. But on the evening of August 24, 1970, members of the group drove a van filled with ammonium nitrate and fuel oil and detonated it outside the Sterling Hall building of the University of Wisconsin in Madison. A postdoctoral student in chemistry, Robert Fassnacht, who was working late, was killed in the explosion. The Weathermen had been trying to destroy the Army Mathematics Research Center. They believed that their violence was morally justified because its goal was to end greater violence and gross injustice by the United States in Vietnam.

Nor was this the first time an American president had spoken of a war on terrorism. In his 1986 speech to the United Nations General Assembly President Ronald Reagan said, "The United States believes that the understandings reached by the seven industrial democracies at the Tokyo summit last May make a good start towards an international accord in the war on terrorism."[10] The phrase "war on terrorism" had also been fairly widely used much earlier by the press to describe the efforts by Russian, European, and eventually American governments to stop assassination attempts by international anarchists in the late nineteenth century.[11]

Of much more recent memory were other, metaphorical, wars. In his State of the Union Address on January 8, 1964, President Lyndon Johnson declared a "War on Poverty," which was designed to address the plight of 35 million Americans living in poverty that year. In 1971, President Richard Nixon declared a "War on Drugs." He called for an "all-out offensive" on the problem of drug abuse in America and created the Office of National Drug Control Policy to respond to the problem.

This war was, of course, different. On September 12, 2001, NATO declared the action against the United States to be an attack against all nineteen members of the alliance. This was the first time in the history of the Western alliance that NATO invoked Article 5 of the Washington Treaty, which stipulates that an armed attack against one member of NATO will be considered an attack against every member of NATO. At the same time, NATO and its erstwhile enemy, Russia, intensified their cooperation. It was clear that we were no longer in the realm of a metaphorical war.

The depth of support from around the world was unprecedented. In London the band outside Buckingham Palace movingly played "The Star-Spangled Banner." A headline of France's main daily newspaper, *Le Monde,* famously declared, *"Nous sommes tous Américains"*[12] (We are all Americans). German Chancellor Gerhard Schroeder, who later won reelection largely on the strength of his opposition to the American-led invasion of Iraq, promised the United States *"uneinge-schränkte solidarität"* (unlimited solidarity).[13]

Here was a chance to recast international relations. Countries that had been allies and those that had been rivals throughout the Cold War could have been united against the threat of transnational terrorism. They were anxious to be used in this way. We accepted their condolences but not their offers of support. We did not use the mechanism of NATO or any other international institution to fashion or implement a response. We felt strong enough to react on our own, and so we did. An undersecretary of defense later explained that the United States had been "so busy developing its war plans that it did not have time to focus on coordinating Europe's military role."[14]

A year after the attack, NATO held a summit meeting in Prague. Lord George Robertson, the secretary-general of NATO and former British defense secretary, had very high hopes for the meeting. The plans for the summit envisioned the adoption of a comprehensive package of measures to combat terrorism and even the creation of a NATO Response Force, a technologically advanced, flexible, and interoperable force that would be available for immediate deployment following a decision by the NATO Council. Robertson hoped that NATO would become the focal point of the international fight against terrorism and demonstrate that NATO had changed to adapt to the new security environment. The meeting was intended both to discuss the expansion to former members of the Warsaw Pact and to demonstrate the strength of the traditional Atlantic alliance. As it turned out, the summit was dominated by the contentious issue of a possible war with Iraq. Secretary of Defense Donald Rumsfeld's remark that "the mission determines the coalition, not the coalition the mission" was seen as a deliberate effort to undermine NATO, the very embodiment of the Atlantic alliance. That remark was eclipsed in unpopularity only by Secretary

Rumsfeld's subsequent dismissal of France and Germany (which opposed war in Iraq) as "old Europe" in favor of the "new Europe" of the east, which was more supportive of the American administration's plans to invade Iraq. When asked later why he did not use NATO to go into Iraq, Rumsfeld said, "It hasn't crossed my mind."[15]

It was soon widely believed in other countries that the United States was ignoring the interests of everyone but itself. While all governments are expected to think of their own interests first and foremost, alliance leaders and superpowers are also expected to take into account the interests of others. By offering immediate and unconditional support to the United States, Western leaders were expressing genuine sentiments, but they were also expecting that in return they would be consulted by the United States. They were soon disappointed.[16] These feelings were not limited to the elites. A Pew Research Center poll in May 2003 found that more than 70 percent of citizens in such generally friendly countries as Canada, Spain, the Netherlands, and Russia believed that the United States does not take the interests of others into account; 85 percent of the French, 66 percent of the Germans, and 55 percent of the British felt the same way.[17]

The shared interest in combating terrorism and the declared willingness of NATO to dedicate itself to that end could have been used to transform international institutions into an effective means of pooling diverse and complementary resources for a common purpose. In so doing, the security community that had emerged since the Second World War and that had effectively eliminated the legitimacy of the use of force to resolve conflicts among its members could have been extended to other countries anxious to join. To have invested in remaking the international order in this way, however, would have required a willingness to consult others and ultimately to constrain the exercise of American power. Unlike the Truman administration at the end of the Second World War, which took a long-range view of American interests and used the opportunity afforded by the end of the war to remake international institutions, the Bush administration focused on the short-term response and led a "coalition of the willing" into Afghanistan and later Iraq.

There are any number of reasons that an American president of any ideological huc might have responded to the 9/11 attacks with a declaration of war. The enormity of the attacks seemed to call for it.

Moreover, there is no more effective means of mobilizing a country domestically than by declaring war. Rivals come together, differences are forgotten, and the country rallies first behind the leader and later behind the boys who fight in its name. There is another, more pragmatic reason. The accretion of power to the executive that inevitably occurs in time of war has always been an attractive by-product for national leaders.

The public was also overwhelmingly in favor of a declaration of war, though it is perhaps reasonable to point out that no other options were made available to it. Had it been proffered a list of options, it might have responded differently. Polls indicated that most Americans considered the country to be in a state of war.[18] There was overwhelming popular support for a resort to military force in response to the attacks.[19] The American public was also overwhelmingly confident that the United States would find and punish the people responsible for the attacks.[20]

To declare war on what is, after all, a tactic does not appear to make a great deal of sense. One would never hear of war being declared on, say, precision-guided bombing. It's not so much the tactic that ought to be the focus of our attentions as those who deploy the tactic. Later, the war on terrorism became the Global War on Terror (GWOT), which is an even more nebulous notion. Terror, like fear, is an emotion, so declaring war on an emotion is hardly a strategy conducive to success. When the president was not declaring war on terrorism or terror, he was declaring war on evil. At a meeting with King Abdullah of Jordan, President Bush said, "I have assured His Majesty that our war is against evil, not against Islam."[21] Two months later he gave the same message to the Warsaw Conference: "We do not fight Islam, we fight against evil."[22] In January 2002, the president told a town meeting in California, "Our war is a war against evil."[23] On another occasion the president assured Americans, "We will rid the world of evildoers."[24]

There were, of course, alternatives available to declaring war on terrorism, terror, and evil. The administration might, for example, have declared war on al-Qaeda or on Afghanistan, the state that harbored it. Had it done so, there would have been some clear matrices of success or failure by which progress could have been measured. One might even have been able to know, for example, when the war was over. The scale of the atrocity and the desire to respond in sufficiently epic terms, however, suggested that a war against a state or an organization wasn't enough. The United States wanted to wage war not just on al-Qaeda but on "every terrorist group of global reach."[25]

The problem with a declaration of war is that warfare conjures up notions of victory and defeat. Yet, as was obvious at the time and as we have begun to realize since, it is very difficult ever to declare victory in a war on terrorism or terror, much less evil. We succeeded in defeating the Taliban in Afghanistan, but that has not brought us victory in the war on terrorism. Indeed, at the time, Americans believed that toppling the Taliban but failing to capture bin Laden and his aides would constitute failure.[26] We have succeeded in severely curtailing the freedom of operation of the al-Qaeda leadership. We have captured many, but by no means all, of its leaders and destroyed its command, communication, and training systems, yet this has not brought us victory in the war on terrorism.

If victory means making the United States invulnerable to terrorist attack, we are never, ever going to be victorious. Here's why casting a conflict in terms of a war one cannot win is a big mistake. By dispatching any operative into any Starbucks, subway station, or shopping mall in the country and blowing it up, a terrorist group could demonstrate that the most powerful country in the history of the world has not been able to beat it. This is making it much too easy for the terrorists.

Terrorists want to be considered soldiers at war with an enemy. Most aspire to garner enough support for their cause that they can, one day, field a real army. The concept of jihad, as invoked by Islamic extremists, for example, is all about war. Terrorists constantly refer to themselves as soldiers. Sidique Khan, the teacher's aide from Leeds who blew up a London Underground train, declared, "We are at war and I am a soldier. Now you too will feel the reality of this situation."[27] Dermot Finucane remembers how proud he was that his brother John, a member of the IRA, was getting a military funeral. Terrorists constantly use military forms of address to one another and military forms of organization and discipline. In 1981, the ten republican prisoners jailed in Northern Ireland did not starve themselves to death to force the British out of Ireland. They did not starve themselves slowly to death to unite the island of Ireland. They starved themselves to death in order to win political prisoner status for themselves. The ultimate goal of any war must be to deny the adversary what it is that he wants. Terrorists want to be considered at war with us, so to concede this to them is to grant them what they want, instead of doing our utmost to deny them what they want.

Terrorists like to be considered soldiers at war both because of the legitimacy they believe it brings their cause and for the status they believe it confers on them. For the United States to declare war on a bunch of radical extremists living under the protection of an impoverished Afghanistan is to elevate their stature in a way that they could not possibly hope to do themselves. Terrorists want to be on a "wanted" poster. (When Dermot Finucane finally made it onto a "wanted" poster, he was disappointed to have to share the honor with thirty-five others.) To be elevated to the status of public enemy number one is just what a terrorist group wants. It gives the group stature among its potential recruits, which in turn wins it more followers. Declaring war on terrorists, in effect, hands it the renown it seeks.

The language of warfare also induces what Michael Howard has called a "war psychosis." People expect immediate action. Certainly, the Bush administration felt compelled to undertake immediate action in response to the attacks of 9/11 rather than wait for the Pentagon to produce carefully calibrated war plans. But the experience of other countries in combating terrorism makes abundantly clear that successful counterterrorist campaigns require, above all, patience and a long time horizon. The Provisional IRA emerged in the early months of 1970. It finally declared an end to its terrorist campaign and destroyed its arsenal thirty-five years later, in 2005. It took an enormous amount of patience and careful planning by the British government to get to that point.

The other point, of course, is that a declaration of war has standing in international and domestic law. A declaration of war prompts the expectation in the international community that one will abide by the international conventions on the conduct of warfare. The most famous of these are known as the Geneva Conventions. They have a long lineage in international relations. Efforts to regulate the conduct of warfare have been around as long as warfare itself, but historically agreements bound the participants only in the conduct of a particular war. The first effort to establish international standards for all wars was launched by the Swiss businessman Henri Dunant, who founded the International Red Cross in 1863. Dunant was appalled by the carnage caused by the Battle of Solferino in northern Italy. He visited Emperor Napoleon III and persuaded him to order the unconditional release of all captured doctors. In 1864 Dunant invited thirteen countries to attend a conference on the humane conduct of war. The result of the conference was the first Geneva Convention, which provided for the neutrality of military hospitals and medical transports; the treatment of wounded soldiers and medical staff as nonbelligerents; the return of prisoners to their home country if they were unable to fight; and the adoption of the white flag with a red cross as a symbol of neutrality.

In 1899, the first Geneva Convention was supplemented by treaties on the use of asphyxiating gases and expanding bullets. In 1906, the second Geneva Convention, which extended the principles to war at sea, was signed. In 1929, after the trauma of the First World War, two more Geneva Conventions were signed, dealing with the treatment of the wounded and of prisoners of war. The atrocities of the Second World War, both on the battlefield and in prisoner-of-war camps, provided a further impetus to efforts to regulate the conduct of war. The result was the 1949 Geneva Convention, which modernized the earlier conventions and added another, pertaining to the treatment of civilians in time of war. In 1977, two further protocols were added, extending the protections to other forms of warfare, such as civil wars and wars of self-determination. Terrorism is not specifically mentioned. The Geneva Conventions are not the only agreements pertaining to the conduct of war; there are also a number of international laws and agreements, but the efforts to contain the atrocities of war represented by the Geneva Conventions have widespread international legitimacy and overwhelming support among democratic states.

When the United States declared a war on terrorism, the international community expected that the United States would be bound by the rules of warfare and in particular by the international conventions on treatments of civilians, the wounded, and prisoners. The White House counsel and subsequently the attorney general, Alberto Gonzales, however, argued that the war on terrorism was a "new paradigm [that] renders obsolete Geneva's strict limitations on questioning of enemy prisoners and renders quaint some of its provisions."[28] The White House adopted the term "enemy combatant" and used it as a blanket category to cover Afghan fighters and foreign mujahedin fighting in Afghanistan, as well as foreigners arrested in the United States. The rubric was also extended to Americans captured both in the field and, most controversially, in the United States. At the time many in the State Department argued vehemently against discarding international conventions and later believed that the abuses of prisoners carried out in Iraq and Afghanistan were a direct consequence of the decision to abandon the accepted norms of behavior. The Abu Ghraib prisoner abuse scandal in turn did an incalculable amount of damage to America's moral standing in the world and the effort to win support for its campaign against terrorism.

By declaring war yet refusing to be bound by the agreed constraints on warfare and refusing to conduct the war through existing international institutions, the United States alienated its allies and confirmed the worst views of neutrals and adversaries. In 2001, for example, according to a poll conducted by the Pew Research Center, three out of four Indonesians had a positive view of the United States. Two years later, four out of five had a negative view.[29] A BBC poll in summer 2003 revealed that the vast majority of Jordanians and Indonesians considered the United States to be more dangerous than al-Qaeda. A majority in India, Russia, South Korea, and Brazil saw the United States as more dangerous than Iran.[30] The U.S. government believed that the atrocity committed against it was so great that it could not afford to have any constraints on the exercise of its power in response. Ironically, it was precisely the unbridled deployment of that unrivaled power that alienated its allies, turned neutrals against it, swelled the ranks of its adversaries and destroyed its chances of achieving its long-term objective, that is, the containment of the resort to terrorism.

Warfare, of course, also implies the deployment of the military. Again, the experience of other countries in countering terrorism makes very clear that the military is too blunt an instrument to be relied upon exclusively to counter terrorism effectively.

The war in Afghanistan was the first step in the war on terrorism. It had massive domestic popular support and overwhelming international support as well. Public support for military action in Afghanistan was a heady 94 percent.[31] When the Taliban refused to turn over bin Laden and the leadership of al-Qaeda, the United States dismissed all responses short of complete compliance as insincere prevarication and immediately inserted American and British special forces into the country to make contact with local opponents of the Taliban regime.

On October 7, 2001, less than a month after the attacks on New York and Washington, U.S. and British forces began an aerial bombing campaign targeting al-Qaeda and Taliban forces. The campaign was initially entitled "Operation Infinite Justice" but was quickly renamed Operation Enduring Freedom when it was pointed out that only God could dispense "infinite justice." The paltry Taliban air defenses were soon destroyed (the United States did not lose a single aircraft to enemy fire). Within a few days, most al-Qaeda training sites had been badly damaged. Kabul fell on November 12, and the al-Qaeda fighters retreated to the Tora Bora cave complex. Kundūz fell on November 25, and on December 7, Mullah Muhammad Omar, the leader of the Taliban, slipped out of the former stronghold of Kandahar, the last Taliban-controlled city. Meanwhile, by the time the tribal forces backed by U.S. special operations troops and air support took over the last defense post of the cave complex at Tora Bora on December 17, it became apparent that the al-Qaeda leadership had also slipped away. The war in Afghanistan succeeded in toppling the brutal Taliban regime but did not capture either the Taliban or al-Qaeda leadership, nor has it brought peace to the country.

The war in Afghanistan taught the lesson that has already been taught many times previously: that winning battles does not necessarily equate with winning wars, especially when it comes to fighting terrorists. The Russians had not been able to translate overwhelming military force into victory in Chechnya. The Israelis had not been able to translate their overwhelming military force into success in Lebanon or the occupied territories. The Peruvian government had also failed to achieve success against the Shining Path through the use of military force. As pointed out earlier, a seventy-man intelligence unit within the Peruvian police force was able to achieve what wave after wave of military deployment had failed to accomplish, the destruction of the Shining Path. These cases suggest that military force alone cannot win against terrorism, no matter how glaring the asymmetry in power. There are a few Latin American cases in which the military was successfully deployed against terrorism domestically, but never by a democracy.

In Chechnya, despite fighting two all-out wars between 1994 and

1996 and 1999 and 2002, the formidable armed might of the Russian Army was unable to defeat terrorism. The Russian Army, moreover, was able to operate without many of the constraints on the use of force imposed on armies in more mature democracies. Casualty figures range from 40,000 to 70,000 on all sides, yet terrorism continues.[32] Ominous, too, is the fact that the conduct of the war has radicalized the terrorist movement in Chechnya. While initially Chechen terrorists were nationalists seeking independence from the Russian Federation, Chechen terrorist groups have now been infiltrated by radical Islamists and consequently are becoming more absolutist, less willing to constrain their violence, and less likely to accept a negotiated settlement. Some of their actions, such as the Beslan school massacre, which killed 331 people, including 186 children, rank among the most heinous acts of terrorism ever.

No country has as much depth of experience in fighting terrorism as Israel. Yet in spite of having a superbly trained, equipped, and motivated army, Israel was unable to defeat Hezbollah in Lebanon. Israel initially invaded Lebanon in 1982 to displace the Palestinian presence there, but by 1985 Hezbollah had succeeded in driving Israel back to a "security zone" along the southern border. For fifteen more years, Israeli forces clashed with Hezbollah before finally withdrawing from Lebanon altogether in May 2000. In the course of this fighting, 21,000 civilians, 2,100 Lebanese fighters, and more than 900 Israeli soldiers are estimated to have been killed.[33] During the conflict the Israeli Army won many of the battles, often suffering one casualty for every ten inflicted, but they were unable to translate these military victories into political success. Moreover, Israel was willing to accept far fewer casualties than the adversary was. Hezbollah was well aware of this difference and exploited it skillfully. In one prisoner exchange in January 2004, for example, seven hundred Lebanese and Palestinian prisoners were exchanged for one Israeli businessman and the bodies of three dead Israeli soldiers. When Israel finally withdrew from Lebanon in 2000, Hezbollah was a stronger organization than when Israel had first crossed the border in 1982.

There are a number of reasons why it was difficult for Israel to prevail in Lebanon. Hezbollah proved to be a resilient and skillful organization. It had powerful state sponsors in Iran and Syria. The Lebanese state was so weak as to be ineffectual and hence unable to serve as a useful ally of Israel even if it had wanted to. Moreover, the fact that Israel did not control the territory of Lebanon meant that it was unable to develop an effective intelligence network. The actions of the Israeli Army and Hezbollah's success against it served to generate more support for Hezbollah among the population at large. Moreover, Israel was constrained by domestic opinion at home. Israelis were both uncomfortable with the role of their democratic state as an army of occupation and unwilling to bear significant casualties among their citizen soldiers. Israel was also constrained by international opinion abroad, which was deeply critical of many of Israel's more forceful actions. These same factors are likely to constrain any other democracy in its effort to use military force against terrorists.

There have, however, been some success stories. In a number of countries, especially in Latin America, the military has been successfully deployed to defeat terrorist groups. In these instances, the military operated in a fashion that is entirely inconsistent with the principles of liberal democracy. Argentina provides one of the more notorious examples. After the death of Juan Perón, a state of emergency was declared and the military acted with impunity. A military junta assumed power in a coup in March 1976. Later that year, the military launched what was known as "the Process of National Reconstruction," better known as *"el Proceso,"* or "the Process," in an effort to stamp out left-wing terrorism, of which Perón was believed to have been fairly tolerant. The two main terrorist groups operating at the time, the Montañeros and the People's Revolutionary Army (ERP), exploited the vacuum left by Perón's death. As so often happens with the use of violence, the goal was soon broadened from defeating terrorism to exterminating all political opposition. The scale of human rights violations and "disappearances" that ensued was staggering. People suspected of being terrorists, related to terrorists, or sympathetic to terrorists were taken prisoner and never heard from again. The various units of the security forces competed with one another in their zeal to exterminate the terrorists. As one army commander, General Luciano Menéndez, famously said, "We are going to have to kill 50,000 people; 25,000 subversives, 20,000 sympathizers, and we will make 5,000 mistakes."[34] The final death toll is unclear, but it is believed to be the case that between 10,000 and 30,000 people were killed in the name of *"el Proceso."*[35] More than a thousand people were directly involved in the interrogation, torture, and murder of suspects between 1976 and 1979. Terrorist attacks stopped.

Argentina is not the only example. In Chile the Movement of the Revolutionary Left (MIR) waged a terrorist campaign against the state between 1965 and 1989. Its base was in the countryside, where it forcibly seized land for the peasantry and from there moved to the cities to launch campaigns of urban guerrilla warfare. There, as in Argentina, the military was deployed domestically against terrorism, and again gross violations of human rights resulted. The Chilean military believed the state to be threatened by terrorism, especially after the leftist Salvador Allende was elected president. He was ousted, with American assistance, in a military coup in 1973. The new regime immediately set about quelling all opposition with ruthless brutality. The junta promptly established the National Directorate of Intelligence (DINA) to eradicate terrorist subversion. Much of the initial repression was fueled by a mysterious "Plan Z," thought to be a plot hatched by Communists to take over the army. Troops were ordered to uncover the plot and eliminate those involved. Officers showing insufficient zeal were peremptorily dismissed. The plan was probably fabricated as an excuse for repression. Most of the terrorist leadership was killed or captured by the end of 1974, but MIR emerged again briefly in 1980 and again was soon suppressed. The Chilean government did succeed in eliminating terrorism but at a price of gross violation of human and civil rights. The cost in human lives is difficult to calculate precisely. A public monument located in the General Cemetery of Santiago has the names of 4,000 victims who were executed or "disappeared" for political reasons. A February 1995 report by the Corporation for Reparation and Reconciliation listed 2,095 extrajudicial executions and deaths under torture, and an additional 1,102 disappearances.[36]

In Brazil, too, the military successfully defeated a number of terrorist groups. As in a number of other Latin American countries, Brazilian terrorist groups started out in the countryside, trying to establish a mass base, and then moved into the cities to wage urban guerrilla warfare. Indeed, the manual of the urban guerrillas widely read by terrorist groups throughout the world, *Minimanual of the Urban Guerrilla*, was written by Carlos Marighella, the leader of Action for National Liberation (ALN), one of the largest of Brazil's terrorist groups. The threat from terrorism in the mid-1960s caused the Brazilian government to evolve from a moderate military regime engaged in fostering economic stability into an ever more repressive military dictatorship determined to restore order. Brazilian terrorists proved particularly adept at kidnapping high-profile individuals, and in these instances the government negotiated concessions to win the release of the prisoners. Simultaneously the military intelligence service engaged in a brutal counterterrorist campaign that included the use of death squads, torture of prisoners, and widespread arrests. One of the government's most significant successes occurred in November 1969, when Marighella and a band of his followers were located and killed in a shootout. By the end of 1971, the tactic of urban guerrilla warfare had been abandoned in Brazil.

The lessons of Latin American counterterrorism suggest that if the military is deployed domestically and freed from constraints it can indeed defeat terrorism. It is free to operate in ways not open to democracies. Indeed, the democratic government of Uruguay was replaced by military rule in 1973 precisely because of the failure of the government to respond effectively to the terrorism of the Tupamaros. In this instance the Uruguayan military was encouraged to pull off a coup by the neighboring military regime in Brazil, which felt that the Tupamaros posed a threat to its security. With the unbridled use of force, the military did defeat the Tupamaros.

The tactics of the Argentinean, Brazilian, and Chilean military governments, however, are simply not available to democratic governments. Those governments eradicated insurgent terrorism but in so doing replaced it with what was in effect state terrorism, the wanton abuse of force. No government could practice such tactics and remain a democracy, since the rule of law is replaced by the rule of force.

In declaring a war on terrorism, therefore, the U.S. government did not have in mind the kind of war on terrorism practiced by Latin American generals. It had in mind the legitimate conduct of war as on the western front against the Nazis. But the problem was that it was not facing an enemy like the Nazis. President Bush has frequently compared al-Qaeda's ideology to that of fascism, Stalinism, and Nazism, but he has done so to equate the fanaticism and immorality of its ideology, not its military battalions. Using military armies against the Nazis could work because they were deploying military ranks against us, but al-Qaeda deployed a handful of individual suicide bombers against the United States; thus, massed armies are not the best way to get them.

As the Cypriot nationalist George Grivas, head of the terrorist group EOKA, said of a British field marshal who was waging a campaign against him, "Harding persisted in his error: he underrated his enemy on the one hand and overrated his forces on the other. But one does not use a tank to catch field-mice—a cat will do the job better."[37] Declaring a war on terrorism, and dispatching an army to fight it, is very much a case of using a tank to catch a field mouse.

Some might reasonably argue that the experiences of Latin American countries and countries such as Russia and Israel have little relevance for the United States, as our polities and our cultures are so different. The same argument can hardly be made of our closest ally, the United Kingdom, our partner in what Winston Churchill first called the "Special Relationship." Few countries have had the depth of experience in counterterrorism and counterinsurgency as the United Kingdom. Many of the colonial movements seeking independence from Britain resorted to terrorist tactics at one point or another. Initially, Britain relied simply on superior military force, but, as in India, this strategy was ultimately unsuccessful. After the Second World War, Britain was faced with a range of insurgencies in opposition to colonial rule. In Malaya and Kenya, Britain was deemed to have been successful. The Cyprus conflict ended with compromise, and in Aden the British withdrew and Marxist insurgents took power.

On the basis of its extensive experience, the British military devised what were known as the Thompson Principles, six principles of counterinsurgency warfare. These are:

1. The primacy of the political
2. Coordination of government machinery
3. Obtaining intelligence
4. Separating the insurgent from his base of support
5. Neutralizing the insurgent
6. Postinsurgency planning

Armed with these principles, with years of experience, and with a professional, highly trained, and widely respected military, Britain faced the emergence of the Provisional IRA in Northern Ireland in 1970.

There is no doubt that the IRA was a very different type of terrorist group from al-Qaeda, but in fact, Britain enjoyed a great many advantages that the United States does not have. The internal security forces of the state, the Northern Ireland police force, and the locally recruited regiments of the British Army were all entirely on the side of the British. Moreover, the British troops spoke the same language as the terrorists and the community from which they derived their support, which greatly facilitated intelligence gathering. What's more, the army was operating close to home in a geographically constrained area without difficult logistical support issues to contend with. In spite of all these advantages, a $5 billion annual subvention from the British Treasury, and the fact that the government was prepared to deploy up to 30,000 British troops on top of the local security forces, the British discovered that they could not defeat the IRA, which had only a few hundred members.

James Callaghan, home secretary in Harold Wilson's Labor government, ordered the deployment of British troops on August 14, 1969, in response to a request from the prime minister of Northern Ireland, James Chichester-Clark. The British government soon learned that it is altogether easier to deploy troops than to remove them. The deployment was intended to be a temporary measure, but thirty-five years later, the troops were still there. After the initial deployment it was feared that any withdrawal of troops might appear to constitute a victory for the terrorists, so the troops remained. The troops were sent in to restore order in the wake of disturbances caused by the civil rights movement, but also to protect the minority Catholic population from Protestant mobs and the actions of the undisciplined and highly partisan police force. Their arrival was initially welcomed by the Catholic community. The IRA was nowhere to be found.

Irrespective of the good intentions of the military, the arrival of the heavily armed soldiers and military vehicles onto civilian streets soon transformed the situation. The Provisional IRA was created in early 1970 to defend the Catholic community. The military soon found itself on the side of law and order but in a divided society that made it partisan. The presence of the military on the streets enabled the IRA to portray the situation as one of British imperialism and provided target practice for novice terrorists. Early in the conflict, three events involving the military served to alienate the Catholic population, win recruits for the IRA, and win admiration for the IRA, even from people who were not prepared to support their methods.

Faced with marauding mobs and a complicit police force, Catholics barricaded themselves into "no-go" areas. Realizing the danger of permitting the IRA to recruit and train with impunity, the British Army launched "Operation Motorman," the biggest military operation in Ireland in the twentieth century. Thirty-one thousand troops were deployed to pull down the barricades. The operation succeeded in breaking up the no-go areas and turning their inhabitants into enemies of the army. This operation was soon followed by the biggest political miscalculation of the entire conflict, the introduction of internment without trial. Again, it was the military that implemented the policy, carrying out nighttime raids throughout Catholic areas and terrorizing whole neighborhoods, not to mention the families of those arrested. The fact that the policy was enforced almost entirely against Catholics, who by no means enjoyed a monopoly on the use of illegal violence, and the fact that a great many of those interned were innocent of any connection with the IRA again infuriated the local population, turning it against the British government and into the arms of the IRA.

The third military action that proved to be both a tragedy in itself as well as a recruitment bonanza for the IRA was the incident known as "Bloody Sunday." On January 30, 1972, British soldiers of the Parachute Regiment, apparently believing themselves to be under attack, opened fire on civil rights marchers, killing thirteen on the spot. TV images of terrified youngsters ducking for cover and priests waving white handkerchiefs as they carried the wounded to safety completed the alienation of the population the military had recently arrived to protect. The heavy-handed tactics in which soldiers are trained can have an enormously powerful and negative effect when deployed in a civilian context, as the British military soon discovered. Its very physical presence, complete with weaponry and armored cars, cannot help but instill fear, incite resentment, and intimidate.

As often happens in such conflicts, the military themselves were among the first to appreciate the realities of the situation. The British Army did not enjoy the deployment in Northern Ireland, seeing it as a distraction from the more important task for which it had been trained, defending Europe from the Soviet Union. In 1978 the commander of the land forces in Northern Ireland, General J. M. Glover, wrote a secret intelligence estimate of the IRA. The report was bitterly criticized because it concluded that, Britain's overwhelming military strength notwithstanding, the IRA could not be defeated militarily. The report also rejected the government's view that the members of the IRA were thugs and criminals: "Our evidence of the caliber of rank and file terrorists does not support the view that they are merely mindless hooligans drawn from the unemployed and unemployable."[38] Glover concluded:

> The Provisionals' campaign of violence is likely to continue while the British remain in Northern Ireland. . . . PIRA will probably continue to recruit the men it needs. They will still be able to attract enough people with leadership talent, good education and manual skills to continue to enhance their all-round professionalism. The movement will retain popular support sufficient to maintain secure bases in the traditional Republican areas."[39]

Subsequent events would bear out Glover's analysis.

The British government had not declared a war on terrorism in Northern Ireland, but its deployment of the military in the province permitted the IRA to cast the situation as a war and itself the legitimate adversary of the British Army. The presence of the army in a civilian setting and the heavy-handed tactics that necessarily go along with this garnered popular support for the IRA in its role as adversary of the British Army. The presence of the military on the ground did help to curtail IRA violence, and after the first few years the military and the terrorists arrived at a military stalemate punctuated by particular atrocities by the IRA and successful security operations by the army. The resolution of the problem and the end of the terrorist campaign of the IRA, however, was brought about only by years of painstaking negotiation and engagement with the grievances that fueled the support for the terrorists. The fact that 30,000 British soldiers supported by thousands more local security forces could not defeat a few hundred members of the IRA would certainly suggest that the American military operating thousands of miles from home, in an alien culture, and often without the support of reliable local security forces, is unlikely to defeat every terrorist group of global reach.

The second major mistake of the post-9/11 period was the conflation of two very distinct security issues: the threat from al-Qaeda and the threat from Saddam Hussein. Reasonable people have disagreed on the wisdom of the war in Iraq, but from a counterterrorist point of view there can be little doubt that it was a terrible mistake. There were three sets of arguments presented in support of the war. The first was that Hussein had weapons of mass destruction that he might himself use or give terrorists to use against us. This argument had widespread support in the United States, especially among conservatives who regretted not finishing Hussein off the last time, in the first Gulf War. The second set of arguments was that Hussein was a genocidal maniac who brutalized his countrymen so that as a humanitarian gesture he should be stopped. This argument appealed to liberals, especially those who felt that the West had unconscionably stood by and done nothing to stop genocide in Rwanda. Then there was the argument that Hussein was linked to al-Qaeda. In a famous speech at the United Nations in February 2003, Secretary of State Colin Powell laid out the American case for invasion. The bulk of his case rested on evidence of Iraqi development of weapons of mass destruction. He also argued that the fact that the Jordanian-born terrorist Abu Mus'ab al-Zarqawi had operated in the northeast corner of Iraq and had spent two months in Baghdad, where he had received medical treatment, was evidence of collusion between Hussein and bin Laden.[40]

Reports from those in the administration, such as counterterrorism coordinator Richard Clarke, and Treasury Secretary Paul O'Neill, as well as those who interacted with them, such as German Chancellor Gerhard Schroeder, all attest to the fact that immediately after the 9/11 attack senior members of the administration believed that there had to be a link between Hussein and al-Qaeda and started to anticipate taking action against Iraq. Deputy Defense Secretary Paul Wolfowitz, in particular, pushed hard for attacking Iraq right away. In a memo dated September 17, he argued that if there were even a 10 percent chance that Saddam Hussein had been behind the 9/11 attacks, maximum priority should be placed on eliminating that threat. He also argued that the odds in fact were far greater than one in ten.[41]

The American public continued to believe that Iraq was implicated in the September 11 attacks long after the evaporation of any evidence suggesting a link. A *Washington Post* poll in August 2003 found that 69 percent of Americans believed that Saddam Hussein "was personally involved in the September 11 terrorist attacks," down from 78 percent in the days following the attack. A whopping 82 percent believed that Hussein "has provided assistance to Osama bin Laden and his terrorist network."[42] Large numbers of Americans continue to believe that Saddam Hussein helped to plan the 9/11 attacks and that several of the attackers were Iraqis. In fact, none was.[43]

The public's misperception was in large part attributable to statements from the president and senior members of the administration indicating a connection. Those within the government and those outside who studied al-Qaeda knew of bin Laden's deep-seated animosity toward the secular, corrupt regime of Saddam Hussein. They knew that, as mentioned earlier, bin Laden had offered to fight Hussein to eject him from Kuwait. They also knew, as the 9/11 Commission reported, that bin Laden was sponsoring anti-Saddam Islamists in Iraqi Kurdistan and trying to attract them to join forces with him.[44] Nevertheless, in the absence of hard evidence of any link between Iraq and al-Qaeda, senior members of the administration repeatedly implied that there was evidence of a link. Vice President Dick Cheney, for example, repeatedly referred to allegations of a meeting in Prague between 9/11 hijacker Mohamed Atta and a senior Iraqi intelligence officer. He told reporters in December 2001, March 2002, and September 2003 that reports of this meeting were credible.[45] They were not. In September 2002, Defense Secretary Rumsfeld asserted that American intelligence had "bulletproof" evidence of links between al-Qaeda and Saddam Hussein.[46] As late as September 2003, Vice President Cheney described Iraq as "the geographic base of the terrorists who have had us under assault for many years, but most especially on 9/11."[47] The president was obliged to disavow these comments and said clearly on September 17, 2003, "No, we've had no evidence that Saddam Hussein was involved with September the eleventh."[48]

Once the occupation of Iraq occurred and the troops failed to discover the existence of any weapons of mass destruction, the administration was obliged to retreat to the other rationales for the war: the link with terrorism and the humanitarian removal of a brutal dictator.

Given the political predilections of this particular administration, the first argument had more resonance. The war in Iraq was then recast as the central front in the war on terror. In the words of the president, "The terrorists regard Iraq as the central front in their war against humanity. And we must recognize Iraq as the central front in our war on terror."[49] Speeches by members of the administration on the Iraq war are suffused with references to the 9/11 attacks. In his famous speech on board the USS *Abraham Lincoln* under a "Mission Accomplished" banner, in which he declared the "end of major combat" in Iraq, President Bush stated, "The liberation of Iraq is a crucial advance in the campaign against terror. . . . We have not forgotten the victims of September the eleventh—the last phone calls, the cold murder of children, the searches in the rubble. With those attacks the terrorists and their supporters declared war on the United States. And war is what they got."[50] Two years later, he told troops assembled in Fort Bragg, "The troops here and across the world are fighting a global war on terror. The war reached our shores on September the eleventh, 2001. . . . Iraq is the latest battlefield in this war."[51] The 9/11 Commission investigated the allegations of connections between al-Qaeda and Saddam Hussein's regime and concluded that there was none of any significance.[52]

By waging war in Iraq and conflating our enmity with al-Qaeda and our enmity with Saddam Hussein, we have created a self-fulfilling prophecy. In October 2004, an erstwhile rival of bin Laden and one of the leaders of the Iraqi insurgency, al-Zarqawi, pledged his allegiance and that of the terrorist group Tawhid wal-Jihad to bin Laden in a statement posted on the Internet and entitled "Oath of loyalty of leader Abu Mus'ab al-Zarqawi towards the Sheikh of the Mujahadeen, Osama bin Laden."[53] In fall 2005, in a communication between al-Qaeda's second in command, Ayman al-Zawahiri, and al-Zarqawi, we ironically appear to have uncovered a case of an attempt by the al-Qaeda leadership to moderate al-Zarqawi's violence.[54]

The insurgency in Iraq is fueled by opposition to our occupation of the country. The insurgents are made up of local nationalists determined to oust us from Iraq and foreign fighters who see our army and want to eject it from the region. The little information we have on these insurgents all suggests that, far from being hardened members of terrorist groups, they have been recruited and radicalized by our presence. They find the claims that the United States is occupying Iraq to defend New York and deploying an army to import democracy to be so implausible that they do not believe them. Instead, they believe the claims of those who say the U.S. Army is a self-interested army of occupation interested only in dominating the region and exploiting its oil wealth.

Though the American public was strongly supportive of the government's action, the international community was appalled. The United States insisted that Iraq was indeed the central front of the war on terrorism and invaded without the sanction of the United Nations. The war on Iraq deflected the attention of the military away from Afghanistan and the search for the perpetrators of the September 11 attacks as well as away from the vital task of rebuilding the country devastated first by war and then by the Taliban. Moreover, our invasion seemed to confirm the view of our adversaries that we were in fact at war with Islam. Just as the Soviet war in Afghanistan had proved to be a mobilizing force for the mujahedin, so the U.S. invasion of Iraq has proved to be a beacon for a new generation of Islamic radicals. The United States played right into the hands of its enemies.

International support for the United States collapsed. The trend held in all types of countries: friendly, neutral, and hostile. In France the number viewing the United States unfavorably soared from 34 percent in the summer of 2002 to 67 percent in March 2003. In Germany the figure went from 35 percent to 71 percent in the same period. In Russia the number soared from 33 percent to 68 percent, in Indonesia from 56 percent to 83 percent, in Turkey from 55 percent to 84 percent, in Pakistan from 69 percent to 81 percent, in Lebanon from 59 percent to 71 percent, and in Jordan from 75 percent to 99 percent.[55]

The widespread unpopularity of the war in Iraq has undermined international support for America's war on terrorism and the country's credibility in general. A significant percentage of people in France (57 percent) and Germany (49 percent) have come to agree with the view that is widespread in the Muslim world, namely, that the United States is exaggerating the threat from terrorism. By contrast, only 13 percent of Americans think so. In a March 2004 survey, solid majorities in France and Germany and 44 percent in Britain maintained that the war on terror was not a sincere effort to reduce terrorism. Believing in U.S. competence and unwilling to accept U.S. sincerity, citizens of other countries have come to conclude that the United States must have other motives. Majorities of those who doubt American sincerity in seven of the nine countries surveyed in 2004 believe that America's real motive is to control Middle East oil. Almost as many believe that America's motivation is world domination.[56] In effect, they find al-Qaeda's propaganda more credible than ours.

If the two mistakes of this period were declaring war on terrorism and painting Saddam Hussein and Osama bin Laden with the same brush and the first missed opportunity was the unwillingness to mobilize a willing international community behind a campaign against al-Qaeda, the second significant missed opportunity was the chance to educate the American public to the realities of terrorism and to the implication of the United States' global preeminence. Far from trying to educate the public, U.S. leaders played to their fears. While asserting that Muslims in general were in no way responsible, the government summarily picked up about 1,200 Arab Americans and detained them for months without access to counsel or other protections. Rather than attempting to put the terrible atrocity of 9/11 into perspective, it fanned the outrage. Rather than countenance the possibility that certain of its actions might have fueled resentment toward it, it divided the world into good and evil, and those who were not with the United States were with the terrorists.

We might have used the opportunity to think carefully about the question so many Americans were asking: Why do they hate us? Instead of asserting, in essence, that it was because they are evil and we are good, the American public might have been helped to understand the perspective of the powerless. Americans might have been helped to understand that the purity of their motives, unquestioned in our own minds, is not self-evident to others. We might have had a national conversation about the price of being a global superpower, of being the most powerful country in history. Other great powers before the United States have bred resentment, and not because they were more self-interested or less competent than the United States. Other empires, however, have been run by a whole segment of the population in the imperial bureaucracies made up of the younger sons of the wealthy, or the adventurous in search of opportunity, who lived in their colonies overseas. The United States has sought to run its empire by exporting its movies and television shows, not its sons.

We have believed that the superiority of our values and our system of government is so self-evident that only the ignorant or the evil could reject it. Rather than use the shock of the attacks, and the thirst for explanation so evident among the American public, to explore the complexities of our global position, our vulnerability to terrorism, and the best means of countering it, we declared that those who were not with us were against us. Rather than discuss how we as a society could develop resilience to terrorism and devise a policy to contain it, we simply resolved to smash it. Rather than use the opportunity to examine ourselves, we retreated to simplistic formulas of good and evil.

In responding to the attacks of 9/11 with a declaration of war on terror, the United States mirrored the behavior of its adversary. Bin Laden has ignored the rich complexity and nuanced teachings of Islam and superimposed a highly simplified, Manichean view of good and evil: he represents the good servant of Allah; the United States represents the infidel. In response the U.S. government adopted the same black-and-white view of the world, only in its view it represents goodness and he represents evil. Nowhere was this similarity more in evidence than in the unfortunate use of the term "crusade" in describing our war on terror. A few days after the attack, President Bush told reporters that "This crusade, this war on terrorism, is going to take a while."[57] The word might have been dismissed as an unfortunate slip of the tongue had it not been repeated in a set speech to the troops in Alaska some months later. In that instance, the president said of the Canadians, "They stand with us in this incredibly important crusade to defend freedom."[58]

While Westerners may see the Crusades as a romantic military episode in ancient history, in the Middle East today the Crusades are well remembered. The charter of Hamas, for example, deals at some length with the fate of the Crusaders who held Jerusalem for two hundred years before being expelled by the Muslim warrior Saladin. Hamas regards the Israeli occupation of Jerusalem today along the same lines. By their own account, the Crusaders slaughtered 70,000 Muslims when they conquered Jerusalem in 1099, and while they probably exaggerated the number, the memory runs very deep. By using the term "crusade" President Bush appeared to many in the Middle East to demonstrate that the U.S. war on terrorism was actually a war of Christianity against Islam, just as bin Laden has sought to cast it.

One of the striking features of bin Laden's many statements is the endless litany of grievances against the West. He never takes into account the suffering he has inflicted on others, even of the hundreds of innocent Africans killed and injured in the attacks on the American Embassy in Nairobi in 1998. In our response to bin Laden, it appears that for us, too, only our suffering, only our grievances, matter. In fighting back at al-Qaeda, we inadvertently killed a large number of civilians. By August 2002, the estimated number of Afghan civilian deaths from U.S. bombings was between 3,125 and 3,620; that is, significantly more than the number of civilians killed by al-Qaeda on 9/11.[59] These numbers never became a topic of discussion, much less a cause of concern, in this country. We were so taken with the extent of our own suffering that we didn't consider the suffering we were inflicting on others. It goes without saying that a significant difference between the civilian casualties in both cases is that the ones we suffered were intended while the ones we inflicted were accidental. The suffering of the victims, however, was undoubtedly the same.

In all his statements bin Laden has purported to be the defender of Muslims against American aggression. He claims his actions are in reaction to ours and that he seeks only to stop us from inflicting suffering on others. In just the same way, we claim that we are the defenders and he is the aggressor, that his attack on us was completely unprovoked and that we wish only to stop those who inflict terror on others. On the day of the attack the president said, "A great people has been moved to defend a great nation."[60] A few days later he said, "We did not seek this conflict but we will win it."[61] For his part, bin Laden repeatedly claims to be the defender against the American aggressor. He argued, "Our acts are reaction to your own acts, which are represented by the destruction and killing of our kinfolk in Afghanistan, Iraq and Palestine . . . the one who starts injustice bears greater blame."[62]

One of the most frequently used words in President Bush's speeches on the war on terrorism is "freedom." "America was targeted for attack because we're the brightest beacon for freedom and opportunity in the world."[63] "Our enemies murder because they despise our freedom and our way of life."[64] "Either you stand for freedom or you stand with tyranny."[65] "We're responding to a global campaign of fear

with a global campaign of freedom. And once again we will see freedom's victory."[66] Bin Laden, however, also claims to be fighting for
freedom and dismisses American claims to the contrary. In his address
to the American people shortly before the presidential election in 2004,
he said, "I say to you that security is an indispensable pillar of human
life and that men do not forfeit their security, contrary to Bush's claim
that we hate freedom. If so, then let him explain to us why we don't
strike, for example, Sweden? And we know that freedom-haters don't
possess defiant spirits like those of the 19—may Allah have mercy on
them. No, we fight because we are free men who don't sleep under oppression. We want to restore freedom to our nation, just as you lay
waste to our nation so shall we lay waste to yours."[67]

Just as bin Laden seems to be supremely confident that Allah is
on his side, our leaders have expressed equal conviction that God is on
ours. In the words of the president, "Embedded in every soul is the
deep desire to live in freedom. I understand freedom is not America's
gift to the world; freedom is Almighty God's gift to each man and
woman in this world. . . . May God bless the people of this great state.
May God bless our troops. And may God continue to bless the United
States of America."[68] By invoking God on our side in the war on terrorism, we facilitate seeing the conflict in the cosmic terms in which
our enemies see it. It encourages us, too, to "absolutize" the conflict,
to demonize the enemy, and to dismiss all responses short of all-out
victory. It helps us, in other words, to see the conflict in the terms in
which bin Laden sees it.

The president put it this way: "In fact, we're not facing a set of
grievances that can be soothed and addressed. We're facing a radical
ideology with unalterable objectives: to enslave whole nations and intimidate the world. No act of ours invited the rage of the killers—and
no concession, bribe or act of appeasement would change or limit their
plans for murder."[69] In so saying the president delegitimized any effort
to engage with the grievances that might have fueled support for bin
Laden. By invoking God on our side, we are inclined to see ourselves
representing all that is good in the world and the enemy representing
all that is evil: "We believe in human rights, and the human dignity of
every man, woman, and child on this Earth. The terrorists believe that
all human life is expendable. They share a hateful ideology that rejects
tolerance and crushes all dissent. They envision a world where women

are beaten, children are indoctrinated, and all who reject their ideology of violence and extremism are murdered."[70] Hearing this just confirms the terrorists in their view that God is on their side and that this perversion of their perspective must be deliberate. In bin Laden's words, "Had he been truthful about his claim for peace . . . he also would not have lied to people and said that we hate freedom and kill for the sake of killing. Reality proves our truthfulness and his lie."[71] By invoking God in our response, therefore, we are again playing into the hands of the terrorists and sharing the view of cosmic conflict propounded by our opponents.

By using the extreme language of conviction that bin Laden uses, by declaring war, even a crusade, against him in response to his war against us, we are mirroring his actions. We are playing into his hands, we are elevating his stature, we are permitting him to set the terms of our interactions. Given that he has a very weak hand and we have a very strong one, we should not be letting him set the parameters of the game.

The goal of any combatant in warfare is to deny the adversary the objectives he seeks. As argued earlier, terrorists have both primary and secondary objectives; al-Qaeda's rhetoric combines both practical policy objectives and grand religious visions. But as I have argued, like other terrorists al-Qaeda seeks three objectives: revenge, renown, and reaction. The first it can get for itself; the other two it must get from others. By declaring a war on terror, far from denying it its objectives, we are conceding its objectives, and this is why the war on terror can never be won.

Bin Laden has made it very clear in all his statements that he wants revenge on the United States for its actions in the Muslim world and our support of Israel. By bringing our army to him, we are making it easy for him and those who follow him or are inspired by him to exact this revenge. Moreover, by placing our troops in Afghanistan and Iraq, we are ensuring that there will be many other actions to be avenged, whether it is the killing of civilians in air strikes, the abuse of prisoners or desecration of corpses in Afghanistan, or military operations and prisoner abuse in Iraq, those hurt by these actions are likely to swell the ranks of those seeking vengeance. Thanks to the role of the media, evidence of these abuses is presented for all the world to see, so that those seeking revenge are not just those who have suffered but also those who identify with those who have suffered and are radicalized by the experience.

There is no more sure route to renown than to be declared the greatest enemy of the most powerful country in the world. By offering millions of dollars for his head and declaring that we wanted him "dead or alive," we have elevated the stature of Osama bin Laden in a way he could only have dreamed of. It is, of course, the case that his success in pulling off the 9/11 attacks guaranteed him considerable glory in many circles. Reacting to the attack in the way we did, however, we greatly expanded those circles. If we succeed in killing him, we will turn him into a martyr and his renown will be consolidated for generations to come. If we don't capture him, he can continue to defy us and demonstrate our weakness. At this point it would be very hard for bin Laden to lose the war on terror.

A wiser response would have been to do everything in our power to capture him. Instead of relying on unreliable local forces whose interests we little understood, we should have focused our efforts on the caves of Tora Bora. Had we captured him alive, we would have had an extraordinary opportunity to demonstrate to the world the strength of the American commitment to the rule of law. Had we captured bin Laden alive and then resisted the very human urge to exact revenge and instead handed him over to an international court of impeccable rectitude and reputation for trial on charges against humanity, we would have deprived him of glory and demonstrated, even to the skeptical, the vast difference between his values and ours.

There is no greater affront to terrorists than to be ignored. They deliberately attempt spectacular attacks in an effort to gain attention. The risk of ignoring a terrorist action, of course, is the fear that it might incite the terrorists to carry out even more devastating attacks in order to get attention. So ignoring terrorists is not a feasible option, especially in a democracy, in which the public demands action in the face of atrocity. By pursuing terrorists like the criminals they are, however, outside the limelight and with painstaking and necessarily covert action, one can undermine their effectiveness without raising their profiles.

Terrorists have repeatedly and quite explicitly told us that they want to provoke a reaction, and the more extreme the reaction, the better for them. It will get them attention; and it will alienate the uncommitted and win recruits to their cause. On September 25, 1968, a leading Brazilian newspaper, *Jornal do Brasil,* published a manifesto spelling out the aims of the Brazilian terrorist group ALN. This is the group that was led by Carlos Marighella, author of the *Minimanual of the Urban Guerilla.* The manifesto declared the terrorist group's aim to create a crisis in the country that would cause the government to adopt a military response. This in turn would lead to a mass uprising against the regime in which power would pass to the armed people. By responding to the 9/11 attacks with a declaration of war, we played right into the hands of the terrorists: we conceded the very objectives, revenge, renown, and reaction that they were seeking, and we ensured that we could not win.

The urge to declare war in response to an atrocity on the scale of September 11 is very powerful, and the decision to do so is very understandable. I have argued, however, that it is also very unwise. In the chapter that follows, I will spell out an alternative strategy, a strategy that replaces the very ambitious goals to "rid the world of the evil-doers" and "to root terrorism out of the world"[72] with the more modest and more achievable goal of containing the threat from terrorism. This strategy is based on the lessons that can be derived from the experience of other countries, and especially other democracies, in countering terrorism.

EIGHT

WHAT IS TO BE DONE?

Happy is he who learns from others' mistakes.[1]

—Osama bin Laden

Ireland forces upon us these great social and great religious questions—
God grant that we may have the courage to look them in the face and to
work through them.[2]

—William Ewart Gladstone, 1844

THE BOMBING AT CLERKENWELL PRISON IN DECEMBER 1867, the details of which were recounted in chapter 2, was followed by widespread arrests (including that of a police informant hired to spy on the terrorists), and rumors of impending atrocities were rampant. Fenians were alleged to be planning to dynamite the gas works and the railway lines, to blow up the Crystal Palace, and even to attack the British fleet. Protection for the royal family was increased dramatically, and the police and the public became preoccupied by society's vulnerability to attack from the sewers. The newspapers fanned the public hysteria. *The Banner of Ulster* declared, "Of all the fiendish ferocities ever perpetrated in any country, none exceeds that recently committed in the heart of London."[3] *The Impartial Observer* said it was "the most frightful crime of modern times."[4] The government was compelled to respond and put out a call for volunteers to act as special constables. More men volunteered than during either of the subsequent world wars.

Five men and a woman were soon charged with the crime and brought to trial. The weakness of the Crown's case was quickly evident as the case against two of the six collapsed and three others were acquitted for lack of evidence. One man, Michael Barrett, who presented several witnesses to support his alibi that he had been in Glasgow at the time of the explosion, was convicted and sentenced to death. Queen Victoria was furious that the government was not taking a stronger line. In a letter to the home secretary, the queen wrote that she was grieved "to see the failure of the evidence against all but one of the Clerkenwell criminals . . . it seems dreadful for these people to escape . . . one begins to wish that these Fenians should be lynch-lawed and on the spot."[5]

At his trial Michael Barrett did not fit the profile of the mindless murderer. He gave a thoughtful and eloquent forty-five-minute speech from the dock, delivered without hesitation and without notes. *The Daily Telegraph* noted that he "was evidently a man of high intelligence."[6] *The Times* remarked favorably on his "look of determination and frank courage."[7] One of the lawyers for the other defendants said of him, "A less murderous countenance than Barrett's indeed, I do not remember to have seen. Good humor was latent in every feature."[8] Even the lord chief justice was unconvinced of the justice of the result. Some members of the House of Commons, such as John Bright and John Stuart Mill, requested clemency, but the prevailing sentiment was that even if Barrett had not committed the crime, he was clearly a Fenian and deserved to be hanged. When Barrett's mother approached her local member of Parliament for help in seeking a reprieve, he told her that her son and all other Fenians should be hanged, and the sooner the better.[9] On May 26, 1868, five months after the explosion, Michael Barrett was hanged before a crowd of about two thousand onlookers in the last public execution in England.

A few days after the Clerkenwell explosion, during the height of the public and media hysteria, William Ewart Gladstone, then MP for South Lancashire and shortly to become leader of the Liberal Party, gave a speech in which he tried to press upon his listeners his belief that

Irish violence was the product of Irish grievance and that it was the duty of the British people to address these grievances. He also reminded his audience that if the public were excited, the excitement would influence a jury and even a judge.[10] Gladstone's was a lone voice in trying to look behind the violence. While others cried for blood, Gladstone sought to find out why Irishmen felt driven to violence against England.

Gladstone became prime minister of England for the first time a year after the Clerkenwell explosion with a mission to pacify Ireland. He had no illusions that it would be easy, but through the Irish Church Act of 1869 and the Irish Land Act of 1870 he sought to address the underlying religious and social issues that fueled support for Irish nationalist violence. He soon concluded that political change was also necessary, and in 1886 he introduced his first unsuccessful Home Rule Bill for Ireland. In 1893, the year before he retired, he tried again and introduced the second, and again unsuccessful, Home Rule Bill for Ireland. Gladstone did not succeed in his mission of pacifying Ireland. Too many others preferred a straightforward coercive response to Irish violence.

Nevertheless, Gladstone's endeavor to look behind the violence and to understand the factors that fueled it and his effort to introduce social, political, and religious reforms to alleviate the conditions that breed support for violence is a model of what can be done in the face of terrorism. Gladstone failed to pacify Ireland, but had he succeeded the history of Britain and Ireland over the past hundred years would have been very different.

Nearly fifty years after Michael Barrett's death, on August 1, 1915, at the funeral for another Fenian, Jeremiah O'Donovan Rossa, a young Padraig Pearse, who would soon lead the next Irish insurrection, gave one of the most famous speeches in the annals of Irish nationalism: "Life springs from death; and from the graves of patriot men and women spring living nations . . . the fools, the fools, the fools! They have left us our Fenian dead, and while Ireland holds these graves, Ireland unfree shall never be at peace."[11] Almost sixty years later, in 1973, the next generation of Fenians, this time called the IRA, planted a bomb outside the Old Bailey in London, right at the spot on which Michael Barrett had been executed more than a century earlier.

Governments are invariably placed under enormous pressure to react forcibly and fast in the wake of a terrorist attack. This response is not likely to be most conducive to long-term success against terrorists. Nor is there a simple solution to terrorism. Terrorism is a complicated, multifaceted phenomenon, but it is also one that can be rationally understood. An efficacious response is likely to be just as complicated as the problem. In the well-known words of H. L. Mencken, "For every complex problem, there is a solution that is simple, neat, and wrong." Gladstone's government recognized this long ago and introduced political, social, and religious reforms as well as coercive policies in an effort to redress the problem of Irish terrorism. One does not need to go back as far as Gladstone to find examples of countries, even fully fledged democracies, which have had to contend with a threat from terrorism. Indeed, some of our allies who were anxious to help us were somewhat perturbed by the impression they gathered from Americans that terrorism was unknown before 9/11. They argued that they had acquired a good deal of experience that might just be useful to us.

In looking at the counterterrorism experience of other democracies, one point becomes clear: their policies improved with time. Whether it was Britain in dealing with the IRA, the Peruvian government in dealing with the Shining Path, the Italian government responding to the Red Brigades, or India responding to Sikh terrorism in the Punjab, each of these governments learned from its early mistakes and significantly improved the effectiveness of its counterterrorism policies over time. The United States is in the fortunate position of being able to learn from others' mistakes, but it appears instead to prefer to learn from its own. In this chapter, therefore, I will spell out some of the lessons that I think can be derived from the experience of others to enable the United States successfully to contain the threat from terrorists.

SIX RULES FOR COUNTERACTING TERRORISM

Rule 1: Have a Defensible and Achievable Goal

The first point about which one must be clear is the purpose of the strategy. If the goal is to defeat terrorism or eliminate terror, not to mention evil, the goal simply cannot be attained. On the other hand, had our government declared its goal on the evening of September 11 simply to be to capture those responsible for the attacks, it might very well have been successful. This goal would have required a different political and military strategy in Afghanistan, and it would have kept us out of Iraq. Due to the impact of our response to 9/11 on al-Qaeda, and in particular the fact that the movement now has many of the characteristics of a diffuse and inspirational ideology rather than a military organization, even if we were to capture the remainder of those responsible we would not have defeated terrorism.

As a result, our task today is in many ways more difficult than it was in fall 2001. Rather than having the objective of the defeat of terrorism, today our goal should be to contain the threat from terrorists. Unlike the goal of eliminating terrorism, the goal of containing the terrorist threat is achievable. The particular brand of terrorism that currently poses a threat to us is terrorism used by Islamic militants; therefore, our goal today should be to stop the spread of Islamic militancy. In order to contain the spread of Islamic militancy, we must isolate the terrorists and inoculate their potential recruits against them.

If we were to keep this more modest and more concrete goal firmly in sight and plan accordingly, we would be able to ensure that our short-term tactics did not undermine the effort to realize our long-term objectives. If the goal is to prevent the spread of Islamic militancy, we should take pains to ensure, for example, that our coercive policies against the presumed perpetrators of violence do not harm or alienate the broader populations in which our actions take place. The prevention of the spread of Islamic militancy is ultimately a political rather than a military goal, and, as Thucydides said long ago and British counterinsurgency strategy reiterated more recently, it is imperative to keep the political goal firmly in mind. We need to ensure that military actions do not make political goals harder to accomplish.

The nature of this goal, moreover, is such that unlike taking a beachhead or bombing a training site, it does not lend itself to unrealistic expectations that it can be accomplished overnight. The nature of this goal affords the political leadership the time and the opportunity to educate the public to the nature of the threat we face and the careful steps that must be taken to counter it.

One of the perennial difficulties faced by other democracies in attempting to formulate effective counterterrorist strategies has been the difficulty of coordinating across different bureaucracies. The difficulty of coordination seems to be endemic to complex organizations of any nationality and every function. In India, Northern Ireland, Peru, Sri Lanka, and Turkey both the military and the police forces were engaged in counterterrorism, and all initially experienced considerable difficulties coordinating their responses across different types of bureaucracies. Even those countries in which counterterrorism policy was firmly in the hands of the police force, such as France, Japan, Italy, and Spain, there were chronic problems of coordination across different agencies. In countries that have been least successful in combating terrorism, such as Russia and Colombia, the problems of poor coordination are rampant. In the Colombian case this is because the state has been too weak to enforce coordination and in Russia because myriad security units—some regional, some national, some police, and some military—all appear to be operating on their own. Having a coherent, clearly articulated objective provides a goal against which all acts can be measured and helps to elaborate a division of labor to ensure mutually reinforcing pursuit of the shared objective.

Successful counterterrorism almost invariably requires a combination of coercive and conciliatory policies. It is imperative for success to ensure that these policies do not undermine one another by being used against the wrong audiences. Coercive policies should be restricted to the few actual perpetrators of the violence, while conciliatory policies ought to be focused on their potential recruits. To use coercive policies too broadly, as we have been prone to do, serves to alienate those we should be trying to conciliate, while conciliating the perpetrators of the violence is likely to be successful only if they have clearly understood and negotiable political objectives.

If we keep the goal of halting the spread of Islamic militancy firmly in mind, we are less likely to be distracted by anger at atrocities along the way; the immediate urge to retaliate is more likely to be satisfied with an appeal to the longer-term objective. Similarly, fears of being accused of being soft on terrorism or of rewarding terrorists are likely to be ameliorated if the goal is to end their appeal. A number of policies, such as legislation granting leniency in return for information, have proven to be successful when offered to members of an organization that is on the defensive, as the Red Brigades were when Italy introduced its *pentiti* (repenters) legislation. This policy has been less successful when offered to members of a group who are feeling in the ascendant. The policy can have political costs by appearing not to punish adequately the perpetrators of terrorist violence, but again, if the goal is to halt the spread of militancy and we are confident of acquiring invaluable information to further the achievement of that objective, then concerns of rewarding terrorism are less likely to resonate.

Rule 2: Live by Your Principles

There are a number of principles that should guide the United States' counterterrorist campaign. The first of these was succinctly expressed by President Bush on September 20, 2001: "We are in a fight for our principles, and our first responsibility is to live by them."[12] In this the president was quite right. There is, nevertheless, a widespread and quite fallacious view that democracies are peculiarly vulnerable to terrorism and that the freedoms granted citizens in democratic societies can be exploited by terrorists and therefore must be curtailed. In the wake of terrorist attacks, governments invariably respond with emergency legislation and the public is generally quite happy to sacrifice some liberty in the name of security. The perspective of Benjamin Franklin on this point is not often quoted. He said, "They who would give up an essential liberty for temporary security deserve neither liberty nor security."[13] Support for emergency legislation is generally won with the argument that it is a temporary expedient, but, as Laura Donohue has demonstrated in her work on the United States and the United Kingdom, the one iron law of emergency legislation is that temporary legislation is rarely temporary.[14]

Quite aside from the many reasons of principle why it is unwise to abandon liberal democratic values and practices in the face of a terrorist threat, there are a number of pragmatic reasons as well. To alter one's government in response to a terrorist threat is to concede a victory to the adversary. It is to reward the adversary's action by demonstrating its power. It is to provide them with a reaction. It is to pass on the opportunity to demonstrate the strength of our commitment to the rule of law and to model the behavior we advocate for others.

If we are prepared to abandon our principles as soon as they are threatened, it demonstrates to those whose support we should be focused on winning that we have double standards, one for ourselves and one for others. We detain Arab Americans but not others. Or we hold others to standards such as the Geneva Conventions that we are not prepared to uphold ourselves. It undermines the legitimacy of our position and makes more credible the claims of our enemies that our democratic ideals are a mere smokescreen for baser motives.

During the Revolutionary War, General George Washington understood both the principled and pragmatic position on these points. More Americans died in British prison ships in New York Harbor than in all the battles of the Revolutionary War. According to the Department of Defense, there were 4,435 battle deaths during the Revolutionary War, while estimates of the number of deaths on prison ships range from 7,000 to 11,644. The British justified the appalling treatment of the Americans on the grounds that they were merely rebels. In an indignant letter that might have been written on behalf of an enemy combatant in Guantánamo, Abu Ghraib, or Bagram today, General Washington wrote to General Lord Howe on January 13, 1777, in protest:

> You may call us rebels, and say that we deserve no better treatment. But remember, my Lord, that supposing us rebels, we still have feelings as keen and sensible as loyalists, and will, if forced to it, most assuredly retaliate upon those upon whom we look as the unjust invaders of our rights, liberties and properties.[15]

As it happened, Washington opted not to retaliate. Instead, after the capture of 221 British prisoners at Princeton, Washington wrote to the American officer in charge, "Treat them with humanity, and let then have no reason to complain of our copying the brutal example of the British army in their treatment of our unfortunate brethren."[16] Instead Washington used the issue as an object lesson for his men on the importance of the principles they were fighting for. According to the historian David Fischer, Washington regularly reminded his men that they were fighting for liberty and freedom, which were rights of all humanity and therefore ought to be extended even to their enemies.[17]

Our government in the post-9/11 days might have decided that the rebels we confronted were entitled to the protections of the Geneva Conventions. Our government might have decided, as General Washington did, that, as defenders of democracy and individual freedom, we were bound to treat our prisoners humanely and might have used the opportunity to demonstrate to our soldiers and the world the difference between us and our adversaries. Had our government so decided, the abuse of prisoners that took place in our prisons would never have happened. The photographic evidence of this abuse, which has been shown throughout the world, has done incalculable damage to America's moral standing. It has undermined our legitimacy in the eyes of our allies and the noncommitted and confirmed our perfidy in the eyes of everyone else.

We will never know just how many young men were moved to join terrorist groups in anger and outrage at these photographs, or how many others resolved that they would never lift a finger to help us in our campaign against terrorism. I believe that we can safely assume that the numbers are very large. These photographs, and the failure to repudiate them conclusively by holding the most senior people responsible, has made the crucial task of driving a wedge between the terrorists and the communities that produce them immeasurably more difficult.

In the campaign against terrorism, our ethics and our interests are completely aligned. Our democratic principles, far from constraining our ability to respond to terrorism, are among the strongest weapons in our arsenal. All we have to do is remember them.

Rule 3: Know Your Enemy

There is no more important requirement for the success of any encounter than knowing your enemy. There is simply no substitute for good intelligence. The centrality of good intelligence to the successful conduct of warfare has long been recognized. Sun-tzu, the Chinese military strategist thought to have lived in the fourth century B.C., wrote, "Nothing should be as favorably regarded as intelligence; nothing should be as generously rewarded as intelligence; nothing should be as confidential as the work of intelligence."[18]

We must know how and where terrorists operate, how they organize themselves, how they communicate with one another, how they finance and plan their operations. Our post-9/11 counterterrorist campaign has actually been fairly successful in this regard. We have captured significant numbers of the leaders of al-Qaeda, including many of the masterminds of the 9/11 attacks. We have completely disrupted their ability to communicate with one another, and we have disrupted their organization by forcing the leadership to expend most of its time, energy, and resources on avoiding detection. We have successfully seized a great many of their assets and made it altogether more difficult for them to transfer significant amounts of money to finance large-scale operations.

In response they have simply adapted. The threat from al-Qaeda has changed. We are no longer facing a well-funded, well-led, well-trained, and well-run organization. Instead, the ideology that inspired al-Qaeda now inspires radicalized Muslims in a wide range of countries from the Middle East to the heart of Europe. Some of these groups have connections through individuals to al-Qaeda, many do not. Al-Qaeda may offer advice and occasional expertise but it does not direct or finance their operations. One of the biggest advantages of the tactic of terrorism is that it is so inexpensive. The 9/11 operation was the most expensive terrorist attack in history, and it cost its organizers, as mentioned earlier, an estimated $500,000 (it cost the insurance industry alone between $25 billion and $50 billion[19]). Subsequent operations in London, Madrid, Bali, and Casablanca have been self-financed and cost only a few thousand dollars each. Turning off the flow of money to al-Qaeda has hurt the organization and weakened it, but it has not and will not stop terrorist attacks, though it does reduce the likelihood of a recurrence of sophisticated attacks such as those on 9/11.

While our intelligence operations have enjoyed some successes against al-Qaeda and especially against what might be called "al-Qaeda central," we have been singularly unsuccessful in gleaning good intelligence on a range of equally important issues. We need to understand the basis of al-Qaeda's strength. We need to understand the nature of al-Qaeda's appeal. We need to understand the importance it attaches to the various goals it articulates. Does it really wish to establish a caliphate, or would it be satisfied if the United States withdrew from the Middle East? Would it continue to fight until Israel was annihilated or would it stop fighting if it were to succeed in bringing down the Saudi regime and introducing Sharia law in Saudi Arabia? We have no idea.

If we do not even know what our enemies are fighting for, we cannot hope to counter them effectively. We have come to believe our own rhetoric that they are driven by uncontrolled evil and limitless ambition to harm us. We have tended to imagine all the terrible things they could do to us and then to attempt the impossible task of defending against all of them. Instead, we need to figure out, on the basis of sound intelligence, the things they have (or might soon have) both the motive and the capability to do to us and defend ourselves accordingly. We also need to figure out how we can most effectively weaken them.

Every government that has faced a threat from terrorism has found that good intelligence has been the most crucial weapon in its armory. This has been true across all types of terrorist movements and across all types of governments, from Rómulo Betancourt's campaign against the FALN in Venezuela in the 1960s to France's campaign against the GIA (Groupe Islamique Armé) in the 1990s. I have already mentioned the key role played by DIRCOTE, the small, specialized intelligence agency with the Peruvian police force that was so crucial to the capture of Abimael Guzmán. Israel too has relied heavily on intelligence for information leading to the prevention of particular attacks or the location of terrorist leaders in the West Bank and the Gaza Strip. In Northern Ireland, over time, the British security services developed a highly efficient intelligence operation based largely on informants that enabled them to prevent planned attacks. The security services there claimed that by the early 1990s, 70 percent of all planned IRA operations were abandoned on security grounds. Of the remaining 30 percent, 80 percent were prevented or interdicted by the security forces.[20] Good intelligence also afforded the opportunity to ambush terrorist operatives, as the SAS did in Loughgall in 1987, killing eight IRA members, and undercover army commandos did in Coagh in 1991. In all these cases intelligence was acquired by the sophisticated use of advanced technologies as well as the extensive use of personal informants. We have been highly successful in developing the former and have completely failed to develop the latter, relying instead on often dubious information extracted from those we have captured.

Good intelligence not only helps to weaken the capabilities of the adversary by providing information on planned operations or location of hideouts, it also provides crucial information on the internal dynamics of the group. Terrorist groups operate under conditions of considerable uncertainty and often suffer from quite understandable bouts of paranoia. When operations and individuals are betrayed, the group often turns against its own. As members of terrorist groups tend to have impeccable intelligence on one another, they can be very effective in eliminating suspected collaborators with cold ruthlessness. For example, in the period 1979–1981, more members of the IRA were murdered by their colleagues as informants than were killed by the security forces.[21]

In the Punjab the success of the Indian government in infiltrating Sikh terrorist groups served to weaken the movements by sowing distrust among the membership. One of the abiding characteristics of terrorist groups is their fissiparous tendencies, that is, their tendency to split into smaller groups. Most well-known terrorist groups, whether they be nationalist groups such as the IRA or social revolutionary groups such as the Red Army Faction, are surrounded by smaller offshoots that have split off over some ideological or personal issue (and most often it is a personal issue wrapped up as an ideological one). These splits weaken the movement, distracting attention from the central campaign it is waging by requiring scarce resources like trained members to be lost, as when an expert bomb maker joins a splinter group, leaving people outside the control of the leadership with vital information about the core group. One of the most effective means of weakening a terrorist group is to encourage these splits. In order to do so, we must have intelligence operatives deep inside these groups participating in the internal debates and learning about the leanings as well as the plans of the membership.

There is no doubt that penetrating terrorist groups is no easy task. Developing a good intelligence network takes time, connections, language skills, cultural knowledge, and deep engagement in the region the groups come from. It is even more difficult when, as at present, so many new ad hoc groups are forming that appear to be linked only by personal connection and radical ideology. Nevertheless, if John Walker Lindh can be accepted by the Taliban, and Jose Padilla by al-Qaeda, then other Americans, with a very different agenda, must also be able to join radical jihadi groups. If Richard Reid, the so-called Shoe Bomber, can be recruited in prison and prisons are becoming what Jessica Stern has called "gateway organizations," we should have our operatives permeating these avenues to militant Islam.

As Israel's very different experience in intelligence gathering in Lebanon and the West Bank can attest, it is a great deal more difficult to acquire good intelligence in a territory one does not control. Never-theless, there is no real alternative. We must either gather this intelli-gence ourselves or persuade enough people on the ground to gather it for us. Within the United States the best possible source of information on the emergence of small groups of Islamic militants along the lines of their European counterparts in Britain, Spain, the Netherlands, France, Germany, and Belgium is the loyal Muslim population of this country. If we treat them as suspect by rounding up and detaining large num-bers of them, if we pay lip service to tolerance while practicing racial profiling, we are likely to deprive ourselves of invaluable information, quite aside from any real civil liberties concerns we may have.

If anything, we appear to know less about the nature of our adver-saries in the war on terrorism than we did when we began. We take as a given that their demands are so extreme as to be nonnegotiable, but it would be worth finding out if that is, in fact, the case. Yet suggestions that their demands might be negotiable are treated with deep suspi-cion, and suggestions that we actually talk to the terrorists are consid-ered tantamount to treason. It seems to me that this issue is of such importance that it needs to be demonstrated rather than simply as-serted that their demands indeed are nonnegotiable. Even if we could get over the public's inhibition against talking to the terrorists it would not be altogether easy to do so. The hammer of American military power that descended on al-Qaeda in the fall of 2001 had the effect of shattering the organization and sending splinters throughout the world, so it is not entirely clear to whom one could talk. That said, Ayman al-Zawahiri has clearly emerged as the chief spokesman and strategist of the al-Qaeda leadership, and while it is far from clear that he has the authority to carry his followers with him, the opportunity to engage him is one that should not be missed, no matter how much oppro-brium we hold for him.

I have no illusions about how unpopular a suggestion this is likely to be. Governments always resist talking to terrorists for fear that it will seem to confer legitimacy on them, or to reward their terrorism. It is also the case that many governments have successfully defeated ter-rorist groups without ever engaging them. Nevertheless, it is also the case that Britain ended the IRA's terrorism only through negotiating with the terrorists and that the cease-fire currently enjoyed in Sri Lanka is a result of government talks with the hated Tamil Tigers. The difference between the Red Brigades and RAF, on the one hand, and the LTTE and IRA, on the other, is that the first pair both had nonnegotiable goals and were isolated from their communities. The second pair had political and hence negotiable goals and a significant degree of support in their communities. As I mentioned in the first chapter (see Figure 1), the two key characteristics of all terrorist groups are the nature of the goals they seek and the nature of their relationship to their community. Al-Qaeda appears to have nonnegotiable goals and a significant degree of community support. The focus of our intelligence, and indeed all other counterterrorist policies at the moment, ought to be, first, to establish if that indeed is the nature of their goal and, second, to isolate them from their community of support.

Wars are easier to begin than to end; they tend to last much longer than an objective assessment of the interests of the participants suggest that they should. The same is true of terrorism and counterterrorist campaigns.[22] In some cases one side has overwhelming power and simply wins the conflict, but this is rarely the case. The First World War, for example, ended in 1918 on terms that had essentially been available two years earlier. The Boer War could have ended on the same terms as it eventually did eighteen months earlier. The IRA finally called an end to its campaign seven years after the Good Friday Agreement, and the broad terms of that agreement could have been available many years earlier. There are a variety of reasons for this. The costs of wars are such that participants feel they need to continue fighting to justify the costs already borne. Wars and terrorist campaigns tend to be prolonged by an unlikely alliance of hawks on both sides and generally require an alliance of doves on both sides in order to make peace.

In the case of terrorist groups, delay can be caused by unwillingness to negotiate. Talks with terrorists are not simply an opportunity for negotiating concessions, they are also an invaluable opportunity for gaining information about the opponent. Governments tend to be reluctant to get involved in talks with terrorists as they do not want to confer legitimacy on an illegal group or to reward its violent activity. Nevertheless, many states have, in fact, talked to terrorists, although most have been inconsistent in their willingness to do so. The Khasavyurt Accord brought the first Chechen war to an end with the promise of resolving the status of Chechnya, but the outbreak of the second Chechen war and Vladimir Putin's assumption of power and firm refusal to negotiate have meant a bloody prolongation of the conflict.

Throughout the conflict in Northern Ireland, the British government held talks with the IRA. These talks often took place during a time when the government had an official line of refusing to talk to terrorists. From the first secret talks in 1972, which served mainly to demonstrate to each side the extent of the differences between them, the meetings helped the British government size up its opponent. In 1975, a series of meetings was held between the British government and the IRA while the movement maintained a cease-fire. The IRA subsequently concluded that it had been tricked into the meetings. Initially it was led to believe that Britain was looking for a way to extricate itself from the province, but it concluded that the talks had been a ruse by the government to gather intelligence and encourage splits within the movement by trying to draw some members into constitutional politics. The years of direct and indirect public and private talks finally paid off in the signing of the 1998 Good Friday Agreement.

By overcoming our reluctance to talk, we could discover a great deal about our adversaries, about the importance they assign to particular goals, about how they make decisions, and about their assessment of their own position. Such talks do not have to be public, nor do they have to be direct. They could be conducted through intermediaries, but it is very difficult to know your enemies if you don't try to engage them.

There are any number of examples of how our ignorance of our enemies has served only to strengthen them. In his speech to the United Nations in February 2003, when Colin Powell painted the portrait of Abu Mus'ab al-Zarqawi as bin Laden's man in Iraq, he suddenly transformed al-Zarqawi, a hitherto largely unknown two-bit Jordanian thug, into a leader of a global movement. At the time al-Zarqawi was not remotely in the same league as the highly trained, highly educated, experienced leadership of al-Qaeda. By offering a $25 million reward for him, we soon elevated him into the senior ranks. In fact, it took al-Zarqawi a year and a half to declare allegiance to bin Laden in a statement posted on Islamist Web sites.[23] Two months later, in December 2004, bin Laden, in an audiotape, accepted al-Zarqawi's fealty and pronounced him the "emir" of al-Qaeda in Iraq and instructed Muslims to listen to him.[24]

By knowing your enemies, you can find out what it is they want. Once you know what they want, you can then decide whether to deny it to them and thereby demonstrate the futility of their tactic, give it to them, or negotiate and give them a part of it in order to cause them to end their campaign. By knowing your enemies, you can make an assessment not just of their motives but also of their capabilities and of the caliber of their leaders and their organizations. Any information one could glean from such encounters would be useful. If one concludes definitively that their demands are nonnegotiable, the focus of one's policy must be to isolate them from their communities and go after them with targeted coercive policies. On the other hand, one might learn that their demands are, in fact, negotiable, and this could once again help to direct counterterrorist policy. The most likely outcomes would be to discover that they are not a unitary actor and that some have negotiable demands and others do not. Then the direction of policy should be to exploit these differences and sow dissent among them.

In short, there is nothing to lose and a great deal to gain by knowing one's enemies. The best way to do so is to invest decisively and heavily in a comprehensive intelligence strategy.

Rule 4: Separate the Terrorists from Their Communities

The first point, as I have said, is to be clear about the goal we seek: we wish to contain the threat from terrorists. Today this means that we need to stop the spread of Islamic militancy. In order to stop the spread of Islamic militancy, we must understand the nature of its appeal and endeavor to counter it. This means that the focus of our counterterrorism strategy should not be, as it has been until now, on the actual perpetrators of the violence but rather on the potential recruits of the terrorist groups, the communities from which they derive their support. Terrorist groups thrive in complicit societies. Without recruits they cannot grow. If they are isolated from their communities, they become infinitely weaker as they become dependent upon crime to derive a means of support, and this in turn exposes them to capture. If they are isolated from their communities, they cannot travel safely, internal rivalries become more intense, paranoia grows, and the group becomes more susceptible to defection and is at greater risk of betrayal. It becomes more difficult for them to operate, and in particular it becomes more difficult to operate sophisticated weapons arsenals or training grounds.

Our policies in the years since 9/11 have been focused on the perpetrators of the violence. Our focus has been on stopping them, not figuring out what motivates them or how they manage to win recruits. Our use of force against them has appeared to many on the ground to be indiscriminate, and because of this we have intensified their relationships with their communities and alienated their communities from us. In so doing we have won them recruits and safe houses and ensured that they will not be turned over to us. Had we more wisely seen it as a two-step process whereby we would first isolate them from their community and then go after the perpetrators with highly discriminate coercive policies, there would today be far less support for Islamic militancy and far more support for the United States.

Our purpose in alienating the terrorists from their communities is not to win a popularity contest. The reality is that the extent of our wealth and strength will always breed resentment. We do not need to be loved; great powers rarely are. The only threshold we need to reach is that ordinary members of society not be prepared to support those who wish to oppose us by killing our civilians. That is not such a high threshold to achieve. Nevertheless, if by our actions we seem to confirm the view of us held by the terrorists themselves, if our behavior seems more in keeping with their account of our motives than with our own, then we will strengthen our adversaries immeasurably.

As mentioned earlier, terrorism requires a combination of an alienated individual, a complicit society, and a legitimizing ideology. Of the three, it is the society that is most susceptible to influence by us. Individuals become alienated and radicalized in a host of ways, and we cannot intercede to prevent this. We can challenge ideologies, whether they be Salafism or communism, but we are not in the best position to influence these debates. The level at which we can intervene and at which we potentially have all the resources needed to intervene effectively is at the level of the societies that produce the extremists. This is where our attention needs to be focused.

If our goal is to contain the threat from terrorists and the focus of our attention is the communities from which the terrorists derive their support, we have some criteria to consider when contemplating policies.

There are surely few who would dispute the appropriateness of the goal of containing the spread of Islamic militancy; the dispute is over how best to do so. Our approach has been to play to what we consider to be our strength—our military prowess—and to stop the spread of Islamic militancy by capturing or killing all the Islamic militants. The problem with this approach is that in our efforts to capture and kill them our use of overwhelming force is in fact generating more of them. This is emphatically the case with the war in Iraq, which has radicalized a whole generation of young jihadists who have been led to believe that we are establishing a base in the Middle East with which to exploit the resources and dominate the politics of the region.

Secretary of Defense Rumsfeld showed that he understood the difficulty in an October 16, 2003, memo to four of his subordinates. He asked, "Today, we lack metrics to know if we are winning or losing the global war on terror. Are we capturing, killing or deterring and dissuading more terrorists every day than the madrassas and the radical clerics are recruiting, training and deploying against us?"[25] He was, in effect, describing a competitive battle for the hearts and minds of potential recruits. Capturing the culprits is one approach, and it has the advantage of being action oriented and decisive and using America's great military strength.

The other approach is to engage in the war of ideas and in effect to try to inoculate the broader community against the appeal of the militants. This approach has less appeal to policy makers as it is more intangible, is likely to take a long time to produce results, appears to reward those close to the terrorists, and insufficiently repudiates the evil of the atrocity. Moreover, it requires a deep engagement with the region across a range of policy areas as well as linguistic and cultural familiarity that are surprisingly rare in the halls of our foreign and intelligence services.

The leaders of al-Qaeda are acutely conscious of the fact that they are engaged in a war of ideas with us. Through their extensive use of the new media, from the Internet to audio- and videotapes, they have sought to compensate for their military weakness and engage in this battle. The term "hearts and minds" was coined in the British counter-insurgency experience in Malaya and much discredited by the U.S. campaign in Vietnam; nevertheless, it remains a crucial component in the current campaign against terrorism. It is a term that has even been used by the terrorists: "I say to you that we are in a battle, and that more than half of this battle is taking place in the battlefield of the media. And that we are in a media battle in a race for the hearts and minds of our Umma [community]."[26]

In a missive captured in fall 2005 from al-Qaeda's second in command, Ayman al-Zawahiri, to Abu Mus'ab al-Zarqawi, one of the leaders of the Iraqi insurgency, the elder terrorist sought to teach the younger firebrand the importance of this aspect of their war. This extraordinary document, dated July 2005 and captured by U.S. intelligence sources in Iraq and posted on the Web site of the Office of the Director of National Intelligence, spells out the strategy being pursued by al-Qaeda in Iraq and proffers advice on how to achieve its objectives:

> If we look at the two short-term goals, which are removing the Americans and establishing an Islamic amirate in Iraq, or a caliphate if possible, then we will see that the strongest weapon which the mujahedeen enjoy—after the help and granting of success by God—is popular support from the Muslim masses in Iraq, and the surrounding Muslim countries. So, we must maintain this support as best we can, and we should strive to increase it. . . . In the absence of this popular support, the Islamic mujahed movement would be crushed in the shadows. . . . Therefore, the mujahed movement must avoid any action that the masses do not understand or approve.[27]

He then goes on to counsel against attacks on Shias and gruesome beheadings of hostages on the grounds that the Muslim public are troubled by these tactics.

If al-Qaeda believes that its greatest strength is the popular support it enjoys among the Muslim populations, our energies should be focused on undermining that support. On the contrary, almost everything we have done has served to strengthen that support.

Conducting a war of ideas is a more nebulous and less energizing concept than waging a "real" war of bombs and bullets. The two kinds of warfare also require somewhat different mind-sets. The heavy sacrifices expected of those who participate in conventional warfare require certitude about the rectitude of one's own position in order to justify those sacrifices. In order to win a war of ideas, however, one has to engage with the adversaries and even concede at times that they may have a point.

The fact that someone who has committed heinous crimes makes allegations against us does not mean that those allegations are without foundation and should be dismissed out of hand. If our audience is the broader community to which he is appealing, then we need to listen and to respond to the allegations. Nowhere is the gulf between al-Qaeda's argument and ours more in evidence than in the question of the impact of economic sanctions on Iraq. In his statements over the years bin Laden regularly invoked the hundreds of thousands of Iraqi children killed by American sanctions. "A million innocent children are dying as we speak, killed in Iraq without any guilt."[28] Americans simply dismissed these claims as the outrageous rantings of a diabolical fanatic. Economic sanctions, after all, are benign; they are a means of putting pressure on a pariah government without using force. Americans saw our sanctions as evidence of our restraint, and if they caused hardship for Iraqi civilians it was because Saddam Hussein was impeding their implementation in the humanitarian way we had intended.

The fact is that the UN sanctions did cause the deaths of hundreds of thousands of Iraqi children. A UNICEF report issued in 1999 indicated that 500,000 children under the age of five died between 1991 and 1998 in Iraq due largely to the impact of the sanctions.[29] The British medical journal The Lancet reported, "Infant mortality rose from 47 per 1,000 live births during 1984–89 to 108 per 1,000 in 1994–99, and under five mortality rose from 56 to 131 per 1,000 live births."[30] Two successive UN officials in charge of the program resigned to protest the humanitarian catastrophe over which they were presiding. Hans von Sponeck explained, "I can no longer be associated with a program that prolongs suffering of the people and which has no chance to meet even the basic needs of the civilian population." Later he said, "Lawlessness of one kind does not justify lawlessness of another kind . . . how long must the civilian population be exposed to such punishment for something that they've never done?"[31] Earlier,

Fred Halliday, a thirty-year veteran of the United Nations, had also resigned, insisting that "4,000 to 5,000 children [are] dying unnecessarily every month due to the impact of sanctions because of the breakdown of water and sanitation, inadequate diet and the bad internal health situation." Halliday went on to describe the complete breakdown in civil society in Iraq as a result of the privations imposed by sanctions, and, remarking on the growth of fundamentalist Islamic thinking, he declared, in 1998, "We are pushing people to take extreme positions."[32]

It is imperative that we listen to the allegations being made against us and that we examine the impact of our policies on the ground. Repeated public opinion polls have indicated that the American people did not blame the Iraqi people for the actions of their leader, yet the economic sanctions we imposed on Iraq punished Iraqi civilians. Indeed, the number of Iraqis who died as a result of economic sanctions was greater than the number of people who have been killed by every kind of weapon of mass destruction throughout history, including the bombing of Hiroshima and Nagasaki.[33] We cannot hope to win a war of ideas if our actions appear to be so completely at variance with our stated principles.

We must also engage with the grievances that spawn the pools of resentment from which terrorist groups draw. Many of these grievances are political and are difficult to redress. Extremists, however, have been very successful at exploiting such conflicts as the Arab-Israeli problem and the dispute between India and Pakistan over Kashmir. No reasonable person expects us to resolve these disputes, and our support for Israel will always be unpopular. Nevertheless, if we are seen to hold our allies to the same standards of behavior as we hold our adversaries and if we make a concerted effort to facilitate resolution of these political disputes, we will garner the respect of moderate Arab opinion.

The other political arena in which we should act if we wish to drive a wedge between the extremists and the societies that enable their behavior is the domestic politics of our allies in the Middle East. There can be little doubt that many of our allies in the region do not share our commitment to democracy and the rule of law. If we want their populations to believe that we are committed to the principles we espouse, we must be seen to be an advocate for political reforms. We should demonstrate that we are aware that elections alone do not constitute democracy and that democracy cannot successfully be imposed from without. Instead, we should support the development of a resilient civil society and moderate opposition political parties. We should see the election of those who disagree with us as evidence of our success, not our failure. Again, this is a very long-term process, but our commitment to the process will undermine the argument of those who proselytize by pointing to the significant disparity between our principles and our practices.

As the richest country in the world, we have an enormous comparative advantage in the campaign against terrorists. We should use it. We should adopt a comprehensive development agenda to address the underlying or permissive causes of terrorism. It has often been said that Americans prefer big ideas to small ones, as evidenced by the support for the Marshall Plan after World War II, the mobilization behind John F. Kennedy's plan to put a man on the moon, or indeed the support for President Bush's plan to eliminate terrorism. What better way to demonstrate the difference between us and those who attacked us on 9/11 than to respond by redressing economic and social inequities among the populations they claim to represent?

We should have no illusions that these actions would impress, much less mollify, the perpetrators of the violence, but they would not be the target of our policies. In the worst-case scenario, a comprehensive development plan would fail to deprive terrorists of support. It would nevertheless significantly improve the quality of life of a great many people and in all probability develop markets for U.S. products too. On the other hand, if the war on terrorism fails, as I have argued it is bound to do, the lives of many people and the quality of life of a great many more will have been destroyed.

As I have pointed out earlier, there is no direct link between poverty and terrorism, and many of the perpetrators of jihadi violence today have above-average levels of education. The societies that support them, however, are societies that have experienced social and economic dislocation and in which perceptions of relative deprivation and political exclusion are acute. In many instances, ranging from Peru to Egypt, well-meaning policies such as providing opportunities for education have backfired because they were carried out in isolation. Providing opportunities for education while failing to offer opportunities for em-

ployment for those who have been educated and whose expectations
have consequently been raised has proven to be a particularly dangerous mistake. In developing a comprehensive development agenda, it is
imperative that the various policies be coordinated and consistent with
the overall objective.[34]

It turns out that perhaps one of our most successful counterterrorist policies was one that we implemented quite unwittingly and not
under the guise of countering terrorism. Indonesia, the country with
the largest Muslim population in the world (almost 200 million), has
proven to be a hotbed of support for al-Qaeda. The local militant Islamic group Jemaah Islamiyah has been implicated in numerous terrorist attacks including a number of attacks on Western targets. A bomb
outside the Sari Club and another at the nearby Paddy's Bar on October 12, 2003, killed 202 people. When interrogators asked Amrozoi,
one of the accused bombers, why he wanted to bomb the club, he repeatedly told them it was because he "hated Americans." Another of
the accused, Imam Samudra, elaborated:

> I hate America because it is the real center of international terror-
> ism, which has already repeatedly tyrannized Islam. I carry out jihad
> because it is the duty of a Muslim to avenge, so the American ter-
> rorists and their allies understand that the blood of the Muslim
> community is not shed for nothing.[35]

In the years since the attack, Jemaah Islamiyah has been seriously
weakened by a combination of government action and internal divisions. In October 2005, three suicide bombers blew up three Western
restaurants, killing themselves and nineteen others. This attack had
none of the sophistication that marked the attack in 2003 and appears
to have been carried out by a previously unknown group of jihadis.[36]
The difference in the two attacks illustrates the declining fortunes of
the jihadi movement in Indonesia.

In December 2004, Indonesia was devastated by the Indian Ocean
earthquake and subsequent tsunami. The natural disaster is estimated
to have cost 280,000 lives, with tens of thousands injured and a million people made homeless. Casualties in Indonesia are estimated at
130,000 dead, 100,000 injured, and 400,000 to 700,000 displaced.
The United States initially offered $35 million in assistance. That was

quickly increased to $350 million, and in February 2005 President Bush pledged $950 million in assistance. A public opinion poll conducted by the Pew Global Attitudes Survey found that 79 percent of Indonesians said they had a more favorable view of the United States as a result of the American relief efforts. The number of Indonesians who had a favorable opinion of the United States increased from 15 percent in 2003 to 38 percent in 2005.[37] Consistent with this change is the subsequent finding that 35 percent of the Indonesian public had confidence in Osama bin Laden as a world leader in 2005, down from 58 percent in 2003.[38] By its humanitarian efforts to alleviate the suffering caused by the tsunami in Indonesia, the United States has undermined popular support for terrorism against the United States.

The prospects of success for any policy initiatives that we undertake are likely to be significantly enhanced if we engage in a concerted effort to explain our policies and the reasoning behind them. This requires a sustained and significant commitment to public diplomacy. There have been a number of recent reports spelling out details of how our conduct of public diplomacy might be overhauled.[39] There can be no doubt that if we are to separate the terrorists from their communities, we must make our case to these communities. This again is an area in which our wealth, our media, and our technological skills can be a considerable advantage. These advantages will gain us nothing, however, if we do not take the time to study the languages and cultures of the societies with which we are dealing. Currently, the public diplomacy budget stands at three tenths of one percent of the Defense Department budget.[40] The complete failure to seize the opportunity to make our case to the Islamic world since 9/11 is difficult to understand. The position of undersecretary of state for public diplomacy has remained vacant for long stretches and been rotated among a series of well-meaning and talented individuals, none of whom has had extensive experience in the cultures s/he is supposed to engage.

For a campaign of public diplomacy to have any chance of success, it must be a great deal more than window dressing. It must have a comprehensive, coordinated, well-funded plan developed and implemented by disinterested people who are intimately familiar with the nuances of the societies we seek to influence. Its success will not be measurable on a timeline consistent with electoral politics in the United States, and therefore our political leaders need to develop a bipartisan consensus so that the implementation of these policies is not exploited for short-term political advantage.

The most sophisticated, best-articulated, and best-funded public diplomacy campaign, however, will probably come to nothing if the arguments that are being made are inconsistent with what people are experiencing. If the United States continues to pursue policies that are widely unpopular and that appear to be inconsistent with what it is saying, our actions will speak louder than our words. As long as American troops remain on the ground in Iraq, and as long as we are unable to deliver security, stability, and a decent standard of living to Iraqis, those who argue that we are there either to dominate the region or to acquire Iraqi oil are going to find a willing audience.

If we succeed in separating the terrorists from the communities that produce them, there will be real limits to the damage they can do to us. We will never be able to stop their attacking a soft Western target in some part of the world, but we can prevent their pulling off a spectacular attack that requires sophisticated and coordinated planning. If we are able to isolate them, we can then focus our coercive policies on tracking them down and disabling them. We will not be able to isolate them unless we can persuade others that what they say about us is wrong.

Rule 5: Engage Others in Countering Terrorists with You

Historically, most terrorist action occurred within countries or across neighboring countries. Terrorism was adopted as a tactic to address a local grievance, but very often the issue had international implications. In the case of nationalist movements, terrorism may have affected two neighboring states, as when a group wanted to secede from one country and join another, for example in the disputed Indian and Pakistani claims to Kashmir or the desire of some Northern Irish Catholics to secede from the United Kingdom and join the Republic of Ireland. On other occasions, neighboring countries are involved because of the desire of a terrorist group to create a homeland consistent with the location of an ethnic group, such as the Basques in Spain and France or the Kurds in Turkey, Iraq, and Syria.

Though the groups emerged locally, there has often been an international component, as when nationalist groups have relied for support on those who have emigrated abroad. Sikhs in North America have generously supported Sikh nationalists in India's Punjab. The Tamil and Kurdish diaspora has also been a consistent source of support for the LTTE and the PKK, while Irish Americans have supported the IRA. In a few cases the ideology of terrorist groups has been internationalist, as was the case of the social revolutionary groups in Europe in the 1970s. A German group called itself the Red Army Faction because it perceived itself to be just one faction of an international Communist army. Terrorism also became international when states sponsored terrorists overseas as a covert instrument with which to conduct their foreign policy. In some cases, such as the Iranian and Syrian support for Hezbollah, the support has not even been so covert.

Nevertheless, the transnationalism of recent terrorists appears to have gone a considerable step further. In the case of the London bombing, for example, young men born in England were radicalized by what they had heard of American actions in Iraq. Never having been either to America or to Iraq, they murdered commuters in London. This is indeed the globalization of terrorism, in which a global conflict ignites a local terrorist group. We simply cannot hope to counter these types of groups on our own, yet we are quite vulnerable to them. The 9/11 attacks were planned by a cell in Hamburg. Richard Reid was recruited in a British jail. Zacharias Moussaoui, a would-be member of the 9/11 team, found his calling in a London mosque. Ahmad Rassam, who planned to blow up Los Angeles International Airport, was linked to a network of radicals in France. We will need extensive cooperation and intelligence sharing with other countries in order to monitor the activities of known and emerging cells of radical militants.

This cooperation is more likely to be successful if other countries believe in the legitimacy of our position and believe that they are consulted by us in defining the problem and devising a response. Inevitably, domestic norms and domestic legislation will impede action in particular cases, but the terrorists themselves are very adept at operating freely across borders, so we must become equally adept at traversing borders in response.

We should make it a priority to establish effective multilateral institutions that will facilitate the tracking of terrorists. This must go beyond our insisting on specific actions on the part of other countries. Instead, we must develop broadly acceptable norms and procedures so that sharing of information is automatic. The experience of other countries dramatically demonstrates the effectiveness of such collaborative arrangements. As long as Kashmiri separatists could find safe haven in Pakistan, Basques in France, and republicans in southern Ireland, these movements thrived. Once the French and Irish governments were persuaded of the legitimacy of the Spanish and British counterterrorist policies and agreed to prevent the terrorists from operating freely from their side of the border, the terrorist groups were greatly weakened. In the case of Northern Ireland, Britain got this support only after it finally recognized that the Republic of Ireland also had an interest in the question and gave formal recognition to the Irish dimension to the Northern Irish conflict.

There are any number of ways in which engaging the international community in the campaign to contain the terrorist threat can strengthen our hand. At a practical operational level, it can help us to track and capture militants, curtail their funding, and impede their operations. At a political level, it can enhance the legitimacy of our position by casting the conflict as one between those who believe in the rule of law and those who don't, rather than simply one of the strong against the weak or the United States against the rest.

Members of the international community can also play an important role as a broker in negotiations, as the Norwegians did in brokering the Oslo accords or as the United States did in facilitating the Northern Ireland peace process. The international community can also help to address social problems, as in the World Bank and the Inter-American Bank's funding of the Peruvian microdevelopment projects designed to address some of the socioeconomic grievances that fueled support for the Shining Path.

Given that the international community shares our interest in combating terrorism, if not our assessment of the best way to do so, there are clearly areas of mutual agreement. One of these areas is "loose nukes." There is considerable international consensus on the dangers inherent in the fact that there remain numerous unsecured sites in which the former Soviet Union worked on the development of nuclear, chemical, and biological weapons. Securing these sites is probably the best available means of enhancing our security at the lowest cost. Yet the U.S. government program to do so has been poorly run and seriously underfunded. This is an issue that must be addressed, and the

U.S. government, unaccountably, has lacked either the will or the interest to do so. As such, it is an ideal issue with which to engage the international community.

The Cooperative Threat Reduction (CTR) program was established in 1991 to secure nuclear, chemical, and biological weapons sites in the former Soviet Union. The USSR had the most intensive biological weapons program in history, with the result that stores of dangerous pathogens, such as anthrax, smallpox, and Ebola virus, remain in unsecured sites in parts of the world in which terrorist groups with a declared interest in acquiring them are known to be operating. In 2003, the General Accounting Office reported that security projects were under way at only four of the forty-nine known biological sites and that only two sites had been secured against external threats. The CTR, which is responsible for securing nuclear and chemical as well as biological facilities, has been funded at approximately $1 billion a year since the 1990s, in spite of the recommendation of a bipartisan panel in January 2001 to triple the funding. Given the real need for action on this front and our unwillingness to act, this seems to be an area that we should be prepared to engage others in addressing.

A second area in which a division of labor would make eminent sense is managing the aftermath of military operations. The Europeans have more extensive experience than we have at postwar reconstruction (even if we are daily acquiring more experience). Other countries are actively engaged in postwar reconstruction in Afghanistan. NATO currently has more than 12,000 troops stationed there. In order to secure support for postwar reconstruction, however, we are going to have to be prepared to consult our allies more broadly during prewar planning. Today we are in the curious position in which behind-the-scenes cooperation is actually better than anyone cares to admit publicly. The unpopularity of the U.S.-led war on terrorism is such that allied governments have no desire to publicize the degree to which they are helping us, preferring instead for the cooperation to take place quietly. Small groups of French and German special forces, for example, are in Afghanistan and Pakistan searching for the remnants of the al-Qaeda leadership but without announcing this fact for fear of domestic unpopularity. It cannot be in our interest for our allies to conceal the extent to which they are helping us.

The international community, of course, is not the only other entity that needs to be engaged. As I have mentioned, local communities need to be engaged and can be the most powerful force in the repudiation of terrorism. In Egypt, for example, when significant segments of the public concluded that terrorist attacks against tourists, as occurred at Luxor in 1997, were at variance with the Islamic tradition of protection for visitors and deeply damaging to the tourist industry as well, they helped to put pressure on al-Gama'a al-Islamiyya to stop these attacks.

A recent example occurred in Israel. A nineteen-year-old Israeli soldier, Eden Natan-Zada, who was affiliated with the right-wing Kach group, opened fire on a bus carrying Palestinians to protest the Israeli pullout from Gaza. At the time he was AWOL from the army. The Israeli public emphatically repudiated the attack. The media immediately referred to it as a terrorist act (language not usually heard when Israelis kill Palestinians), and the attacker was labeled a terrorist. The prime minister called Natan-Zada a "bloodthirsty murderer and terrorist." The Ministry of Defense refused to allow him to be buried among soldiers, as he had sullied the honor of the IDF (Israeli Defense Force), and the mayor of his hometown refused to allow him to be buried there. Those among the right-wing settler community who might have been inclined to be more sympathetic felt compelled to condemn the action. This kind of complete repudiation by a community of someone claiming to be acting in its name is striking.

We cannot know for sure if this kind of response will deter another young Israeli extremist from acting in the same way, but it is hard to believe that it could not. This young man may have succeeded in exacting revenge, but he certainly got no renown, nor did he succeed in provoking the desired reaction. If the local communities from which terrorists come were to respond in this way, there can be little doubt that terrorism would hold less attraction for young men seeking glory.

We do not just need to engage the broader members of a community, we also need to mobilize moderates. When engaging members of the local community in this way, we have to be careful that they are not delegitimized by virtue of being associated with us. We must not have as a price of our support the insistence that the moderates we attempt to mobilize will be uncritical of us. There is no surer way of undermining them. We need to engage them and engage with their criticisms of our policies and our practices. We must demonstrate in our reaction to them that we respect the right of others to oppose us. We simply do not accept their right to express their opposition through terrorism.

Again, the experience of other countries provides many examples of how governments have successfully mobilized moderates against extremists. The Italian government's ability to defeat the Red Brigades was immeasurably enhanced by the role played by the Italian Communist Party. In Northern Ireland the British government endeavored to strengthen the hand of the moderate nationalist party the SDLP (Social Democratic and Labour Party) as a counterweight to the IRA. Later, after the leader of the SDLP, John Hume, had engaged the leader of Sinn Féin, Gerry Adams, in talks, the government concentrated on strengthening the hand of the pragmatists within the republican movement itself, such as Adams.

In another example, the Indian government assisted in the development of moderate political parties to represent the Sikhs as a counterweight to those who were prepared to deploy violence to achieve their political objectives. Similarly, in Spain, the government sought to strengthen the moderate Basque Nationalist Party in an effort to demonstrate the advantages of political approaches to conflict resolution. For a time the government also permitted the emergence of the political party Herri Batasuna as a means of encouraging the ETA to pursue political means, but it revoked that recognition once it decided that Batasuna was no more than a front for ETA.

A recent example from Spain demonstrates how the Spanish government has responded to the terrorist attacks in Madrid by working with the moderate leaders of Spain's one million Muslims. On the first anniversary of the bombing at Atocha Station, which occurred on March 11, 2004, and killed 192 people, Mansur Escudero Bedate, secretary general of the Islamic Commission of Spain, issued a fatwa against bin Laden, al-Qaeda, and all who use the Koran to try to justify terrorism.

It is worth pointing out that the experience of others indicates one very clear lesson: that the mobilization of moderates should never extend to the point of supporting one group that is prepared to use violence against another. This tactic invariably backfires. Indeed, one has only to look to U.S. support of the mujahedin in Afghanistan as a counterweight to the Soviet Union for evidence of the folly of this approach. Prime Minister Anwar Sadat of Egypt assisted in the development of the movement that eventually murdered him in his effort to develop a counterweight to Communist parties. In Lebanon too, Israel unwittingly assisted in the creation of Hezbollah as radicals within the Amal movement resisted peace negotiations. Similarly, in the West Bank and Gaza, Israel turned a blind eye to the activities of the Muslim Brotherhood in the belief that the group was more moderate than Fatah, but the result was the emergence of Hamas, which was considerably less moderate.

The lesson from other countries suggests the wisdom of engaging with moderate opinion and mobilizing and encouraging a moderate alternative to violence. It is not crucial that this moderate voice be supportive of the U.S. position, but it is crucial that it oppose violent forms of political change.

Terrorist groups are often quite keenly aware of the threat posed to them by moderate leaders of their own community. The Tamil Tigers in particular have been ruthless in targeting moderate Tamil leaders for assassination. The Red Brigades also turned against the reformist Italian Communist Party, of which they were as critical as of the conservative Christian Democrats. The Red Brigades' murder in 1979 of Guido Rossi, a popular Communist Party activist, proved to be a major miscalculation. Spontaneous demonstrations and strikes in protest at Rossi's murder erupted in all the major factories of Genoa, previously a stronghold of support for the Brigadistas.

Terrorist groups often do make mistakes and go too far, even for their own supporters. Most commonly, this happens when they start killing moderate leaders or particularly vulnerable populations, such as children. Such mistakes offer a hugely important opportunity for governments to mobilize opinion against the terrorists. In the past, governments have very rarely seized this opportunity. Most often, governments react with severe security measures or by introducing draconian counterterrorist legislation and promptly lose the moderate support they had the opportunity to gain. If governments keep their eye on the objective of isolating the terrorists and preventing the spread of their ideology, they will capitalize on these terrorist atrocities and use them to further that objective rather than acceding to the provocation of the terrorists.

On the morning of July 7, 2005, British Prime Minister Tony Blair was attending the G8 Summit in Gleneagles, Scotland, when four suicide bombers attacked the London transport system, killing 56 people. Blair's early and apparently unscripted comments were a very model of how a democratic leader should respond to a terrorist attack. Far from elevating the rhetoric and engaging in the language of warfare or revenge, he spoke calmly of crime scenes and police work and of Britain's quiet determination to defend its values and way of life. The communication between terrorists and their audience is a constant narrative of blame, a constant contest to assume the role of victim to the other's aggressor. Blair simply refused to engage in this dialogue and in so doing modeled a different way for democratic leaders to respond to terrorism. In subsequent and clearly scripted speeches, Prime Minister Blair's remarks did slip back into the more familiar and less constructive response mode generally adopted by democratic leaders.

The British government again displayed the good judgment that accompanies experience with countering terrorism when the IRA finally called off its military campaign and decommissioned its arsenal. Rather than treating IRA disarmament as the concession it was and employing the language of victory for political advantage, Blair disavowed triumphalism and instead used language that would help the IRA supporters of disarmament deal with their hard-line critics.

The task of countering terrorism will be rendered much easier if we are prepared to engage others, and to pay the price necessary to engage others, in the effort to contain them.

Rule 6: Have Patience and Keep Your Perspective

Some terrorist groups have lasted for generations; some have lasted only a few years. A list of the groups active in, say, 1970 reveals some very familiar names and many more that have long since been forgotten. Those that have lasted the longest have tended to be those that have close ties to their communities. These groups tend to be ethnic or nationalist groups seeking political change. Some of these groups too are no longer active. The IRA finally declared an end to its military campaign, and the PKK was defeated by the action of the Turkish government, though the latent threat of resurgent terrorism among disenfranchised Kurds remains real. The social revolutionary movements that posed a considerable threat to several Western democracies in the 1970s have all disintegrated through a combination of effective police work, popular repudiation, and strategic mistakes by the terrorists.

Given the nature of the threat posed to us by al-Qaeda and the global jihadi networks it has spawned, it is highly unlikely that these groups will disappear quickly. The duration of the threat they pose to us will in large part be determined by the nature of their relationships with the communities from which they come and that in turn will depend upon our success in separating them from those communities. As many of the grievances that fuel these groups involve profound socioeconomic realities and deeply intractable political problems, such as the Arab-Israeli issue, they are unlikely to be redressed quickly. Concerted effort on our part to address the grievances that fuel the animosity against us will not bring immediate results but will serve to stem the growth of resentment and to roll back the perceived legitimacy of resorting to terrorist tactics.

The language of warfare connotes action and immediate results. We need to replace this language with the language of development and construction and the patience that goes along with it.

Terrorism in one form or another, therefore, is probably here to stay. The impact of globalization means that terrorist acts will be easier to plan and conduct, weapons will be easier to acquire and transport, and the enemy will be easier to reach than in the past. Nevertheless, the likelihood that terrorist groups could inflict real harm on us remains very low. The possibility that a terrorist group could set off a bomb in an American subway, stadium, or shopping mall will always be there. The probability that terrorists will kill as many Americans as drunk drivers do in any given year is tiny.

In thinking about the terrorist threat we face, we should always remember the words of Ayman al-Zahawiri himself: "However far our capabilities reach, they will never be equal to one thousandth of the capabilities of the kingdom of Satan that is waging war on us." We can reject his characterization of us without rejecting his basic point, that the terrorists will never have one thousandth of our strength. We need to bear this in mind as we contemplate the threat and plan our response: we are infinitely stronger than they are. This does not give us license for complacency, but it does give us the luxury of adopting a deliberative response and a long time horizon. It also requires that we not embolden them by confirming their belief in our cowardice by exaggerating the threat they pose to us.

The only way that terrorists could inflict real and lasting damage on us is if they were to acquire a weapon of mass destruction, and not just any weapon of mass destruction. A dirty bomb or a chemical weapon could inflict serious damage but pose no real threat. The one way they could truly harm us is if they were to acquire and deploy a biological or nuclear weapon. The likelihood of this was always very low. It is even lower today because we have deprived al-Qaeda, at least, of its base in Afghanistan and deterred other states from offering it sanctuary. Moreover, while the war on terror may have generated many new recruits for the terrorist cause, these new recruits are joining small ad hoc groups and not those with sophisticated organizations and training sites. The threat nevertheless remains, and, as I have mentioned, one of the easiest and least expensive ways of reducing it is to secure immediately all known facilities where these weapons are stored. In contemplating this threat, it is also worth remembering that compared to twenty years ago, when the Soviet nuclear arsenal had the power to obliterate the United States, we are far less vulnerable to nuclear attack than we have been for a very long time.

The adoption of terrorism as a tactic is to engage in psychological warfare against a stronger enemy. Terrorism is an attractive tactic because it is easy and because it makes the weak seem stronger, but if we can recognize terrorists' essential weakness, enhance societal resilience, and calibrate our reaction to the actual risk we face, then we will make the task of the terrorists more difficult.

On September 16, 2001, President Bush declared our goal to be "to rout terrorism out of the world." He said, "We will rid the world of the evil-doers."[41] The truth is, we won't. But if we have a more modest agenda—if our goal is to contain the threat from terrorism and if in doing so we play to our strengths and abide by our principles—then we can definitely succeed.

WHERE ARE WE NOW?

In considering U.S. counterterrorist policy since September 11, it is very clear that we have not followed these six rules. We set ourselves an unattainable goal, we have been seen to abandon many of the principles that have guided our democracy, the inadequacies of our intelligence operations have been exposed, our actions have served to strengthen ties between terrorists and the communities from which they come, we have failed to engage others in the campaign against terrorists, and we have failed to demonstrate either patience or a sense of perspective.

That said, American counterterrorism policy is clearly improving with time. In responding to the attacks of 9/11, we have repeated the pattern evident in other democracies. The first reaction is almost always to demonstrate resolve by the adoption of a draconian response that goes largely unchallenged by the public. The second phase is one of polarization, in which the Right demands more tough measures and denounces opponents as unpatriotic while the Left objects to any coercive measures at all. The third phase is one of more reasoned reflection and comes about when the draconian measures have ceased to produce the desired results and the adversary has demonstrated the implacability of his commitment to harming us. It looks as though the United States is now entering this third and more constructive phase. Had we looked around in the fall of 2001, we would have seen that this is how democratic states respond to terrorism and could then have avoided the first two phases; instead, convinced of the uniqueness of our position, we could not bring ourselves to learn from others. Instead, we have learned from our own mistakes, as others before us have done. We are becoming, slowly, more adept at countering terrorism.

In thinking about counterterrorism policies, the question should never be, as it so often is, Who's tough on terrorism, who's soft on terrorism? Invariably, opposition parties become immobilized for fear of being tainted with being *soft* on terrorism. What matters, of course, is what is *effective* against terrorism. There are two questions that should be asked of any counterterrorist proposal. The first is "Is it effective?" If the answer is "yes," the second should be "At what cost?"

The United States responded to the terrorist attacks of September 11 by passing the PATRIOT Act as well as a joint resolution authorizing the use of military force against those responsible.[42] The government then invaded Afghanistan and Iraq and determined that the U.S. conduct of the war on terrorism was not bound by the Geneva Conventions. These actions were undoubtedly tough on terrorism—but were they effective? Partisans like to declare that the answer to such a question is clear-cut, but it rarely is. It is easy to declare an action good or bad, to tout the benefits without conceding the costs; it is more difficult to try to establish the ratio between the good and the bad.

Take the invasion of Afghanistan. This action had overwhelming domestic and international support. The invasion destroyed al-Qaeda's base of operations and drove its leadership into hiding; it succeeded in toppling the brutal Taliban regime and replaced it with an elected assembly. (There was a 70 percent turnout in the October 2004 presidential election and a 50 percent turnout in the September 2005 legislative elections.) These are major accomplishments. There have also been serious costs. Accurate estimates are impossible to come by, but most estimates put the number of Afghan civilian casualties far higher than the number of Americans killed on September 11. Social conditions before the invasion were appalling, and they remain so. (Afghanistan is ranked 173 out of 178 in the human development index.[43]) The situation of opium production, however, is a great deal worse. Afghanistan had 82,000 hectares of land cultivating poppy in 2000, when the Taliban banned opium production. The ban was a near-complete success, and the amount of land under poppy cultivation dropped to 7,600 hectares in 2001. In 2004, there were 131,000 hectares of land under opium poppy cultivation in Afghanistan. Eighty-seven percent of the world's opium production now takes place in Afghanistan, up from 12 percent at the time of the U.S. invasion.[44] The U.S. government is spending one billion dollars a month on military operations in Afghanistan, but more American soldiers were killed in 2005 than in the three previous years combined. In April 2005, the Taliban launched a comeback, and today there are an estimated 1,800 warlords who maintain private militias in the country.[45] The most senior leaders of al-Qaeda and of the Taliban, moreover, remain at large. The invasion of Afghanistan cannot yet fairly be described as a success in the campaign against terrorism; the ratio of good to bad is very low.

By contrast, the ratio of good to bad in the war in Iraq is very high. Whatever the virtue of the other arguments in favor of the war in Iraq, from the point of view of counterterrorism the invasion of Iraq was a calamitous mistake. As detailed in the last chapter, the Iraq war, far from being an effective policy against terrorism, immeasurably strengthened the hand of our adversaries and weakened our own. We have alienated the international community and united our enemies against us. We have provided a training ground for our adversaries, spawned a new generation of terrorists convinced that we are at war with Islam, and failed to bring security to the country. The inadequacy of our postwar planning was grossly negligent. We appear never to have taken the time to challenge the assumptions on which we based our policy; instead, we simply assumed that the policy would be effective and never inquired as to the cost.

Domestically, the PATRIOT Act has become the lightning rod for criticism of the administration's counterterrorism policy. The provocative name of the act has invited challenges, and the act is regularly denounced as evidence of the abandonment of treasured democratic principles. It is too soon to say whether or not the act has been effective, as claims on both sides of this point are rarely accompanied by reliable evidence. The fact is that the act did remove a number of bureaucratic and legal encumbrances to effective information sharing between law enforcement and intelligence agencies. This strikes me as an entirely appropriate response and a necessary step to effective intelligence gathering. Other controversial aspects of the act, such as requiring libraries to provide information on their patrons, should be dropped simply on the grounds of being ineffective.

Where the U.S. government did violate fundamental principles and behave in a manner wholly unworthy of the country's traditions was in the decision that the Geneva Conventions do not apply to the war on terror and the indefinite detention and mistreatment of suspects that resulted. These decisions were quite unrelated to the PATRIOT Act. Leaving aside the question whether any democracy worthy of the name should ever engage in torture—in my view the answer is no—the question that should have been asked is whether or not torture is effective. Again, we appear casually to have assumed that being tough meant being effective. There is, unfortunately, a great deal of empirical evidence available on the effectiveness of torture. Practitioners at least as far back as the Spanish Inquisition have kept impeccable records of their tortures and the results they induced. If we had examined the effectiveness of torture, we would have found that the evidence is mixed. If we had then inquired as to the cost in terms of undermining our moral legitimacy both at home and abroad, not to mention the shakiness of the legal position, we would surely never have sanctioned torture.

Since September 11, 2001, the effectiveness of our counterterrorism policy has improved as we have seen that strength does not easily translate into victory and that the problem we face is primarily a political one. We have passed through the phase in which authority is unquestioningly ceded to the executive in the interests of security; we have begun to question the effectiveness of our policies and to count the costs. We must continue to do so.

WHAT IS TO COME?

We are likely to encounter terrorism in the future, just as we have in the past. We are going to have to learn to live with it and to accept it as a price of living in a complex world. Through improved security procedures and enhanced intelligence, we must protect ourselves against the most dangerous weapons and most sophisticated attacks. We must always remember, however, that terrorists cannot derail our democracy by planting a bomb in our midst. Our democracy can be derailed only if we conclude that it is inadequate to protect us. I have argued here, however, that far from being inadequate, our democratic principles are our strongest weapons. In the case of counterterrorism, our ethics and our interests are clearly aligned.

The most recent attacks in London, Madrid, and the Netherlands all suggest that the Muslim diaspora in Europe will produce the next wave of terrorist attacks. Figures on the number of Muslims in Europe range from 15 million to 23 million, with unknown numbers of illegal immigrants accounting for the discrepancy. This is about 5 percent of the population and excludes the 68 million to 70 million Muslims in Turkey. By 2015, the European Muslim population is expected to double. Most European countries have large, diverse Muslim populations, and many of these Muslims are unassimilated. Over the years, different European countries have adopted different policies toward their immigrant populations. Germany, Austria, and Switzerland perceived Muslim immigrants as temporary guest workers and made few efforts at integration. As a result, parallel societies developed. Britain and the Netherlands embraced multiculturalism, but in practice this helped to entrench Muslim communities that functioned apart from the culture of the host country. France, on the other hand, practiced a policy of integration, providing full citizenship though promoting secularization, but this approach failed to prevent segregation too. None of these countries successfully integrated their Muslim immigrants. There are enormous ethnic, religious, gender, and generational differences within this Muslim population. Very few support radical Islam. The few who do differ in social, educational, and geographic background. They follow a trajectory of becoming politically aware, usually through coverage of an issue such as Bosnia or Iraq, then become radicalized and then religious. Marc Sageman has demonstrated that jihadists become drawn into the movement through social networks. This is no different from the young Communists in the seventies. In the words of one of the latter, "What pushed me on was the solidarity towards those *compagni* that I had known, people who were committing their lives through this venture, to this struggle, and with whom I had shared a part of myself."[46] Adrift between two cultures, young Muslims are vulnerable to the attractions of a simple, electronically disseminated view of the world and their place in it. Through group solidarity, they negate the alienation they feel. By becoming jihadists, they can avenge the indignities they suffer and gain glory in the eyes of their community. They pose a particular threat to us because of their ability to exploit modern technologies, the ease with which they move among us, and the difficulty of distinguishing them from their millions of peaceful coreligionists.

The same ideology that motivated Michael Barrett in the 1860s motivated Seamus Finucane in the 1970s. Nationalism has never ceased in its attraction to those prepared to fight for the "freedom" of their group. This sense of nationalism is as keenly felt in Sri Lanka, Chechnya, India, Spain, and Iraq. Today, however, the "national" group that young men of the European diaspora identify with is religious and transnational. Their exploitation of new technologies enables them to generate and sustain a sense of belonging to this wider community. In a metaphor that is often used by Muslim extremists, a Jemaah Islamiyah Web site declared, "One Muslim to another is like a single body. If one part is in pain, the other part will also feel it."[47] The fusion of nationalism and religion, as we have seen in Iraq, Chechnya, and Kashmir, is a troubling development, as religious groups have always been the most absolutist and nationalist groups have always been most successful in maintaining ties to broader communities. Moreover, it is of course harder to predict where the theater of operations will be when the cause is transnational. We can predict, based on past patterns of behavior, that the terrorists will hit where we are not looking.

In Europe a generation ago, young, educated, alienated idealists such as Mara Cagol who sought to change the world were mobilized by communism and a powerful sense of solidarity. Today young, educated, alienated idealists such as Omar Sheikh, Ziad Jarrah, and Sidique Khan are mobilized by jihadism and a powerful sense of solidarity. We do not know what ideology will mobilize the next generation of young idealists who want to change the world, who are prepared to sacrifice themselves and others in pursuit of their extremist ambition. We can be quite confident, however, that there will be another generation mobilized by yet another extremist ideology designed to protest the inequities evident around them. We should be equally confident that we can withstand the threat they pose.

ACKNOWLEDGMENTS

The many shortcomings of this book are my responsibility. Such strengths as it has are due in large part to the help I have received from a number of others. I would like to acknowledge just some of them.

I have benefited greatly from the unerring editorial eye and wise counsel of my friend Sarah Flynn, and from the insight, energy and charm of my agent, Michael Carlisle.

I wrote this book at the Radcliffe Institute for Advanced Study, a vibrant hotbed of intellectual inquiry. Drew Gilpin Faust generously gave me the time I needed to write, Or-Corinne Chapman gave me invaluable research and logistical assistance, Silvia Suteu provided additional research assistance, and my friends and colleagues at Radcliffe encouraged me all along the way. I am profoundly grateful to each of them.

I have had the considerable pleasure of teaching with and learning from two extraordinary colleagues and friends, Stanley Hoffmann and Philip Heymann. My views on the subjects examined in this book, as well as on many other matters, have benefited from their influence. I have also greatly enjoyed and benefited from being questioned constantly by my students at Harvard, who leave no assertion unchallenged and no argument undefended. I am in their debt.

I would like to thank my editor at Random House, Will Murphy, for his incisive editorial comments and Matt Kellogg for shepherding the book through to production. I would also like to thank Jonathan Karp for his engagement with this book from the outset.

I owe my biggest debt of gratitude to my husband, Thomas R. Jevon, for his irrepressible enthusiasm for this project and his unfailing generosity in cheerfully picking up the pieces on the home front. This book is dedicated to our three children, Ciara, Fiona, and Rory, whose mother's enduring preoccupation with terrorists remains a source of occasional annoyance and constant amusement.

March 20, 2006

GLOSSARY

Abu Sayyaf Group (ASG): A small Muslim separatist group operating in the southern Philippines, which split from the larger Moro National Liberation Front in the early 1990s.

Ação Libertadora Nacional (ALN) (Action for National Liberation): A revolutionary movement formed in Brazil in 1967. Led by Carlos Marighella, the group engaged in urban guerrilla activity. Declined after Marighella's death in 1969.

Action Directe: A French social revolutionary terrorist group active in French cities in the 1980s.

Adams, Gerry (1948–): Leader of the Irish republican movement. President of Sinn Féin and member of Parliament for West Belfast since 1983.

African National Congress (ANC): South Africa's governing party since the first free election in South Africa in 1994. Dedicated to majority rights. Formed in 1912, abandoned nonviolence in 1960.

al-Aqsa Martyrs Brigades: Militant Palestinian group associated with Arafat's Fatah movement. Specializes in suicide terrorism. Originally named after the al-Aqsa Mosque, one of Islam's holiest sites and an icon for the Palestinian movement. Emerged shortly after the outbreak of the al-Aqsa Intifada in 2000.

al-Dawa: Shia Islamic party founded in late 1950s and supported by Iran.

al-Fatah (Palestine National Liberation Movement): Military wing of the Palestinian Liberation Organization, founded in 1959 by Yasser Arafat.

al-Gama'a al-Islamiyya (Islamic Group) (IG): Egypt's largest militant group, active since the 1970s. The group's spiritual leader, Sheikh Umar Abd al-Rahman, is serving a life sentence in the United States for his role in the 1993 World Trade Center attack. In 1998, the group signed Osama bin Laden's fatwa calling for attacks against the United States.

al-Ghamidi, Ahmad al-Haznawi (1980–2001): Born in Saudi Arabia. One of the hijackers of United Airlines flight 93 (which crashed in Pennsylvania) on September 11, 2001.

al-Qaeda (The Base): Radical Islamic movement founded in Afghanistan in the 1980s. Led by Osama bin Laden. Responsible for the September 11, 2001, and many other terrorist attacks.

al-Qurashi, Abu Ubeid: Aide to Osama bin Laden and al-Qaeda spokesman based in London. Wrote for the now-defunct al-Qaeda Web site and online magazine, al-Ansar.

al-Riyashi, Reem (1981–2003): First Palestinian mother to be a suicide bomber in January 2004. Claimed by both Hamas and al-Aqsa.

al-Zarqawi, Abu Mus'ab (1966–): Jordanian leader of the Iraqi insurgency group Jama'at al-Tawhid wal Jihah (Unification and Holy War Group), also known as al-Qaeda in Iraq.

al-Zawahiri, Ayman (1951–): Egyptian doctor, formerly leader of Egyptian Islamic Jihad, second in command of al-Qaeda.

Amir, Yigal: Right-wing Israeli who assassinated Prime Minister Yitzhak Rabin in November 1995.

Arafat, Yasser (1929–2004): Chairman of the Palestine Liberation Organization (PLO), founder of al-Fatah, recipient of the 1993 Nobel Peace Prize along with Shimon Peres and Yitzhak Rabin.

Asahara, Shoko (1955–): Founder and leader of Aum Shinrikyo in Japan. Convicted, among other crimes, of the 1995 sarin gas attack on the Tokyo subway. Sentenced to death in 2004. Appeal pending.

Assassins: A violent radical Muslim sect that operated from the eleventh to thirteenth centuries.

Atta, Mohamed (1968–2001): Egyptian leader of the September 11, 2001, attack team. Piloted American Airlines flight 11 into the North Tower of the World Trade Center.

Aum Shinrikyo (Aum, Supreme Truth): Japanese religious millenarian cult, established in 1987 by Shoko Asahara. Released sarin gas on the Tokyo subway in March 1995.

Baader, Andreas (1943–1977): Leader of the Red Army Faction, also known as the Baader-Meinhof Gang, in West Germany in the early 1970s. Sentenced to life imprisonment, Baader committed suicide in jail in October 1977.

Baader-Meinhof Gang: Popular name of the Red Army Faction.

Ba'ath Party: Founded in 1945 as a left-wing, secular, pan-Arab nationalist political party. Came to power in Syria and Iraq in 1963. Subsequently split into rival groups in 1966. After the overthrow of Saddam Hussein's Ba'athist regime in 2003, occupying authorities banned the Iraqi party.

Barayev, Movzar (1975–2002): Chechen separatist, leader of the Special Purpose Islamic Regiment (SPIR), killed during the seizure of the Dubrovka Theater in Moscow, which he led in October 2002.

Barrett, Michael (1841–1868): Irish nationalist, member of the Fenians, hanged in 1868 for the Clerkenwell bombing.

Basayev, Shamil Salmanovich (1965–): Chechen leader, briefly prime minister (1998), currently leader of Islamic International Peacekeeping Brigade (IIPB) and Riyadus-Salikhin Reconnaissance and Sabotage Battalion of Chechen Martyrs (RSRSBCM). Believed to have been responsible for the Beslan school siege in 2004.

Baumann, Bommi (1948–). Member of the German terrorist group the June 2nd Movement. The Movement's name was a reference to June 2, 1967, the date on which German police killed Benno Ohnesorg, a German university student attending his first political demonstration.

Begin, Menachem (1913–1992): Prime minister of Israel (1977–1983). Leader of the Irgun movement in the 1940s. Awarded Nobel Peace Prize in 1978.

Benchellali, Menad (1975–): Radical Islamist arrested in France on terrorism charges. Known as "the chemist" because of his alleged chemical weapons training.

Betancourt, Rómulo (1908–1981): President of Venezuela (1945–48, 1959–64).

bin al-Shibh, Ramzi: Born in Yemen in 1973, captured in Pakistan in 2002, now in U.S. custody. A key member of al-Qaeda who helped plan the September 11, 2001, attacks.

bin Laden, Osama (1957–): Founder and leader of al-Qaeda. Born in Saudi Arabia; his citizenship was revoked in 1994. Son of a construction magnate, he studied management and economics at King Abdul Aziz University. He established al-Qaeda in the 1980s to aid the mujahedin in Afghanistan against the Soviet Union. Declared war on the United States in 1996. Believed to be in hiding.

Black September: A terrorist group set up following Jordan's expulsion of PLO guerrillas in the "Black September" of 1970. Responsible for the kidnapping and murder of the Israeli Olympic team in Munich in 1972. Al-Fatah dissolved Black September in December 1974.

Brigate Rosse (Red Brigades) (BR): Italian social revolutionary terrorist group active in the 1970s and early 1980s. Responsible for the kidnap and murder of the elder statesman Aldo Moro in 1978.

Cellules Communistes Combattantes (CCC) (Communist Fighting Cells): A small social revolutionary group active in Belgium in the mid-1980s.

Clan na Gael (Irish Family): Organization formed by Irish republican sympathizers in the United States in the late nineteenth century. Maintained close ties to the Fenians and to the IRB.

Continuity IRA (CIRA): A splinter group from the IRA formed in 1994 in opposition to the Northern Irish peace process

Contras: A U.S.-backed force that opposed the left-wing Sandinista government of Nicaragua between 1979 and 1990. Disbanded following the electoral defeat of the Sandinistas in 1990.

Curcio, Renato (1941–): Leader of the Red Brigades in Italy.

Devrimci Sol (Dev Sol) (Revolutionary Left): Small Turkish Marxist-Leninist group, formed in 1978 and split into two factions in the early 1990s. Dev Sol's original founder changed the group's name to DHKP-C. The group has continued to conduct violent attacks against Turkish government targets as well as against Western interests in Turkey.

Dirección de Inteligencia Nacional (DINA): Chilean Intelligence Service until late 1977, when it was renamed the Central Nacional de Informaciones. Acted as a secret police force under the direction of Augusto Pinochet, head of the military government that ruled Chile from 1973 to 1990.

Dohrn, Bernardine (1942–): A leader of and spokesperson for the Weather Underground.

Ejército Revolucionario del Pueblo (People's Revolutionary Army) (ERP): Armed wing of the Argentinean Workers Revolutionary Party; founded in 1969, led by Mario Roberto Santucho. Active 1973 to 1977.

Euskadi ta Askatasuna (Basque Fatherland and Liberty) (ETA): Basque nationalist group founded in 1959 and still operating in Spain with the aim of establishing an independent homeland encompassing the Spanish Basque provinces of Vizcaya, Guipúzcoa, and Álava, the autonomous region of Navarra, and the southwestern French provinces of Labourd, Basse-Navarre, and Soule.

Fuerzas Armadas Revolucionarias de Colombia (Revolutionary Armed Forces of Colombia) (FARC): Established in 1964 by the Colombian Communist Party, the FARC, led by Manuel Marulanda Vélez (*nom de guerre* of Pedro Antonio Marín), is Latin America's oldest and largest terrorist group.

Fenian Brotherhood (Fenians): Nineteenth-century Irish republican organization dedicated to the use of force to gain independence for Ireland. The name is taken from the mythical hero Fionn MacCumhall and his warriors, the Fianna. The term Fenians is loosely used to describe the republican movement incorporating several separate organizations.

Grivas, George Theodore (1898–1974): Leader of the Greek Cypriot terrorist group Ethnike Organosis Kypriakou Agonos (EOKA), advocated union with Greece and led the guerrilla campaign against British rule in the 1950s. After Cyprus's independence in 1959, he formed the paramilitary organization EOKA-B, opposed to President (and Archbishop) Makarios.

Groupe Islamique Armé (Armed Islamic Group) (GIA): Formed in 1982. An Islamic extremist group based in Algeria and operative in North Africa and France.

Grupo de Resistencia Anti-Fascista Primero de Octubre (GRAPO): A small extremist Marxist-Leninist group formed in Spain in 1975. Vehemently anti-American, the group also advocates the overthrow of the Spanish government.

Guevara, "Che" (1928–1967): Born Ernesto Guevara de la Serna, the Argentine revolutionary and guerrilla leader served in Fidel Castro's government in Cuba in the early 1960s. He was captured and shot in 1967 while training guerrillas for an uprising against the Bolivian government.

Guzmán, Abimael (1934–): Founder and leader of Peru's Maoist terrorist group, the Shining Path. A former philosophy professor, he was captured in 1992. Often referred to by his followers as "Chairman Gonzalo" and the "Fourth Sword of Marxism," following Marx, Lenin, and Mao.

Habash, George (1925–): Marxist Palestinian and founder in 1968 of the Popular Front for the Liberation of Palestine (PFLP).

Hamas (Islamic Resistance Movement): Radical Islamic Palestinian group formed in late 1987 with the goal of establishing an Islamic Palestinian state in Israel. Hamas's strength is concentrated in the Gaza Strip and the West Bank, and it competes for support with the secular PLO and the smaller Palestinian Islamic Jihad. In January 2006 Hamas won a surprise victory in Palestinian parliamentary elections.

Hanif, Assaf Mohammed (1979–2000): British suicide bomber who blew up a bar in Tel Aviv in April 2003. Believed to have been recruited by Hamas.

Harakat-ul-Mujahidin (HUM): An Islamic militant group based in Pakistan that operates primarily in Kashmir. Signed bin Laden's 1998 fatwa against the United States. Its longtime emir, Fazlur Rehman Khalil, was replaced by the popular commander Farooq Kashmiri in 2000. Coalition air strikes destroyed HUM terrorist training camps in fall 2001.

Hussain, Hasib (1986–2005): One of four British suicide bombers who attacked the London transport system on July 7, 2005, killing themselves and fifty-two others.

Hezbollah (Party of God): Radical Shiite organization formed in Lebanon in the early 1980s, dedicated to opposing Israel and establishing an Islamic state in Lebanon. Currently led by Secretary General Hassan Nasrallah, supported by Iran and Syria.

Idris, Wafa (1975–2002): A Red Crescent volunteer, the first female Palestinian suicide bomber when she exploded her backpack in the middle of a Jerusalem market. Al-Aqsa Martyrs Brigades claimed responsibility for the attack.

Irgun: Zionist organization founded in Palestine in 1931 to fight for the establishment of a Jewish state. Led for a time by Menachem Begin, later prime minister of Israel (1977–1983).

Irish Republican Army (IRA): Formed in the early twentieth century to fight for Irish independence from Britain. The "Old" IRA split in late 1969 into the "Provisionals" and the "Officials." The "Provisionals" soon became synonymous with IRA and waged a thirty-five-year-long violent campaign for Irish unity. They called an end to their campaign in summer 2005.

Irish Republican Brotherhood (IRB): The IRB was a militant Irish republican organization that grew out of the Fenian movement in the mid–nineteenth century and was the precursor of the contemporary IRA. The IRB organized the Easter Rising of 1916 but was gradually replaced by the IRA in the course of the war of independence. Disbanded in 1924.

Islamic International Peacekeeping Brigade (IIPB): Chechen terrorist group created in 1998 by Shamil Basayev; he leads it jointly with the Arab mujahedin leader Abu al-Walid. Its membership includes Chechens, Arabs, and other foreign fighters. Involved in the seizure of the Dubrovka Theater in Moscow in October 2002.

Izz al-Din al-Qassam Brigades (al-Qassam): The military wing of Hamas, named after Sheikh Izz al-Din al-Qassam (1882–1935).

Jama'at al-Tawhid wal-Jihad (Unification and Holy War Group) (JTJ): Islamist terrorist network in Iraq formed by Abu Mas'ab al-Zarqawi in the late 1990s. In 2004 the group changed its name to al-Qaeda in Iraq.

Japanese Red Army (JRA): Small Japanese social revolutionary terrorist group operative for thirty years from the early 1970s. The only known terrorist group to be led by a woman, Fusako Shigenobu, arrested in 2000. Responsible for the Lod Airport massacre in 1972.

Jarrah, Ziad (1975–2001): Lebanese member of the September 11, 2001, attack team. Piloted United Airlines flight 93 (which crashed in Pennsylvania).

Jaish-e-Mohammed (Army of Mohammed) (JEM): Radical Islamic group based in Pakistan. Founded in 2000 by Maulana Masood Azhar with the goal of uniting Kashmir with Pakistan.

Jemaah Islamiyah (JI): Islamic terrorist group based in Southeast Asia. Its goal is to create an Islamic state comprising Brunei, Indonesia, Malaysia, Singapore, the southern Philippines, and southern Thailand. Linked to al-Qaeda and responsible for Bali bombings in 2002 and 2005.

Jihad Mosque: The Jihad Mosque soccer team was started in 1998 by Muhsin Kawasmeh, a sixteen-year-old in Hebron. Beginning in 2002, it provided eight volunteers for suicide missions out of its eleven-man team.

Kach (also Kahane Chai): Far-right Israeli terrorist group founded in the early 1970s by Rabbi Meir Kahane (1932–1990) and dedicated to restoring the biblical state of Israel. Banned by Israel in 1994, the group officially disbanded; unofficially, however, it remains active.

Khaled, Leila (1944–): Famous female terrorist and member of the PFLP. In August 1969, Khaled was part of a team that hijacked TWA flight 840. In September 1970, Khaled and Patrick Arguello, a Nicaraguan, attempted the hijack of El Al flight 219.

Khan, Mohammad Sidique (1974–2005): British-born leader of the four British suicide bombers who attacked the London transport system on July 7, 2005, killing themselves and fifty-two others.

Kherchtou, L'Houssaine (1964–): Moroccan member of al-Qaeda; testified as a government witness in the "embassy bombing" trial in 2001, which tried and convicted four men accused of bombing U.S. embassies in Africa in 1998.

Kumaratunga, Chandrika (1945–): Fourth president of Sri Lanka (1994–2005).

Liberation Tigers of Tamil Eelam (Tamil Tigers) (LTTE): A large Sri Lankan guerrilla and terrorist group founded in 1976 and led by Velupillai Prabhakaran. It began armed conflict in 1983 to achieve an independent Tamil state. Currently observing a tenuous cease-fire.

Lindh, John Walker (1981–): "The American Taliban." An American captured in Afghanistan in November 2001, while fighting for the Taliban. In 2002, he was sentenced to twenty years in prison for supplying services to the Taliban and for carrying explosives.

Lindsay, Germaine (Jamal) (1985–2005): Jamaican-born, one of the four British suicide bombers who attacked the London transport system on July 7, 2005, killing themselves and fifty-two others.

Mac Sweeney, Terence (1879–1920): Nationalist lord mayor of Cork; died on hunger strike in Brixton prison in 1920, during Ireland's war of independence against Britain.

Majallar al-Ikhwan al-Musalamin (Muslim Brotherhood): Islamist organization in the Middle East. The original Muslim Brotherhood was founded by Hassan al-Banna in 1928 in Egypt, where it remains the largest political opposition group. Branches of the Muslim Brotherhood have since been founded in Syria, Jordan, Palestine, Kurdistan, and Iraq.

Marighella, Carlos (1911–1969): Brazilian revolutionary, member of the ALN, author of *Minimanual of the Urban Guerrilla* (1969).

Marín, Pedro Antonio (1928–): The leader of Colombia's FARC, better known as Manuel Marulanda Vélez.

Masood Azhar, Maulana (1968–): Militant Islamic leader, founder of Jaish-e-Mohammad (JEM), dedicated to uniting Kashmir with Pakistan.

Mawdudi, Sayyid Abul A'la (1903–1979): One of the most influential Muslim theologians of the twentieth century and founder of Jamaat-e-Islami, which was founded in prepartition India to promote Islamic values and practices. Together, Mawdudi and Qutb are considered the founding fathers of the global Islamic revival movement.

McGuinness, Martin (1950–): One of the leaders of the Irish republican movement. Chief negotiator for Sinn Féin; onetime IRA leader; elected MP for Mid Ulster in 1997; became education minister in the Northern Ireland Assembly in 1998.

Meinhof, Ulrike (1934–1976): Leader with Andreas Baader of the Red Army Faction (Baader-Meinhof Gang) in West Germany. Committed suicide in prison.

Mohammed, Khalid Shaikh (1965–): Architect of the September 11, 2001, attacks. Senior Kuwaiti member of al-Qaeda. Captured in Pakistan in 2003. Currently held by the United States in an unknown location.

Movimiento de Izquierda Revolucionaria (Movement of the Revolutionary Left) (MIR): Left-wing revolutionary movement founded in Chile in the 1960s; engaged in sporadic terrorist attacks in the 1970s and 1980s.

Movimiento Revolucionario Túpac Amaru (Túpac Amaru Revolutionary Movement) (MRTA): Peruvian Marxist-Leninist revolutionary movement formed in 1982. Best known for its seizure of the Japanese Embassy in Lima in 1996.

Mugabe, Robert Gabriel (1924–): Leader of Zimbabwe since 1980: prime minister (1980–1987) and, since 1987, executive president. Founder and leader of the Zimbabwe African People's Union (ZAPU) liberation movement.

Narodnaya Volya (People's Will): A Russian revolutionary anarchist group active between 1878 and 1883. Responsible for the assassination among others of Tsar Alexander II in 1881.

Nasrallah, (Sayyed) Hassan (1960–): Lebanese secretary general of Hezbollah.

Nepalese Communist Party (Communist Party of Nepal–Maoists): Maoist terrorist group founded in 1994 and led by Pushpa Kamal Dahal. The group's objective is to take over the Nepalese government and transform Nepal into a Communist society.

New People's Army (Communist Party of the Philippines): Military Maoist wing of the Philippine Communist Party, formed in 1969, dedicated to overthrowing the government. Its leaders, Jose Maria Sison and Luis Jalandoni, live in the Netherlands.

Öcalan, Abdullah (1948–): Founder (in 1974) and leader of the Kurdish terrorist group PKK. Captured in 1999 and sentenced to life in prison.

Okamoto, Kozo (1948–): Member of the Japanese Red Army (JRA). Sole survivor of the Lod Airport attack team in 1972. Sentenced to life in prison by Israel but released in 1985 in a prisoner exchange with the PFLP-GC, he fled to Libya. Subsequently arrested in Lebanon; granted asylum in 2000.

Omar, Mullah Muhammad (1959–): Leader of the Taliban and Afghanistan's de facto head of state from 1996 to 2001. He has been in hiding since the U.S. invasion in 2001.

Palestinian Islamic Jihad (PIJ): Formed in the Gaza Strip in the late 1970s by Fathi Shaqaqi as a branch of the Egyptian Islamic Jihad, the group is active in the West Bank and Gaza and dedicated to the creation of an Islamist Palestinian state and the destruction of Israel.

Palestine Liberation Organization (PLO): Political and military umbrella organization dedicated to creating an independent Palestinian nation state. Formed by the Arab League in 1964 and led by Yasser Arafat from 1969 to 2004. Arafat was succeeded by Mahmood Abbas, who was elected president of the Palestinian Authority in 2005.

Partiya Karkerên Kurdistan (Kurdistan Workers' Party) (PKK): Large terrorist group founded by Abdullah Öcalan in 1974 and operating with the goal of an independent Kurdish state in Kurdish areas of Turkey, Iraq, and Iran.

Popular Front for the Liberation of Palestine (PFLP): Secular left-wing Palestinian group founded in 1967 by George Habash; opposed the Oslo peace process.

Popular Front for the Liberation of Palestine–General Command (PFLP–GC): Palestinian terrorist group opposed to the PLO. Split from the PFLP in 1968; led by Ahmad Jibril, former captain in the Syrian Army.

Prabakharan, Vellupillai (1954–): Leader of the LTTE (Tamil Tigers); sole surviving founder of the organization.

Premadasa, Ranasinghe (1924–1993): President of Sri Lanka (1989–1993); assassinated by the LTTE (Tamil Tigers).

Provisional IRA (PIRA): In December 1969, the IRA split into two groups. The Provisional IRA, or "Provos," soon became the largest group synonymous with "IRA." The group declared an end to its campaign of violence to secure a united Ireland in 2005.

Qaddafi, Muammar Abu Minyar al- (c. 1942–): Leader of Libya since 1969.

Qutb, Sayyid (1906–1966): Egyptian Islamic theologian, theoretician, and writer. Influenced the development of Islamic fundamentalism, especially the concept of jihad (holy war) and the view of the illegitimacy of secular rule. Executed in 1965 for plotting to overthrow the state.

Rantisi, Abdul Aziz (1947–2004): Pediatrician and leader of Hamas. Assassinated by an Israeli missile attack.

Rassam, Ahmad (c. 1967–): Algerian convicted of plotting to blow up the Los Angeles International Airport on the eve of the millennium. Sentenced to twenty-two years in prison.

Real IRA (RIRA): Militant offshoot of the IRA, formed in 1998 in opposition to the Northern Irish peace process.

Resistência Nacional Moçambicana (Renamo): Right-wing force opposed to the FRELIMO government of Mozambique. Founded in 1975 and currently led by Afonso Dhlakama.

Revolutionary Organization 17 November (17 November): Small radical leftist group operating in Greece. Founded in 1975 and named for the student uprising in Greece in November 1973. Most of the leadership were arrested in 2002 and were sentenced to multiple terms of life imprisonment in December 2003.

Riyadus-Salikhin Reconnaissance and Sabotage Battalion of Chechen Martyrs (RSRSBCM): Chechen group, led by Shamil Basayev, involved in siege of the Dubrovka Theater in Moscow in 2002. The name translates as "Requirements for Getting into Paradise."

Rossa, Jeremiah O'Donovan (1831–1915): Irish Fenian leader who inspired generations of Irish republicans.

Rote Armee Fraktion (Red Army Faction) (RAF): German social revolutionary terrorist group, sometimes known as the Baader-Meinhof Gang, operative in Germany in the late 1960s and 1970s. Officially dissolved in 1998.

Salafiya Jihadia (Jihad for Pure Islam): Moroccan extremist Islamist movement responsible for suicide bombings in Casablanca in 2003.

Salim, Mamduh Mahmud (1958–): Sudanese, reputed to be al-Qaeda's chief of finance, arrested in Munich, Germany, in 1998 on charges of trying to obtain nuclear materials.

Santucho, Mario Roberto (1936–1976): Leader of the People's Revolutionary Army (ERP) in Argentina. Killed in 1976.

Sendero Luminoso (Shining Path): Maoist terrorist group in Peru, founded in the late 1960s and led by Abimael Guzmán. Began armed operations in 1980. Seriously weakened by arrest of the leadership in 1992.

Sendic Antonaccio, Raúl (1926–1989): Founder and leader of the Tupamaros, a terrorist group active in Uruguay in the 1960s and 1970s.

Shanab, Ismail Abu (1950–2003): Third-ranking Hamas leader in Gaza. Assassinated in an Israeli helicopter missile attack in 2003.

Sharif, Omar Khan (c. 1976–2003): British jihadist, one of two suicide bombers who attacked a bar in Tel Aviv in April 2003.

Sheikh, Omar (Ahmed Omar Saeed Sheikh) (1973–): British citizen and radical Islamist member of Jaish-e-Mohammed (JEM); convicted of the murder of *Wall Street Journal* reporter Daniel Pearl in Pakistan in 2002. Sentenced to death in 2002; appeal pending.

Shigenobu, Fusako (1945–): Leader of the Japanese Red Army. Only woman to lead a terrorist group. Forged an alliance between the JRA and the PLFP in 1971. Arrested in 2000. Currently in prison in Japan.

Sicarii: Literally, "dagger men." Jewish zealots violently opposed to Roman rule in the first century after Christ.

Sinn Féin (Ourselves): Commonly rendered "Ourselves Alone." Political party dedicated to Irish independence established in 1905 by Arthur Griffith. Currently the political arm of the IRA, which seeks the unification of Ireland, and the largest Catholic political party in Northern Ireland.

South Lebanese Army (SLA): Pro-Israeli Lebanese militia during the Lebanese civil war (1975–1990). Founded in 1976.

Special Purpose Islamic Regiment (SPIR): Chechen group dedicated to independence. Led by Movzar Barayev until his death in the seizure of the Dubrovka Theater in Moscow in 2002. Barayev was succeeded by Khamzat Tazabayev, who was reported killed in 2004.

Stern Gang (Lehi): Splinter group of the Irgun, founded in 1940 by Abraham Stern. Sought to expel British forces and Arab people from Palestine, but it refused to observe a truce during the war with Germany. One Lehi leader, Yitzhak Shamir, subsequently became prime minister of Israel (1983–1984; 1986–1992).

Suthanthirap Paravaikal (Birds of Freedom): The female wing of the Tamil Tigers (LTTE) in Sri Lanka.

Taliban: The Taliban, whose name means "students of Islamic knowledge," came to power in the course of the Afghan civil war. An Islamist and Pashtun nationalist movement led by Mullah Mohammed Omar, the Taliban effectively ruled most of Afghanistan from 1996 to 2001 and enforced a strict interpretation of Sharia. After the U.S. invasion, the Afghan Interim Authority (AIA) replaced the Taliban government in December 2001.

Tanweer, Shehzad (1982–2005): One of four British suicide bombers who attacked the London transport system on July 7, 2005, killing themselves and fifty-two others.

Thugi: Large, violent Hindu cult that operated in India in the thirteenth through nineteenth centuries.

Tsuchiya, Masami (1965–): Chief chemist of Aum Shinrikyo. Sentenced to death in 2004 for his role in sarin gas attack; appealing the ruling.

Umkhonto we Sizwe (MK): Military wing of the African National Congress (ANC) whose name means "Spear of the Nation." Founded in 1961; suspended operations in 1990.

União Nacional para a Independência Total de Angola (UNITA): Angolan national liberation movement founded by Jonas Savimbi in 1966 to fight for independence from Portuguese colonial rule.

Weather Underground Organization (The Weathermen): A violent offshoot of the SDS (Students for a Democratic Society) student protest movement. Active in the United States in the early 1970s.

Yassin, Sheikh Ahmed (1936–2004): Founder and spiritual leader of Hamas. Assassinated by Israeli helicopter gunship.

Zealots: Violent Jewish group opposed to Roman rule in the Judaea Province in the first century A.D.

NOTES

EPIGRAPH

1. Cited in Rex A. Hudson, "The Sociology and Psychology of Terrorism: Who Becomes a Terrorist and Why?" (Washington, D.C.: Federal Research Division, Library of Congress, 20540-4840, September 1999).

INTRODUCTION

1. This oft-quoted expression dates to John Bradford, a sixteenth-century Englishman, who commented on seeing a group of criminals being led to their execution. He was burned at the stake a few years later.
2. Benjamin Franklin told his cosignatories, "We must all sign together or most assuredly we will all hang separately." The Irish signatories were executed by firing squad.
3. F. S. L. Lyons, *Ireland Since the Famine* (Glasgow: Collins/Fontana, 1973), p. 375.
4. The nomenclature of the IRA can be confusing to the uninitiated. The generic term, IRA, for Irish Republican Army, is the most commonly used in Ireland. In December 1969, however, a split in the IRA led to the emergence in the ensuing months of two groups, the "Provisional" IRA, or "Provos" for short, and the "Official" IRA. The IRA before the split became known as the "Old" IRA. In the course of "The Troubles," the term given to the Northern Irish conflict, as the Provisionals became the most dominant group, the qualifier "Provisionals" was gradually dropped and the term "IRA" returned. In the early 1990s, two further splinter groups emerged, the "Real" IRA and "Continuity" IRA, each claiming to be the true heirs of the historical IRA.
5. Table 4 in Robert Art and Louise Richardson (eds.), *Democracy and Counter-*

terrorism Lessons from the Past (Washington, D.C.: United States Institute of Peace, 2006).

6. Comisión de la Verdad y Reconciliación Perú, *Informe Final,* tomo 1, Primera parte: *El proceso, los hechos, las víctimas* (Lima: Navarrete, 2003).

7. This account of the campaign against the Shining Path is necessarily abbreviated. For a fuller account of the Peruvian counterterrorist campaign against the Shining Path, see David Scott Palmer, "Peru and the Shining Path," in Robert Art and Louise Richardson (eds.), *Democracy and Counterterrorism: Lessons from the Past* (Washington, D.C.: United States Institute of Peace, 2006).

8. Abu Ubeid al-Qurashi, al-Ansar, no. 4, March 12, 2002. Quoted in Middle East Media Research Institute Special Dispatch no. 353. Available on the MEMRI Web site, www.memri.org/bin/articles.cgi?Area=sd&ID=SP35302, accessed March 17, 2006.

PART ONE: THE TERRORISTS

EPIGRAPH

1. Speech by Yasser Arafat at the United Nations General Assembly, New York, November 13, 1974. Available on the MidEastWeb.org Web site, www.mideast web.org/Arafat_at_un.htm, page accessed May 18, 2006.

CHAPTER 1: WHAT IS TERRORISM?

1. Maximilien Marie Isidore de Robespierre (1758–1794), Member, National Assembly and Committee on Public Safety, Speech, Paris, February 1794. In Mayo W. Hazeltine, ed., *Orations: From Homer to William McKinley,* vol. viii (New York: Collier and Son, 1902), pp. 3279–84. Available on TheGreatBooks .com Web site, www.thegreatbooks.com/sources/defenseofterrorism.html, page accessed March 21, 2006.

2. Al-Qaeda Statement, October 10, 2001. Reprinted in Barry Rubin and Judith Colp Rubin (eds.), *Anti-American Terrorism and the Middle East* (Oxford: Oxford University Press, 2002), pp. 251–253.

3. CNN, February 5, 2005. Transcript of interview of Osama bin Laden with al-Jazeera correspondent Tayseer Alouni in October 2001. Available on the CNN Web site, archives.cnn.com/2002/WORLD/asiapcf/south/02/05/binladen .transcript/index.html, page accessed March 17, 2006.

4. Osama bin Laden, interview with John Miller of ABC News, May 1998. Available on PBS Online and WGBH's *Frontline* Web site, www.pbs.org/wgbh/ pages/frontline/shows/binladen/who/interview.html, page accessed March 17, 2006.

5. Interview with Chairman Gonzalo in *El Diario,* July 1988, p. 19. Available on the Shining Path Web site, www.blythe.org/peru-pcp/docs_en/interv.htm, page accessed July 26, 1997.

6. Interview aired on ABC News *Nightline,* July 28, 2005. Available on the ABC News Web site, abcnews.go.com/Nightline/International/story?id=990187& page=1, page accessed March 17, 2006.

7. Transcript of remarks to Jordanian officials. Available on the Web site of the U.S. Embassy in New Delhi, newdelhi.usembassy.gov/wwwhpr0514b.html, page accessed June 15, 2005.

8. Abu Ubeid al-Qurashi, al-Ansar, no. 4, March 12, 2002. Available on the MEMRI Web site, www.memri.org/bin/articles.cgi?Area=sd&ID=SP35302, page accessed March 17, 2006.

9. B. Rubin and J. C. Rubin (eds.), *Anti-American Terrorism and the Middle East,* p. 261.

10. Shamil Basayev, interview on ABC News *Nightline,* July 27, 2005. Available at www.jamestown.org/publications_details.php?volume_id=409&issue_id=3424 &article_id=2370102, page accessed March 17, 2006.

11. Osama bin Laden, interview, al-Jazeera, 1998 (specific date unknown). Available on the *Telegraph* Web site, www.news.telegraph.co.uk/news/main.jhtml ?xml=/news/2001/10/07/wbin07.xml, page accessed March 21, 2006.

12. Osama bin Laden, "Message to America," October 30, 2004. Available on the al-Jazeera Web site, english.aljazeera.net/NR/exercs/79C6AF22-98FB-4A1C-B21F-2BC36E87F61F.htm, page accessed March 17, 2006.

13. Speech by Yasser Arafat to UN General Assembly, New York, November 13, 1974, *Le Monde Diplomatique.* Available on the *Monde Diplomatique* Web site, MondeDiplo.com/focus/mideast/a2288, page accessed June 20, 2005.

14. Julie Wolf, "People & Events; The Iran Contra Affair." Available on PBS Online, www.pbs.org/wgbh/amex/reagan/peopleevents/pandde08.html, new content 1999–2000 PBS Online/WGBH, page accessed June 15, 2005.

15. Bin Laden, interview with ABC's John Miller of ABC News, May 1998.

16. Nelson Mandela, *Long Walk to Freedom* (Boston: Little, Brown, 1994), p. 240.

17. Bin Laden, "Message to America," October 30, 2004.

18. Basayev on ABC News *Nightline,* June 27, 2005.

19. I have included eighty groups in this table. These are the forty groups designated by the State Department as "Foreign Terrorist Organizations" and the thirty-seven groups listed by the State Department as "Other Terrorist Groups." In addition, I have included three groups that are now defunct, the Red Army Faction, Action Directe, and the CCC, because they are mentioned several times in the text.

Any effort to categorize terrorist groups requires a number of caveats:

Determining whether a group is close to or isolated from its community is often a judgment call. In some instances, terrorist groups or their proxies compete in elections, as in the elections to the Palestinian Authority or the Northern Ireland Assembly. In other cases, its degree of support can be gauged in other ways by looking at public opinion polls or university elections.

It is also often hard to tell whether a group has transformational or temporal goals. This is particularly the case when a group, such as Hezbollah or Hamas, or indeed al-Qaeda, has both.

It is also the case that terrorist groups are not static and can move from one category to another. This happens most often through splits in the organization, as in the IRA, but it can also happen when there is popular repudiation of the terrorist group, as in the Egyptian al-Gama'a al-Islamiyya.

This table makes abundantly clear, however, that the most dangerous category is a terrorist group with transformational goals and close ties to the community.

20. See Andrew Silke (ed.), *Terrorists, Victims and Society: Psychological Perspectives on Terrorism and its Consequences* (London: Wiley, 2003). Max Taylor, *The Terrorist* (London: Brassey's, 1988). Walter Reich (ed.), *Origins of Terrorism: Psychologies, Ideologies, Theologies, States of Mind* (Washington, D.C.: Woodrow Wilson Center Press, 1998). Max Taylor and Edith Quayle, *Terrorist Lives* (London: Brassey's, 1994).

21. Peter Taylor, *Loyalists: War and Peace in Northern Ireland* (New York: TV Books, 1999), p. 8.

22. On the PKK, see R. Hudson, "The Sociology and Psychology of Terrorism: Who Becomes a Terrorist and Why?" (Washington, D.C.: Federal Research Division, Library of Congress, 20540-4840, 1999), p. 47. On Islamist groups, even those that recruit for martyrdom operations, see Anne Marie Oliver and Paul Steinberg, *The Road to Martyrs' Square: A Journey into the World of the Suicide Bomber* (Oxford: Oxford University Press, 2005), p. 119, and Diego Gambetta, *Making Sense of Suicide Missions* (Oxford: Oxford University Press, 2005), p. 107.

23. Quoted in "Suicide Terrorism: Martyrdom and Murder," *The Economist,* June 8, 2004. Available at www.economist.com/displaystory.cfm?story_id=2329785, page accessed March 17, 2006.

24. Bruce Hoffman, "The Logic of Suicide Terrorism," *Atlantic Monthly,* June 2003, pp. 40–47. R. Pape, "The Strategic Logic of Suicide Terrorism," *American Political Science Review* 97 (2003): 343–361. Luca Ricolfi, "Palestinians 1981–2003," in Diego Gambetta (ed.), *Making Sense of Suicide Missions* (Oxford: Oxford University Press, 2005), pp. 76–130.

25. Cited by Gregg Zoroya in "Woman Describes the Mentality of a Suicide Bomber," *USA Today,* April 22, 2002.

26. See chapter 5 for more detailed coverage of suicide bombings. Also, Louise Richardson, "Blasts from the Past," *Financial Times,* July 5, 2005.

27. Bernard Lewis, *The Assassins* (New York: Basic, 2002).

28. George W. Bush, "Address to a Joint Session of Congress and the American People," September 20, 2001. Available on the White House Web site, www.white house.gov/news/releases/2001/09/20010920-8.html, page accessed March 17, 2006.

29. Albert Camus, *Caligula and Three Other Plays* (New York: Vintage Books, 1958).

30. Osama bin Laden, "Declaration of War Against the Americans Occupying the Land of the Two Holy Places," August 1996. Available on PBS Online and WGBH's *NewsHour* Web site, www.pbs.org/newshour/terrorism/international/fatwa_1996.html, page accessed March 17, 2006.

31. Prabakharan interview, *The Week,* India, March 23, 1986. Available on the LTTE Web site, www.eelam.com/interviews/leader_march_86.html, page accessed March 17, 2006.

32. Nasra Hassan, "An Arsenal of Believers Talking to the Human Bombs," *The New Yorker,* November 19, 2001.

33. Cited in Raimondo Catanzaro (ed.), *The Red Brigades and Left Wing Terrorism in Italy* (New York: St. Martin's Press, 1991), p. 185.

34. Cited in Garrett O'Boyle, "Theories of Justification and Political Violence: Examples from Four Groups," *Terrorism and Political Violence* 14, no. 2 (Summer 2002), p. 32.

35. Mohamed Elmasry, president of the Canadian Islamic Congress, in Hicham Safieddine, "Adult Israelis Seen as 'Targets' by Foe," *Toronto Star,* October 23, 2004.

36. Osama bin Laden, "Letter to the American People," printed in English in *The Observer,* Sunday, November 24, 2002.

37. Hassan, "An Arsenal of Believers Talking to the Human Bombs."

38. Taylor, *Loyalists: War and Peace in Northern Ireland,* p. 92.

39. Bin Laden, interview with John Miller of ABC News, May 1998.

40. Alan Cullison, "Inside Al Qaeda's Hard Drive," *The Atlantic Monthly,* September 2004, pp. 55–70.

41. Osama bin Laden, audiotape broadcast on al-Arabiya, April 15, 2004. Available on the BBC News Web site, news.bbc.co.uk/2/hi/middle_east/3628069.stm, page accessed March 17, 2006.

42. On the IRA hunger strikers, see D. Beresford, *Ten Men Dead: The Story of the 1981 Hunger Strike* (London: HarperCollins, 1987), and Padraig O'Malley, *Biting at the Grave: The Irish Hunger Strikes and the Politics of Despair* (Boston: Beacon Press, 1990).

43. See Gambetta, *Making Sense of Suicide Missions.* Oliver and Steinberg, *The Road to Martyrs' Square.* Pape, "The Strategic Logic of Suicide Terrorism." Hassan, "An Arsenal of Believers Talking to the Human Bombs."

44. Oliver and Steinberg, *The Road to Martyrs' Square,* p. 155

CHAPTER 2: WHERE HAVE TERRORISTS COME FROM?

1. Yassar Arafat, speech at the UN general Assembly, December 13, 1988. Available on the MidEastWeb.org Web site, www.mideastweb.org/arafat1988.htm, page accessed May 18, 2006.

2. This account relies heavily on Patrick Quinlivan and Paul Rose, *The Fenians in England, 1865–1872* (London: John Calder, 1982).

3. Ibid., p. 95.

4. Ibid., p. 96.

5. The seminal piece comparing the three ancient groups is David C. Rapoport, "Fear and Trembling: Terrorism in Three Religious Traditions," *American Political Science Review,* 78, 3 (1984): 658–677. I have relied heavily on his account.

   On the Fenians, see T. W. Moody (ed.), *The Fenian Movement* (Cork: Learning Links, 1978), and F. S. L. Lyons, *Ireland Since the Famine* (Glasow: Collins, 1973). On the anarchists, see James Joll, *The Anarchists* (Cambridge, Mass.: Harvard University Press, 1980).

6. There were, in fact, a number of different groups, some called Sicarii and some Zealots. I have followed Rapoport in treating them as one, though others vigorously object to doing so. See Morton Smith, "Zealots and Sicarii, Their Origins and Relation," in *Harvard Theological Review* 64, no. 1 (January 1971): 1–19. For another treatment of the Sicarii as early terrorists, see Richard A. Horsley, "The Sicarii: Ancient Jewish Terrorists," *The Journal of Religion* 59, no. 4 (October 1979): 435–458.

7. Rapoport, "Fear and Trembling," p. 670.

8. Josephus, cited in ibid.

9. Margaret Thatcher, speech to the American Bar Association, July 15, 1985: "And we must find ways to starve the terrorist and the hijacker of the oxygen of publicity on which they depend." Full text available at www.margaretthatcher.org/Speeches/displaydocument.asp?docis=106096&doctyp=1, page accessed June 23, 2005.

10. On the assassins, see Bernard Lewis, *The Assassins, A Radical Sect in Islam* (London: Weidenfeld and Nicolson, 1967), and Marshall G. S. Hodgson, *The Secret Order of Assassins: The Struggle of the Early Nizari Ismailis Against the Islamic World* (Philadelphia: University of Pennsylvania Press, 2005).

11. On the Thugi, see W. H. Sleeman, *The Thugs or Phansigars of India* (Philadelphia: Carey and Hart, 1839). Captain Sleeman was a British officer charged with combating the Thugi. His grandson Colonel James Sleeman also wrote an account: J. L. Sleeman, *Thugs; or a Million Murders* (London: S. Low and Marston, 1933). See also Hiralal Gupta, "A Critical Study of the Thugs and Their Activities," *Journal of Indian History* 38 (1959): 167–176.

12. Sleeman. *Thugs; or a Million Murders.*

13. Rapoport, "Fear and Tremblings," p. 662.

14. Ibid., p. 664.

15. Sleeman, *Thugs; or a Million Murders,* p. 1.

16. "Report of Saint-Just, February 26, 1794," cited in Hippolyte Taine, *The French Revolution,* trans. John Durand (Indianapolis: Liberty Fund, 2002), p. 910, fn. 22.

17. Marx to Engels in Manchester, December 14, 1867, in Marx/Engels, *Collected Works,* vol. 42: Marx-Engels Correspondence, 1867 (London: Lawrence & Wishart, 1975–2005), p. 501.

18. Engels to Marx, December 19, 1867, *Marx/Engels Collected Works,* vol. 42, p. 505.

19. See Richard E. Rubenstein, *Alchemists of Revolution: Terrorism in the Modern World* (New York: Basic Books, 1987).

20. See, e.g., bin Laden audiotape, broadcast by al-Arabiya, April 15, 2004. Available on the BBC News Web site, news.bbc.co.uk/2/hi/middle_east/3628 069.stm, page accessed March 17, 2006.

21. James Joll, *The Anarchists* (Cambridge, Mass.: Harvard University Press, 1980). Paul Avrich, *Anarchist Portraits* (Princeton, N.J.: Princeton University Press, 1990).

CHAPTER 3: WHAT CAUSES TERRORISM?

1. Osama bin Laden, "Message to America," October 30, 2004. Available on the al-Jazeera Web site, english.aljazeera.net/NR/exeres/79C6AF22-98FB-4A1C-B21F-2BC36E87F61F.htm, page accessed March 17, 2006.

2. Ibid.

3. George Paynter, interviewed by the BBC, July 16, 2002. Available on the BBC News Web site, news.bbc.co.uk/1/hi/uk/1804710.stm, page accessed March 17, 2006.

4. David Shead, head referee of the European Arm Wrestling Federation, cited in Yosri Fouda and Nick Fielding, *Masterminds of Terror* (New York: Arcade, 2003), p. 55.

5. Fouda and Fielding, *Masterminds of Terror,* p. 56.

6. "Omar Sheikh's Diaries, Part II," *The Indian Express,* October 11, 2001.

7. Osama bin Laden, "Dinner Party Tape," December 13, 2001. Available on the CNN Web site, archives.cnn.com/2001/US/12/13/tape.transcript/, page accessed March 17, 2006.

8. Karl Rove, "Remarks of Karl Rove at the New York Conservative Party," June 22, 2005. Available on the *Washington Post* Web site, www.washingtonpost.com/wp-dyn/content/article/2005/06/24/AR2005062400097.html, page accessed April 10, 2006.

9. The most influential psychological studies of aggression and violence have been associated with Freud, Fromm, Lorenz, Pavlov, and Skinner.

10. Michael Baumann, *How It All Began* (Vancouver: Pulp Press, 1997). Donatella Della Porta, *Social Movements, Political Violence and the State* (Cambridge: Cambridge University Press, 1995). Kevin Toolis, *Rebel Hearts: Journeys Within the IRA's Soul* (New York: St. Martin's Press, 1995). Peter Taylor, *The Loyalists: War and Peace in Northern Ireland* (New York: TV Books, 1999).

11. "Omar Sheikh's Diaries, Part II," *The Indian Express,* October 11, 2001.

12. "Tamil National Leader Hon. V. Pirapaharan's Interview," *The Week,* India, March 23, 1986. Available on the LTTE Web site at www.eelam.com/interviews/leader_march_86.html, page accessed March 17, 2006.

13. Interview with Chairman Gonzalo in *El Diario,* July 1988, p. 19. Available on

the Shining Path Web site, www.blythe.org/peru-pcp/docs_en/interv.htm, page accessed July 26, 1997.

14. Osama bin Laden, statement, October 7, 2001.

15. Osama bin Laden, "Message to America," October 30, 2004. Translation in Bruce Lawrence, ed., *Messages to the World: The Statements of Osama bin Laden* (New York: Verso, 2005) p. 239.

16. George W. Bush, "Address to Joint Session of Congress," September 20, 2001. Available on the White House Web site, www.whitehouse.gov/news/releases/2001/09/20010920-8.html, page accessed March 17, 2006.

17. Osama bin Laden, interview broadcast on al-Jazeera, 1998. Full English text July 10, 2001. Available on the *Telegraph* Web site, www.news.telegraph.co.uk/news/main.jhtml?xml=/news/2001/10/07/wbin07.xml, page accessed March 17, 2006.

18. Mark Juergensmeyer, *Terror in the Mind of God* (Berkeley: University of California Press, 2000), p. 74.

19. Osama bin Laden, interview with John Miller of ABC News, May 1998. Available on PBS Online and WGBH's *Frontline* Web site, www.pbs.org/wgbh/pages/frontline/shows/binladen/who/interview.html, page accessed March 17, 2006.

20. Seamus Finucane to Kevin Toolis in *Rebel Hearts: Journeys Within the IRA's Soul* (New York: St. Martin's Press, 1995), p. 104.

21. Bin Laden, broadcast on al-Jazeera, 1998. Full English text July 10, 2001.

22. Osama bin Laden, interview with Peter Arnett of CNN, March 1997.

23. Marc Sageman, *Understanding Terror Networks* (Philadelphia: University of Pennsylvania Press, 2004).

24. Gilles Keppel, *Muslim Extremism in Egypt: The Prophet and the Pharaoh* (Berkeley: University of California Press, 1995).

25. Peter Bergen and Swati Pandey, "The Madrassa Myth," *The New York Times,* June 14, 2005.

26. Jerrold M. Post, "Notes on a Psychodynamic Theory of Terrorist Behavior," *Terrorism: An International Journal* 7, 3 (1984): 242–256.

27. Jillian Becker, *Hitler's Children: The Story of the Baader-Meinhof Terrorist Gang* (Philadelphia: J. B. Lippincott, 1977).

28. Jerrold Post et al., "The Terrorists in Their Own Words: Interviews with 35 Incarcerated Middle Eastern Terrorists," *Terrorism and Political Violence* 15, no. 1 (Spring 2003): 176.

29. Donatella Della Porta, *Social Movements, Political Violence and the State* (Cambridge: Cambridge University Press, 1995), especially chap. 6.

30. "Life History" 12:35 in Donatella Della Porta, *Social Movements, Political Violence and the State,* p. 146.

31. Anne Marie Oliver and Paul Steinberg, *The Road to Martyrs' Square* (Oxford: Oxford University Press, 2005). Kevin Toolis, *Rebel Hearts: Journeys Within the IRA's Soul* (New York: St. Martin's Press, 1995).

32. Eamon Collins, *Killing Rage* (London: Granta, 1997), p. 78.

33. "Tamil National Leader Hon. V. Pirapaharan's Interview."

34. *Patterns of Terrorist Violence* (Washington, D.C.: U.S. Department of State, April 2003), p. 77.

35. Bush, "Address to Joint Session of Congress," September 20, 2001.

36. Louise Richardson, "State Sponsorship: A Root Cause of Terrorism?" in Tore Bjorgo (ed.), *Root Causes of Terrorism: Myths, Reality and Ways Forward* (London: Routledge, 2005), pp. 189–197.

37. Alan Krueger and Jitka Maleckova, NBER Working Paper no. w9074, National Bureau of Economic Research, Cambridge, Mass., 2002. See also Krueger and Maleckova, "Does Poverty Cause Terrorism?" *The New Republic,* June 24, 2004, pp. 27–34.

38. Human Development Report 2005, *Inequality and Human Development* (New York: United Nations Development Programme), p. 55, available at the United Nations Development Programme Web site, hdr.undp.org/reports/global/2005/, page accessed January 5, 2006.

39. Ted Robert Gurr, *Why Men Rebel* (Princeton, N.J.: Princeton University Press, 1970).

40. As a mother of three children, I generally come home from work without treats for my children. They do not expect any and are reasonably well behaved. If I were to bring home three candy bars and give one to each of my children one day, they would all be delighted, very appreciative, and very well behaved (for a short time, at least). If I were to bring home four candy bars and give one each to my daughters and two to my son, I would have two furious children, outraged by the injustice done to them. Their objective condition would be better than if I brought home no candy bars and no different than if I had given each child one, but in this instance they would be outraged. This, in essence, is relative deprivation.

41. *The World Factbook* (Washington, D.C.: CIA), updated on January 10, 2006. Appendices: "Field Listing—Unemployment Rate." Available at the CIA Web site, http://www.cia.gov/cia/publications/factbook/fields/2129.html, page accessed March 17, 2006.

42. *2005 World Population Data Sheet* (Washington, D.C.: 2005), Population Reference Bureau.

43. Scott Atran, "Genesis of Suicide Terrorism," *Science,* March 7, 2003. Available on the *Science* magazine Web site, www.sciencemag.org/cgi/content/abstract/299/5612/1534, page accessed April 10, 2006.

44. Bin Laden, interview with John Miller of ABC News, May 1998.

45. Barry Rubin and Judith Colp Rubin, *Anti-American Terrorism and the Middle East* (Oxford: Oxford University Press, 2002), pp. 169–172.

46. Judy Aita, "Bombing Trial Witness Describes Nairobi Surveillance Mission," February 23, 2001, U.S. Department of State. Available at the Department of State Web site, usinfo.state.gov/is/Archive_Index/Bombing_Trial_Witness_Nairobi_Surveillance_Mission.html, page accessed January 23, 2006.

47. In recent years, the Republic of Ireland has often ranked highest on the globalization index. The IRA's terrorism has emerged in the quite distinct economy in Northern Ireland.

48. "Index of Globalization," *Foreign Policy Magazine,* January/February 2001, pp. 56–65; January/February 2002, pp. 38–51; January/February 2003, pp. 60–72; March/April 2004, pp. 54–69; May/June 2005, pp. 52–60.

49. Quoted in Jessica Stern, *Terror in the Name of God: Why Religious Militants Kill* (New York: HarperCollins, 2003), pp. 40–41.

50. Bruce Hoffman, *Inside Terrorism* (New York: Columbia University Press, 1998), p. 91.

51. *Patterns of Global Terrorism 2003* (Washington, D.C.: U.S. Department of State, April 2004).

52. John Kifner, "Israelis Investigate Far Right; May Crack Down on Speech," *The New York Times,* November 8, 1995.

53. On Aum Shinrikyo, see D.W. Brackett, *Holy Terror: Armageddon in Tokyo* (New York: Weatherhill, 1966), and Ian Reader, *Religious Violence in Contemporary Japan: The Case of Aum Shinrikyo* (Honolulu: University of Hawaii Press, 2000).

54. Osama bin Laden, interview with Peter Arnett of CNN, March 1997. Available on the FindLaw Web site, files.findlaw.com/news.findlaw.com/cnn/docs/binladen/binladenintvw-cnn.pdf, page accessed March 17, 2006.

55. Ibid.

56. Osama bin Laden, "Declaration of War Against the Americans Occupying the Land of the Two Holy Places," August 1996. Available on PBS Online and WGBH's *NewsHour* Web site, www.pbs.org/newshour/terrorism/international/fatwa_1996.html, page accessed March 17, 2006.

CHAPTER 4: THE THREE Rs: REVENGE, RENOWN, REACTION

1. The account is based on interviews with various members of the Finucane family in Kevin Toolis's fine book *Rebel Hearts; Journeys with the IRA's Soul* (New York: St. Martin's Griffin, 1997), pp. 84–191.

2. Among those who make this point is Robert Pape in "The Logic of Suicide Terrorism," *American Conservative,* July 18, 2005, available on the *American Conservative* Web site, amconmag.com/2005_07_18/article.html, page accessed March 20, 2006. When I talk to groups, this point is regularly made to me too by members of the audience.

3. The publication of a book by Alan Dershowitz, *Why Terrorism Works* (New Haven, Conn.: Yale University Press, 2002), sparked a debate on this issue.

4. Hannah Arendt, "Reflections on Violence," *The New York Review of Books,* February 27, 1969. Available on the *New York Review of Books* Web site, www.nybooks.com/articles/11395, page accessed March 20, 2006.

5. Osama bin Laden, in "Dinner Party Tape," December 13, 2001. Available on the CNN Web site, archives.cnn.com/2001/US/12/13/tape.transcript/, page accessed March 17, 2006.

6. See the account in David A. Korn, *Assassination in Khartoum* (Bloomington: Indiana University Press, 1993).

7. Peter Taylor, *Behind the Mask: The IRA and Sinn Fein* (New York: TV Books, 1997), p. 127.

8. Gurutz Jáuregui, "Del nacionalismo sabiniano a la guerra revolucionaria (1963–1965)," in Antonio Elorza et al., *La Historia de ETA* (Madrid: Temas de Hoy, 2000).

9. Taylor, *Behind the Mask*, p. 127.

10. Ibid., p. 305.

11. Barry Rubin and Judith Colp Rubin (eds.), *Anti-American Terrorism and the Middle East* (Oxford: Oxford University Press, 2002), p. 21.

12. Quoted in Donatella Della Porta, *Social Movements, Political Violence and the State: A Comparative Analysis of Italy and Germany* (Cambridge: Cambridge University Press, 1995), p. 150.

13. Interview posted on FARC's Web site. Available at www.farcep.org/pagina_ ingles/interview/rrp111082001.html, page accessed July 27, 2005.

14. Al-Safir, February 16, 1985, in Rubin and Rubin, *Anti-American Terrorism and the Middle East*, pp. 50–54.

15. Ibid.

16. Robert C. Tucker, ed., *The Marx-Engels Reader* (New York: Norton, 1972), p. 160.

17. Osama bin Laden, interview with Peter Arnett of CNN, March 1997. Available on the FindLaw Web site, files.findlaw.com/news.findlaw.com/cnn/docs/ binladen/binladenintvw-cnn.pdf, page accessed March 17, 2006.

18. Interview with *El Diario*, Peru, July 1988, p. 54. Available on the NY Transfer Web site, www.blythe.org/peru-pcp/docs-en/interv.htm, page accessed July 26, 1997.

19. Interview with Paul Reyes by Luis Enrique González of *Prensa Latina*, July 20, 2001. Available on the FARC Web site, www.farcep.org/pagina_ingles/interview/ rrp111082001.html, page accessed July 27, 2005.

20. Interview with Anita Pratap, *Sunday Magazine*, India, March 11–17, 1984. Also available on the LTTE Web site, www.eelam.com/interviews/leader_ march_84.html, page accessed March 20, 2006.

21. ABC News *Nightline*, July 28, 2005. Available on the ABC News Web site, abc news.go.com/Nightline/International/story?id=990187&page=1, page accessed March 17, 2006.

22. Anne Marie Oliver and Paul Steinberg, *The Road to Martyrs' Square* (Oxford: Oxford University Press, 2005), p. 148.

23. Ibid., p. 146.

24. Ibid., p. 79.

25. "Communiqué on the Attempted Assassination of Hans Neusel, State Secretary in the German Ministry of the Interior in Cologne on 27 July 1990," in Yonah Alexander and Dennis A. Pluchinsky, *Europe's Red Terrorists: The Fighting Communist Organizations* (London: Frank Cass, 1992), pp. 70–74.

26. "Communiqué on the Assassination of Dr José Ramón Muñoz in Zaragoza on 27 March 1990," in Alexander and Pluchinsky, *Europe's Red Terrorists,* pp. 127–129.

27. Taylor, *Behind the Mask,* pp. 151–152.

28. Peter Taylor, *Loyalists, War and Peace in Northern Ireland* (New York: TV Books, 1999), pp 91–92.

29. Quoted in Della Porta, *Social Movements, Political Violence and the State,* p. 155.

30. Ibid.

31. Osama bin Laden, "Message to America," October 30, 2004. Available on the al-Jazeera Web site, english.aljazeera.net/NR/exeres/79C6AF22-98FB-4A1C-B21F-2BC36E87F61F.htm, page accessed March 17, 2006.

32. Osama bin Laden, audiotape, broadcast on al-Arabiya, April 15, 2004.

33. Osama bin Laden, "Declaration of War Against the Americans Occupying the Land of the Two Holy Places," August 1996. Available on PBS Online and WGBH's *NewsHour* Web site, www.pbs.org/newshour/terrorism/international/fatwa_1996.html, page accessed March 17, 2006.

34. Bin Laden, "Dinner Party Tape," December 13, 2001.

35. Osama bin Laden, statement on al-Jazeera, November 3, 2001.

36. Osama bin Laden, interview on al-Jazeera, December 27, 2001.

37. James Glanz, "In Jordanian Case, Hints of Iraq Jihad Networks," *The New York Times,* July 29, 2005, p. 1. Available on the *New York Times* Web site, www.nytimes.com/2005/07/29/international/middleeast/29jihad.html?ex=128 0289600&en=1d46093d6dfa901f&ei=5090&partner=rssuserland&emc=rss, accessed March 20, 2006.

38. Jerrold M. Post, Ehud Sprinzak, and Laurita M. Denny, "The Terrorists in Their Own Words: Interviews with 35 Incarcerated Middle Eastern Terrorists," *Terrorism and Political Violence* 15, no. 1 (Spring 2003): 178.

39. Della Porta, *Social Movements, Political Violence and the State,* p. 159.

40. Ibid., p. 158.

41. Rubin and Rubin, *Anti-American Terrorism and the Middle East,* p. 274.

42. Interview with *El Diario,* Peru, July 1988, p. 54. Available on the NY Transfer Web site, www.blythe.org/perupcp/docs-en/interv.htm, page accessed July 26, 1997.

43. Jean Marcel Bougereau, "Memoirs of an International Terrorist: Conversations with Hans Joachim Klein," in *The German Guerrilla* (Orkney: Cienfuegos Press), p. 36.

44. Jerrold Post, "The Socio-cultural Underpinnings of Terrorist Psychology: When Hatred Is Bred in the Bone," in Tore Bjorgo (ed.), *Root Causes of Terrorism: Myths, Reality and Ways Forward* (New York: Routledge, 2005), p. 61.

45. Kevin Cullen, "From Terrorist to Priest," *The Boston Globe Sunday Magazine,* August 7, 2005, p. 20.

46. Post, Sprinzak, and Denny, "The Terrorists in Their Own Words," p. 177.

47. Kevin Cullen, "From Terrorist to Priest."

48. Bin Laden, interview with Peter Arnett of CNN, March 1997.

49. Interview with Anita Pratap, *Sunday Magazine,* India, March 11–17, 1984.

50. Interview aired on ABC News *Nightline,* July 28, 2005.

51. Interview with *El Diario,* Peru, July 1988, p. 54. Available on the NY Transfer Web site, www.blythe.org/perupcp/docs-en/interv.htm, page accessed July 26, 1997.

52. Osama bin Laden statement, November 3, 2001. In "Bin Laden Rails Against Crusaders and UN." Available on the BBC News Web site, news.bbc.co.uk/1/hi/world/monitoring/media_reports/1636782.stm, page accessed March 20, 2006.

53. Bin Laden, interview with Peter Arnett of CNN, March 1997.

54. Ed Moloney, *A Secret History of the IRA* (New York: W.W. Norton, 2002), pp. 121–122.

55. Tim Pat Coogan, *The IRA: A History* (Boulder, Colo.: Roberts Rinehart, 1994), pp. 299–302; William Whitelaw, *Whitelaw Memoirs* (Anrum Press: London, 1989), pp. 99–100; Sean Mac Stiofain, *Memoirs of a Revolutionary* (Edinburgh: Gordon Cremonesi, 1975), p. 281.

56. Della Porta, *Social Movements, Political Violence and the State,* p. 146.

57. "Interview with Mullah Omar Mohammad," September 21, 2001, in Barry Rubin and Judith Colp Rubin (eds.), *Anti-American Terrorism in the Middle East: A Documentary Reader* (Oxford: Oxford University Press, 2002), pp. 247–249.

58. Ayman al-Zawahiri, *Knights Under the Prophet's Banner,* Summer 2001, translation by FBIS (Foreign Broadcast Information Service).

59. Al-Ansar is al-Qaeda's online magazine. Abu Ubeid al-Qurashi is thought to be a leader of al-Qaeda. Al-Ansar, issue 4. Translation by the Middle East Media Research Institute, report 353, March 12, 2002.

60. Eamon Collins, *Killing Rage* (London: Granta, 1997), pp. 59–60.

61. See especially Bernard Lewis, *What Went Wrong: Western Impact and Middle Eastern Response* (Oxford: Oxford University Press, 2002).

62. Bin Laden, "Declaration of War Against the Americans Occupying the Land of the Two Holy Places," August 1996, p. 19.

63. Al-Qurashi, Middle East Media Research Institute, report no. 353, March 12, 2002. Available on the MEMRI Web site, memri.org/bin/opener.cgi?Page=archives&Area=sd&ID=SP35302, page accessed July 29, 2005.

64. Osama bin Laden, audiotape, April 15, 2004. Available on the CNN Web site, www.cnn.com/2004/WORLD/asiapcf/04/15/binladen.tape/, page accessed March 20, 2006. Osama bin Laden, interview on al-Jazeera, 1998. Available on the *Telegraph* Web site, www.news.telegraph.co.uk/news/main.jhtml?xml=/news/2001/10/07/wbin07.xml, page accessed March 20, 2006.

65. Osama bin Laden, "Fatwa Urging Jihad Against Americans," February 23, 1998. Available on the MidEastWeb.org Web site, www.mideastweb.org/osamabinladen2.htm, page accessed May 18, 2006.

66. Sayyid Qutb, *Milestones,* excerpted in Rubin and Rubin (eds.), *Anti-American Terrorism and the Middle East,* p. 32.

CHAPTER 5: WHY DO TERRORISTS KILL THEMSELVES?

1. "It is a sweet and glorious thing to die for one's country." Quintus Horatius Flaccus (Horace), *Odes*, III.ii.13.
2. George La Hir, writing of Verdun in *The New York Times*, 1916, cited in Jeremy Black (ed.), *The Seventy Great Battles in History* (London: Thames and Hudson, 2005), p. 236.
3. Quoted in Sandra Laville and Dilpazier Aslam, "Mentor to the Young and Vulnerable," *The Guardian*, July 14, 2005. Available on the *Guardian* Web site, www.guardian.co.uk/attackonlondon/story/0,16132,1528112,00.html, page accessed March 20, 2006.
4. Quoted in Sandra Laville and Ian Cobain, "From Cricket-Lover Who Enjoyed a Laugh to Terror Suspect," *The Guardian*, July 13, 2005. Available on the *Guardian* Web site, www.guardian.co.uk/attackonlondon/story/0,16132,1527 429,00.html, page accessed March 20, 2006.
5. Merari makes this argument in his lectures to students whom we have jointly taught at Harvard Law School.
6. See Stephen Frederic Dale, "Religious Suicide in Islamic Asia: Anti-colonial Terrorism in India, Indonesia and the Philippines," *Journal of Conflict Resolution* 32, 1 (March 1988): 37–59, on which this account is based.
7. Robert A. Pape, *Dying to Win: The Strategic Logic of Suicide Terrorism* (New York: Random House, 2005), p. 139.
8. Stephen Hopgood, "Tamil Tigers, 1987–2002," p. 44, and Luca Ricolfi, "Palestinians, 1981–2003," p. 82, in Diego Gambetta (ed.), *Making Sense of Suicide Missions* (Oxford: Oxford University Press, 2005).
9. Rohan Gunaratna, "The LTTE and Suicide Terrorism," *Frontline* (India) 17, 3 (February 5–8, 2000).
10. About 90 percent of Tamils are Hindu, but the Tamil Tigers are avowedly secular.
11. Sumantra Bose, *States Nations Sovereignty: Sri Lanka, India and the Tamil Eelam Movement* (New Delhi: Sage, 1994), p. 118.
12. Stephen Hopgood, "Tamil Tigers, 1987–2002," p. 74.
13. Charu Lata Joshi, "Ultimate Sacrifice: Faced with Harassment and Economic Deprivation, Young Tamils Are Ready to Give Up Their Lives," *Far Eastern Economic Review*, June 1, 2000, pp. 64–67.
14. Cited in P. Schalk, "Resistance and Martyrdom on the Process of State Formation in Tamililam," in J. Pettigrew (ed.), *Martyrdom and Political Resistance* (Amsterdam: VU University Press, 1997), p. 79.
15. One has to imagine that the logistics of this are difficult.
16. Amy Waldman, "Masters of Suicide Bombing: Tamil Guerrillas of Sri Lanka," *The New York Times*, January 14, 2003.
17. Cited in Joshi, "Ultimate Sacrifice."
18. Ibid.
19. Ibid.
20. Christoph Reuter, *My Life as a Weapon: A Modern History of Suicide Bombing* (Princeton, N.J.: Princeton University Press, 2004).

21. Ibid., p. 57.
22. Ariel Merari, "Social, Organizational and Psychological Factors in Suicide Terrorism," in Tore Bjorgo (ed.), *Root Causes of Terrorism: Myths, Reality and Ways Forward* (New York: Routledge, 2005), p. 72.
23. Diego Gambetta (ed.), *Making Sense of Suicide Missions* (Oxford: Oxford University Press, 2005), p. 288.
24. See Peter Hill, "Kamikaze 1943–45," in Gambetta (ed.), *Making Sense of Suicide Missions*, pp. 1–42.
25. Ibid., pp. 24–25.
26. Ibid., p. 23.
27. For excellent accounts see David Beresford, *Ten Men Dead: The Story of the 1981 Hunger Strike* (London: Harper Collins, 1987), and Padraig O'Malley, *Biting at the Grave: The Irish Hunger Strikes and the Politics of Despair* (Boston: Beacon Press, 1990).
28. Anne Marie Oliver and Paul Steinberg, *The Road to Martyrs' Square* (Oxford: Oxford University Press, 2005), p. 119.
29. Daniel Pipes, "Arafat's Suicide Factory," *New York Post*, December 9, 2001.
30. Quoted in Gregg Zoroya, "Woman Describes the Mentality of a Suicide Bomber," *USA Today*, April 22, 2002.
31. Robert Pape asserts in *Dying to Win* that there were 315 suicide attacks worldwide between 1980 and 2003 (p. 15). There were about 400 between the U.S. invasion of Iraq in 2003 and June 2005 (*The Washington Post*, July 17, 2005). The most extensive quantitative analysis of suicide attacks has been conducted by Pape in *Dying to Win*. His numbers, however, are lower than those of most other analysts familiar with the cases. Nevertheless, the general point about the scale of the tactic in Iraq compared to elsewhere remains.
32. The most detailed analysis of the foreign insurgents in Iraq is a September 2005 study by Andrew Cordesman and Nawaf Obaid of the Centre for Strategic and International Studies (CSIS). They argue that of the 3,000 foreign insurgents, 600 are Algerians, 550 Syrians, 500 Sudanese, 400 Egyptians, 350 Saudis. Most other reports have assumed the Saudis to be the largest contingent.
33. Aparisim Ghosh, "Inside the Mind of an Iraqi Suicide Bomber," *Time*, July 4, 2005.
34. Ibid.
35. Ibid.
36. Barbara Victor, *Army of Roses: Inside the World of Palestinian Women Suicide Bombers* (New York: Rodale [St. Martin's], 2003), p. 19.
37. Quoted by Victor in ibid., p. 30.
38. Libby Copeland, "Female Suicide Bombers: The New Factor in Mideast's Deadly Equation," *The Washington Post*, April 27, 2002; Avishai Margalit, "The Suicide Bombers," *The New York Review of Books*, January 16, 2003.
39. Victor, *Army of Roses*, p. 33
40. Cited by Victor in *Army of Roses*, p. 266.
41. "Homicide Bomber-Mom Kills Four at Gaza Border," Fox News, January 14,

2004. Available on the Fox News Web site, www.foxnews.com/story/0,2933, 108329,00.html, page accessed April 10, 2006.

42. Quoted by Victor in *Army of Roses,* p. 242.

43. Manuela Dviri, "My Dream Was to Be a Suicide Bomber. I Wanted to Kill 20, 50 Jews, Yes, Even Babies," *The Telegraph* (London), June 26, 2005.

44. Victor, *Army of Roses,* p. 112.

45. This is the argument of Barbara Victor in *Army of Roses.*

46. Manuela Dviri, "My Dream," June 26, 2005.

47. Quoted by Victor in *Army of Roses,* p. 253.

48. Victor, *Army of Roses,* p. 35.

49. Cited in Rohan Gunaratna, "The LTTE and Suicide Terrorism," *Frontline* (India), February 5–8, 2000.

50. *The Daily Star* (Beirut), February 8, 2002. Cited in Haim Malka, "Must Innocents Die? The Islamic Debate over Suicide Attacks," *Middle East Quarterly,* Spring 2003. Available on the Middle East Forum Web site, www.meforum .org/article/530, page accessed April 10, 2006.

51. Stathis Kalyyvas and Ignacio Sánchez-Cuenca, "Killing Without Dying: The Absence of Suicide Missions," in Gambetta (ed.), *Making Sense of Suicide Missions,* p. 211.

52. See Ayman al-Zawahiri, *Knights Under the Prophet's Banner,* serialized in *al-Sharq al-Awsat* (London), December 2–10, 2001, trans. Foreign Broadcast Information Service, document FBIS-NES-2001-1202, maintained online by the Federation of American Scientists, http://fas.org/irp/world/para/aymanh_ bk.html, and available online at www.liberalsagainstterrorism.com/wiki/index .php/Knights_Under_the_Prophet's_Banner, page accessed July 13, 2005.

53. Pape, *Dying to Win,* p. 190.

54. Nasra Hassan, "An Arsenal of Believers," *The New Yorker,* November 19, 2001, pp. 36–41.

55. Ibid.

56. Quoted by Victor in *Army of Roses,* p. 112.

57. Hassan, "An Arsenal of Believers."

58. Ibid.

59. Ariel Merari, "Social, Organizational and Psychological Factors in Suicide Terrorism," in Tore Bjorgo (ed.), *Root Causes of Terrorism: Myths, Reality and Ways Forward* (New York: Routledge, 2005). Nasra Hassan also described these training sessions in "An Arsenal of Believers."

60. Oliver and Steinberg, *The Road to Martyrs' Square,* p. 31

61. Luca Ricolfi, "Palestinians, 1981–2003," p. 113.

62. Oliver and Steinberg, *The Road to Martyrs' Square,* pp. 153–154.

63. Merari, "Social, Organizational and Psychological Factors in Suicide Terrorism."

64. Public Opinion Poll 15, Palestinian Center for Policy and Survey Research, March 2005. Available on the Palestinian Center for Policy and Survey Re-

search Web site, www.pcpsr.org/survey/index.html, page accessed March 20, 2006.

65. Public Opinion Poll 54, Jerusalem Media and Communications Centre, May 2005. Available on the Jerusalem Media and Communications Centre Web site, www.jmcc.org/publicpoll/results/2005/index.htm, page accessed March 20, 2006.

66. Public Opinion Poll 9, Palestinian Center for Policy and Survey Research, October 2003. Available on the Palestinian Center for Policy and Survey Research Web site, www.pcpsr.org/survey/index.html, page accessed March 20, 2006.

67. Hassan, "An Arsenal of Believers."

68. Cited by Christoph Reuter in *My Life Is a Weapon*, trans. Helena Ragg Kirkby (Princeton, N.J.: Princeton University Press, 2004), p. 155.

69. Victor, *Army of Roses*, p. 37.

70. Ibid., p. 206.

71. Nasra Hassan, "An Arsenal of Believers."

72. Thomas L. Friedman, "Marines Release Diagram on Blast," *The New York Times*, October 28, 1983.

73. Aparisim Ghosh, "Inside the Mind of an Iraqi Suicide Bomber," *Time*, July 4, 2005, pp. 22–29.

74. Oliver and Steinberg, *The Road to Martyrs' Square*, p. 122.

75. Ronald Reagan, *An American Life* (New York: Simon and Schuster, 1990), p. 465.

76. Texts of the statements can be found on www.bbcnews.com.

77. "Statement Claiming London Attacks," July 7, 2005. Available on the BBC News Web site, news.bbc.co.uk/1/hi/uk/4660391.stm, page accessed May 24, 2006.

78. One of the four, Germaine Lindsey, was born in Jamaica.

79. Quoted in Laville and Cobain, "From Cricket-Lover Who Enjoyed a Laugh to Terror Suspect."

PART TWO: THE COUNTERTERRORISTS

EPIGRAPHS

1. George W. Bush, "Address to a Joint Session of Congress and the American People," September 20, 2001. Available on the White House Web site, www.whitehouse.gov/news/releases/2001/09/20010920-8.html, page accessed March 17, 2006.

2. Osama bin Laden, "Sermon for the Feast of the Sacrifice," February 11, 2003; Middle East Media Research Institute, Special Dispatch Series, no. 476, March 5, 2003.

CHAPTER 6: WHAT CHANGED AND WHAT DID NOT ON SEPTEMBER 11, 2001

1. George W. Bush, "Address to a Joint Session of Congress and the American People," September 20, 2001. Available on the White House Web site, www.white house.gov/news/releases/2001/09/20010920-8.html, page accessed March 17, 2006.

2. Lord Campbell, House of Commons, March 19, 1868, *Hansard Parliamentary Debates,* vol. 193.

3. Terry McDermot, *Perfect Soldiers: The Hijackers: Who They Were, Why They Did It* (New York: HarperCollins, 2005), p. 234.

4. Text in McDermot, *Perfect Soldiers,* p. 231.

5. This account relies on McDermot, *Perfect Soldiers.*

6. Yosri Fouda and Nick Fielding, *Masterminds of Terror* (New York: Arcade Publishing, 2003), pp. 98–100.

7. *Patterns of Global Terrorism 2000* (Washington, D.C.: U.S. Department of State, April 2001).

8. *Patterns of Global Terrorism 1999* (Washington, D.C.: U.S. Department of State, April 2000).

9. Frantz Fanon, *The Wretched of the Earth* (New York: Grove Press, 1963).

10. McVeigh was actually pulled over by an Oklahoma Highway Patrol officer for driving without a license. He was linked to the bombing as he was about to be released two days later.

11. NBC News, *Meet the Press,* transcript for Sunday, September 14, 2003. Available on the MSNBC Web site, www.msnbc.msn.com/id/3080244/, page accessed March 20, 2006.

12. CBS News Poll, conducted October 25–28, 2001. Available on the Polling Report Web site, www.pollingreport.com/terror7.htm, page accessed February 14, 2006.

13. Osama bin Laden, "Sermon on the Feast of the Sacrifice," February 11, 2003, Middle East Media Research Institute, Special Dispatch Series, no. 476, March 5, 2003.

14. George W. Bush, "Address to the Nation," September 11, 2001. Available on the White House Web site, www.whitehouse.gov/news/releases/2001/09/20010911-16.html, page accessed March 20, 2006.

15. George W. Bush, "President Addresses Military Families," Nampa, Idaho, August 24, 2005. Available on the White House Web site, www.whitehouse.gov/news/releases/2005/08/20050824.html, page accessed March 20, 2006.

16. Harris Poll, conducted September 19–24, 2001. Available on the Polling Report Web site, www.pollingreport.com/terror8.htm, page accessed February 14, 2006.

17. Ipsos-Reid Poll, conducted September 11, 2001. Available on the Polling Report Web site, www.pollingreport.com/terror10.htm, page accessed February 14, 2006.

18. Figures from the Centers for Disease Control and Prevention (CDC), "Total Deaths Data Set, United States 2001, by Cause and Age Group." Available on the CDC Web site, apps.nccd.cdc.gov/ardi/HomePage.aspx, page accessed September 26, 2005. "CDC, Alcohol-Attributable Deaths Report, United States

2001." Available on the CDC Web site, apps.nccd.cdc.gov/ardi/Report.aspx?
T=AAM&P=9d3057a6-5cda-416d-ba10-41c7b0cbd521&R=c22869f8 a1d3
48a8-8095-9142c6de5baf&M=1d04dc84-f775-4032-9ab3-75bc10221b2b,
page accessed March 20, 2006. National Highway Traffic Safety Administration FARS data. Available on the MADD Web site, madd.org/stats/0,1056,
1298,00.html, page accessed March 21, 2006.

19. Bush, "Address to a Joint Session of Congress and the American People," September 20, 2001.

20. Pew Research Center survey, conducted by Princeton Survey Research Associates, August 14–25, 2002. Available on the Polling Report Web site, www
.pollingreport.com/terror5.htm, page accessed February 14, 2006.

21. Bush, "Address to a Joint Session of Congress and the American People," September 20, 2001.

22. George W. Bush, "Address to National Endowment for Democracy," October
6, 2005. Available on the White House Web site, www.whitehouse.gov/news/
releases/2005/10/20051006-3.html, page accessed March 21, 2006.

23. See Mark Juergensmeyer, "Religion as a Cause of Terrorism," in Peter Neumann and Louise Richardson (eds.), *Democracy and Terrorism: The Root
Causes of Terrorism* (New York: Routledge, 2006).

24. "President Bush Delivers Graduation Speech at West Point," June 1, 2002.
Available on the White House Web site, www.whitehouse.gov/news/releases/
2002/06/20020601-3.html, page accessed March 21, 2006.

25. ABC News Poll, conducted October 8–9, 2001. Available at the Polling Report
Web site, www.pollingreport.com/terror8.htm, page accessed February 14,
2006.

26. Murray Sayle, "Nerve Gas and Four Noble Truths," *The New Yorker,* April 1,
1996, p. 71.

27. "Factory Bombing: A Matter of Evidence," BBC News, May 5, 1999. Available
on the BBC News Web site, news.bbc.co.uk/1/hi/world/africa/336375.stm, page
accessed April 10, 2006.

28. John McWethy, "Bin Laden Set to Strike Again?," ABC News, June 16, 1999.
Transcript 99061601-j04. Available on the ABC News Web site, www.transcripts
.tv/search/do_details.cfm?ShowDetailID=17293, page accessed March 21, 2006.
"Afghan Alliance—UBL Trying to Make Chemical Weapons," Parwan Payam-e
Mojahed, December 23, 1999. Parwan Payam-e-Mojahed is an online weekly
magazine published by the Northern Alliance.

29. Muhammad Salah, "Bin Laden Front Reportedly Bought CBW from E. Europe," *al-Hayah,* April 20, 1999. Muhammad Salah, "US Said (to Be) Interrogating Jihadist over CBW," *al-Hayah,* April 21, 1999.

30. Guido Olimpio, "Islamic Group Said Preparing Chemical Warfare on the
West," *Corriere della Sera,* July 8, 1998. Yosef Bodansky, *Bin Laden: The Man
Who Declared War on America* (Roseville, Calif.: Prima, 2001), p. 326.

31. Pamela Hess, "Al Qaeda May Have Chemical Weapons," United Press International, August 19, 2002. *Insight,* CNN, August 19, 2002. Available on CNN's

Insight Web site, transcripts.cnn.com/TRANSCRIPTS/0208/19/i_ins.01.html, page accessed on March 21, 2006.

32. Eric Croddy, "Chemical Terrorist Plot in Rome?," CNS Research Story, March 11, 2002. Available on the Center for Nonproliferation Studies Web site, cns.miis.edu/pubs/week/020311.htm, page accessed March 21, 2006.

33. Alan Cullison and Andrew Higgins, "Computer in Kabul Holds Chilling Memos," *The Wall Street Journal,* December 31, 2001. "Report: Al Qaeda Computer Had Plans for Bio-Weapons," Reuters, December 21, 2001.

34. Barton Gellman, "Al Qaeda Near Biological, Chemical Arms Production," *The Washington Post,* March 23, 2003.

35. Gwynne Roberts, "Militia Defector Claims Baghdad Trained al Qaeda Fighters in Chemical Warfare," *The Sunday Times* (London), July 14, 2002.

36. Joby Warrick, "An al Qaeda 'Chemist' and the Quest for Ricin," *The Washington Post,* May 5, 2004.

37. Chris Summers, "Questions over Ricin Conspiracy," BBC News, April 13, 2005. Available on the BBC News Web site, news.bbc.co.uk/1/hi/uk/443 3499.stm, page accessed March 21, 2006.

38. Richard Norton Taylor, "Ricin Plot: London and Washington Used Plot to Strengthen Iraq War Push," *The Guardian,* April 14, 2005. May Ridden, "With Poison in Their Souls," *The Observer,* April 17, 2005.

39. The eleventh volume of this 5,000-page tome is devoted to instructions on how to construct chemical and biological weapons.

40. Al J. Venter, "Elements Loyal to bin Laden Acquire Biological Agents 'Through the Mail,'" *Jane's Intelligence Review* 11, no. 8 (August 1, 1999): 1.

41. "Prague Discounts an Iraqi Meeting," *The New York Times,* October 21, 2001.

42. "Al Qaeda: Anthrax Found in al Qaeda Home," *Global Security Newswire,* December 10, 2001. Available on the NTI/Global Security Newswire Web site, www.nti.org/d_newswire/issues/thisweek/2001_12_10_biow.html, page accessed March 21, 2006. "Walker Lindh: Qaeda Planned More Attacks," CNN, October 3, 2002. Available on the CNN Web site, archives.cnn.com/2002/LAW/10/03/walker.lindh.documents/index.html, page accessed March 21, 2006.

43. Judith Miller, "Labs Suggest Qaeda Planned to Build Arms, Officials Say," *The New York Times,* September 2002. Michael Gordon, "US Says It Found Qaeda Lab Being Built to Produce Anthrax," *The New York Times,* March 23, 2002. Dominic Evans, "US Troops Found Afghan Biological Lab," Reuters, March 22, 2002.

44. At the time, de Villepin was interior minister. He was speaking at a bioterrorism conference in Lyon. "Al Qaeda Made Biological Weapons in Georgia—French Minister," *Moscow News,* January 3, 2005.

45. James Gordon, "Feds Find Poison Plot vs. Gulf Troops," *The Daily News* (New York), February 10, 2003. Available on the Global Security Web site, www.globalsecurity.org/org/news/2003/030210-poison01.htm, page accessed March 21, 2006. Mike Toner, "Humble Bean Produces a Deadly Toxin," *Atlanta Journal-*

Constitution, March 21, 2003, p. 10A. Maria Ressa, "Reports: Al Qaeda Operative Sought Anthrax," CNN, October 10, 2003. Available on the CNN Web site, edition.cnn.com/2003/WORLD/asiapcf/southeast/10/10/alqaeda.anthrax/, page accessed March 21, 2006. Judith Miller, "US Has New Concerns About Anthrax Readiness," *The New York Times,* December 28, 2003.

46. David C. Rapoport, "Terrorism and Weapons of the Apocalypse," *National Security Studies Quarterly* 5, no. 3 (1999): 57.

47. Ibid., p. 52.

48. Fox News/Opinion Dynamics Poll, September 19–20, 2001. Available on the Polling Report Web site, www.pollingreport.com/terror9.htm, page accessed February 15, 2006.

49. Fox News/Opinion Dynamics Poll, June 4–5, 2002. Available on the Polling Report Web site, www.pollingreport.com/terror6.htm, page accessed February 14, 2006.

50. Osama bin Laden, interview with al-Jazeera, 1998. English text available at www.news.telegraph.co.uk/news/main.jhtml?xml=/news/2001/10/07/wbin07.xml, filed July 10, 2001, page accessed March 21, 2006.

51. Riyad Alam al Din, "Report Links Bin Laden, Nuclear Weapons," *al-Watran al-Arabi,* November 12, 1998; Emil Torabi, "Bin Laden's Nuclear Weapons," *The Muslim Magazine,* Winter 1998, www.muslimmag.org, page accessed on July 13, 1999, no longer available.

52. Benjamin Weiser, "US Says bin Laden Aide Tried to Get Nuclear Weapons," *The New York Times,* September 26, 1998.

53. "Arab Security Sources Speak of a New Scenario for Afghanistan: Secret Roaming Networks That Exchange Nuclear Weapons for Drugs," *al-Sharq al-Awsat,* December 24, 2000.

54. Ibid.

55. "N-weapons May Be in US Already," *Daily Telegraph* (Sydney, Australia), November 14, 2001.

56. "Al-Qaeda Does Not Have Our Nuclear Bombs Insists Ukraine," *The Scotsman,* February 11, 2004; "Al-Qaeda Said to Possess Nuclear Arms," Associated Press, February 9, 2004.

57. "Osama Bin Laden's Bid to Acquire Weapons of Mass Destruction Represents the Greatest Threat That Western Civilization Has Faced," *The Mail on Sunday* (London), June 23, 2002.

58. Fox News/Opinion Dynamics Poll, November 14–15, 2001. Available on the Polling Report Web site, www.pollingreport.com/terror7.htm, page accessed February 14, 2006.

59. Adam Nathan and David Leppard, "Al Qaeda's Men Held Secret Meetings to Build a Dirty Bomb," *The Sunday Times* (London), October 14, 2001.

60. Uthman Tizghart, "Does bin Laden Really Possess Weapons of Mass Destruction? Tale of Russian Mafia Boss Simon Mogilevich Who Supplied Bin Laden with the Nuclear 'Dirty Bomb,'" *al-Majallah* (London), November 25, 2001.

61. Ed Johnson, "Report: al Qaeda Made Bomb in Afghanistan," Associated Press, January 30, 2003.

62. Nick Felding, "Bin Laden's Dirty Bomb Quest Exposed," *The Sunday Times*, (London), December 19, 2004.

63. "The case against Jose Padilla," Online NewsHour, June 1, 2004. Available on PBS Online and WGBH's *NewsHour* Web site, www.pbs.org/newshour/bb/terrorism/jan-june04/padilla_06-01.html, page accessed March 21, 2006.

64. Osama bin Laden made this assertion in an interview with Rahilullah Yusufzai, who reports for both *Time* magazine and ABC News. See "Wrath of God," *Time Asia*, vol. 153, no. 1. Available on the *Time Asia* Web site, www.time.com/time/asia/asia/magazine/1999/990111/osama1.html, page accessed March 21, 2006.

65. Hamid Mir, "Osama Claims He Has Nukes: If US Uses N-Arms It Will Get Same Response," *Dawn* (Pakistan), November 10, 2001. (There have been doubts expressed about the authenticity of this interview.)

66. Jamie McIntyre, "Zubaydah: Al Qaeda Had 'Dirty Bomb' Know How," CNN, April 22, 2002. Available on the CNN Web site, archives.cnn.com/2002/US/04/22/zubaydah.dirty.bomb/index.html, page accessed March 21, 2006. "Al-Qaeda Claims Dirty Bomb Know-How," BBC, April 23, 2002. Available on the BBC Web site, news.bbc.co.uk/1/hi/world/americas/1945765.stm, page accessed March 21, 2006.

67. Max Delany, "Under Attack al Qaeda Makes Nuclear Claim," *The Moscow News*, March 3, 2004.

68. John Mueller and Karl Mueller, "Sanctions of Mass Destruction," *Foreign Affairs*, 78, no. 3 (1999): p. 51.

69. David C. Rapoport, "Terrorism and Weapons of the Apocalypse," *National Security Studies Quarterly*, 5, no. 3 (1999): p. 52.

70. Pew Research Center for the People and the Press. Available at the Pew Research Center Web site, people-press.org/reports/print.php3, page ID 441. Released April 11, 1996. Page accessed October 5, 2005.

71. Report of the work of Michael J. Flanagan and Michael Sivak in Sid Perkins, "Unfounded Fear: Scared to Fly After 9/11? Don't Reach for the Car Keys," *Science News Online*, vol. 163, no. 2, week of January 11, 2003, p. 20. Available at www.sciencenews.org/articles/20030111/fob3.asp, page accessed March 21, 2006.

72. Garrick Blalock, Vrinda Kadiyali, and Daniel H. Simon, "The Impact of 9/11 on Driving Fatalities: The Other Lives Lost to Terrorism," *Cornell News*, February 25, 2005. Available on the *Cornell News* Web site, www.news.cornell.edu/stories/March05/Sept11driving.pdf, page accessed March 21, 2006.

CHAPTER 7: WHY THE WAR ON TERROR CAN NEVER BE WON

1. General George Grivas, leader of the Greek Cypriot terrorist group EOKA (1955–1958), referring to the actions of the British Army in Charles Foley (ed.), *The Memoirs of General Grivas* (New York: Praeger, 1965), p. 53.

2. Bommi Baumann, a leading member of the German terrorist group the June 2nd Movement, explains how he was radicalized by the shooting of a New Left student, Benno Ohnesorg, during demonstrations against a visit by the shah of Iran in June 1967. Bommi Baumann, *Wie Alles Anfing. How It All Began*, 2nd ed., trans. Helene Ellenbogen and Wayne Parker (Vancouver: Pulp Press, 1981), p. 40.

3. George W. Bush, "Statement by the President in His Address to the Nation," September 11, 2001. Available on the White House Web site, www.whitehouse .gov/news/releases/2001/09/20010911-16.html, page accessed March 20, 2006.

4. George W. Bush, "Address to a Joint Session of Congress and the American People," September 20, 2001. Available on the White House Web site, www.white house.gov/news/releases/2001/09/20010920-8.html, page accessed March 17, 2006.

5. Authorization for Use of Military Force, September 18, 2001. Public Law 107-40 (SJ Res 23), 107th Congress. Joint Resolution.

6. Osama bin Laden, "Fatwa Urging Jihad Against Americans," February 23, 1998. Available on the MidEastWeb.org Web site, www.mideastweb.org/osamabinladen2 .htm, page accessed May 18, 2006.

7. George W. Bush, "Remarks by the President upon Arrival," The South Lawn, September 16, 2001. Available on the White House Web site, www.white house.gov/news/releases/2001/09/20010916-2.html, page accessed March 21, 2006.

8. See, e.g., CBS News/New York Times Poll, September 20–23, 2001. Available at the Polling Report Web site, www.pollingreport.com/terror9.htm, page accessed January 10, 2006.

9. The full texts of this and other Weathermen communiqués are available at www.sunrisedancer.com/radicalreader/library/weatherman/weatherman45.asp, page accessed September 24, 2005.

10. Ronald Reagan, Address to the 41st Session of the U.N. General Assembly in New York, September 22, 1986. Available on the Ronald Reagan Presidential Library Web site, www.reagan.utexas.edu/archives/speeches/1986/092286a.htm, page accessed March 21, 2006.

11. See, e.g., "The War on Terrorism," *The New York Times*, April 2, 1881.

12. Jean-Marie Colombani, "Nous sommes tous Américains," *Le Monde* (Paris), September 12, 2001, p. 1.

13. Stephen F. Szabo, *Parting Ways: The Crisis in German-American Relations* (Washington D.C.: Brookings, 2004), p. 15, and related to the author by some of those who were present.

14. Douglas Feith, as quoted by Fred Kaplan in "Bush's Many Miscalculations," *Slate*, September 9, 2003.

15. "Secretary Rumsfeld Media Availability En Route to Poland," U.S. Department of Defense, News Transcript, September 22, 2002.

16. See, e.g., Stephen F. Szabo, *Parting Ways: The Crisis in German-American Relations* (Washington, D.C.: Brookings, 2004), p. 16.

17. Pew Research Center, Global Attitudes Survey, May 2003. Available on the Pew Research Center Web site, www.google.com/search?hl=en&lr=&q=pew+global+attitudes+survey+May+2003, page accessed on March 21, 2006.

18. Los Angeles Times Poll, September 13–14, 2001. Available on the Polling Report Web site, www.pollingreport.com/terror10.htm, page accessed January 10, 2006.

19. CBS News/New York Times Poll, September 20–23, 2001. Available on the Polling Report Web site, www.pollingreport.com/terror9.htm, page accessed January 10, 2006. Pew Research Center, November 13–19, 2001. Available on the Polling Report Web site, www.pollingreport.com/terror7.htm, page accessed January 10, 2006.

20. ABC News/Washington Post Poll, September 13, 2001. Available on the Polling Report Web site, www.pollingreport.com/terror10.htm, page accessed January 10, 2006. CBS News/New York Times Poll, September 20–23, 2001. Available on the Polling Report Web site, www.pollingreport.com/terror8.htm, page accessed January 10, 2006.

21. George W. Bush, "Remarks by President Bush and His Majesty King Abdullah of Jordan in a Photo Opportunity," the Oval Office, September 28, 2001. Available on the White House Web site, www.whitehouse.gov/news/releases/2001/09/20010928-4.html, page accessed March 20, 2006.

22. George W. Bush, "President Bush: 'No Nation Can Be Neutral in this Conflict,'" Remarks by the President to the Warsaw Conference on Combatting Terrorism, November 6, 2001. Available on the White House Web site, www.whitehouse.gov/news/releases/2001/11/20011106-2.html, page accessed March 21, 2006.

23. George W. Bush, "President Holds Town Hall Forum on Economy in California," Ontario Convention Center, Ontario, California, January 5, 2002. Available on the White House Web site, www.whitehouse.gov/news/releases/2002/01/20020105-3.html, page accessed March 21, 2006.

24. Bush, "Remarks by the President upon Arrival."

25. Bush, "Address to Joint Session of Congress and the American People," September 20, 2001.

26. *Investor's Business Daily/Christian Science Monitor* poll conducted by TIPP, the polling arm of TechnoMetrica Market Intelligence, November 7–11, 2001. Available at the Polling Report Web site, www.pollingreport.com/terror7.htm, page accessed January 10, 2006.

27. "London Bomber: Text in Full," September 1, 2005. Available on the BBC News Web site, news.bbc.co.uk/1/hi/uk/4206800.stm, page accessed March 21, 2006.

28. Alberto R. Gonzales, Memorandum, "Decision Re Application of the Geneva Convention on Prisoners of War to the Conflict with Al Qaeda and the Taliban," January 25, 2002. Available on the *Newsweek* Web site, msnbc.msn.com/id/4999148/site/newsweek, page accessed May 17, 2005.

29. The Pew Global Attitudes Project, June 23, 2005. Available on the Pew Research Center Web site, pewglobal.org/reports/display.php?ReportID=247, page accessed March 21, 2006.

30. BBC poll. Available on the BBC News Web site, www.bbc.co.uk/pressoffice/pressreleases/stories/2003/06_june/16/news_poll_america.shtml, page accessed May 19, 2006.

31. ABC News/Washington Post Poll, October 7, 2001. Available on the Polling Report Web site, www.pollingreport.com/terror8.htm, page accessed January 10, 2006.

32. For estimates on casualty figures, see Robert Art and Louise Richardson (eds.), *Democracy and Counterterrorism: Lessons from the Past* (Washington, D.C.: U.S. Institute of Peace, 2006), Table 4.

33. Congressional Research Service, no. 1B89118, updated June 10, 2005. Available on the Federation of American Scientists Web site, www.fas.org/sgp/crs/mideast/IB89118.pdf, page accessed March 21, 2006.

34. *Report on the Situation of Human Rights in Argentina* (Washington, D.C.: Organization of American States, Inter-American Commission on Human Rights, 1980), p. 135n.

35. Guillermo Rojas, *30,000 desaparecidos: realidad, mito y dogma* (Buenos Aires: Editorial Santiago Apostol, 2003); *Nunca Mas, A Report by Argentina's National Commission on Disappeared People* (London: Faber & Faber, 1986).

36. Report available on the Italian Amnesty International Web site, www.amnesty.it/Allibtop/1996/AMR/222000196.htm (no longer available).

37. Foley (ed.), *The Memoirs of General Grivas*, p. 71.

38. Text of report in Sean Cronin, *Irish Nationalism: A History of its Roots and Ideology* (Dublin: Academy Press, 1980), appendix XVIII, paragraph 16c.

39. Ibid., paragraphs 64–65.

40. U.S. Secretary of State Colin Powell, Address to the U.N. Security Council, February 5, 2003.

41. *9/11 Commission Report: Final Report of the National Commission on Terrorist Attacks Upon the United States (Official Edition)* (Washington, D.C.: Claitor's Law Books and Publishers Division, July 22, 2004), pp. 335–336.

42. *Washington Post* Poll: Saddam Hussein and the September 11 Attacks, September 6, 2003. Available on the *Washington Post* Web site, http://www.washingtonpost.com/wp-srv/politics/polls/vault/stories/data082303.htm, page accessed October 20, 2005.

43. "Iraq, 9/11, Al Qaeda and Weapons of Mass Destruction: What the Public Believes Now, According to Latest Harris Poll," Harris Poll no. 14, February 18, 2005. Available on the HarrisInteractive Web site, http://www.harrisinteractive.com/harris_poll/printerfriend/index.asp?PID=544, page accessed October 20, 2005.

44. *9/11 Commission Report*, p. 62.

45. NBC News, *Meet the Press*, December 9, 2001. NBC, March 24, 2002. NBC

News, *Meet the Press,* September 14, 2003. This was the Prague meeting mentioned in the last chapter at which Atta was alleged to have been given a vial of anthrax.

46. Eric Schmitt, "Threats and Responses: Intelligence: Rumsfeld Says U.S. Has 'Bulletproof' Evidence of Iraq's Links to Al Qaeda," *New York Times,* September 28, 2002, p. 9.

47. *Meet the Press* transcript for Sunday, September 14, 2003. Available on the MSNBC Web site, www.msnbc.msn.com/id/3080244/, page accessed March 20, 2006.

48. George W. Bush on *Fox News Sunday,* September 17, 2003. Available on the Fox News Web site, www.foxnews.com/story/0,2933,97527,00.html, page accessed March 21, 2006.

49. George W. Bush, "President Bush Discusses War on Terror at National Endowment for Democracy," October 6, 2005. Available on the White House Web site, www.whitehouse.gov/news/releases/2005/10/20051006-3.html, page accessed March 21, 2006.

50. George W. Bush, "Remarks of the President," May 1, 2003. Available on the White House Web site, www.whitehouse.gov/news/releases/2003/05/2003 0501-15.html, page accessed March 21, 2006.

51. George W. Bush, "President Addresses Nation, Discusses Iraq, War on Terror," Fort Bragg, North Carolina, June 28, 2005. Available on the White House Web site, www.whitehouse.gov/news/releases/2005/06/20050628-7.html, page accessed March 21, 2006.

52. *9/11 Commission Report,* p. 65.

53. Pepe Escobar, "Zarqawi and al Qaeda, Unlikely Bedfellows," *Asia Times,* October 22, 2004.

54. Letter from al-Zawahiri to al-Zarqawi, October 11, 2005. Available on the Office of the Director of National Intelligence Web site, www.dni.gov/release_letter_101105.html, page accessed March 21, 2006.

55. The Pew Global Attitudes Project, June 23, 2005. Available on the Pew Research Center Web site, pewglobal.org/reports/display.php?ReportID=247, page accessed March 21, 2006.

56. Pew Research Center, *Global Opinion: The Spread of Anti-Americanism, Trends 2005,* chap. 7. Available on the Pew Research Center Web site, pewtrust .org/pdf/trends2005.pdf, page accessed March 21, 2006.

57. Bush, "Remarks by the President on Arrival," the South Lawn, September 16, 2001.

58. George W. Bush, "President Rallies the Troops in Alaska," February 16, 2002. Available on the White House Web site, www.whitehouse.gov/news/releases/2002/02/20020216-1.html, page accessed March 21, 2006.

59. Tom Templeton and Tom Lumley, "9/11 in Numbers," *The Observer* (London), August 18, 2002.

60. Bush, "Statement by the President in His Address to the Nation," September 11, 2001.

61. George W. Bush, "Radio Address of the President to the Nation," September 29, 2001. Available on the White House Web site, www.whitehouse.gov/news/releases/2001/09/20010929.html, page accessed March 21, 2006.

62. Osama bin Laden, April 2004, in an audiotape offering conditional reconciliation with Europe. Available on the BBC News Web site, news.bbc.co.uk/2/hi/middle_east/3628069.stm, page accessed March 21, 2006.

63. George W. Bush, "Statement by the President in His Address to the Nation," September 11, 2001.

64 George W. Bush, "President Addresses Military Families," Nampa, Idaho, August 24, 2005. Available on the White House Web site, www.whitehouse.gov/news/releases/2005/08/20050824.html, page accessed March 21, 2006.

65. Bush, "President Rallies the Troops in Alaska."

66. George W. Bush, "President Discusses War on Terror at National Endowment for Democracy," October 6, 2005. Available on the White House Web site, www.whitehouse.gov/news/releases/2005/10/20051006-3.html, page accessed March 21, 2006.

67. Osama bin Laden speech in a videotape sent to al-Jazeera, October 30, 2004. Available on the al-Jazeera Web site, english.aljazeera.net/NR/exeres/79C6AF22-98FB-4A1C-B21F-2BC36E87F61F.htm, page accessed March 17, 2006.

68. Bush, "President Bush Addresses Military Families."

69. Bush, "President Discusses War on Terror at National Endowment for Democracy," October 6, 2005.

70. Bush, "President Addresses Military Families," Nampa, Idaho, August 24, 2005.

71. Osama bin Laden in a tape offers "Conditional Reconciliation with Europe," April 15, 2004. Available on the BBC News Web site, news.bbc.co.uk/1/hi/world/middle_east/3628069.stm, page accessed March 21, 2006.

72. Bush, "Remarks by the President on Arrival," the South Lawn , September 16, 2001.

CHAPTER 8: WHAT IS TO BE DONE?

1. Osama bin Laden, "Message to America," October 30, 2004. Available on the al-Jazeera Web site, english.aljazeera.net/NR/exeres/79C6AF22-98FB-4A1C-B21F-2BC36E87F61F.htm, page accessed March 17, 2006.

2. William Ewart Gladstone, letter to his wife, in J. L. Hammond, *Gladstone and the Irish Nation* (London: Longmans, Green, 1964), p. 51.

3. *The Banner of Ulster*, December 17, 1867. Cited in Patrick Quinlivan and Paul Rose, *The Fenians in England, 1865–1872* (London: John Calder, 1982), p. 97.

4. *Impartial Reporter*, May 7, 1868. Cited in Quinlivan and Rose, *The Fenians in England*, p. 97.

5. Queen Victoria to Gathorne Hardy, the Lord Cranbrook, May 1, 1868. Cited in Quinlivan and Rose, *The Fenians in England*, p. 133.

6. Cited in Qunilivan and Rose, *The Fenians in England*, p. 117.

7. *The Times* (London), April 21, 1868, cited in Quinlivan and Rose, *The Fenians in England*, p. 117.

8. Cited in Quinlivan and Rose, *The Fenians in England,* p. 117.

9. Quinlivan and Rose, *The Fenians in England,* p. 135.

10. J. L. Hammond, *Gladstone and the Irish Nation* (London: Longmans, Green, 1964), p. 80.

11. Padraic H. Pearse, *Political Writings and Speeches* (Dublin: Talbot Press, 1966), p. 137.

12. George W. Bush, "Address to a Joint Session of Congress and the American People," September 20, 2001. Available on the White House Web site, www.white house.gov/news/releases/2001/09/20010911-16.html, page accessed March 20, 2006.

13. Benjamin Franklin, Pennsylvania Assembly: Reply to the Governor, November 11, 1775, in *The Papers of Benjamin Franklin,* ed. Leonard W. Larabee, vol. 6, (New Haven: Yale University Press, 1963), p. 242.

14. Laura K. Donohue, *Counterterrorist Law and Emergency Powers in the United Kingdom, 1922–2000* (Dublin: Irish Academic Press, 2001).

15. George Washington, 1732–1799. The Writings of George Washington from the Original Manuscript sources, vol. 7, Electronic Text Center, University of Virginia Library.

16. David Hackett Fischer, *Washington's Crossing* (Oxford: Oxford University Press, 2004), p. 379.

17. Ibid., p. 276.

18. Sun-tzu, sixth century B.C., *The Art of War,* transl. by R. L. Wing in *The Art of Strategy: A New Translation of Sun Tzu's Classic* The Art of War (New York: Doubleday, 1998), p. 151.

19. Tom Templeton and Tom Lumley, "9/11 in Numbers," *The Observer* (London), August 18, 2002.

20. Peter R. Neumann, *Britain's Long War: British Strategy in the Northern Irish Conflict, 1969–1998* (New York: Palgrave, 2003), p. 157.

21. Louise Richardson, "Britain and the IRA," in Robert Art and Louise Richardson (eds.), *Democracy and Counter-terrorism: Lessons from the Past* (Washington, D.C.: USIP, 2006).

22. Louise Richardson, "How Terrorist Campaigns End: Lessons from War Termination," paper delivered at the International Studies Association Annual Convention, New Orleans, La., March 25, 2002.

23. David Ensor, "U.S. Officials: Al-Zarqawi Group's Statement Credible," CNN, October 18, 2004. Available on the CNN Web site, www.cnn.com/2004/WORLD/meast/10/18/al.zarqawi.statement/index.html, page accessed March 21, 2006.

24. "Voice on Tape Is bin Laden, Say US Investigators," MSNBC, December 28, 2004. Available on the MSNBC Web site, www.msnbc.msn.com/id/6759167/, page accessed March 21, 2006.

25. October 16, 2003. Text available on the *USA Today* Web site, www .usatoday.com/news/washington/executive/rumsfeld-memo.htm, page accessed March 21, 2006.

26. Letter from al-Zawahiri to al-Zarqawi, Office of the Director of National Intelligence, October 11, 2005. Available on the Office of the Director of National Intelligence Web site, www.dni.gov/release_letter_101105.html, page accessed March 21, 2006.

27. Ibid.

28. Osama bin Laden, October 7, 2001. Available on the MidEastWeb.org Web site, www.mideastweb.org/osamabinladen3.htm, page accessed March 21, 2006.

29. "Iraq Surveys Show 'Humanitarian Emergency,'" UNICEF Information Newsline, August 12, 1999. Available on the UNICEF Web site, www.unicef .org/newsline/99pr29.htm, page accessed May 25, 2006.

30. Mohamed M. Ali and Iqbal H. Shah, "Sanctions and Childhood Mortality in Iraq," *The Lancet,* 355, issue 9218 (May 27, 2000): 1851–1857.

31. Open letter to Mr. Peter Hain, *The Guardian,* January 3, 2001.

32. BBC News, September 30, 1998. Available on the BBC News Web site, news.bbc.co.uk/1/hi/world/middle_east/183499.stm, page accessed March 21, 2006.

33. John Mueller and Karl Mueller, "Sanctions of Mass Destruction," *Foreign Affairs,* 78, no. 3 (1999): 43–53.

34. For details on the kinds of policies that might be included in a comprehensive development plan, see the Madrid Agenda produced by the Club de Madrid on March 11, 2005. The background papers upon which the agenda is based provide a wealth of detailed policy recommendations.

35. Greg Fealy, "Hating Americans: Jemaah Islamiyah and the Bali Bombings," *IIAS Newsletter* 31 (July 2003): 3.

36. Raymond Bonner, "Bali Suicide Bombers Said to Have Belonged to Small Gang," *The New York Times,* October 7, 2005, p. A3.

37. Pew Global Attitudes Survey, June 23, 2005. Available on the Pew Research Center Web site, pewglobal.org/reports/display.php?ReportID=247, page accessed March 21, 2006.

38. Pew Global Attitudes Project, July 14, 2005. Available on the Pew Research Center Web site, pewglobal.org/reports/display.php?ReportID=248, page accessed March 21, 2006.

39. Report of the Independent Task Force Sponsored by the Council of Foreign Relations, "Finding America's Voice: A Strategy for Reinvigorating U.S. Public Diplomacy," New York, 2003; The Djerejian Report, "Changing Minds, Winning Peace: A New Strategic Direction for U.S. Public Diplomacy in the Arab and Muslim World," Report of the Advisory Group on Public Diplomacy for the Arab and Muslim World, Washington, D.C., 2003.

40. Djerejian Report, p. 25.

41. "Remarks by the President upon Arrival," the South Lawn, September 16, 2001. Available on the White House Web site, www.whitehouse.gov/news/ releases/2001/09/20010916-2.html, page accessed March 21, 2006.

42. The vote on the resolution authorizing force was 420–1 in the House and in the

Senate 98–0. The vote on the PATRIOT Act was 357–66 in the House and 98–1 in the Senate.

43. "Security with a Human Face: Challenges and Responsibilities," UNDP National Human Development Report, 2004, UNDP—Afghanistan, February 2005.

44. United Nations International Drug Control Programme, *Annual Opium Poppy Survey, Afghanistan 2001, 2004.*

45. Peter Barron, "Afghanistan Struggles to Keep Warlords Off the Ballot," *The Christian Science Monitor,* September 8, 2005.

46. Interview cited in Raimondo Catanzaro (ed.), *The Red Brigades and Left Wing Terrorism in Italy* (New York: St. Martin's Press, 1991), p. 185.

47. Cited in Fealy, "Hating Americans: Jemaah Islamiyah and the Bali Bombings," p. 3.

BIBLIOGRAPHY

Aita, Judy. "Bombing Trial Witness Describes Nairobi Surveillance Mission." Washington, D.C.: United States Department of State, February 23, 2001. Available on the State Department Web site, usinfo.state.gov/is/Archive_Index/Bombing_Trial_Witness_Describes_Nairobi_Surveillance_Mission.html, page accessed May 17, 2006.

al Din, Riyad Alam. "Report Links Bin Laden, Nuclear Weapons." *Al-Watran al-Arabi,* November 12, 1998.

Alexander, Yonah, and Dennis A. Pluchinsky. *Europe's Red Terrorists: The Fighting Communist Organizations.* London: Frank Cass, 1992.

Allison, Graham. *Nuclear Terrorism: The Ultimate Preventable Catastrophe.* New York: Times Books, 2004.

al-Qurashi, Abu Ubeid, "Al-Qa'ida Activist, Abu 'Ubeid Al Qurashi: Comparing Munich (Olympics) Attack 1972 to September 11." Middle East Media Research Institute report no. 353, March 12, 2002. Available on the MEMRI Web site, memri.org/bin/articles.cgi?Page=subjects&Area=jihad&ID=SP35302, page accessed May 17, 2006.

al-Zawahiri, Ayman. *Knights Under the Prophet's Banner.* Trans. FBIS (Foreign Broadcast Information Service), Summer 2001. Available on the Liberals Against Terrorism Web site, www.liberalsagainstterrorism.com/wiki/index.php/knights_Under_the_Prophet's_Banner, page accessed May 17, 2006.

Annual Opium Poppy Survey, Afghanistan 2001, 2004. United Nations International Drug Control Programme, Vienna.

"Arab Security Sources Speak of a New Scenario for Afghanistan: Secret Roaming Networks That Exchange Nuclear Weapons for Drugs." *Al-Sharq al-Awsat,* December 24, 2000.

Arendt, Hannah. "Reflections on Violence." *The New York Review of Books,* February 27, 1969. Available on the *New York Review of Books* Web site, www.nybooks.com/articles/11395, page accessed July 22, 2006.

Art, Robert, and Louise Richardson, eds. *Democracy and Counterterrorism: Lessons from the Past.* Washington, D.C.: U.S. Institute of Peace, 2006.

Atran, Scott. "Genesis of Suicide Terrorism." *Science,* March 7, 2003. Available on the *Science* magazine Web site, www.sciencemag.org/cgi/content/abstract/299/5612/1534, page accessed May 17, 2006.

Avrich, Paul. *Anarchist Portraits.* Princeton, N.J.: Princeton University Press, 1990.

Baumann, Bommi. *Wie Alles Anfing. How It All Began,* 2nd ed. Trans. Helene Ellenbogen and Wayne Parker. Vancouver: Pulp Press, 1981.

Becker, Jillian. *Hitler's Children: The Story of the Baader-Meinhof Terrorist Gang.* Philadelphia: J. B. Lippincott, 1977.

Benjamin, Daniel, and Steven Simon. *The Age of Sacred Terror, Radical Islam's War Against America.* New York: Random House, 2003.

Beresford, David. *Ten Men Dead: The Story of the 1981 Hunger Strike.* London: HarperCollins, 1987.

Bergen, Peter. *Holy War, Inc: Inside the Secret World of Osama bin Laden.* New York: Free Press, 2001.

——, and Swati Pandey. "The Madrassa Myth." *The New York Times,* June 14, 2005.

bin Laden, Osama. "Letter to the American People." Trans. *The Observer,* November 24, 2002.

Black, Jeremy (ed.). *The Seventy Great Battles in History.* London: Thames and Hudson, 2005.

Blalock, Garrick, Vrinda Kadiyali, and Daniel H. Simon. "The Impact of 9/11 on Driving Fatalities: The Other Lives Lost to Terrorism." Ithaca, N.Y.: Cornell University, February 25, 2005. Online. Available on the Cornell University Web site, www.news.cornell.edu/stories/March05/Sept11driving.pdf, page accessed May 17, 2006.

Bodansky, Yosef. *Bin Laden: The Man Who Declared War on America.* Roseville, Calif.: Prima, 2001.

Bonner, Raymond. "Bali Suicide Bombers Said to Have Belonged to Small Gang." *The New York Times,* October 7, 2005.

Bose, Sumantra. *States Nations Sovereignty: Sri Lanka, India and the Tamil Eelam Movement.* New Delhi: Sage, 1994.

Bougereau, Jean Marcel. "Memoirs of an International Terrorist: Conversations with Hans Joachim Klein." In *The German Guerrilla: Terror, Reaction, and Resistance.* Sanday, England: Cienfuegos Press, 1981.

Brackett, D. W. *Holy Terror: Armageddon in Tokyo.* New York: Weatherhill, 1966.

Burke, Jason. *Al-Qaeda: The True Story of Radical Islam.* London: I. B. Taurus, 2003.

Camus, Albert. *Caligula and Three Other Plays.* New York: Vintage Books, 1958.

Catanzaro, Raimondo. *The Red Brigades and Left Wing Terrorism in Italy.* New York: St. Martin's Press, 1991.

Chaliand, Gérard (ed.). *Guerrilla Stratégios.* Berkeley: University of California Press, 1982.

"Changing Minds, Winning Peace: A New Strategic Direction for U.S. Public Diplomacy in the Arab and Muslim World ('The Djerejian Report')." Report of the Advisory Group on Public Diplomacy for the Arab and Muslim World, Washington, D.C., 2003.

Charters, David (ed.). *The Deadly Sin of Terrorism: Its Effect on Democracy and Civil Liberties in Six Countries.* Westwood, Conn.: Greenwood Press, 1994.

Clark, Robert P. *The Basque Insurgents: ETA 1952–1980.* Madison: University of Wisconsin Press, 1984.

Clarke, Richard A. *Against All Enemies: Inside America's War on Terror.* New York: Free Press, 2004.

Clyde, R. Mark, et al. CRS Issue Brief for Congress, Lebanon. Congressional Research Service, Library of Congress, updated June 10, 2005.

Collins, Eamon. *Killing Rage.* London: Granta, 1997.

Congressional Research Service, no. 1B89118, Library of Congress, updated June 10, 2005.

Coogan, Tim Pat. *The IRA: A History.* Boulder, Colo.: Roberts Rinehart, 1994.

Copeland, Libby. "Female Suicide Bombers: The New Factor in Mideast's Deadly Equation." *The Washington Post,* April 27, 2002.

Council on Foreign Relations. *The War on Terror: A Foreign Affairs Book.* New York: Council on Foreign Relations, 2003.

Crenshaw, Martha. "The Causes of Terrorism." *Comparative Politics,* 13, no. 4 (July 1981): 379–400.

Crenshaw, Martha (ed.). *Terrorism in Context.* University Park: Pensylvania State University Press, 1995.

Croddy, Eric, Matthew Osborne, and Kimberly McCloud. "Chemical Terrorist Plot in Rome?" Center for Nonproliferation Studies Research Story, March 11, 2002. Available on the CNS Web site, cns.miis.edu/pubs/week/020311.htm, page accessed May 17, 2006.

Cronin, Audrey Kurth, and James M. Ludes (eds.). *Attacking Terrorism: Elements of a Grand Strategy.* Washington, D.C.: Georgetown University Press, 2004.

Cronin, Sean. *Irish Nationalism: A History of its Roots and Ideology.* Dublin: Academy Press, 1980.

Cullen, Kevin. "From Terrorist to Priest." *The Boston Globe Sunday Magazine,* August 7, 2005, p. 20.

Cullison, Alan. "Inside Al Qaeda's Hard Drive." *The Atlantic Monthly,* September 2004, pp. 55–70.

———, and Andrew Higgins. "Computer in Kabul Holds Chilling Memos." *The Wall Street Journal,* December 31, 2001.

Dale, Stephen Frederic. "Religious Suicide in Islamic Asia: Anti-colonial Terrorism in India, Indonesia and the Philippines." *Journal of Conflict Resolution,* 32, no. 1 (March 1988): 37–59.

Dartnell, Michael Y. *Action Direct: Ultra-Left Terrorism in France, 1979–87.* London: Frank Cass, 1995.

Delany, Max. "Under Attack al Qaeda Makes Nuclear Claim." *The Moscow News,* March 3, 2004.

Della Porta, Donatella. *Social Movements, Political Violence and the State: A Comparative Analysis of Italy and Germany.* Cambridge: Cambridge University Press, 1995.

Dershowitz, Alan. *Why Terrorism Works.* New Haven, Conn.: Yale University Press, 2002.

Donohue, Laura K. *Counterterrorist Law and Emergency Powers in the United Kingdom, 1922–2000.* Dublin: Irish Academic Press, 2001.

Dviri, Manuela. "My Dream Was to Be a Suicide Bomber. I Wanted to Kill 20, 50 Jews, Yes, Even Babies." *The Telegraph* (London), June 26, 2005.

Dwyer, Jim, et al. *Two Seconds Under the World.* New York: Crown, 1994.

English, Richard. *Armed Struggle: The History of the IRA.* London: Macmillan, 2003.

Escobar, Pepe. "Zarqawi and al Qaeda, Unlikely Bedfellows." *Asia Times,* October 22, 2004.

Esposito, John L. *Unholy War: Terror in the Name of Islam.* Oxford: Oxford University Press, 2002.

Evans, Dominic. "US Troops Found Afghan Biological Lab." Reuters, March 22, 2002.

Fanon, Frantz. *The Wretched of the Earth.* New York: Grove Press, 1963.

Farrell, William R. *Blood and Rage: The Story of The Japanese Red Army.* Lexington, Mass.: Lexington Books, 1990.

Fielding, Nick. "Bin Laden's Dirty Bomb Quest Exposed." *The London Times Online,* December 19, 2004.

"Finding America's Voice: A Strategy for Reinvigorating U.S. Public Diplomacy." Report of the Independent Task Force Sponsored by the Council of Foreign Relations, New York, 2003.

Fischer, David Hackett. *Washington's Crossing.* Oxford: Oxford University Press, 2004.

Foley, Charles (ed.). *The Memoirs of General Grivas.* New York: Praeger, 1965.

Foley, Greg. "Hating Americans: Jemaah Islamiyah and the Bali Bombings." *IIAS Newsletter* 31 (July 2003): 3–4.

Fouda, Yosri, and Nick Fielding. *Masterminds of Terror.* New York: Arcade, 2003.

Franklin, Benjamin. *The Papers of Benjamin Franklin.* Ed. Leonard W. Larabee. Vol. 6. New Haven: Yale University Press, 1963.

Friedman, Thomas L. "Marines Release Diagram on Blast." *The New York Times,* October 28, 1983.

Gambetta, Diego (ed.). *Making Sense of Suicide Missions*. Oxford: Oxford University Press, 2005.

Garddner, J. Starkie. *Armour in England from the Earliest Times to the Seventeenth Century*. Whitefish, Mont.: Kessinger Publishing Company, 2004.

Gellman, Barton. "Al Qaeda Near Biological, Chemical Arms Production." *The Washington Post*, March 23, 2003.

Ghosh, Aparisim. "Inside the Mind of an Iraqi Suicide Bomber." *Time*, July 4, 2005, pp. 23–29.

Gonzales, Alberto R. "Memorandum: Decision Re Application of the Geneva Convention on Prisoners of War to the Conflict with Al Qaeda and the Taliban," January 25, 2002. Available at http://msnbc.msn.com/Id/4999148/sIte/newsweek.

Gordon, James. "Feds Find Poison Plot vs. Gulf Troops." *The Daily News* (New York), February 10, 2003.

Gordon, Michael. "US Says It Found Qaeda Lab Being Built to Produce Anthrax." *The New York Times*, March 23, 2002.

Greenberg, Karen J. *Al Qaeda Now: Understanding Today's Terrorists*. Cambridge: Cambridge University Press, 2005.

Guevara, Che. *Guerrilla Warfare*. Introduction by Marc Becker. Lincoln: University of Nebraska Press, 1998.

Gunaratna, Rohan. *Inside Al Qaeda Global Network of Terror*. New York: Columbia University Press, 2002.

———. "The LTTE and Suicide Terrorism." *Frontline* (India), February 5–8, 2000.

Gurr, Ted Robert. *Why Men Rebel*. Princeton: Princeton University Press, 1970.

Hammond, J. L. *Gladstone and the Irish Nation*. London: Longmans, Green, 1964.

Hassan, Nasra. "An Arsenal of Believers: Talking to the Human Bombs." *The New Yorker*, November 19, 2001.

He Hir, J. Bryan, *Liberty and Power: Dialogue on Religion & U.S. Foreign Policy in an Unjust World*. Washington, D.C.: Brookings, 2004.

Hess, Pamela. "Al Qaeda May Have Chemical Weapons." United Press International, August 19, 2002.

Heymann, Philip B. *Terrorism, Freedom, and Security: Winning Without War*. Cambridge, Mass.: MIT Press, 2003.

Hill, Peter. "Kamikaze 1943–45." In *Making Sense of Suicide Missions*, ed. Diego Gambetta. Oxford: Oxford University Press, 2005.

Hodgson, Marshall G. S. *The Secret Order of Assassins: The Struggle of the Early Nizari Isma'ilis Against the Islamic World*. The Hague: Mounton & Company, 1955.

Hoffmann, Bruce. *Inside Terrorism*. New York: Columbia University Press, 1998.

———. "The Logic of Suicide Terrorism." *The Atlantic Monthly*, June 2003, pp. 40–47.

Horsley, Richard A. "The Sicarii: Ancient Jewish Terrorists." *The Journal of Religion*, 59, no. 4 (October 1979): 435–458.

Hudson, R. *The Sociology and Psychology of Terrorism: Who Becomes a Terrorist and Why?* Washington, D.C.: Federal Research Division, Library of Congress, 20540-4840, 1999.

Human Development Report 2005. New York: United Nations Development Programme. Available on the United Nations Development Programme Web site, hdr.undp.org/reports/global/2005/, page accessed January 5, 2006.

Hupta, Hiralal. "A Critical Study of the Thugs and their Activities." *Journal of Indian History,* 38 (1959): 167–176.

Jaber, Hala. *Hezbollah Born with a Vengeance.* New York: Columbia University Press, 1997.

Jacquard, Roland. *In the Name of Osama bin Laden: Global Terrorism and the Bin Laden Brotherhood.* Durham, N.C.: Duke University Press, 2002.

Jáuregui, Gututz. "Del nacionalismo sabiniano a la guerra revolucionaria (1963–1965)." In *La Historia de ETA,* ed. Antonio Alorza et al. Madrid: Temas de Hoy, 2000.

Johnson, Ed. "Report: al Qaeda Made Bomb in Afghanistan." Associated Press, January 30, 2003.

Joll, James. *The Anarchists.* Cambridge, Mass.: Harvard University Press, 1980.

Joshi, Charu Lata. "Ultimate Sacrifice: Faced with Harassment and Economic Deprivation, Young Tamils Are Ready to Give up Their Lives." *Far Eastern Economic Review,* June 1, 2002, pp. 64–67.

Juergensmeyer, Mark. "Religion as a Cause of Terrorism." In *Democracy and Terrorism: The Root Causes of Terrorism.* ed. Peter Neumann and Louise Richardson. New York: Routledge, 2006.

———. *Terror in the Mind of God.* Berkeley: University of California Press, 2000.

Kaplan, Fred. "Bush's Many Miscalculations." *Slate,* September 9, 2003.

Keppel, Gilles. *Jihad: The Trail of Political Islam.* Cambridge, Mass.: Harvard University Press, 2002.

———. *Muslim Extremism in Egypt: The Prophet and the Pharaoh.* Berkeley: University of California Press, 1995.

———. *The War for Muslim Minds: Islam and the West.* Cambridge, Mass.: Harvard University Press, 2004.

Khosrokhavar, Farhad. *Suicide Bombers: Allah's New Martyrs.* Trans. David Macey. London: Pluto, 2002.

Kifner, John. "Israelis Investigate Far Right; May Crack Down on Speech." *The New York Times,* November 8, 1995.

Korn, David A. *Assassination in Khartoum.* Bloomington: Indiana University Press, 1993.

Krueger, Alan, and Jitka Maleckova. "Does Poverty Cause Terrorism?" *The New Republic,* June 24, 2004.

———. "Education, Poverty, Political Violence and Terrorism: Is There a Causal Connection?" *NBER* Working Paper no. 9074. Cambridge, Mass.: National Bureau of Economic Research, 2002.

Krumwiede, Heinrich-W., and Peter Walelmann (eds.). *Civil Wars: Consequences and Possibilities for Regulation.* Baden-Baden: Nomos Verlagsgesellschaft, 2000.

———. *Voices of Terror.* New York: Reed, 2004.

Laqueur, Walter. *No End to War: Terrorism in the Twenty-First Century.* New York: Continuum, 2003.

Lawrence, Bruce (ed.). *Messages to the World: The Statements of Osama bin Laden.* New York: Verso, 2005.

"Letter from al-Zawahiri to al Zarqawi." Washington, D.C.: Office of the Director of National Intelligence, October 11, 2005. Available on the Web site of the Director of National Intelligence, www.dni.gov/Privacy_Security_Notice.html, page accessed May 17, 2006.

Lewis, Bernard. *The Assassins.* New York: Basic Books, 2002.

———. *What Went Wrong?: Western Impact and Middle Eastern Response.* Oxford: Oxford University Press, 2002.

Lyons, F. S. L. *Ireland Since the Famine.* Glasgow: Collins/Fontana, 1973.

Mac Stiofain, Sean. *Memoirs of a Revolutionary.* Edinburgh: Gordon Cremonesi, 1975.

"The Madrid Agenda." Madrid: Club de Madrid, March 11, 2005. Available at english.safe-democracy.org/agenda/the-madrid-agenda.html, page accessed May 17, 2006.

Malka, Haim. "Must Innocents Die? The Islamic Debate over Suicide Attacks." *Middle East Quarterly,* Spring 2003. Available at www.meforum.org/article530.

Mandela, Nelson. *Long Walk to Freedom.* Boston: Little, Brown, 1994.

Margalit, Avishai. "The Suicide Bombers." *The New York Review of Books,* January 16, 2003.

Marighella, Carlos. *Minimanual of the Urban Guerrilla.* Montreal: Abraham Guillen Press 2002.

Marx/Engels Collected Works (MECW), vol. 42; *Marx-Engels Correspondence 1867.* London: Lawrence & Wishart, 1975–2005.

McDermot, Terry. *Perfect Soldiers: The Hijackers: Who They Were, Why They Did It.* New York: HarperCollins, 2005.

McIntyre, Jamie. "Zubaydah: Al Qaeda Had 'Dirty Bomb' Know-How." *CNN,* 22 April 2002. Available on the CNN Web site, www.cnn.com/2002/us/04/22/zubaydah.dirty.bomb, page accessed May 17, 2006.

McWethy, John. "Bin Laden Set to Strike Again?" ABC News, June 16, 1999.

Merari, Ariel. "Social, Organizational and Psychological Factors in Suicide Terrorism." In *Root Causes of Terrorism: Myths, Reality and Ways Forward,* ed. Tore Bjorgo. New York: Routledge, 2005.

Miller, Judith. "Labs Suggest Qaeda Planned to Build Arms, Officials Say." *The New York Times,* September 14, 2002.

———. "US Has New Concerns About Anthrax Readiness." *The New York Times,* December 28, 2003.

Mir, Hamid. "Osama Claims He Has Nukes: If US Used Narms It Will Get Same Response." *Dawn* (Pakistan), November 10, 2001.

Moloney, Ed. *A Secret History of the IRA.* New York: W.W. Norton, 2002.

Moody, T. W. (ed.). *The Fenian Movement.* Cork: Learning Links, 1978.

Mueller, John, and Karl Mueller. "Sanctions of Mass Destruction." *Foreign Affairs,* 78, no. 3 (1999): pp. 43–53.

Nathan, Adam, and David Leppard. "Al Qaeda's Men Held Secret Meetings to Build a Dirty Bomb." *Sunday Times* (London), October 14, 2001.

Neumann, Peter R. *Britain's Long War: British Strategy in the Northern Irish Conflict, 1969–1998.* New York: Palgrave, 2003.

9/11 Commission Report: Final Report of the National Commission on Terrorist Attacks Upon the United States (Official Edition). Washington, D.C.: Claitor's Law Books and Publishers Division, July 22, 2004.

Nunca Mas (Report by Argentina's National Commission on Disappeared People). Buenos Aires: Faber & Faber, 1986.

O'Boyle, Garrett. "Theories of Justification and Political Violence: Examples from Four Groups." *Terrorism and Political Violence,* 14, no. 2 (Summer 2002): 32.

O'Malley, Padraig. *Biting at the Grave: The Irish Hunger Strikes and the Politics of Despair.* Boston: Beacon Press, 1990.

"Omar Sheikh's Diaries." *The Indian Express,* October 11, 2001.

Olimpio, Guido. "Islamic Group Said Preparing Chemical Warfare on the West." *Corriere della Sera,* July 8, 1998.

Oliver, Anne Marie, and Paul Steinberg. *The Road to Martyrs' Square: A Journey into the World of the Suicide Bomber.* Oxford: Oxford University Press, 2005.

Organization of American States, Inter-American Commission on Human Rights. "Report on the Situation of Human Rights in Argentina." Washington, D.C., 1980.

Pape, Robert A. *Dying to Win: The Strategic Logic of Suicide Terrorism.* New York: Random House, 2005.

———. "The Strategic Logic of Suicide Terrorism." *American Political Science Review,* 97 (2003): 343–361.

Patterns of Global Terrorism 1999. Washington, D.C.: U.S. Department of State, April 2000.

Patterns of Global Terrorism 2000. Washington, D.C.: U.S. Department of State, April 2001.

Patterns of Global Terrorism 2001. Washington, D.C.: U.S. Department of State, April 2002.

Patterns of Terrorist Violence 2002. Washington, D.C.: U.S. Department of State, April 2003.

Patterns of Terrorist Violence 2003. Washington, D.C.: U.S. Department of State, April 2004.

Pearse, Padraic H. *Political Writings and Speeches.* Dublin: Talbot Press, 1966.

Pipes, Daniel. "Arafat's Suicide Factory." *New York Post,* December 9, 2001.

Post, Jerrold M. "Notes on a Psychodynamic Theory of Terrorist Behavior." *Terrorism: An International Journal*, 7, no. 3 (1984): 242–256.

———. "The Socio-cultural Underpinnings of Terrorist Psychology: When Hatred Is Bred in the Bone." In *Root Causes of Terrorism: Myths, Reality and Ways Forward*, ed. Tore Bjorgo. New York: Routledge, 2005.

———, et al. "The Terrorists in Their Own Words: Interviews with 35 Incarcerated Middle Eastern Terrorists." *Terrorism and Political Violence* 15, no. 1 (Spring 2003): 176.

Prendergast, Alan. "A Simple Case: How a Drunk Driving Fatality Got Lost in the System," September 25, 2003. Available on the Westword Web site, www .westword.com/issues/2003-09-25/news/news.html, page accessed May 17, 2006.

Quinlivan, Patrick, and Paul Rose. *The Fenians in England, 1865–1872*. London: John Calder, 1982.

Rapoport, David C. "Fear and Trembling: Terrorism in Three Religious Traditions." *American Political Science Review* 78, no. 3 (1984): 658–677.

———. *Inside Terrorist Organizations*. New York: Columbia University Press, 1988.

———. "Terrorism and Weapons of the Apocalypse." *National Security Studies Quarterly* 5, no. 3 (1999): 57.

Rashid, Ahmed. *Taliban: Militant Islam, Oil and Fundamentalism in Central Asia*. New Haven, Conn.: Yale University Press, 2001.

Raufer, Zavier. "The Red Brigades: A Farewell to Arms." *Studies in Conflict and Terrorism* 16 (1993): 315–325.

Reader, Ian. *Religious Violence in Contemporary Japan: The Case of Aum Shinrikyo*. Honolulu: University of Hawaii Press, 2000.

Reagan, Ronald. *An American Life*. New York: Simon and Schuster, 1990.

Reich, Walter (ed.). *Origins of Terrorism Psychologies, Ideologies, Theologies, States of Mind*. Washington, D.C.: Woodrow Wilson Center Press, 1998.

Ressa, Maria. "Reports al Qaeda Operative Sought Anthrax." CNN, October 10, 2003. Available on the CNN Web site, edition.cnn.com/2003/world/asiapcf/ southeast/10/10/alqaeda.anthrax/, page accessed May 17, 2006.

Reuter, Christoph. *My Life Is a Weapon*. Trans. Helena Ragg Kirkby. Princeton, N.J.: Princeton University Press, 2004.

Richardson, Louise. "Blasts from the Past." *Financial Times*, July 5, 2005: 26–7.

———. "Britain and the IRA." In *Democracy and Counter-terrorism: Lessons from the Past*, eds. Robert Art and Louise Richardson. Washington, D.C.: USIP, 2006.

———. "Buying Biosafety: Is the Price Right?" *New England Journal of Medicine*, May 20, 2004, pp. 2121–23.

———. "How Terrorist Campaigns End; Lessons from War Termination." Paper delivered at the International Studies Association Conference, New Orleans, La., March 2002.

———. "State Sponsorship: A Root Cause of Terrorism?" In *Root Causes of Terrorism: Myths, Reality and Ways Forward*, ed. Tore Bjorgo. London: Routledge, 2005.

Ridden, May. "With Poison in Their Souls." *The Observer* (London), April 17, 2005.

Roberts, Gwynne. "Militia Defector Claims Baghdad Trained al Qaeda Fighters in Chemical Warfare." *The Sunday Times* (London), July 14, 2002.

Rojas, Guillermo (ed.). "30,000 desaparecidos: realidad, mito y dogma: historia verdera y manipulación ideológica." Buenos Aires: Santiago Apostol, 2003.

Rubenstein, Richard E. *Alchemists of Revolution: Terrorism in the Modern World.* New York: Basic Books, 1987.

Rubin, Barry, and Judith Colp Rubin (eds.). *Anti-American Terrorism and the Middle East.* Oxford: Oxford University Press, 2002.

Sageman, Marc. *Understanding Terror Networks.* Philadelphia: University of Pennsylvania Press, 2004.

Salah, Muhammad. "Bin Laden Front Reportedly Bought CBW from E. Europe." *Al-Hayah,* April 20, 1999.

———. "US Said [to Be] Interrogating Jihadist over CBW." *Al-Hayah,* April 21, 1999.

Sayle, Murray. "Nerve Gas and Four Noble Truths." *The New Yorker,* April 1, 1996.

Schalk, P. "Resistance and Martyrdom on the Process of State Formation in Tamililam." In *Martyrdom and Political Resistance,* ed. J. Pettigrew. Amsterdam: VU University Press, 1997.

Schmid, Alex P., and Ronald Crelinsten (eds.). *Western Responses to Terrorism.* London: Frank Cass, 1993.

Silj, Alessandro. *Never Again Without a Rifle: The Origins of Italian Terrorism.* Trans. Salvator Attanasio. New York: Karz, 1979.

Silke, Andrew (ed.). *Research on Terrorism: Trends, Achievements and Failures.* London: Frank Cass, 2004.

———. *Terrorists Victims Society: Psychological perspectives on Terrorism and Its Consequences.* London: Wiley, 2003.

Sleeman, J. L. *Thugs; or a Million Murders.* London: S. Low and Marston, 1933.

Sleeman, W. H. *The Thugs or Phansigars of India.* Philadelphia: Carey and Hart, 1839.

Smith, Morton. "Zealots and Sicarii, Their Origins and Religion." *Harvard Theological Review* 64, no. 1 (January 1971): 1–19.

Stern, Jessica. *Terror in the Name of God: Why Religious Militants Kill.* New York: HarperCollins, 2003.

———. *The Ultimate Terrorists.* Cambridge, Mass.: Harvard University Press, 1999.

Stern, Steve J. *Shining and Other Paths: War and Society in Peru, 1980–1995.* Durham, N.C.: Duke University Press, 1998.

Strickland, Matthew. *War and Chivalry: The Conduct and Perception of War in England and Normandy, 1066–1217.* Cambridge, England: Cambridge University Press, 1996.

Sun-tzu, sixth century B.C. *The Art of War*. Trans. R. L. Wing. *The Art of Strategy: A New Translation of Sun Tzu's Classic* The Art of War. New York: Doubleday, 1998.

Swamy, M. R. Narayan. *Inside an Elusive Mind: Prabhakaran*. Delhi: Konark, 2003.

Szabo, Stephen F. *Parting Ways: The Crisis in German-American Relations*. Washington, D.C.: Brookings, 2004.

"Tamil National Leader Hon. V. Pirapaharan's Interview." *The Week* (India), March 23, 1986. Available on the LTTE Web site, www.eepam.com/interviews/LEADER_MARCH_86_html, page accessed July 30, 2005.

Taylor, Max, and Edith Quayle. *Terrorist Lives*. London: Brassey's, 1994.

Taylor, Maxwell. *The Terrorist*. London: Brassey's, 1988.

Taylor, Maxwell, and John Horgan (eds.). *The Future of Terrorism*. London: Frank Cass, 2000.

Taylor, Peter. *Behind the Mask: The IRA and Sinn Fein*. New York: TV Books, 1997.

———. *Loyalists: War and Peace in Northern Ireland*. New York: TV Books, 1999.

Taylor, Richard Norton. "Ricin Plot: London and Washington Used Plot to Strengthen Iraq War Push." *The Guardian* (London), April 14, 2005.

Templeton, Tom, and Tom Lumley. "9/11 in Numbers." *The Observer* (London), August 18, 2002.

Tizghart, Uthman. "Does bin Laden Really Possess Weapons of Mass Destruction? Tale of Russian Mafia Boss Simon Mogilevich Who Supplied Bin Laden with the Nuclear 'Dirty Bomb.' " *Al-Majallah* (London), November 25, 2001.

Toner, Mike. "Humble Bean Produces a Deadly Toxin." Fox News Service, March 20, 2003.

Toolis, Kevin. *Rebel Hearts: Journeys Within the IRA's Soul*. New York: St. Martin's Press, 1995.

Torabi, Emil. "Bin Laden's Nuclear Weapons." *Muslim Magazine*, Winter 1998; www.muslimmag.com (no longer available).

Tout, T. F. *The History of England from the Accession of Henry III to the Death of Edward III (1216–1377)*. London: Longmans, Green, 1905.

Tucker, Jonathan B. (ed.). *Toxic Terror: Assessing Terrorist Use of Chemical and Biological Weapons*. Cambridge, Mass.: MIT Press, 2000.

Tucker, Robert C. *Marx-Engels Reader*. New York: Norton, 1972.

Venter, A. J. "Elements Loyal to bin Laden Acquire Biological Agents 'Through the Mail.' " *Intelligence Review*, August 1999.

Victor, Barbara. *Army of Roses: Inside the World of Palestinian Women Suicide Bombers*. New York: Rodale (St. Martin's), 2003.

Waldman, Amy. "Masters of Suicide Bombing: Tamil Guerrillas of Sri Lanka." *The New York Times*, January 14, 2003.

Warrick, Joby. "An al Qaeda 'Chemist' and the Quest for Ricin." *The Washington Post*, May 5, 2004.

Washington, George. *The Writings of George Washington from the Original Manu-script Sources.* Vol. 7, *1745–1799.* Charlottesville, Va.: Electronic Text Center, University of Virginia Library.

Weinberg, Leonard. "Turning to Terror: The Conditions Under Which Political Parties Turn to Terrorist Activities." *Comparative Politics,* 23, no. 4 (July 1991): 423–438.

Weiser, Benjamin. "US Says bin Laden Aide Tried to Get Nuclear Weapons." *The New York Times,* September 26, 1998.

Whitelaw, William. *Whitelaw Memoirs.* London: Anrum Press, 1989.

Wieviorka, Michel. *The Making of Terrorism.* Chicago: University of Chicago Press, 1988.

Wilkinson, Paul. *Terrorism Versus Democracy: The Liberal State Response.* London: Frank Cass, 2001.

The World Factbook. Washington, D.C.: CIA. Available on the CIA Web site, www.cia.gov/cia/pubications/factbook/fields/2129.html, page accessed February 5, 2006.

Zoroya, Gregg. "Woman Describes the Mentality of a Suicide Bomber." *USA Today,* April 22, 2002.

INDEX

Abbot, Minnie, 22
Abdullah, King of Jordan, 175
Abu Aisha, Darine, 123
Abu Ghraib scandal, 179
Abu Sayyaf Group, 11
Abu Shanab, Ismail, 60
Abu-Surur, 88, 130
Abu Zubayda, 164
Action Directe, 11, 41, 76
Action for National Liberation (ALN), 101, 183–84
Adams, Gerry, 78, 99, 229
Aden, 65, 185
Afghanistan, 64, 133
    al-Qaeda's loss of sanctuary in, 158, 159, 167, 180, 233
    Islamic militants in, 54, 66, 145, 164–65, 166, 177
    postwar reconstruction in, 227
    Soviet invasion and war in, 65–66, 103, 145, 192, 229
    U.S. policy in, 18, 52, 54, 55, 92, 157, 174, 175–76, 179–80, 197, 204, 229, 234–35

WMD labs in, 153, 154, 156, 158, 161–62, 163
Africa, 56, 61
African National Congress (ANC), 8–9, 53, 54
airplanes, 167–68
    as bombs, xviii–xix, 124
    hijackings of, 17, 64, 76, 77, 106
Akhras, Ayat al-, 123, 130
al-Aqsa Martyrs Brigades, 15, 113, 117, 120–21, 122, 130
Albrecht, Susanne, 46
Alexander II, Tsar of Russia, 34
al-Fatah, 7, 96, 120, 121, 230
al-Gama'a al-Islamiyya (Islamic Group), 49, 57, 228
Algeria, Algerians, 49, 58, 118, 156, 163
alienation, 35, 40–41, 61, 69, 78–79, 141, 186, 198–99, 216
al-Jazeera, 43, 44, 93, 128, 132, 160–61
Allende, Salvador, 52, 183

al-Qaeda, xx, 4, 44–47, 58–59,
    99–101, 145, 171, 212–15, 222,
    227, 229
  Afghanistan sanctuary lost by, 158,
    159, 167, 180, 233
  bin Laden's relationship with, xxi,
    45–46
  Bush's views on, 149, 184
  goals of, 81, 197, 213, 218
  groups linked to, 77, 83, 191,
    214–15
  Iraq linked with, xix, 154, 166, 167,
    170, 189–92, 215, 218
  Islamic fundamentalism of, 49, 120
  and morality of terrorism, 18–19
  Padilla's links with, 163, 211
  renown of, 94–95, 97, 197
  state sponsorship and, 53, 54
  suicide bombing by, 105, 106, 113,
    118, 120, 184–85
  U.S. counterterrorism and, 175–76,
    177, 179–80, 189–98, 208–9,
    213, 214–15, 218–19, 232–37
  in war of ideas, 217–19
  WMDs and, 148, 153–54, 156–67
  see also bin Laden, Osama;
    September 11 attacks
al-Qaeda Europe, 105, 132–33
al-Qassam, 16, 126, 128
al-Shifa Pharmaceutical Factory, 153
Amal movement, 230
American Revolution, xiii, 1, 207
Amir, Yigal, 62
Amrozoi (bomber), 222
anarchism, 25, 32, 34–36, 172
Angola, 54
Ansar al-Islam, 118, 158
Ansar al-Sunna, 118
anthrax, 154–58, 227
"Antxon" (ETA leader), 79
Arab Americans, 193, 206
Arab-Israeli peace efforts, 62, 226
Arabs, 10, 26, 56, 232
Arafat, Yasser, 1, 7, 21, 47, 120, 121

Arendt, Hannah, 75
Argentina, 46, 182–83, 184
Arivuchcholai, Kantharuban, 111
Arnett, Peter, 63, 86
Asahara, Shoko, 45, 47, 152
Ashe, Thomas, 116
Assad, Hafez al-, 120–21
Assassins, 15, 23, 25–27, 33, 107
Atta, Mohamed, 47, 56, 118, 157, 190
audience, 5, 36, 141–42
Aum Shinrikyo, xxi, 11, 45, 47, 76,
    160
  Tokyo subway attack by, 62, 95, 151,
    152–53, 155, 158
Austria, 237
Azhar, Maulana Masood, 78
Aznar, José María, 133

Baader, Andreas, 46
Baader-Meinhof Gang (Red Army
    Faction; RAF), 11, 16–17, 41, 48,
    76, 89, 211, 213, 225
  biological weapons of, 155
  leaders and followers in, 46–47
  Marxism-Leninism of, 49, 82
Bahrain, 53
Bakunin, Mikhail, 31, 32, 34
Barayev, Movzar, 83
Barrett, Michael, 22, 201–2, 238
Basayev, Shamil, 4, 6, 9, 83, 87, 98
Basque Nationalist Party, 229
Basques, 8, 13, 49, 56, 224
  see also ETA
Baumann, Bommi, 170
Baumann, Michael, 42
Becker, Jillian, 48
Begin, Menachem, 10
Beirut, 65, 112–13
Belfast, 8, 49, 91, 97
Belgium, 41, 76, 212
Benchellali, Menad, 156
Bergen, Peter, 47
Berlin bombing, 51
Betancourt, Rómulo, 210

bin al-Shibh, Ramzi, 18–19
bin Laden, Osama, 3, 7–8, 9, 30, 35,
    43–47, 54, 99–100, 141, 176, 179,
    194–98, 200, 219, 229
  on American cowardice, 65, 99, 131
  on American responsibility, 6, 17–18
  background of, 47, 58
  on causes, 38, 40, 43–45
  fatwas of, 16, 65, 83, 84, 171
  goals of, 63, 84–85, 86
  Hussein linked to, xix, 166, 189–92
  as leader, xxi, 45–46, 47, 214, 223
  on morality of terrorism, 4, 16–19
  Muslim humiliation and, 102–3
  renown of, 95–98
  revenge and, 43, 91–92
  on Twin Towers, 5, 77, 144–45
  wealth of, 47, 56, 58–59
  WMDs and, 153–54, 159, 161–64
  Zarqawi's links to, 191, 214–15
biological weapons, 151, 153–61, 165,
    226–27
Birds of Freedom, 109
Black and Tans, xiii–xiv
Black September Palestinians, 17, 78
Black Tigers, 109–12, 124
Black Tigresses, 109, 110
"Black Widows," 128
Blair, Tony, 156–57, 230–31
Blanqui, Auguste, 31
blister agents, 151
blood agents, 151
  see also cyanide
Bloody Friday, 91
Bloody Sunday massacre (1972), xiv,
    89–90, 91, 187
Boer War, 213
bombing, 15, 101
  see also suicide bombing; specific
    sites
Bosnia, 42, 238
botulinum toxin, 155, 157, 158
Bradford, John, xii
Branch Davidians, 76

Brazil, 46, 101, 179, 183–84, 199
Brehon law, 115–16
Bright, John, 201
British Army, 73, 89, 90, 97, 186–88,
    207
Bulgaria, 78, 155
Burke, T. H., 33
Burns, Lizzy, 32
Bush, George W., 15, 44, 149, 194–96,
    221, 233
  on freedom, 137, 139, 146, 195–96
  on principles, 206
  on September 11 attacks, 3, 54–55,
    146, 167, 191
  transformation of, 168
  war declared by, 170, 174–79, 184
  WMDs and, 159

Cagol, Mara, 79–80, 239
caliphate, restoration of, 80, 85, 209,
    218
Callaghan, James, 186
Campbell, Lord, 139
Camus, Albert, 16
Canada, 33, 174
Carlos (The Jackal), 96
Carter, Jimmy, 65, 101
Castro, Fidel, 52
"Catechism of the Revolution"
    (Nechayev), 79
Cavendish, Lord Frederick, 33
CCC, 41, 76
Chechens, Chechnya, 4, 13, 49, 83, 95,
    180–81, 213–14, 238–39
  female suicide bombers in, 120, 128
  WMDs and, 156, 161, 163
chemical weapons, 151 54, 156,
    158–61, 164, 165
  in Iran-Iraq War, 159, 166
  "loose," 226–27
  types of, 151–52
  in World War I, 151, 159
Cheney, Dick, 144, 190
Chichester-Clark, James, 186

children, killing of, 16, 18, 22, 37, 128, 181, 219–20, 230
Chile, 52, 183, 184
Christianity, 23, 195
  see also Irish Catholics; Protestants
Churchill, Winston, 185
CIA, 142, 144, 145
Civil War, U.S., xiii, 13, 33, 143, 155
Clan na Gael (Irish Family), 33
Clarke, Richard, 189
Clarke, Terence (Cheeky), 78, 81
Clerkenwell explosion, 21–22, 31–32, 139, 200–202
CNN, 86
Cold War, 51, 148, 150, 159, 173
Collins, Eamon, 49, 102
Colombia, 205
  see also FARC
colonialism, 1, 143, 185
Committee of Public Safety, 29
communism, 148, 155, 225, 230, 238
Communist Party, Italian, 229, 230
Communist Party, Nepalese, 11, 49, 76
Communist Party of the Philippines, see New People's Army
communities, 11, 13–14, 228
  humiliation of, 102
  terrorists isolated from, 48–49, 215–24, 232
  see also enabling communities
Congress, U.S., 170–71
conservatives, 40, 56, 189
Contras, Nicaraguan, 7, 51–52
Cooperative Threat Reduction (CTR), 227
Corporation for Reparation and Reconciliation, 183
counterterrorism, xii, xix–xx, xxii, 36, 137–239
  coercion vs. conciliation in, 205–6
  conflation of al-Qaeda and Hussein as mistake of, 170, 189–92
  defensible and achievable goal for, 203–6

education of Americans as missed opportunity in, 170, 193–99
  engaging others in, 224–31
  knowledge of enemy in, 208–15
  and living by principles, 206–8, 220–21, 233–34
  multilateral, 224–31
  patience and perspective in, 231–33
  public resilience and, 148
  separating terrorists from their communities in, 215–24, 232
  six rules for, 203–33
  suicide bombings and, 106
  understanding the appeal of terrorism in, xx, 40
  U.S. current standing in, 233–37
  U.S. declaration of war against terrorism in, 170–88, 194
  U.S. failure to mobilize international community in, 170, 192–93
  U.S. learning from the experience of other countries in, xxii
counterterrorism, goals of, 217, 233–34
  defensible and achievable, 203–6
crusades, 194–95
Cuba, 51, 52
Cullison, Alan, 154
Curcio, Renato, 42–43, 79, 80
cyanide, 151, 153, 154, 158
"cyberterrorism," use of term, 4
Cyprus, 185
Czech Republic, 157

Daraghmeh, Hiba, 123
Dar es Salaam, U.S. embassy bombed in, 59, 153
Death of a Nation (movie), 42
"Declaration of a State of War, A" (1970), 171–72
Declaration of Independence, U.S., xiii
Declaration of War (1996 fatwa), 16, 65, 171
Defense Department, U.S., 177, 207, 223

Deir Yassin, 10
Della Porta, Donatella, 42
democracy, xxii, 9–10, 50, 51, 67, 85,
    137, 206, 207, 220–21, 234, 237
  definition of terrorism and, 8
  problem of coordinating
      counterterrorist strategies in,
      204–5
  radical Islamic group's use of, xxi
  reaction and, 99–101
  September 11 attacks and, 146, 147
Democratic Party, U.S., 65, 156
Dershowitz, Alan, 75
deterrence, 106, 148, 164
Dev Sol, 82–83
"Dinner Party Tape," 92
DIRCOTE, xx–xxi, 210
dirty bombs, 162–63, 165
Dohrn, Bernardine, 171–72
Donahue, Laura, 206
Dostoevsky, Fyodor M., xi
Dublin, xiii–xiv, xv, 74
  Phoenix Park murders in, 33
Dunant, Henri, 177–78
Dviri, Manuela, 122

Easter Rising (1916), xii–xiii, 116
Ebola virus, 157, 227
Egypt, 47, 53, 56, 57, 58, 60, 100, 145,
    157, 229–30
  al-Gama'a al-Islamiyya in, 49, 57,
      228
Eid, Guy, 78
Elizabeth, Empress of Austria, 36
enabling communities, xxii, 13–14, 48,
    49, 69, 213, 216
  suicide bombings and, 106, 112, 115
Encyclopedia of Jihad, The (al-Qaeda
    manual), 157
"enemy combatant," 178–79
Engels, Friedrich, 31–32
EOKA, 169, 185
ERP (People's Revolutionary Army),
    46, 182

Escudero Bedate, Mansur, 229
ETA (Euskadi ta Askatasuna), 8, 48,
    76, 79, 82, 99, 229
ethnonationalist terrorist conference,
    xvi–xvii
Evans, Martha, 22

Fadl, Jamal Ahmad al-, 59, 161
FALN, 210
Fanon, Frantz, 30, 143
FARC (Fuerzas Armadas
    Revolucionarias de Colombia), 46,
    58, 124
  goals of, 82, 86–87
Fassnacht, Robert, 172
Fenians, 31–34, 37, 200–202
Finucane, Dermot, 72–74, 176
Finucane, John, 72, 73, 176
Finucane, Martin, 72–73
Finucane, Pat, 72, 74
Finucane, Rosie, 73
Finucane, Seamus, 73, 238
Finucane family, 42, 72–74
Fischer, David, 207
Fort Detrick, Md., Level 4 lab at,
    156
France, 25, 173, 227
  Action Directe in, 11, 41, 76
  Basques in, 224, 226
  biological weapons in, 155, 156
  counterterrorism in, 108, 205, 210,
      226
  Hague embassy seizure and, 77–78
  Iraq war and, 174, 192
  Lebanon's relations with, 65, 83,
      112–13, 131
  Muslims in, 149, 212, 225, 238
Franco, Francisco, 8
Franklin, Benjamin, xii–xiii, 206
freedom, 137, 139, 146–47, 195–96,
    206, 207
freedom fighters, 6–10
French and Indian War, 155
French Revolution, 23, 29–30

fundamentalism, 76
  Islamic, 17, 49, 53, 63–69, 77, 97,
    120, 126, 220

Gadallah, Suhad, 122
Gandhi, Rajiv, 108
Gaza, 49, 57, 117, 128, 210, 231
  culture of martyrdom in, 97, 107
  Israeli pullout from, 228
General Accounting Office, U.S., 227
Geneva Conventions, 177–78, 207,
    234, 236
Georgia, 156, 158
German Ideology, The (Marx), 85
Germany, 42, 48, 161, 227
  Iraq war and, 173, 174, 192
  Muslims in, 149, 212, 237
  revenge as motive in, 89, 94
  see also Baader-Meinhof Gang
Ghamidi, Ahmad al-Haznawi al-, 103
Ghosh, Aparisim, 119
GIA (Groupe Islamique Armé), 49,
    210
"Giants, The" (video), 127, 130
Gilmore, Raymond, 81
Gladstone, William Ewart, 200–203
globalization, 57, 60, 144, 232
Glover, J. M., 187–88
Gonzales, Alberto, 178
"Gonzalo Thought," 96
Good Friday Agreement (1998), 213,
    214
GRAPO, 13, 82–83, 89
Great Britain, 10, 25, 33, 108, 185–88,
    200–204, 218, 226
  in Afghanistan, 133, 180
  American Revolution and, 1, 207
  Bloody Sunday and, xiv, 89–90, 91,
    187
  intelligence of, 210, 214
  IRA bombings in, 95, 96, 97
  IRA meetings with, 98–99, 177, 212,
    214
  in Iraq War, 80–81, 133

Ireland ruled by, xiii–xv, 31, 49, 78,
    81, 98–99, 116, 176
  moderates mobilized by, 229
  Muslims in, 149, 212, 237–38
  September 11 attacks and, 142, 173
  Thugi and, 27, 28
  U.S. relations with, 51
  view of U.S. in, 174, 192
  WMDs and, 155, 156–57, 163
  see also British Army; London
Greece, 17 November in, 13, 82–83
Grivas, George, 169, 185
guerrillas, 6–10, 16, 183
Gulf War, first, 189
Guzmán, Abimael, 4, 58, 86, 210
  identification and, 42–43
  as leader, xx–xxi, 45, 46
  renown of, 96, 98

Habash, George, 47
Hague, The, French Embassy seized in,
    77–78
Haifa, 10, 128, 131
Halabja, chemical weapons used in,
    152, 166
Halliday, Fred, 220
Hamas, 24, 44, 53, 57, 60, 76, 194,
    230
  background of leaders of, 47
  and morality of terrorism, 16, 19
  suicide bombing of, 113, 117,
    121–22, 124, 125–26, 130
  Yassin's assassination and, 92
Hanif, Assaf Mohammed, 68
Harakat ul-Mujahidin (HUM), 77, 78,
    83
Harris poll, 147
Harvard University, xi, xv–xviii
Hassan, Nasra, 16, 18
"hearts and minds," 218
Hebron, 89, 127
Heinzen, Karl, 31
Henry V (Shakespeare), 72
Herri Batasuna, 229

Hezbollah, 11, 47, 57, 76, 181–82
    goals of, 83–84
    state sponsorship of, 53, 54, 64, 181, 225
    suicide bombings of, 64–65, 111–14, 125
    tactics of, 64–65
hijackings, 17, 64, 76, 77, 106
Hill, Peter, 114
Hindi, al- (suicide bomber), 130
Hindi, Suhail al-, 88
Hinduism, 23, 27–28
Hiroshima, bombing of, 5, 18, 36, 165, 220
Hitler, Adolf, 30, 36
Hitler's Children (Becker), 48
Horace, 104
Horani, Zaid, 93
hostages, 64, 77, 78, 101, 218
House of Commons, British, 34, 201
Howard, Michael, 177
Howe, Lord, 207
How It All Began (Baumann), 42
human-wave attacks, 112
Hume, John, 229
humiliation, 102–3, 123, 127
hunger strikes, 19, 89, 115–17, 176
Hussain, Hasib, 80, 132, 134
Hussain, Nasser, 38
Hussein, Saddam, 18, 112, 118, 119, 219
    al-Qaeda linked with, xix, 166, 167, 170, 189–92
    chemical weapons used by, 152, 166
    U.S. WMD fears and, 160, 166, 167, 189

identification with others, 39, 41, 42–43, 67–68
Idris, Mabrook, 130
Idris, Salah, 153
Idris, Wafa, 120–21, 123, 129, 130
India, 39, 60, 179, 238
    counterterrorism in, 203, 205, 211, 229
    Kashmir dispute and, 13, 83, 220, 224
    Sikh terrorism in, 56, 203, 211, 225, 229
    suicide bombing in, 107–8
Indian Airlines Airbus IC-814, 77
Indonesia, 60, 179, 192, 222–23
    suicide bombing in, 107–8
intelligence, 208–15
Inter-American Bank, 226
Internet, 47–48, 134, 157, 217–18
Invincibles, 33–34
IRA (Irish Republican Army), xiv–xv, xvi, 14, 17, 32, 45, 46, 48, 49, 67–68, 72–76, 102, 142, 225, 229
    bombings by, 8, 42, 61, 95, 97, 202
    British intelligence about, 210, 211
    British meetings with, 98–99
    disarmament deal and, 177, 231
    goals of, 78, 81, 82, 176, 213
    hunger strikes of, 19, 89, 115–17, 176
    Provisional, 76, 83, 177, 185–88
    renown of, 95, 96, 97
    revenge and, 89–91
Iran, 5, 60, 112
    human-wave attacks and, 112
    revolution in (1979), 23, 29, 52–53, 64, 65
    suicide bombers influenced by, 112, 113, 114
    terrorism sponsored by, 51–54, 64, 181, 225
    U.S. arms-for-hostage deal with, 64
    U.S. hostage crisis in, 64, 101
Iran, Shah of, 42, 64
Iran-Iraq War, 112, 159, 166
Iraq, 5, 18, 51, 57, 78, 133, 238–39
    al-Qaeda linked with, xix, 154, 166, 167, 170, 189–92, 215, 218
    British in, 80–81

Iraq (*cont.*)
    chemical weapons used by, 152, 159,
        166
    hostage taking in, 78
    Kurds in, 152, 166, 224
    Shiite groups in, 53
    suicide bombing in, 105, 106, 109,
        118–20
    U.S. in, 49, 53, 55, 93, 118, 119,
        132, 133, 154, 157, 168, 173,
        174, 189–93, 197, 204, 218,
        224, 225, 234, 235–36
    U.S. sanctions against, 84, 92, 219
    WMDs and, 152, 154, 157, 160,
        166, 167, 189
Ireland, xii–xvi, 60, 116, 224, 226
    unity of, 82
    see also IRA; Northern Ireland
Irgun, 10
Irish Americans, 33, 225
Irish Catholics, xii, xv, 17, 56, 61,
        72–74, 89–91, 102, 186–87, 224
    Bloody Sunday and, xiv, 89–90
    hunger strikes and, 117
Irish Home Rule Party, 32–33
Irish nationalists, 32–34
Irish Republican Brotherhood (IRB),
        32–33
Islam, Muslims, 13, 18–19, 23, 41, 43,
        97–100, 193, 194, 197
    as cause of terrorism, 40, 61–69
    in Chechnya, 83
    in Europe, 61, 149, 212, 237–38
    fundamentalism and, 17, 49, 53,
        63–69, 77, 97, 120, 126, 220
    humiliation of, 102–3
    radical, xxi, 26, 59, 133, 145, 204,
        205, 209, 212, 217, 238; *see
        also specific groups*
    Shia, 26–27, 53, 64, 66, 76, 113,
        130, 218
    suicide bombings and, 19, 64–65, 88,
        107–8, 112–14, 118–34
    Sunni, 66, 113, 114

    in U.S., 61, 149, 212
Islamic Commission of Spain, 229
Islamic Group, *see* al-Gama'a al-
    Islamiyya
Islamic International Peacekeeping
    Brigade (IIPB), 83
Israel, 10, 30, 44, 57, 67, 89, 93, 161,
        194, 209, 230, 232
    Hezbollah and, 64, 83, 84, 181–82,
        230
    intelligence of, 210, 211–12
    Iran's activities against, 52, 53
    and morality of terrorism, 17, 18, 19
    Olympic team of, 17, 77
    suicide bombers and, 113, 114, 118,
        120–23, 125, 128, 130, 131–32
    U.S. relations with, 35, 43–44, 64,
        77, 84, 147, 197
    and winning wars vs. battles, 180,
        181–82, 185
    Yassin assassination and, 47, 92
Italian Communist Party, 229, 230
Italy, 36, 42, 154, 162, 205
    revenge in, 91, 94
    terrorist organizations in, 48
    see also Red Brigades

Jaber, Fayez, 15, 117
Japan, 58, 78, 107, 205
    kamikaze attacks of, 114–15
    Pearl Harbor attacked by, 143, 171
    Red Army in, 11, 77–78, 79, 82
    see also Aum Shinrikyo
Jarrah, Aysel, 139–40
Jarrah, Ziad, 139–40, 239
Jefferson, Thomas, xii–xiii
Jemaah Islamiyah, 158, 222, 238
Jenkins, Brian, 141
Jerusalem, 10, 132, 194
Jews, Judaism, xvii, 10, 23, 24, 30, 49,
        62, 84, 107
jihad, 26, 44, 63, 84, 92, 93, 100, 119,
        121, 176, 217, 221, 222, 232, 239
"Jihad Mosque," 127

Johannesburg, ANC bombings in, 8
Johnson, Lyndon B., 172
Jordan, 56, 57, 93, 100, 179, 192
JRA, 107
Juergensmeyer, Mark, 44, 149
June 2nd Movement, 170
Justes, Les (Camus), 16
Justice Department, U.S., 163

Kach group, 228
Kali, 27–28
kamikaze attacks, 114–15
Kantharuban Arivuchcholai orphanage,
    111
Kashmir, 13, 39, 83, 220, 224, 226,
    238–39
Kazakhstan, 161
Kennedy, John F., 221
Keppel, Gilles, 47
Kerry, John, 159
Khan, Mohammad Sidique, 80, 104–5,
    132, 133, 134, 176, 239
Khartoum, 78, 153, 161
Khasavyurt Accord, 213–14
Kherchtou, L'Houssaine, 59
Khobar, al-, 65
Khomeini, Ayatollah, 52–53, 64
kidnappings, 39, 64, 78, 95, 96
King, Martin Luther, 85
Kinner, Eddie, 18, 90
Koran, 62, 66, 122, 127, 229
Kumaratunga, Chandrika, 109
Kurdish Workers Party, *see* PKK
Kurds, Kurdistan, 49, 152, 166, 190,
    224, 225, 231
Kuwait, 53, 113, 166, 190

Latin America, 58, 180, 182–85
    poverty-terrorism link and, 56
    rural movements in, 25
leadership, 45–47, 85–86
    charismatic, xx–xxi
Lebanon, 54, 57, 64–65, 76, 180, 192
    civil war in, 112, 113

Israeli intelligence on, 211–12
Israeli invasion of, 43–44, 181–82
suicide bombings in, 65, 112–13,
    121, 125, 130, 131–32
TWA flight 847 hijacking and, 64,
    76, 77
U.S. withdrawal from, 65, 99, 131
    see also Hezbollah
legitimizing ideologies, xxii, 18–19, 49,
    106, 112, 216
    Islam as, 133
    nationalism as, 48, 108, 115, 124,
        126, 130–31, 238
Lenin, V. I., 35, 86
Lewis, Bernard, 102
liberals, 40, 56, 189
Libya, 5, 51
Lima, Japanese Embassy in, 77
Lincoln, Abraham, xii
Lindh, John Walker, 157–58, 211
Lindsay, Germaine, 80
Lod Airport attack (1972), 107
London, 36, 173, 202, 209, 225
    Clerkenwell explosion in, 21–22,
        31–32, 139, 200–202
    Harrods bombing in, 61
    ricin lab in, 156–57, 163
    subway bombings in, 68, 80, 105,
        132–34, 176, 225, 231, 237
"Long Live the Gap" (Richardson), xix
Los Angeles International Airport, 154,
    225
LTTE (Liberation Tigers of Tamil
    Eelam), *see* Tamil Tigers
Luxor attack (1997), 228

McCartney, Raymond, 89–90
McCreesh, Raymond, 102
McGuinness, Martin, 99
Machel, Samora, 53
McKinley, William, 36
Mac Sweeney, Terence, 116
McVeigh, Timothy, 143, 157
Madrid bombing, 133, 209, 229, 237

Mafia, 160, 162

Mahler, Horst, 46

Malaya, 185, 218

Mandela, Nelson, 8–9, 10, 53

Maoism, *see* Nepalese Communist
    Party; New People's Army; Shining
    Path

Marighella, Carlos, 46, 99, 183–84,
    199

Marín, Pedro Antonio (Manuel
    Marulanda Vélez), 46

Marines, U.S., 65, 112–13, 130

Markov, Georgi, 155

Marshall Plan, 221

martyrdom, 15, 19, 23, 26–27, 97,
    107, 110, 113–14, 118–31

Marwan, 119, 120

Marx, Jenny, 31

Marx, Karl, 30, 31–32, 34, 85

Marx, Laura, 31

Marxism-Leninism, 49, 63–64, 82–83,
    108

Mawdudi, Sayyid Abul A'la, 64

Meinhof, Ulrike, 16–17, 46

Meins, Holger, 46–47

Mencken, H. L., 203

Menéndez, Luciano, 182

Merari, Ariel, 107, 127

"Message to America" (bin Laden),
    95–96

Middle Ages, 25, 85

Middle East, 13, 55–58, 64, 81
    elimination of boundaries in, 85
    state-sponsored terrorism and, 51, 52
    U.S. policies in, 145, 147, 149, 209

Milestone (Qutb), 66

Mill, John Stuart, 201

Minimanual of the Urban Guerrilla
    (Marighella), 46, 183, 199

Mir, Hamid, 164

moderates, mobilizing of, 229–30

modernization, 55, 57

Mohammed, Khalid Shaikh, 142, 154

Montañeros, 182

Moore, George Curtis, 78

Moro, Aldo, 95

Moroccans, 133, 154

Moscow hostage crisis, 128

Moussaoui, Zacharias, 225

Movement of the Revolutionary Left
    (MIR), 183

Mozambique, 53, 54

MRTA, 82–83

Mugabe, Robert, 10

Muhammad, 66, 86

Muhammad, Ali, 81

mujahedin, xxi, 15, 52, 66, 118, 137,
    145, 166, 179, 191, 229

Munich Massacre (1972), 17, 77,
    94–95

Muñoz, José Ramón, 89

Murad, Abdul Hakim, 142

Murder (Heinzen), 31

Murphy, James, 22

Muslim Brotherhood, 64, 230

mustard gas, 151

mutually assured destruction (MAD),
    148

Nagasaki, bombing of, 5, 18, 36, 165,
    220

Nairobi, U.S. embassy bombed in, 59,
    153, 195

Napoleon I, Emperor of France, 30

Napoleon III, Emperor of France, 36,
    178

Narodnaya Volya (People's Will), 34

Nasrallah, Hassan, 47, 125

Nassr, Muhammad Mahmoud, 131

Natan-Zada, Eden, 228

National Directorate of Intelligence
    (DINA), 183

nationalism:
    as legitimizing ideology, 48, 108,
        115, 124, 126, 130–31, 238
    see also specific groups

NATO, 172–74, 227

Nechayev, Sergey, 79, 99

Nepalese Communist Party, 11, 49, 76
nerve agents, 151–52, 154
    see also sarin
Netanyahu, Benjamin, 132
Netherlands, 174, 212, 237–38
Neusel, Hans, 89
New Jersey, USS, 76
New People's Army, 11, 82
New York Times, 104
Nicaragua, 7, 52
9/11 Commission, 145, 190
Nixon, Richard M., 172
Nkomati Accord, 53
Noel, Cleo, 78
nonviolence, 8, 50, 62
Northern Ireland, 14, 17, 18, 56, 62,
    68, 72–75, 142, 176, 185–88, 205
    Bloody Friday in, 91
    Bloody Sunday in, xiv, 89–90, 91,
        187
    bombings in, 8, 95
    British intelligence in, 210
    British withdrawal from, 98–99
    disorder as goal in, 78
    Harrods bombing and, 61
    moderates in, 229
    peace process in, 83, 226
    secession goal in, 13, 224
Norway, 226
nuclear weapons, 151, 159–62, 164,
    165–66, 233
    "loose," 226–27

O'Brien, Conor Cruise, 8
Öcalan, Abdullah, 45, 47, 108, 129
O'Doherty, Paul, 96
O'Doherty, Shane, 97
Office of the Director of National
    Intelligence, U.S., 218
Ohnesorg, Benno, 169–70
oil, 63, 193
Okamoto, Kozo, 107
Oklahoma City bombing, 76, 143, 157,
    167

Oliver, Anne Marie, 49, 126
Olympic Games, 17, 77, 95, 105
Omar, Muhammad, 99, 180
O'Neill, Paul, 189
Operation Motorman, 187
opium, 164–65, 235
organizational dynamics, reinforcing of,
    79 80
Oslo accords, 226
O'Sullivan, Jeremiah, 22

Padilla, Jose, 163, 211
Paisley, Rev. Ian, 62
Pakistan, 18, 78, 93, 192, 227
    Kashmir dispute and, 83, 220, 224,
        226
Palestine, 43, 57
    Roman rule in, 23–24
Palestine Liberation Organization
    (PLO), 7, 21, 47, 76
Palestinian Islamic Jihad (PIJ), 53, 113,
    117, 121, 126, 127
Palestinians, 25, 46, 53, 93, 113, 114,
    125–28, 181, 228
    criteria for suicide bombers of, 15,
        117
    female suicide bombers of, 110,
        120–24, 130
    goals of, 75, 76
    humiliation of, 102
    identification with, 68
    poverty of, 56, 57
    publicity for, 17, 41, 75, 95
    splits among, 83
    support for suicide bombers of,
        127–28
Pape, Robert, 109
Paris Commune, 31
Parliament, British, 22, 34, 116–17,
    201
Patel, Hasina, 105
patience, counterterrorism and, 231–33
PATRIOT Act, 234, 236
Peace Corps, 144

Pearl, Daniel, 39
Pearl Harbor, Japanese attack on, 143, 171
Pearse, Padraig, 202
Peres, Shimon, 132
Perón, Juan, 182
Perry, William, 65
perspective, counterterrorism and, 231–33
Peru, 205, 210, 226
    MRTA in, 82–83
    Túpac Amaru in, 77
    see also Shining Path
Pew Global Attitudes Survey, 233
Pew Research Center, 174, 179
Phalanges, 83, 84
Philippines, 78, 107–8, 142
    New People's Army in, 11, 82
Phoenix Park murders, 33
PKK (Kurdish Workers Party), xxi, 45, 47, 48, 58, 225, 231
    goal of, 76, 82
    and identifying with others, 67–68
    Marxism-Leninism of, 108
    suicide bombing of, 108, 113, 120, 129
political goals, 4, 13, 23–24, 25, 28, 29–37, 75–76, 131, 213
    religious goals mixed with, 61, 62, 63, 66, 68, 140–41
Popular Front for the Liberation of Palestine (PFLP), 47, 53, 113
popular sovereignty, doctrine of, 30
Post, Jerrold, 48
postwar reconstruction, 227
poverty, 39, 55–56, 57, 221
    suicide bombers and, 117–18
Powell, Colin, 4, 157, 189, 214
Prabakharan, Vellupillai, 16, 42–43, 45, 47, 87, 98
    suicide bombings and, 110, 111, 124
Premadasa, Ranasinghe, 108
principles, living by, 206–8, 220–21, 233–34, 236

Proclamation of Independence, Irish, xii–xiii
Protestant Reformation, 66
Protestants, xiv, xv, 42, 56, 72, 74, 90, 102, 186
psychological explanations, 48–49
psychological impact, 5, 6, 27–28, 141, 147, 165
psychological studies, 14
publicity, 25, 26, 77, 94
    see also renown
Putin, Vladimir, 214

Qaddafi, Colonel, 51, 76
Qassam, Mohammad al-, 88
Qassam Battalion, 89
Qurashi, Abu Ubeid al-, 94–95, 100–101
Qutb, Sayyid, 64, 66, 67

Rabin, Yitzhak, 62
RAF, see Baader-Meinhof Gang
Rahman, Hesmat Abdul, 93
Rantisi, Abdul Aziz, 44, 47, 121–22
Rapoport, David, 27
Rassam, Ahmad, 154, 225
reaction, xxii, 77–81, 98–101, 106, 115, 167, 197, 198–99
    repression as, 78–79
    specific concessions as, 77–78
Reagan, Ronald, 4, 7, 65, 131, 172
recruitment, xix, 6, 47, 57, 58, 68, 69, 93, 96, 186–87, 215–16
    IRA, 89–90
    repression and, 79, 99
    of suicide bombers, 125–26
Red Army, Japanese, 11, 77–78, 79, 82
Red Army Faction, German (RAF), see Baader-Meinhof Gang
Red Brigades, 11, 41, 42–43, 46, 48, 95, 230
    counterterrorism and, 203, 205, 229
    goals of, 76, 99, 213
    Marxism-Leninism of, 49, 82

show of strength of, 79–80
Reid, Richard (Shoe Bomber), 211, 225
"relative deprivation," concept of, 56
religion:
    ancient trilogy and, 23–28
    as cause of terrorism, 40, 61–69,
        140–42, 149
    violence and, 19
Renamo, 53
renown, xxii, 80–81, 94–98, 177, 197
    suicide bombings and, 106, 110–11,
        115, 118, 119–20, 124, 129
repression, 78–79, 99, 145
Republican Party, U.S., 65
revenge:
    as cause, 41–44
    as objective, xxii, 76, 80–81, 88–94,
        106, 115, 118, 124, 128–29,
        197
revolutionaries vs. terrorists, 1, 8
revolutions of 1848, 30–31
Reyashi, Reem al-, 122
Reyes, Paul, 86–87
Richardson, Louise (author):
    background and childhood of, xii–xv
    education of, xii–xiii, xv–xvi
    as Harvard professor, xi, xvii–xviii
ricin, 155–58, 163, 165
Ricolfi, Luca, 109, 126–27
risk factors, 57–59, 69–70
Riyadh, 4, 65
Riyadus-Salikhin Reconnaissance and
    Sabotage Battalion of Chechen
    Martyrs (RSRSBCM), 83
Robertson, Lord George, 173
Robespierre, Maximilien de, 3, 29, 30
Romania, 78
Romans, ancient, 23–24, 25
Roosevelt, Franklin D., 171
Rossa, Jeremiah O'Donovan, 34, 202
Rossi, Guido, 230
Rousseau, Jean-Jacques, 29
Rove, Karl, 40
Rumsfeld, Donald, 173–74, 190, 217

Russia, 98, 161, 172–73, 174, 179,
    192, 205
    nuclear facilities of, 160
    winning battles vs. wars in, 180–81,
        185
Russian anarchism, 25, 32, 34–35
Russian Mafia, 160
Russian Socialist Revolutionary Party,
    34–35
Rwanda, 67, 189
Ryan, Frankie, 97

sabotage, 8, 10
Sadat, Anwar, 10, 229–30
Sageman, Marc, 47, 238
St. Albans, IRA bombing in, 97
Saint Just, Louis de, 29
Saladin, 194
Salim, Mamduh Mahmud, 161
salmonella, 157
Samudra, Imam, 222
Sandinistas, 7
Sands, Bobby, 116, 117
Santucho, Mario Roberto, 46
sarin, 62, 95, 151–52, 155, 158
Saudi Arabia, 46, 53, 57, 100, 118,
    145, 209
    Kuwait invasion and, 166
    U.S. troops in, 35, 63, 84, 92, 146,
        171
Savimbi, Jonas, 54
Schroeder, Gerhard, 173, 189
SDLP (Social Democratic and Labour
    Party), 229
Sendic Antonaccio, Raúl, 46
September 11 attacks (2001), xi, xix,
    xxii, 4, 40, 95, 124, 131, 135,
        139–68, 170–99
    causes of, 43–44
    cost of, 125, 209
    "Dinner Party Tape" and, 92
    ideological justification for, 18–19
    international opinion and, 22–23
    Muslim humiliation and, 102, 103

September 11 attacks (2001) (*cont.*)
  planning of, 225
  reaction to, 99–100, 101
  scale of, 141–43, 145, 147, 167
  state-sponsored terrorism and, 54–55
  U.S. goal after, 203–4
  U.S. response pattern to, 234
  U.S. vulnerability and, 141, 143–44,
    165
  WMDs and, 148, 150–68
Serbs, 42
17 November, 13, 82–83
Shakespeare, William, 72
Sharia, 60, 63, 67, 85, 209
Sharif, Omar Khan, 68
Shawaq al-Aqsa, 121
Sheehan, Michael, 146
Sheikh, Omar (Ahmed Omar Saeed
    Sheikh), 38–40, 42, 47, 77, 78, 239
Shiite Muslims, 26–27, 53, 64, 66, 76,
    113, 130, 218
Shining Path, xx–xxi, 4, 11, 45, 49, 63,
    77, 180, 203, 226
  goals of, 76, 86
  identification and, 42–43, 67–68
  risk factors and, 57–58
Sicarii (Zealots), 23–26, 33, 79, 107
Sikhs, 13, 56, 203, 211, 225, 229
Singapore, 60
Sinn Féin, 81, 116, 229
Somalia, U.S. withdrawal from, 99
soman, 151–52
South Africa, xv, 8–9, 10, 150
  terrorism sponsored by, 52, 53–54
South Korea, 179
Soviet Union, 51, 61, 106, 148,
    153–54, 157, 187, 226–27
  in Afghanistan, 65–66, 103, 145,
    192, 229
  collapse of, 159–60
  WMDs and, 227, 233
Spain, 36, 149, 156, 174, 212, 238
  counterterrorism in, 108, 205, 226,
    229

GRAPO in, 13, 82–83, 89
  Madrid bombing in, 133, 209, 229,
    237
  see also Basques; ETA
Special Purpose Islamic Regiment
    (SPIR), 83
Sri Lanka, 56, 97, 205, 212–13, 238
  lack of democracy in, 50
  suicide bombing in, 108–13
  see also Tamil Tigers
Stalin, Joseph, 36
State Department, U.S., 52, 61, 166, 179
  Office of Counterterrorism of, xix,
    146
states, 26, 67
  terrorism sponsored by, 5, 28, 50–55,
    64, 181, 225
  undermining of, 78
Steinberg, Paul, 49, 126
Stern, Jessica, 60, 211
Stern Gang, 10
substate groups, terrorism as act of, 5, 50
Sudan, 54, 153, 161
suicide bombing, 15, 46, 64–65, 88,
    104–15, 117–34, 184–85
  female, 105, 109, 110, 120–24, 128,
    129, 130
  group solidarity and, 106–7, 126–27
  historical precedents of, 107–14
  in London subway, 68, 80, 105,
    132–34, 176, 225, 231, 237
  morality of, 19
  organizations and individuals in,
    124–34
  variations on, 114–24
  videos and, 127, 129–32, 134
Suleiman, Andalib, 123–24
Sunni Muslims, 66, 113, 114
Sun-tzu, 208
Switzerland, 60, 237
symbolic significance, 4–5
Syria, 112, 113, 118, 131, 224
  terrorism sponsored by, 5, 51, 54,
    181, 225

tabun, 151–52
Tajikistan, 65
Taliban, 99, 154, 158, 163, 176,
     179–80, 192, 211, 235
Tamils, 13, 50, 56, 225, 230
Tamil Tigers (Liberation Tigers of Tamil
     Eelam; LTTE), 16, 42–43, 45, 47,
     48, 50, 58, 98, 213, 225, 230
  goals of, 76, 82, 87
  suicide bombing of, 108–13, 120, 124
Tanweer, Shehzad, 68, 80, 105, 118,
     132, 134
Tawhid wal-Jihad, 191
taxes, responsibility and, 6, 17–18
Taylor, Peter, 14, 42, 78
Tel Aviv, 107, 132
temporal goals, 13
terrorism, causes of, xxii, 38–70
  leaders and followers in, 45–48
  defenders vs. aggressors and, 44–45
  identification as, 41, 42–43, 67–68
  individual-level, 39–45
  religion as, 40, 61–69, 140–42, 149
  revenge as, 41–44
  risk factors and, 57–59, 69–70
  simplicity as, 41
  societal-level, 55–56
  state-level, 50–55
  terrorist organizations and, 48–49
  transnational-level, 60
terrorism, global war on, xix, xxii
  unpopularity of, 173–74, 179,
     192–93, 227
  as unwinnable war, 169–99
terrorism, terrorists:
  characteristics of, 4–6
  future of, 237–39
  misrepresentations of, xv–xvi
  morality of, 4, 15–19
  motivations of, xv, xxii, 216
  negotiations with, 98–99, 212–14
  rationality of, 14–15
  types of, 10–11
  use of term, xxi–xxii, 3–4

terrorism studies, xi, xvii–xx
terrorists, goals of, 11–14, 12, 75–103,
     176–77
  disorder as, 78
  long-term, 75–76, 81, 106
  primary, 76, 82–98
  publicity as, 77
  repression as, 78–79
  revenge as, 76, 80–81, 88–94, 106,
     115, 118, 124, 128–29, 197
  secondary, 76–80
  short-term, 75, 81, 106
  specific concessions as, 77–78
  temporal vs. transformational, 13
  see also political goals; reaction;
     renown
Thatcher, Margaret, 25, 51, 116
Thompson Principles, 185
Thucydides, 204
Thug Buhram, 28
Thugi, 23, 27–28
Time, 164
Tokyo subway, sarin gas in, 62, 95,
     151, 152–53, 155, 158
Toolis, Kevin, 42, 45, 49
Tora Bora cave complex, 180, 198
torture, 236
transformational goals, 13
Treasury, U.S., 153
Trinity College Dublin, xv
Tripoli, U.S. bombing of (1986), 51, 76
Truman administration, 174
Tsuchiya, Masami, 153
Túpac Amaru, 77
Tupamaros, 46, 101, 184
Turkey, 192, 205, 224, 231, 237
  Dev Sol in, 82–83
  see also PKK
Turkmenistan, 65, 161
TWA flight 847, hijacking of, 64, 76,
     77

Ukraine, 161
Umberto I, King of Italy, 36

Umkhonto we Sizwe (MK), 8–9
unemployment, 57, 58
UNICEF, 219
UNITA, 54
United Airlines flight 93, 140
United Kingdom, 13, 51, 57, 142, 185,
    224
  see also Great Britain; Northern
    Ireland
United Nations, 6–7, 45, 189, 192, 214
  sanctions against Iraq and, 219–20
United States, 35–36, 46, 51–57
  Civil War in, xiii, 13, 33, 143, 155
  declarations of war against, 16, 65,
    171–72
  humanitarian efforts of, 221–23
  insularity of, 145–46
  Irish Americans in, 33, 225
  moral issues and, 18
  Muslims in, 61, 149, 212
  specific concessions and, 77, 78
  terrorism sponsored by, 51–52
  see also September 11 attacks
uranium, 161, 162–63
Uribe Vélez, Álvaro, 124
Uruguay, 46, 101, 184
UVF, 90
Uzbekistan, 65

Venezuela, 210
victims:
  audience vs., 5, 36
  civilians as, xx, 4, 6, 25, 26, 36, 37
  Muslims as, 44–45
  of Thugi, 27–28
Victor, Barbara, 121
Victoria, Queen of England, 201
Vietnam War, 218
Villepin, Dominique de, 158
violence, 4, 49
  Arendt's views on, 75
  culture of, 68
  random vs. discriminate, 24
von Sponeck, Hans, 219

Waco, Tex., 76
Walid, Abu al-, 83
war games, xvi–xvii
war psychosis, 177
Washington, George, xii, 207
weapons of mass destruction (WMDs),
    148, 150–68, 189, 220
  biological, 151, 153–61, 165,
    226–27
  chemical, see chemical weapons
  dirty bombs, 162–63, 165
  nuclear, 151, 159–62, 164, 165–66,
    226–27, 233
  U.S. fear of, 150–51, 164–65
Weather Underground, 171–72
West Bank, 49, 57, 97, 230
  Israeli intelligence in, 210, 211–12
Why Terrorism Works (Dershowitz),
    75
Wolfowitz, Paul, 189
World Bank, 226
World Trade Center, 5, 43–44, 77,
    144–45, 148, 156
  1993 attack on, 96, 142, 143
World War I, 36, 151, 159, 178, 213
World War II, 36, 148, 174, 178
  Allied bombing in, 5, 18, 36, 165,
    220
  kamikaze attacks in, 114–15
  Pearl Harbor attack in, 143, 171

Yamada, Yoshiaki, 78
Yassin, Sheikh Ahmed, 47, 92, 121,
    122, 124, 125
Yemen, 59
Yousef, Ramzi, 96

Zarqawi, Abu Mus'ab al-, 118, 120,
    189, 191, 218
  U.S. strengthening of, 214–15
Zawahiri, Ayman al-, 15, 47, 100, 125,
    132, 191, 212, 218, 232
  WMDs and, 154, 164
Zionism, 10, 84, 92, 132–33

ABOUT THE AUTHOR

LOUISE RICHARDSON is executive dean of the Radcliffe Institute for Advanced Study, a senior lecturer in government at Harvard College, and a lecturer in law at Harvard Law School. From 1989 until her appointment to Radcliffe in 2001, she was an assistant and then an associate professor of government at Harvard, specializing in international security. She has been teaching courses on terrorist movements in international relations to Harvard students since the mid-1990s and has received several awards for her teaching. Her lecture audiences have ranged from Harvard/Radcliffe clubs around the country to the annual IDC conference in Milan to the Council on Foreign Relations in Rio de Janeiro. She has appeared on CNN, the BBC, PBS, NPR, and a host of other broadcast outlets. Her work has been featured in a number of international periodicals.

Born in Ireland, now an American citizen, Richardson received a bachelor's and master's degree in history from Trinity College in Dublin, and an M.A. and Ph.D. in government from Harvard University.

ABOUT THE TYPE

This book was set in Sabon, a typeface designed by the well-known German typographer Jan Tschichold (1902–74). Sabon's design is based upon the original letter forms of Claude Garamond and was created specifically to be used for three sources: foundry type for hand composition, Linotype, and Monotype. Tschichold named his typeface for the famous Frankfurt typefounder Jacques Sabon, who died in 1580.